T

Do Not Take From This Room

100 Most Popular
Thriller and Suspense Authors

Biographical Sketches and Bibliographies

Bernard A. Drew

Popular Authors Series

Libraries Unlimited
An Imprint of ABC-CLIO, LLC

A B C  C L I O

Santa Barbara, California • Denver, Colorado • Oxford, England

Library of Congress Cataloging-in-Publication Data

Drew, Bernard A. (Bernard Alger), 1950–
  100 most popular thriller and suspense authors : biographical sketches and bibliographies /
Bernard A. Drew.
     p. cm. — (Popular authors series)
  Includes bibliographical references and indexes.
  ISBN 978-1-59158-699-9 (hbk. : alk. paper) 1. Suspense fiction, American—
Bio-bibliography—Dictionaries. 2. Novelists, American—20th century—Biography—
Dictionaries. I. Title. II. Title: One hundred most popular thriller and suspense authors.
  Z1231.S87 D74
  [PS374.S87]
  016.813'087209—dc22   2009017268

13 12 11 10 9   1 2 3 4 5

This book is also available on the World Wide Web as an eBook.
Visit www.abc-clio.com for details.

ABC-CLIO, LLC
130 Cremona Drive, P.O. Box 1911
Santa Barbara, California 93116-1911

This book is printed on acid-free paper ∞

Manufactured in the United States of America

Contents

Introduction

One hundred chapters, which one to write first? I jumped into a profile of Jerry B. Jenkins, author of a series of futuristic Christian thrillers. And in counterpoint, I next wrote about the series with a Wiccan hero by M. R. Sellars. The next day, I paired a veteran author with a relative newcomer, F. Paul Wilson and Jack DuBrul. Another day, a writer of a series about a police detective and another with a serial killer sequence. Hero and heroine. Businessman and criminal. Politics and romantic suspense. Techno and psychological. All thrillers or suspense novels. All overlapping in various ways with fiction genres, and subgenres, from paranormal to super-normal. Welcome to the world of literature on steroids.

What is a thriller? Jeffery Deaver in a Bookreporter interview offered this definition: "A suspense/thriller novel asks the question, 'What's going to happen?' A traditional mystery novel asks, 'What happened?' In other words, the mystery is a puzzle that the hero (and reader) seek to unravel. A thriller is a carnival ride with the hero (and reader) in the front car."

Whatever the "what" of thrillers, the "how is generally a breathless, adrenaline-charged race from beginning to end, as the hero or heroine faces relentless challenges in a deadly race to defeat evil. For some authors, the suspense is psychological rather than physical, anticipatory rather than actual.

Author David Baldacci in a *Writer's Digest* interview remarked on the ascension of the thriller in post–September 11 times. "As the world becomes a smaller place, people want to *better* understand. People gravitate toward fiction to better understand the facts."

In uncertain, often polarizing times, thrillers can sidle along either side of a political issue. Vince Flynn, author of the Mitch Rapp books, has said the controversial interrogation technique of "waterboarding" is justifiable to garner information from extremists. On the other hand, Barry Eisler, author of the John Rain series, has countered that extreme torture not only does not guarantee useful information, it demeans the American public and places our military personnel in greater jeopardy of retaliation.

Stephen Hunter, author of the sniper Bob Lee Swagger books, appears to believe conflict is best resolved with guns. David Baldacci, conversely, says the urge to kick the living daylights out of the enemy is adrenaline talking, not intelligence.

Mystery and detective novels often have the hero or heroine working to solve a crime. A suspense thriller pumps up the pace. The main characters in thrillers are generally professionals, or at least extremely qualified. They're spies or lawyers or police detectives, assassins or bounty hunters. Present-day and futuristic military duels—the more cutting-edge the weaponry the better—bring science fiction under the thriller umbrella. Some techno novels are modern day, some are post-apocalyptic, some are alternate world. Some fantasy tales involving the paranormal reach into the thriller category. Urban fantasy (whether Andrew Vachss's contemporary crime tales or Laurell K. Hamilton's zombie-hunter exercises) can be considered suspense thrillers. A number of writers who honed their crafts on romances broke into the hardcover market with accentuated suspense in their books.

I selected the 100 authors for this book in consultation with my Libraries Unlimited editor and respected genre experts. All but a handful of the authors included are still active; those who are dead are here because of their influence on the thriller. Ian Fleming and Robert Ludlum took the spy thriller to new heights, and other writers are continuing their characters in new books today. Patricia Highsmith set the pace for modern-day writers of psychological suspense. A lone representative of the western, William W. Johnstone, handled multiple series in his career, several of which are being carried on by new writers.

Choices were made to reflect the breadth of suspense thriller writing. The mix of authors reflects those who are at the peak of several subgenres, including techno, legal, medical, political, and espionage. The writers are veterans; Dan Brown, in fact, may have the fewest books of any author included. But what books they are! If your favorite doesn't appear here, he or she may be in the companion *100 Most Popular Genre Fiction Writers* or may be included in future mystery, science fiction, or romance volumes in this series.

This book was researched through published interviews, examination of author Web pages, feature articles, book reviews, criticism, and other published materials. Complete author bibliographies are offered except in instances of unusually prolific authors Sandra Brown, Nora Roberts (J. D. Robb), Jerry B. Jenkins, and Donald E. Westlake (Richard Stark), in which case, Internet sources of publications are provided.

This book is aimed at students who want to research particular authors or genres or who are looking for more information about favorite writers simply for their own interests. It is also intended as a guide for instructors and librarians in providing a one-source guide to reading interests in the 2000s.

Authors are listed alphabetically. In the cases of W. E. B. Griffin, Jack Higgins, John le Carré, Elizabeth Lowell, Perri O'Shaughnessy, J. D. Robb, James Rollins, M. J. Rose, John Sandford, Michael Slade, and Richard Stark, entries are under well-known pseudonyms, not the authors' real names. Entry headings provide author name, place and date of birth, and a benchmark title or series. Essays examine the authors' writings, series characters (if any), methods of research, habits of writing, and observations on the genre.

Although these biographical essays can't promise the same heart-pounding pace that is the trademark of the writers described, they should open the door to one of today's most dynamic and entertaining literary forms.

References

Barry Eisler blog. http://www.barryeisler.com/2007/11/vince-flynn-left-winger.html (viewed December 29, 2007).

Jeffery Deaver interview, Bookreporter. http://www.bookreporter.com/authors/au-deaver-jeffery.asp#view051200 (viewed November 4, 2007).

Hudson, Audrey, "A Page from His Book" (Vince Flynn interview), http://www.washingtontimes.com/article/20071116/CULTURE/111160101 (viewed December 29, 2007).

"Make Mine a Thompson!" interview with Stephen Hunter. *American Handgunner*, March 2003.

Nance, Kevin, "Thrill Seeker: David Baldacci Uses His Novels, Including His Latest 'Stone Cold,' to Examine Moral Dilemmas." *Chicago Sun-Times*, December 9, 2007.

Vaughn, Michael J., "The Popular Fiction Report." *Writer's Digest*, April 2008.

Jeff Abbott

Crime; Espionage; Thrillers: Legal, Medical

Benchmark Series: <u>Whit Moseley</u>

Dallas, Texas

1963–

Photo credit: Crilly Davis

About the Author and the Author's Writing

"If you ever travel anywhere with Jeff Abbott, insist on driving. Even if it's just to the corner convenience store. Because if he drives like he writes, you'll be so wired by the time you get to your destination that you'll be hunched beneath the dashboard, with your fingers covering your eyes," said Bookreporter reviewer Joe Hartlaub.

Jeff Abbott's 2005 thriller *Panic* snakes Evan Casher, a maker of documentary films, into a twisted world of spies and secret lives. His next book, *Fear* (2006), drops another hero, Miles Kendrick, who is hiding out in the witness protection program because of his testimony against the mob, into the world of illicit clinical tests of pharmaceuticals.

The writer's compelling and convoluted stories also feature climactic endings. "Abbott has a genuine knack for the bang-up finish," observed *Texas Monthly* reviewer Mike Shea.

In *Collision* (2008), Abbott pairs two unlikely men, a corporate consultant and an ex-CIA agent, who must wrestle their way out of a sophisticated frame-up.

The author has methodically worked his way onto the best-seller lists. His first books were traditional paperback original mysteries about Jordan Poteet, a librarian and amateur crime solver. Poteet, a Boston native, has moved to Mirabeau, Texas, to care for his elderly mother in the Agatha and Macavity Award–winning novel *Do unto Others* (1994). When Poteet's fingerprints are found on the baseball-bat murder weapon, he finds himself charged with the murder of a woman who had constantly nagged him about the sensual content of some of the books in the library.

Several themes emerge in the books (and two short stories) featuring Poteet—family relationships, choices, the ability to function under pressure—and Abbott continues to explore these threads in his later suspense novels.

The author switches from first-person to third-person narration, and from rural Texas to the Gulf Coast, for a second series of mysteries about coroner Whit Mosely. Mosely first appeared in a short story, "Salt on the Rim," in the anthology *And the Dying Is Easy.* In the series, he works with police detective Claudia Salazar to solve more crimes that take place in the Lone Star State. Salazar prefers to work within the law's parameters. But Moseley, an elected justice of the peace with no law degree and minimal training, constantly skirts the law in his pursuit of criminals. In *Cut and Run* (2003), Mosely's own mother has taken up with organized crime. A *Publishers Weekly* reviewer remarked on the book's "brutal action and blunt dialogue."

Cut and Run, Abbott said in an interview with Mike Stotter, is about trust. "I … wanted to explore the issue of trust, because that is what Whit and his mother, Eve, don't have, but is what they both need to become whole. Because trust is the foundation of both love and forgiveness."

Born in Dallas, Texas, in 1963, Abbott grew up in Dallas and Austin. When he was sixteen years old, he wrote a 400-page manuscript. It was never published, but it gave him a taste for the craft. He received a bachelor of arts degree in history and English from Rice University in 1985. An avid reader, he has taken inspiration from leading crime writers.

From 1991 to 1998, the author managed communications for IBM and then became a marketing director for Vignette, both in Austin, Texas. He was vice president and creative director for an agency called nFusion in Austin from 2000 to 2003, when he became a full-time writer. He, his wife, and their two sons live in Texas.

Abbott strives for strong characters as well as solid plots in his books. In establishing the substantial, believable background he wants to portray, his research often takes him to unexpected places. The book *A Kiss Gone Bad* includes two characters who once worked in the pornography trade. Through the Internet, the author located a porn producer who turned out to be more personable than he expected. "He gave me a lot of details—funny, human details, even for such an exploitative business as he was in (such as the man's mother working as his accountant while thoroughly disapproving of his oeuvre). Abbott said in a Mystery One Bookstore interview, "He helped me make the characters become more alive, be more precise in their thinking and their view of the world."

Eventually, the author found he had grown beyond certain limitations with his mystery series. "The ideas I was getting for books weren't appropriate for the traditional series I'd written," he said in a BookBrowse interview. "So I had to make a change." He began to write free-standing thrillers.

Where do his plots come from? "Like everyone else, at that secret aisle at Target," he joked.

 # Works by the Author

Panic (2005)
Fear (2006)
Collision (2008)

Jordan Poteet Mysteries

Do unto Others (1994)
The Only Good Yankee (1995)
Promises of Home (1996)
Distant Blood (1996)

Whit Moseley Series

A Kiss Gone Bad (2001)
Black Jack Point (2002)
Cut and Run (2003)

Anthologies

And the Dying Is Easy, edited by Joseph Pittman and Annette Riffle (2001), includes "Salt on the Rim"

High Stakes, edited by Robert J. Randisi (2003), includes "Bet on Red."

The Best American Mystery Stories 2004, edited by Nelson DeMille (2004), includes "Bet on Red"

The World's Finest Crime and Mystery Stories, 5th edition, edited by Ed Gorman and Martin H. Greenberg (2004), includes "Bet on Red"

Death Do Us Part, edited by Harlan Coben (2006), includes "A Few Small Repairs"

Greatest Hits, edited by Robert J. Randisi (2006), includes "Karma Hits Dogma"

Damn Near Dead: An Anthology of Geezer Noir, edited by Duane Swierczynski (2006), includes "Tender Mercies"

For Further Information

Cruz, Gilbert, "Thriller 101." *Entertainment Weekly*, August 26, 2005.

Cut and Run review. *Publishers Weekly*, October 6, 2003.

Hartlaub, Joe, *Panic* review, Bookreporter. http://www.bookreporter.com/reviews2/0451412222.asp (viewed February 4, 2008).

Jeff Abbott interview, BookBrowse. http://www.bookbrowse.com/author_interviews/full/index.cfm?author_number=1204 (viewed January 31, 2008).

Jeff Abbott interview, Mystery One Bookstore. http://www.mysteryone.com/JeffAbbottInterview.htm (viewed January 31, 2008).

Jeff Abbott Web site. http://www.jeffabbott.com/ (viewed November 6, 2008).

Shea, Mike, *Fear* review. *Texas Monthly*, August 2006.

Stotter, Mike, Jeff Abbott interview, Shots magazine. http://www.shotsmag.co.uk/shots21/intvus_21/jabbott.html (viewed January 31, 2008).

David Baldacci

Espionage; Historical Fiction; Thrillers: Political

Benchmark Title: *Absolute Power*

Richmond, Virginia
1960–

Photo credit: John Foley, Opale

About the Author and the Author's Writing

One high-placed fan of David Baldacci's Washington Beltway thrillers, former President Bill Clinton, told *USA Today* in 2007, "I love David Baldacci's books, the dizzying plot twists, the evocative scenes, the compelling characters. His books are riveting thrillers that also enable readers to learn something about important subjects." Former President George H. W. Bush told reporter Carol Memmott he read all the Baldacci books. That's both political sides heard from, and it demonstrates the Virginia-based writer's large and broad following.

Baldacci came to immediate notice with his first novel, *Absolute Power* (1996), which was made into a motion picture starring Clint Eastwood. Luther Whitney, a cat burglar getting along in years, breaks into a billionaire's mansion and unexpectedly witnesses the wife of the house in liaison with the president of the United States. Secret Service agents misinterpret the proceedings (the president is drunk) and shoot the woman—then shape a cover-up to place all blame on an unnamed burglar—Whitney.

"He's much closer to Grisham than to, say, Forsyth; but he's also a first-rate storyteller who grabs readers by their lapels right away and won't let go until they've finished his enthralling yarn," a *Publishers Weekly* reviewer said.

The author was born in Richmond, Virginia, in 1960. He graduated from Virginia Commonwealth University with a bachelor of arts degree in political science. After earning his juris doctorate from the University of Virginia, he worked as a trial and corporate lawyer in Washington, D.C., before becoming a full-time writer. He still lives near the nation's capital, with his wife, Michelle, and their two children.

It is no surprise Baldacci conceived a presidential plot for his first novel. He worked around the corner from the White House, after all. He saw the presidential motorcade more than once; and he conceived his plot one day while bicycling in Alexandria. He wrote the book but had no immediate prospect of placing it.

"It was an outlet for me," he said in an interview with *Fairfax County Times* writer Jason Devaney. "As a trial lawyer, it's a stressful existence. People try to beat up on you every day. So going home at night and writing stuff that I wanted to write was a terrific way for me to have a cathartic experience and get the other stuff out of my system."

As a boy, Baldacci was an avid storyteller; and as a lawyer, he wrote short stories, although he rarely found a market for them. His screenplays fared no better. *Absolute Power*, however, sold to a book publisher almost immediately. Time Warner paid $2 million for film rights. Baldacci appeared on the *Today* show. He quit his day job.

Politics—national and international—became the fodder for Baldacci's novels. *Stone Cold* (2007), for example, follows former government assassin John Carr, who takes a new name (Oliver Stone) and embarks on a new avocation. When he marches in protest outside the White House, he suddenly becomes the object of a Homeland Security counterterrorism agent who is out to kill him.

Terrorism is a natural subject for post–September 11 writers, Baldacci told *Chicago Sun-Times* reporter Kevin Nance. Most prefer to kick butt, rather than work out permanent solutions to world problems. "Terrorism is a lot more complex than we think. It's not just good vs. evil. It's also about how sometimes good people do bad things for the right reasons, and evil people sometimes have redeeming value. I was interested in how they're transformed into instruments of terrorism," he said.

Baldacci admits he's cynical about the honesty of America's leadership. That's reflected in his characters. "We like to have the truth. I think we rarely get it. As time goes on we're more and more manipulated by an ever smaller group of information sources. It's ironic. We live in the information age, but it's very difficult to find the truth."

Thus, he resorts to the thriller—an escape from our current political reality. "The genre of the thriller is a way for very clever people to show what they can do," he told Jeff Zaleski of *Publishers Weekly*. "It's a game between me and the reader."

The author confesses that his biggest struggle is starting a new book. "Being scared to death of the first blank page and turning that fear into energy" is often what gets him started on a new manuscript, he said in a Readers Read interview in 2002.

"I don't write a certain number of hours a day," he said in an interview on the Hatchette Book Group Web site. "I tend to think about things a lot, so when I'm writing, I'm very productive because I've thought everything through in my head. So I can sit down and write 15, 20 or 30 pages in one sitting because it's all there... and I've taken the time to think through all the details."

And it's the details that make Baldacci's novels unusual and fascinating.

Works by the Author

Absolute Power (1996)
Total Control (1997)
The Winner (1997)

The Simple Truth (1998)
Saving Faith (1999)
Wish You Well (2000)
Last Man Standing (2001)
The Christmas Train (2002)
The Whole Truth (2008)

Camel Club Series

The Camel Club (2005)
The Collectors (2006)
Stone Cold (2007)
Divine Justice (2008)

Sean King and Michelle Maxwell Series

Split Second (2003)
Hour Game (2004)
Simple Genius (2007)
First Family (2009)

Juvenile Fiction

Fries Alive (2005)
The Mystery of Silas Finkelbean (2006), sequel to *Fries Alive*

Nonfiction

Origins of Wish You Well (2000)

Adaptations in Other Media

Absolute Power (1997), motion picture based on the novel
McCourt & Stein (2003), USA Network pilot

For Further Information

Absolute Power review, *Publishers Weekly*, October 16, 1995.

David Baldacci interview, BookBrowse. http://www.bookbrowse.com/author _interviews/full/index.cfm?author_number=181 (viewed December 16, 2007).

David Baldacci interview, Bookreporter. http://www.bookreporter.com/autors/ au-baldacci-david.asp (viewed December 16, 2007).

David Baldacci Web site. http://www.davidbaldacci.com/ (viewed November 6, 2008).

Devaney, Jason, "Q&A with David Baldacci." *Fairfax County Times*, November 20, 2007.

Gulli, Andrew F., "Interview: David Baldacci." *Strand Magazine*, February-May, 2009.

Hall, Melissa Mia, "PW Talks with David Baldacci: Seeking the *Stone Cold Truth*." *Publishers Weekly*, September 3, 2007.

"Interview: David Baldacci," Hachette Book Group. http://www.hachettebookgroupusa.com/authors/39/732/interview13777.html (viewed December 16, 2007).

"Interview with David Baldacci," Readers Read, November 2002. http://www.readersread.com/features/baldacci2.htm (viewed December 16, 2007).

Memmott, Carol, "Baldacci's Power Is Absolute." *USA Today*, December 10, 2007.

Nance, Kevin, "Thrill Seeker." *Chicago Sun Times*, December 9, 2007.

Zeleski, Jeff, "A Return to Thrillers: David Baldacci." *Publishers Weekly*, December 10, 2001.

William Bernhardt

Crime; Thrillers: Legal, Political

Benchmark Series: <u>Ben Kincaid</u>

Oklahoma City, Oklahoma

1960–

Photo credit: Robert Mercer

About the Author and the Author's Writing

The president of the United States narrowly avoids death. In Oklahoma City, Oklahoma, on the anniversary of the tragic bombing of the federal building in 1995, he and Senator Ben Kincaid are on the dais when shots ring out. The first lady is dead, and Kincaid's close friend is gravely wounded. The president, enraged, introduces legislation that would suspend the protections of the Bill of Rights. The terrorists must be tracked down at any cost. Kincaid, however, isn't so sure the terrorists aren't, in fact, some powerful forces who inhabit the halls of Congress.

All this takes place in William Bernhardt's taut political thriller *Capitol Conspiracy* (2008). The novel has the edge-of-the-armchair suspense and ripped-from-the-headlines premise expected of the genre, along with, as *Booklist* reviewer Jeff Ayers points out, an intriguing "discussion of our liberties."

William Bernhardt was born in Oklahoma City in 1960, the son of a physician and a teacher. He says on his Web site that he knew he wanted to become a professional writer from the age of seven. He submitted his first work to a publisher when he was eleven. It was several years before anything was accepted. After majoring in English at the University of Oklahoma, which granted him a bachelor of arts degree in 1982, he completed requirements for a juris doctorate at the same institution in 1986. He also attended the University of Toronto in 1983–1984 and Oxford University in 1985. He is a pianist and songwriter and principal in a publishing company, Hawk Publishing Group of Tulsa. He sponsors the Hawk Writing Workshop each summer. He has produced two music CDs and constructed crossword puzzles for the *New York*

Times. He and his wife, attorney Kirsten Ingrid Tucker, married in 1986 and have three children. It's no exaggeration to say Bernhardt is a complex and multitalented man.

Bernhardt wrote his first <u>Ben Kincaid</u> crime novel in 1991. In *Dark Justice*, Kincaid runs a law practice in Tulsa and takes on the case of a tree hugger accused of murder. A later case, *Silent Justice* (2000), involving toxic waste, was inspired by the same real-life case that inspired the nonfiction book *A Civil Action* by Jonathan Harr.

By the time *Capitol Murder* (2006) takes place, Kincaid has successfully run for the U.S. Senate, bringing a whole new political world to the series. Bernhardt admittedly enjoys writing the Kincaid books, but has found a little space brings him a degree of freshness for new novels; and since 2001 he has alternated other novels with the latest adventures in the Kincaid series.

The author was praised for his Wodehousian abilities at humor for *Murder One*. He has also written literary fiction (*The Code of Buddyhood*); a Dickensian holiday novel, *The Midnight before Christmas*; and a collection of short stories.

Two Bernhardt novels, *Dark Eye* (2005) and *Strip Search* (2007), feature a widowed Las Vegas police behavior specialist, Susan Pulaski. Disliked by many officers, who blame Pulaski for her husband's death, she works well with Darcy O'Bannon, an adult math savant and the son of the police chief. Some critics have said Berhnhardt has no business trying to give voice to two characters so distant from his realm of experience. But Pulaksi, the author said in a Bookreporter interview, emerged from his simple observation of women around him. And O'Bannon is a mature version of his own son, an autistic math savant. "Trying to come up with a way to represent the autistic mind on paper took a lot of contemplation," he said, "—and many drafts. And now, in this sequel, you can see how Darcy's voice has evolved as a result of his relationship with Susan."

In *Dark Eye* Bernhardt took great care in his research and portrayal of a serial killer. "What I like most about Edgar is that, even when he is doing the most horrible things, he doesn't think of himself as a bad person. He sees everything he does as an act of kindness; he thinks he's saving the world," Bernhardt said in a *New Mystery Reader* interview.

Bernhardt's profession allows him to explore a variety of themes. As he told *Contemporary Authors*, "My goal is to write books that people will want to read, that will captivate them and carry them to places they have never been before, or make them consider ideas they have not considered."

 # Works by the Author

The Code of Buddyhood (1992)

Double Jeopardy (1995)

The Midnight before Christmas (1998)

Final Round (2001)

Bad Faith (2002)

Dark Eye (2005)

Strip Search (2007), sequel to *Dark Eye*

Nemesis: The Final Case of Eliot Ness (2009)

Ben Kincaid Series

Primary Justice (1991)
Blind Justice (1992)
Deadly Justice (1993)
Perfect Justice (1994)
Cruel Justice (1996)
Naked Justice (1997)
Extreme Justice (1998)
Dark Justice (1999)
Silent Justice (2000)
Murder One (2001)
Criminal Intent (2002)
Death Row (2003)
Hate Crime (2004)
Capitol Murder (2006)
Capitol Threat (2007)
Capitol Conspiracy (2008)

Editor

Legal Briefs: Stories by Today's Best Legal Thriller Writers (1998)
Natural Suspect (2001)

For Further Information

Ayers, Jeff, *Capitol Conspiracy* review, *Booklist*, January 1, 2008.

Strip Search review, *Publishers Weekly*, June 18, 2007.

William Bernhardt entry, Contemporary Authors Online. Reproduced in Biography Resource Center. Farmington Hills, MI: Gale, 2008. http://galenet.galegroup.com/servlet/BioRC (viewed February 28, 2008).

William Bernhardt interview, Bookreporter. http://www.bookreporter/.com/authors/au-bernhardt-william.asp (viewed February 28, 2008).

William Bernhardt interview, New Mystery Reader. http://www.newmysteryreader.com/william_bernhardt.htm (viewed March 7, 2008).

William Bernhardt Web site. http://www.williambernhardt.com (viewed November 6, 2008).

Steve Berry

Adventure; Christian Fiction; Thrillers: Political, Cipher

Benchmark Series: <u>Cotton Malone</u>

Birthplace not identified

1955–

Photo credit: Kelly Campbell Photography

About the Author and the Author's Writing

Author Steve Berry dives deep into history's treasure chest to find inspiration for his thrillers. *The Third Secret* (2005), for instance, incorporates the visions of an obscure Irish bishop, St. Malachy, and his actual A.D. 1139 predictions about future popes—about 90 percent of which came true, the author said in a BookBrowse interview. Although linked to the past, much of Berry's action in the novel takes place in the present, a time when fascination with the doings and secrets of the Catholic Church are high.

"A lot of insiders have written about their Vatican experiences, so if not wholly lifted, the veil of secrecy that perpetually shrouds the Vatican is now more transparent," Berry said. The "third secret" of the novel's title, in fact, relating to a vision of the Virgin Mary relayed at Fatima in 1917, was revealed to only a few in 2000 and became a handy springboard for a modern-day story of the pope's secretary, an Irish priest named Colin Michener, and political manipulations in the highest circles of the church.

Born in 1955, Steve Berry attended Catholic schools before entering college to obtain an undergraduate degree in political science and a postgraduate degree in law. He and his family live in Georgia, where he practices law and sits on the Camden County Board of Commissioners. In his spare time, he plays golf, scuba dives, collects books, and, of course, writes.

Long interested in writing, he completed his first manuscript in 1996. After some eighty-five rejections and several more manuscripts, an editor at Ballantine Books offered a contract for *The Amber Room* (2003). That book and the next, *The Romanov Prophecy,* immediately leapt onto national best-seller lists.

11

Berry writes the kind of history-soaked books that he likes to read. Instead of urging would-be authors to write what they know, he suggests on his Web site to "write what you love." For example, he writes about predictions of the "mad monk" Rasputin figure in *The Romanov Prophecy*. The rest is a matter of good research.

Research, he claims, was both easy and difficult for *The Romanov Prophecy*. On one hand, there were lots of primary and secondary sources available. On the other hand, the primary sources didn't all agree. "I read so many so-called eye witness reports from a variety of participants in the imperial murders," he said on a Random House Web page for the novel.

With *The Templar Legacy*, Berry began a series of books featuring Justice Department agent turned rare book dealer Cotton Malone. "What recurring characters offer … is an ability to grow," Berry said on the Random House Web page for *The Alexandria Link*. "Readers can learn more about these personalities as they face differing situations. Like old friends, the more you see them, the more you know about them."

The Venetian Betrayal pits Malone against Irina Zovastina, the high minister of a Central Asian federation who plans to use bioweapons to further stir the Middle East political pot. The death of Alexander the Great provides a vivid backdrop. Although the hero solves the modern-day puzzle, he never does locate Alexander's still-elusive tomb. In the follow-up, *The Charlemagne Pursuit*, the hero is shocked to learn that his father, Captain Forrest Malone, didn't die in a nuclear submarine accident but instead while on a top-secret mission in the Antarctic.

Berry told a Bookreporter interviewer the writing process is not an easy one. At his current pace of one book a year, he is doing final edits to publish one novel, writing a new manuscript, and researching and plotting a new book for the next year—all at the same time. Sometimes things go smoothly, sometimes not. *The Alexandria Link*, for example, didn't turn out as he expected. "I've found that rarely is the finished book even close to the original plot conception," he said. "This is the kind of thing that drives writers nuts."

It's also the kind of thing that, when done right, vaults writers to the top of the best-seller lists.

Works by the Author

The Amber Room (2003)
The Romanov Prophecy (2004)
The Third Secret (2005)

Cotton Malone Series

The Templar Legacy (2006)
The Alexandria Link (2007)
The Venetian Betrayal (2007)
The Charlemagne Pursuit (2008)
The Paris Vendetta (2009)

For Further Information

Steve Berry interview, *The Alexandria Link,* Random House. http://www.randomhouse.com/catalog/display.pperl?isbn=9780345485755&view-auqa (viewed March 2, 2008).

Steve Berry interview, BookBrowse. http://www.bookbrowse.com/author_interviews/full/index.cfm?author_number=1170 (viewed March 2, 2008).

Steve Berry interview, Bookreporter. http://www.bookreporter.com/authors/au-berry-steve.asp (viewed March 2, 2008).

Steve Berry interview, *The Romanov Prophesy,* Random House. http://www.randomhouse.com/catalog/display.pperl?isbn=9780739320853&view-auqa (viewed March 2, 2008).

Steve Berry Web site. http://www.steveberry.org/berry-bio.htm (viewed November 6, 2008).

Venetian Betrayal review, *Publishers Weekly,* October 8, 2007.

Larry Bond

Adventure; Espionage; Thrillers: Military, Techno

Benchmark Series: <u>First Team</u>

Minnesota
1952–

Photo credit: Chris Carlson

About the Author and the Author's Writing

When Larry Bond served aboard a U.S. Navy destroyer, home-based in Seattle, he was assigned to an antisubmarine unit. "Oh, it's really cool, because when I actually find a sub, I take control," he explained to *Publishers Weekly* reporter Jeff Zeleski. "I'm steering the ship, as a lieutnant j.g., and that's a rush. That is a real rush. I mean the skipper and everyone just stands back and I'm driving, running the whole show."

Bond had the savvy to convert that rush first into board games, then video games, and now Web-based role-playing games. A superstar of the gaming field, Bond's fortuitous meeting with thriller author Tom Clancy led to a modest collaboration—and to Bond's future as a novelist.

Born in 1952, Bond grew up near St. Paul, Minnesota. He earned a degree in quantitative methods from St. Thomas College in 1973 and worked in computer programming for two years before joining the Navy in 1975. He attended Officer Candidate School in Rhode Island and was assigned to a destroyer for four years as an antisubmarine warfare officer. He spent another two years shorebound. In 1981, he left the service to work for a defense consulting firm in the Washington, D.C., area, but remained with Navy Reserve Intelligence until 1984. Bond and his wife, Jeanne, and their daughters live in Virginia.

Games were an old interest of Bond's; he recalls that when he was eight years old, an uncle gave him a copy of *Afrika Corps*—and he was immediately hooked. So, fresh out of uniform, Bond worked with Don Gilman to create the war strategy board game *Harpoon,* which went through several editions and was later converted to a video game.

14

Harpoon is a general audience tactical game that is so accurate in its weaponry details, it is often used in military education. The game went through four editions and garnered a trade association designation, the H. G. Wells Award, three times. The video version, which came out in 1990, was named *Computer Gaming World*'s Wargame of the Year. *Command at Sea* and *Fear God and Dreadnought* extended the game's scope to encompass all possible twentieth-century conflicts.

Tom Clancy played *Harpoon* as he outlined the plot for *The Hunt for Red October*. Clancy picked Bond's brain, they worked out battle scenes together and Bond ended up writing a few pages of the book.

The apprentice soon became a master craftsman as Bond worked with another gamer, Patrick Larkin, on his first independent book, *Red Phoenix* (1989), in which North Korea invades South Korea. Fire team maneuvers, weaponry on the seas, and confrontations in the strategy rooms build huge suspense. Bond and Larkin, a former Reagan administration speechwriter, collaborated on other books, including *Vortex* (1991), about an American assault on South Africa, and *Cauldron* (1993), in which the United States takes on France and Germany.

The Enemy Within (1995), with less techno-fantasy, offers more suspense and less weaponry, as Delta Force Colonel Peter Thorn and FBI Agent Helen Gray track an Irani mastermind, Western-educated and trained General Amir Taleh. Besides changing plot direction, with this book Bond acknowledged the need to create fuller characters, particularly the villain.

"People are interested in the technology, but what they really want are vivid characters that they can connect with," he said in a Bookpage interview. "The planes, the subs, the tanks, are there for the same reason horses are there in a Western."

Bond continues to do extensive research for each book and game. He reads voraciously and has developed a network of contacts within and without the military. He creates detailed outlines and character maps. When writing a book, he attempts to produce 1,500 words each morning.

As a change of pace, Bond provided words to go with photographer f-stop Fitzgerald's images in the book *The Mighty Fallen: Our Nation's Greatest War Memorials,* a tribute to the country's war dead through recognition of its many and various statues and other permanent installations.

In 2004, Bond launched a new book series, <u>First Team</u>, working with author Jim DeFelice. First Team is made up of elite operatives, led by Bob Ferguson. In *Angels of Wrath* (2005), the team faces the terrorist cell known as Seven Angels, a group bent on starting a religious war. *Publishers Weekly*'s reviewer noted that, unusual within the genre, "the book explores the intricacies of Muslim faith and culture with more sensitivity than many similar thrillers."

Given the world dynamics and the United States' presidential election in 2008, Bond's multiculturalism should find a ready audience.

 # Works by the Author

Red Storm Rising, with Tom Clancy (1986)

Red Phoenix, with Patrick Larkin (1989)

Vortex, with Patrick Larkin (1991)

Cauldron, with Patrick Larkin (1993)

The Enemy Within (1995)
Day of Wrath, with Patrick Larkin (1998), sequel to *The Enemy Within*
Dangerous Ground, with Chris Carlson (2005)
Cold Choices (2009)

First Team Series, with Jim DeFelice

Larry Bond's First Team (2004)
Angels of Wrath (2006)
Fires of War (2006)
Soul of the Assassin (2008)

Games

Harpoon First Edition (1981)
Resolution 502 (1982)
Harpoon Second Edition (1983)
Battles of the Third World War (1987)
Harpoon Third Edition (1987)
Computer Harpoon (1990)
Harpoon Data Annex 3.2 (1990)
Harpoon Captain's Edition (1990)
Command at Sea, with Chris Carlson and Ed Kettler (1994)
Command at Sea Second Edition, with Chris Carlson and Ed Kettler (1995)
Harpoon 4, with Chris Carlson (1996)
Command at Sea Third Edition, with Chris Carlson and Ed Kettler (1998)
Fear God and Dreadnought, with Chris Carlson, Ed Kettler, and Michael W. Harris (2001)
Mighty Midgets, with Dave Schueler, Bill Madison, and Chris Carlson (2003)
High Tide, with Jay Wissmann and Chris Carlson (2003)

Contributor

David Copperfield's Tales of the Impossible (1995), includes "Expert Advice"
Tombs (1995), includes "Burial at Sea," with Chris Carlson
Stephen Coonts' Combat, with Dale Brown, Stephen Coonts, and David Hagberg (2001), includes "Lash-Up"

Nonfiction

Command at Sea Player's Handbook, with Chris Carlson and Ed Kettler (1995)
The Mighty Fallen: Our Nation's Greatest War Memorials, with f-stop Fitzgerald (2007)

For Further Information

Buckley, James, "Larry Bond's New Techno-Thriller: Bad Guys with Global Ambitions," BookPage review. http:www.bookpage.com/9603bp/mystery/theenemywithin.html (viewed March 2, 2008).

Larry Bond entry, Contemporary Authors Online, Gale, 2008. Reproduced in Biography Resource Center. Farmington Hills, MI: Gale, 2008. http://galenet.galegroup.com/servlet/BioRC (viewed March 2, 2008).

Larry Bond Web site. http://www.larry-bond.com (viewed November 6, 2008).

Larry Bond's First Team: Angels of Wrath review, *Publishers Weekly*, November 7, 2005.

Mighty Fallen review, Bookreporter, 2007. http://www.bookreporter.com/reviews2/0061170909.asp (viewed March 2, 2008).

Zaleski, Jeff, "Larry Bond: War Games for Grown-Ups," *Publishers Weekly*, March 4, 1996.

Suzanne Brockmann

Crime-Suspense; Espionage; Romance; Science Fiction; Thrillers: Military, Romantic

Benchmark Series: <u>Troubleshooter Inc.</u>

Massachusetts

Birth date not disclosed

About the Author and the Author's Writing

It is one thing to write military thrillers. It is another thing to write romances. It may be unusual to write military romances, the characters simultaneously fighting enemies and courting partners; but it is a true rarity to write military romances with gay heroes. Author Suzanne Brockmann doesn't blink an eye. She has both a long-running military romance series and a gay military romance series, both involving the toughest of the tough, Navy SEALs.

Brockman lives in a writing household; her husband, Ed Gaffney, is also an author (after working for several years as a lawyer). They have two grown children. Suzanne started reading when she was only three. Her first book was Beverly Cleary's *Here Comes the Bus*. She wrote a *Star Trek* novel while in high school just for fun, with no market in mind. She attended Boston University's School of Broadcasting and Film, majored in film and minored in creative writing, but dropped out to perform with a rock and roll band. She has been director, vocal arranger, and a lead singer with the Boston-area a cappella group Serious Fun. She is also a member of PFLAG (Parents, Families, and Friends of Lesbians and Gays) as well as the American Civil Liberties Union and the Human Rights Campaign.

Brockman's first serious attempt at writing was a screenplay. It and later efforts didn't sell, in part because the film industry is a difficult field to break into from the East Coast. Learning from her failures, she focused on the market for romance novels. She wrote four manuscripts before she sold *Future Perfect* in 1993. Since then, she has branched into the genres of military thrillers and crime and received several awards for her writing. Reviewers have praised her ability to craft believable, interesting characters, particularly soldiers.

"I've always been attracted to military heroes," she said in an All About Romance interview. "When I was a kid, I read every book in the library about World War II—it just fascinated me, all those stories of heroism, both on a grand scale and on an individual scale. And I'm a patriot at heart."

Brockmann broke ground in 2004 with *Hot Target*, a novel woven around a gay relationship. With a gay son and several homosexual friends, she asked herself, why not a gay romance? FBI Agent Jules Cassidy is featured in several of the books in her Troubleshooter Inc. series. He not only has a relationship, he marries his lover (legal under Massachusetts law) in *All through the Night*, the twelfth book in the series. Romance is hardly the characters' main concern in this story, however. Cassidy, an agent with a counterterrorism unit, and his life partner, Robin Chadwick, not only run into trouble renovating an apartment but are plagued by a newspaper reporter and stalked by someone opposed to their union. "With her trademark brand of gritty suspense, a cast of complex characters …, polished prose, and a subtle yet sharp sense of humor, RITA Award-winner Brockmann delivers another wonderfully satisfying, unexpected, and thoroughly romantic story," John Charles wrote in a review for *Booklist.*

"I've got to write the stories that I burn to write. And frankly? I believe that I've gained more readers by writing books with vibrant, compelling, honest, and realistic characters like Jules Cassidy and Robin Chadwick," she said in an AfterElton conversation.

The Troubleshooter Inc. series is published by Mira books and features SEAL Team 16. Men from another SEAL Team (10) figure in her Tall, Dark, and Dangerous series (originally issued under the Silhouette Intimate Moments imprint) for Ballantine Books.

Typically, *Defiant Hero,* from the second series follows single-mom Meg Moore's efforts to rescue her daughter, who has been kidnapped by terrorists. A Navy SEAL expert in languages, John Nisson, offers his assistance. Romance builds at about the same speed as the suspense. Sam Starrett and Alyssa Locke have a running romance in the Team 16 books, and the author included them in four short stories that were published as bonuses in selected novels

Beyond solid sales, a sure sign of the success of the books is a publication put together for fans. *Readers Guide to the Troubleshooter Series* not only profiles ongoing characters in the books, it discusses military terminology and rankings and includes interviews with real SEALs.

Brockman says she outlines her books before writing because she often creates intricate plots with several storylines. "I've always been interested in stories that are layered together, with all these people who eventually intersect and individual lives that come together…. Putting a book like that together is kind of like doing a puzzle," she said in a Crescent Blues interview.

The author has a writing style that she labels "deep point of view." She explained in a WritersWrite interview, "I use subjective point of view, but I'm not satisfied with merely showing the reader what that camera sees from its perch atop a character's head. I bring the camera down, inside of that character's head, so we see the world through that character's eyes." Not surprisingly, she uses the character's voice to tell the story.

Brockmann's liberal politics please her readers. "I love the fact that the world I've created in my books—a diverse American world filled with the same variety of people who live in my urban American neighborhood—has been so enthusiastically embraced by readers," she said on her Web site.

Works by the Author

Future Perfect (1993)
Embraced by Love (1995)
Heart Throb (1999)
Bodyguard (1999)

Bantam Loveswept

832. *Forbidden* (1997)
840. *Stand-in Groom* (1997)
Ladies Man (1997), for subscribers only
858. *Time Enough for Love* (1997)
873. *Freedom's Price* (1998), sequel to *Forbidden*
889. *Body Language* (1998)

Harlequin Intrigue

365. *No Ordinary Man* (1996)

Silhouette Desire

1519. *Scenes of Passion* (2003)

Silhouette Intimate Moments

575. *Hero under Cover* (1995)
647. *Not without Risk* (1995)
681. *A Man to Die For* (1995)
831. *Love with the Proper Stranger* (1998)
968. *Undercover Princess* (1999)
1213. *Letters to Kelly* (2003)

Sunrise Key Series

1. *Kiss and Tell* (1996), Bantam Loveswept 787
2. *The Kissing Game* (1996), Bantam Loveswept 817
3. *Otherwise Engaged* (1997), Bantam Loveswept 824

Tall, Dark, and Dangerous (Navy SEALS) Series

1. *Prince Joe* (1996), Silhouette Intimate Moments 720
2. *Forever Blue* (1996), Silhouette Intimate Moments 742
3. *Frisco's Kid* (1997), Silhouette Intimate Moments 759
4. *Everyday, Average Jones* (1998), Silhouette Intimate Moments 872
5. *Harvard's Education* (1998), Silhouette Intimate Moments 884

6. *It Came upon a Midnight Clear* (1998), Silhouette Intimate Moments 896, re-issued as *Hawken's Heart* (2005)

7. *The Admiral's Bride* (1999), Silhouette Intimate Moments 962

8. *Identity: Unknown* (2000), Silhouette Intimate Moments 974

9. *Get Lucky* (2000), Silhouette Intimate Moments 991

10. *Taylor's Temptation* (2001)

11. *Night Watch* (2003)

Troubleshooter Inc. (Navy SEALS) Series

1. *The Unsung Hero* (2000)

2. *The Defiant Hero* (2001)

3. *Over the Edge* (2001)

4. *Out of Control* (2002)

5. *Into the Night* (2002)

6. *Gone Too Far* (2003)

7. *Flashpoint* (2004), paperback edition includes Sam Starrett/Alyssa Locke short story

8. *Hot Target* (2004), hardcover includes Sam Starrett/Alyssa Locke short story

9. *Breaking Point* (2005)

10. *Into the Storm* (2006), includes Sam Starrett/Alyssa Locke short story

11. *Force of Nature* (2007)

12. *All through the Night: A Troubleshooter Christmas* (2007)

13. *Into the Fire* (2008)

14. *Dark of Night* (2009)

15. *Hot Pursuit* (2009)

Precious Gems Series

86. *Give Me Liberty* (1997), written as Ann Brock

Nonfiction

Readers Guide to the Troubleshooter Series (2006)

Force of Nature Extras for Readers and Writers (2007), free promotional book; includes Sam Starrett/Alyssa Locke short story

For Further Information

Charles, John, *All through the Night* review, *Booklist*, October 15, 2007.

Juergens, Brian, "Interview with Bestselling Author Suzanne Brockmann," AfterElton. http://www.afterelton.com/people/2007/10-/suzannebrockmann (viewed January 12, 2008).

Ketteringham, Kristin, "A Chat with Suzanne Brockmann," All About Romance, February 19, 2001. http://www.likesbooks.com/suzannebrockmann.html (viewed January 12, 2008).

"Suzanne Brockmann: A Closer Look at the Successful Romance Author." Associated Content: The People's Media Company, September 24, 2007. http://www.associatedcontent.com/article/383179/suzanne_brockmann_a_closer_look_at.html?cat=38 (viewed March 25, 2009).

"Suzanne Brockmann: SEAL-ed with a Kiss," Crescent Blues. http://www.crescentblues.com/5_3issue/int_brockmann.shtml (viewed January 12, 2008).

Suzanne Brockmann Web site. http://www.suzannebrockmann.com/ (viewed November 6, 2008).

White, Claire E., "A Conversation with Suzanne Brockmann," Writers Write, January-February 2005. http://www.writerswite.com/journal/feb05/brockmann.htm (viewed January 12, 2008).

Dale Brown

Adventure; Crime-Suspense; Espionage; Science Fiction; Thrillers: Military, Techno

Benchmark Series: <u>Patrick McLanahan</u>

Buffalo, New York

1956–

About the Author and the Author's Writing

Dale Brown, one might assume, has a special account with UPS, because he must have adrenalin flown in by the barrel to his home near Lake Tahoe, Nevada. He doesn't need the hormone himself; he pours it directly into his riveting techno thrillers, such as *Storming Heaven* (1990). In that book, Belgian arms dealer Henri Cazaux eludes ATF agents and launches an assault on U.S. airports in Memphis and Dallas-Fort Worth. Only the perseverance of a gruff special operative, Admiral Ian Hardcastle, stands between the terrorist and America's safety. "Cazaux is a fascinating monster," said reviewer Thomas Gaughan in *Booklist*. "His ultimate assault is way over the top, but *Storming Heaven* will be an explosive success with fans of military-techno-thrillers."

The author was born in Buffalo, New York, in 1956. He studied Western European history at Pennsylvania State University, and soon after graduation in 1978, he joined the U.S. Air Force. Beginning as a navigator-bombardier on the B-52 Stratofortress bomber and the F-111A supersonic medium bomber, he ultimately achieved the rank of captain and received the Air Force Commendation Medal, the Combat Crew Award, and the Marksmanship ribbon before leaving the service. In civilian life, Brown flies his own Grumman Gulfstream II and is a director and volunteer pilot for AirLifeLine, a national charitable medical transport organization. He and his second wife, Diane, have one son.

Brown began writing while still in the Air Force. He freelanced for local newspapers and the air base press. Fellow servicemen thought he was preparing for officer's candidate school or working toward a master's degree, but by the time he was discharged, he had two novel manuscripts in hand. Through an agent, he signed a three-book deal with Donald I. Fine. The first book to come out, and what became the first in the <u>Patrick McLanahan</u> series, *Flight of the Old Dog* (1987), was actually the second book he wrote. He followed up with *Silver Tower* (1988), a nonseries book, because he hadn't yet completed the next McLanahan book, *Day of the Cheetah* (1989).

Brown couldn't believe he had a three-book contract. "I never truly believed I'd ever write more than three books—in fact I wasn't even sure *Flight of the Old Dog* was going to sell. So *Day of the Cheetah* was going to be the Old Dog's 'swan song,'"

Brown says on his Megafortress Web site. But *Old Dog* went into more than twenty-five paperback printings, and he has had plenty of opportunity since to flesh out the McLanahan universe.

In the first book of the series, McLanahan is engineer crew leader on a B-52 that is tasked to destroy a Soviet ground-based laser site. McLanahan and his mates take on additional assignments—from China to the Persian Gulf to the Balkans—before the hero retires and strikes out on his own with his freelance Nightstalkers team of commandos.

Many of Brown's books are set a few years in the future. They feature a lot of technical firepower, most of it still in development as Brown writes, and most of it coming into use after the books come out. In an interview with Dan Epstein, Brown said he enjoys no special privileges in gaining access to government air bases to inspect, for example, an antiballistic missile system at Kirkland Air Force Base in Albuquerque. In *Day of the Cheetah,* he described a cockpit technology in which gauges and meters were placed in different positions, some of them visible directly on the windscreen. "I wrote about that and thought-controlled aircraft, which were being experimented with at the Armstrong Laboratories at Wright Patterson Air Force Base," the author told Epstein. "They had a laboratory, which I wasn't allowed into, but they described it [as] experimenting with neural technology for thought-controlled planes."

Brown has written two books based on an interactive Atari game involving Task Force Talon, *Act of War* and *Edge of Battle*. He has also developed the Dreamland series with writer Jim DeFelice, about a later generation of pilots doing the same sorts of things McLanahan did, out of a top-secret research facility in the Nevada desert.

In the initial book, *Dreamland*, Lieutenant Colonel Tecumseh "Dog" Bastian must ferret out a spy who has infiltrated the development center. He gets help from family: daughter Captain Breanna Bastian Stockard and son-in-law, wheelchair-confined Major Jeff "Zen" Stockard. The tense drama culminates in a foray into Somalia with a test Megafortress bomber. "Few novelists can craft an aerial battle scene more strategically" than Brown and DeFelice, said *Publishers Weekly*. In a sequel, *Piranha* (2003), the team hastily puts an experimental undersea robot to work when a crisis erupts in the China Sea.

Brown admits that there's something of himself in his heroes. "Like most first novels, I think, *Flight of the Old Dog* is a 'fantasy autobiography'—the adventures you wished you had. I definitely wanted to be Patrick McLanahan—the lonely, quiet, unassuming guy with a little bit of an attitude that was the acknowledged world expert in strategic attack," he said in an interview for Shop@UKAmazon.com.

His readers obviously share this compassion for his character.

Works by the Author

Silver Tower (1988)

Hammerheads (1990)

Chains of Command (1993)

Storming Heaven (1994)

Fatal Terrain (1997)

Act of War (2005)

Edge of Battle (2006) sequel to *Act of War*

Shadow Command (2008)

Dale Brown's Dreamland Series, with Jim DeFelice

Dreamland (2001)
Nerve Center (2002)
Razor's Edge (2002)
Piranha (2003)
Strike Zone (2004)
Armageddon (2004)
Satan's Tail (2005)
End Game (2006)
Retribution (2007)
Revolution (2008)

Patrick McLanahan Series

Flight of the Old Dog (1987)
Day of the Cheetah (1989)
Sky Masters (1990)
Night of the Hawk (1992)
Shadows of Steel (1996)
The Tin Man (1998)
Battle Born (1999)
Warrior Class (2001)
Wings of Fire (2002)
Air Battle Force (2003)
Plan of Attack (2004)
Strike Force (2007)
Rogue Forces (2009)

Editor

Combat, with Larry Bond, Stephen Coonts, and David Hagberg (2001)

For Further Information

Dale Brown entry, Contemporary Authors Online. Reproduced in Biography Resource Center. Farmington Hills, MI: Thomson Gale, 2008. http://galenet.galegroup.com/serviet/BioRC (viewed January 28, 2008).

Dale Brown interview, Shop@UKAmazon.com. http://genres.ukauthors.com/modules.php?name=News&file=article&sid=176 (viewed February 1, 2008).

Dale Brown Megafortress Web site. http://www.megafortress.com (viewed November 7, 2008).

Dale Brown's Dreamland review, *Publishers Weekly*, May 14, 2001.

Dale Brown's Dreamland Web site. http://www.megafortress.com/dreamland/ (viewed January 28, 2008).

Edge of Battle review, *Publishers Weekly*, March 27, 2006.

Epstein, Dan, Dale Brown interview, UnderGroundOnline. http://www.ugo.com/channels/freestyle/features/dalebrown/default.asp (viewed January 28, 2008).

Gaughan, Thomas, *Storming Heaven* review, *Booklist*, July 1994.

Pitt, David, *Strike Force* review, *Booklist*, May 15, 2007.

Sky Masters review, *Publishers Weekly*, May 31, 1991.

Storming Heaven review, *Publishers Weekly*, August 1, 1994.

Dan Brown

Adventure; Crime; Thrillers: Cipher, Religious, Techno

Benchmark Title: *The Da Vinci Code*

Exeter, New Hampshire

1964–

About the Author and the Author's Writing

With some 60.5 million copies in print in its first three years of publication, Dan Brown's *The Da Vinci Code* is one of the most popular fiction books of all time. It inspired a motion picture in 2006 directed by Ron Howard and starring Tom Hanks and Audrey Tautou. And it engendered a mini industry of spinoff books—most fostering or responding to religious elements of the novel's plot.

As *The Da Vinci Code* opens, series hero Robert Langdon is summoned to the Louvre. A curator has been murdered. Near the body is a puzzling riddle that leads to hidden symbols in the artwork of Leonardo Da Vinci. With assistance from French cryptologist Sophie Neveu, Langdon uncovers a secret society, the Priory of Sion, which for centuries has kept hidden a religious relic. A second hush-hush organization, the fundamentalist Catholic sect Opus Dei, is out to gain the same information as Langdon, and it's a race to see who gets there first.

"Leonardo da Vinci was a man centuries ahead of his time," Brown told *CNN Sunday Morning*. "He was fascinated with secrets. He was one of the first cryptologists, and he devised many ways to keep information secret, and portray it in ways that most people when you look at a painting, don't really see." Brown spun what appear to be hidden meanings in Da Vinci's art into a breath-taking chase.

Brown said he first learned of secret messages in Da Vinci's paintings while studying art at the University of Seville in Spain. He found more details in the Vatican library and the Louvre. Brown and his wife, Blythe, researched the book for more than a year.

The book's plausibility triggered various reactions within a sensitive religious community. Although some supported Brown's research and conclusions and believe they draw logically from the information he uncovered, which has to do with Jesus' relationship to Mary Magdalene; others called him heretical.

"The book suggests—as some feminist scholars have been arguing for a while— that the original Jesus movement was much more welcoming to women, marriage, and sexuality than the church Constantine and Augustine handed on to us," Patrick McCormick wrote in *U.S. Catholic*.

Collin Hansen, writing for *Christianity Today,* criticized the work. "Though un-original in its allegations, *The Da Vinci Code* proves that some misguided theories never entirely fade away. They just reappear periodically in a different disguise."

Gerald O'Collins, a Jesuit writing in *America,* faults Brown's facts and conclusions and suggests the author "belittles the Jewish roots of Christianity."

In response to these charges, Brown first of all stresses that the work is a novel. The grounding—that is, the artwork and architecture and documents and rituals discussed—do exist, but the book is fiction. That the result to many is so realistic is simply the result of the writer's craft.

"This book is not anti-anything," Brown insists on his Web site. "I wrote this story in an effort to explore certain aspects of Christian history that interest me. The vast majority of devout Christians understand this fact and consider *The Da Vinci Code* an entertaining story that promotes spiritual discussion and debate."

Brown knew what he was getting into. "The response from priests, nuns—all sorts of people in the church—for the most part has been overwhelmingly positive. There have been a few people for whom the book was shocking and was upsetting, but less than 1 percent," he told interviewer C. M. McDonald.

Theology aside, it's a great read. "The book moves at a breakneck pace," said *New York Times* reviewer Janet Maslin, "with the author seeming thoroughly to enjoy his contrivances. Virtually every chapter ends with a cliffhanger, not easy, considering the amount of plain old talking that gets done. And Sophie and Langdon are sent on the run, the better to churn up a thriller atmosphere. To their credit, they evade their pursuers as ingeniously as they do most everything else."

Brown in 2007 prevailed in a copyright infringement suit brought in British court by Michael Baigent and Reichard Leigh, authors of a nonfiction book, *Holy Blood, Holy Grail* (1982), from which they claimed Brown borrowed major elements regarding the possible marriage of Jesus and Mary Magdalene. Brown argued that he found the same information in the same sources as the authors.

Brown was born in Exeter, New Hampshire, in 1964. His father taught mathematics. His mother sang sacred music professionally. He attended Phillips Exeter Academy and returned there to teach English after graduating from Amherst College in 1986. This was after a year in California writing songs. His wife, Blythe, is an art historian and assists with his research.

The author admits to enjoying the Indiana Jones action movies and Pink Panther comic capers, as well as *Fantasia, Life Is Beautiful, Annie Hall,* and Zeffirelli's *Romeo and Juliet.* Musically, he sways to Spanish singer Franco de Vita, Sarah Mclachlan, Enya, and the Gypsy Kings. It's a rare day he is not at his desk writing by 4 A.M. He takes hourly breaks to do a few quick stretches and exercises.

Brown's reading interests are largely classical. He enjoys William Shakespeare for his superior wordplay and John Steinbeck for his masterful descriptions. When he decided to write fiction, Robert Ludlum's *The Bourne Identity* gave Brown a blueprint for a high-concept, international suspense novel. Once he had a manuscript, Brown found a publisher for his first book within three weeks.

This book, *Digital Fortress,* published in 1998, takes place within the National Security Agency where an ultra-sophisticated code-breaking computer meets a message it cannot crack. Head cryptographer Susan Fletcher becomes caught up in an accelerating maze of secrecy and lies. The code is so ingenious, so complex, so devious, it threatens to bring down the entire American intelligence network.

The dangers and blessings of technology is a recurring theme in Brown's books. Although he admires science's gains in preventing and curing disease, broadening food sources, and engendering new fuel options, the author said he is at the same time fearful of spacecrafts' ability to deliver precision warheads and distrustful of how genetic engineering might be misused.

Brown followed his first novel with *Angels & Demons*, the first adventure of Harvard symbologist Robert Langdon. Examining a mysterious design branded on a murdered physicist in Switzerland, Langdon is shocked. It is the sign of an ancient brotherhood, the Illuminati, the most powerful and secret organization ever, a rabid enemy of the Catholic Church. With the assistance of Vittoria Vetra, an Italian scientist, Langdon races against time to prevent a disaster at the Vatican.

After another techno-thriller, *Deception Point,* in which a bold scientific deception could influence a presidential election, Brown returned to the Langdon series with *The Da Vinci Code*. Its labyrinthine plot forced Brown to write an outline of more than 100 pages for it. "For me the most astonishing aspect of researching *The Da Vinci Code,*" Brown told BookBrowse, "was the realization that one of history's greatest 'secrets' is not nearly as secret as we think. Clues to its true nature are all around us … in art, music, architecture, legend, and history. In the words of Robert Langdon, 'The signs are everywhere.'"

 # Works by the Author

Fiction

Digital Fortress (1998)
Deception Point (2001)

Robert Langdon Series

Angels & Demons (2000)
The Da Vinci Code (2003)
The Lost Symbol (2009)

Nonfiction

187 Men to Avoid: A Survival Guide for the Romantically Frustrated Woman (1995), written with Blythe Brown, under the name Danielle Brown
The Bald Book (1998), cowritten with Blythe Brown

Adaptations in Other Media

The Da Vinci Code (2006), motion picture
Angels and Demons (2009), motion picture

For Further Information

Adler, Jerry, "Deciphering 'Code,'" *Newsweek*, May 26, 2003.
Angels and Demons review. *Publishers Weekly*, May 1, 2000.

Ayers, Jeff, *Deception Point* review. *Library Journal*, October 1, 2001.

Baigent, Michael, Richard Leigh, and Henry Lincoln. *Holy Blood, Holy Grail.* New York: Delacorte, 1980.

Bock, Darrell L. *Breaking "The Da Vinci Code."* Thomas Nelson, 2004.

Burstein, Daniel. *Secrets of the Code: The Unauthorized Guide to the Mysteries behind "The Da Vinci Code."* CDS Books, 2004.

"Conversation with Dan Brown, author of *The Da Vinci Code*," BookBrowse. http://www.bookbrowse.com/indez.cfm?page=author&authorID=226&view=interview (viewed January 1, 2004).

Court, Ayesha, "'Da Vinci Code' Inspires Fervent Deciphering." *USA Today,* May 8, 2003.

Dan Brown interview, "Meet the Writers," Barnes & Noble. http://btob.barnesandnoble.com/writers/writerdetails.asp?cid=1040938&userid=0H4K V3ZHMT#Interview (viewed Jan. 1, 2004).

Dan Brown Web site. http://www.danbrown.com/ (viewed November 7, 2008).

Digital Fortress review. *Publishers Weekly*, December 22, 1997.

"Fact or Fiction? Cracking *The Da Vinci Code*," *Pages*, September/October 2003.

Garlington, Lela, "Anticipation High for Talk on 'Heretic's Best-Seller," *Journal-Constitution,* October 30, 2003.

Hansen, Collin, "Breaking *The Da Vinci Code*." *Christianity Today,* November 7, 2003. http://www.christianitytoday.com/history/newsletter/2003/nov7.html (viewed January 1, 2004).

"Interview with Dan Brown," *CNN Sunday Morning*, May 25, 2003. http://www.cnn.com/TRANSCRIPTS/0305/25/sm.12.html (viewed January 1, 2004).

Lampman, Jane, "Who Was Mary Magdalene? The Buzz Goes Mainstream." *Christian Science Monitor*, November 14, 2003.

Mariampolski, Ruth, Dan Brown interview, Borders. http://www.bordersstores.com/features/feature.jsp?file=browndan (viewed January 1, 2004).

Maryles, Daisy, "Brown Rocks." *Publishers Weekly,* August 18, 2003.

Maryles, Daisy, "From Angels to Demons." *Publishers Weekly*, January 12, 2004.

Maryles, Daisy, "The Greening of Brown." *Publishers Weekly*, December 15, 2003.

Maryles, Daisy, "Veni, Vidi, Da Vinci." *Publishers Weekly*, March 31, 2003.

Maslin, Janet, "Spinning a Thriller from the Louvre." *New York Times*, March 17, 2003.

McCormick, Patrick, "Painted Out of the Picture: Part of the Best-Selling Appeal of *The Da Vinci Code* Is a Conspiracy That Has Kept Women from Taking Their Rightful Place in the Church." *U.S. Catholic*, November 2003.

McDonald, C. M., Dan Brown interview: *The Da Vinci Code.* http://www.modestyarbor.com/dan_brown.html (viewed January 1, 2004).

Miller, Laura, "The Da Vinci Con." *New York Times Book Review*, February 22, 2004.

Minzesheimer, Bob, "'Code' Deciphers Interest in Religious History." *USA Today,* December 11, 2003.

Mnookin, Seth, "Page-Turner: A Stolen 'Da Vinci'—or Just Weirdness? It's a Real-Life Mystery." *Newsweek,* June 9, 2003.

Morris, Edward, "Explosive New Thriller Explores Secrets of the Church." *BookPage,* April 2003.

O'Collins, Gerald, "Sensational Secrets." *America,* December 15, 2003.

Oldenburg, Don, "'Da Vinci Code' Plaintiffs Fail in Quest to Show Ideas Were Stolen." *Washington Post*, April 8, 2006.

Today show transcript, June 9, 2003. Dan Brown Web page. http://www.danbrown.com/media/todayshow.htm (viewed December 30, 2003).

White, Claire E. "Interview with Dan Brown," Writers Write. http://www.writerswrite/.com/journal/may98/brown.htm (viewed January 1, 2004).

Sandra Brown

Crime-Suspense; Romance; Romantic Suspense; Thrillers

Benchmark Title: *Slow Heat in Heaven*

Waco, Texas

1948–

About the Author and the Author's Writing

Sandra Brown is a Lone Star stater through and through, and it shows in her writing. "I write about Texas—and the South—a lot, because that's what I know," she said in an interview with Sandy Mitchell. "It's also an advantage to have the Texas heroes and history to use. Plus, 'all Texans are liars.' It makes for good stories."

Dozens of her novels have made the *New York Times* best-seller list, but when *The Alibi* reached number one in 1999, it was validation for the author who had made her mark writing category romances.

Born in Waco, Brown grew up in Fort Worth. As a child, the oldest of five sisters, she loved reading and storytelling. She majored in English at Texas Christian University and married Michael Brown after her sophomore year. They have two children and two grandchildren.

She continued her studies at Oklahoma State University and the University of Texas at Arlington, where she now lives. She performed in local theater, managed a cosmetics store, modeled clothing, and appeared in television commercials before joining the syndicated *PM Magazine* as a feature reporter. Spurred by her husband, when her television contract ended, she attended a writer's conference and wrote a romance novel. She lists Tennessee Williams, Taylor Caldwell, and Evelyn Anthony as among the writers who have influenced her own work.

Brown sold her first two books within two weeks of each other and soon had contracts with more than one publisher, writing under four pseudonyms. Raising a family, she was mom morning and night, writer in midday. On her Web site (http://www.sandrabrown.net/), she says she once worked out the plot for a story during a school field excursion to the circus.

"By the time I had written about forty romance books, I was eager to try something new," the author told Phillip Tomasso III of the *Charlotte-Austin Review*. "I made a gradual venture into the mainstream market. Mainstream has enabled me to plot without being constrained by the boundaries of a genre. As a writer, I welcome a challenge with each book that I write. This helps my characters become interesting."

In 1990, *Mirror Image* became the first of a string of her novels to appear on best-seller lists. In 1998, she received the Romance Writers of America Lifetime Achievement Award. She now produces one book a year but finds she puts in just as much work as when she was writing several because she spends more time shaping characters, developing plots, and researching backgrounds.

The Switch (2000), for example, required knowledge of ranching and artificial insemination. "I try and make my settings another character in the story," she said in an interview with Writers Review, "so that my reader gets a real sense of place. I want the reader to vicariously experience the climate, taste the regional food, smell the scents, all of which requires me to experience it myself."

For *Fat Tuesday*, which is set in New Orleans, she and her husband toured the bayou with a Cajun guide and went to Mardi Gras. She even interviewed a former police officer, a man who had left the department under disgrace, to get a true picture of the facets of corruption. For *The Alibi,* she spoke with a county prosecutor in Charleston.

Brown writes at an office away from her home, five days a week (more if under deadline), generally from noon to six. She writes a synopsis for each book for her editor, but seldom refers to it when actually writing. She says she knows the beginning and the ending, but not the route the characters will take to get there.

The author said she is confident, after nearly seventy books, that she has a distinct literary voice and knows what appeals to her readers. At the same time, she writes to satisfy herself; if she gets nervous reading a scene, then her fans are likely to get nervous as well.

Generally, for her story's action plan, the hero and heroine need to have some issue in common. They must be together in a situation. And they must develop an unexpected desire for each other. What pushes it all along? The hero or heroine must be "in very hot water within the first hundred pages," Brown told Skip Hollandsworth of *Texas Monthly*. "You not only face physical danger, but you must face a major psychological, moral dilemma within yourself that will change your life forever." Things accelerate from there. "Anticipation is everything," she added, referring to the compulsory love scenes.

Brown makes up her characters from scratch. "I like creating characters that are unique unto themselves," she said on her Web site. "The characters become so real to me, I can't imagine them looking any differently than how I see them [should they be cast for a movie]."

 ## Selected Works by the Author

For information about other books by the author, see her Web site http://www.sandrabrown.net

Slow Heat in Heaven (1988)
Best Kept Secrets (1989)
Mirror Image (1990)
Breath of Scandal (1991)
French Silk (1992)
Where There's Smoke (1993)
Charade (1994)
The Witness (1995)

Exclusive (1996)
Fat Tuesday (1997)
Unspeakable (1998)
The Alibi (1999)
Standoff (2000)
The Switch (2000)
Envy (2001)
The Crush (2002)
Hello, Darkness (2003)
Sunny Chandler's Return (2004)
White Hot (2004)
Chill Factor (2005)
Ricochet (2006)
Play Dirty (2007)
Smoke Screen (2008)

Adaptations in Other Media

French Silk (1994), television production

For Further Information

Hello, Darkness review. *Publishers Weekly*, July 7, 2003.

Hollandsworth, Skip, "The Woman on Top." *Texas Monthly*, August 2007.

Jones, Daniel, and John D. Jorgenson, eds. Sandra Brown entry. *Contemporary Authors New Revision Series*, volume 63. Detroit, MI: Gale Research, 1998.

Kemp, Barbara E., Sandra Brown entry. *Twentieth-Century Romance and Historical Writers*, 2nd ed., Lesley Henderson, ed. Chicago: St. James Press, 1990.

Mitchell, Sandra, "An Interview with Sandra Brown," MysteryCrimeFiction. http://mysterycrimefiction.suite101.com/article.cfm/an_interview_with_sandra_brown (viewed January 13, 2008).

Sandra Brown interview, Bookreporter. http://www.bookreporter.com/authors/au-brown-sandra.asp (viewed April 5, 2003).

Sandra Brown interview, Novel Journey, August 28, 2007. http://noveljourney.blogspot.com/2007/08/interview-with-nyt-best-selling.html (viewed January 13, 2008).

Sandra Brown interview, Writers Review. http://jez.cc/writersreview/authors/sandra_brown.htm (viewed May 19, 2003).

Sandra Brown Web site. http://www.sandrabrown.net (viewed November 7, 2008).

Tomasso, Phillip III, "An Interview with Bestselling Author Sandra Brown." *Charlotte Austin Review*, January 28, 2001.

von Pier, Sandi, Sandra Brown interview, RebeccasReads.com. http://rebeccasreads.com/interview/authors/092301_brown_interview_svp.html (viewed May 19, 2003).

Edna Buchanan

Crime

Benchmark Series: <u>Britt Montero</u>

Paterson, New Jersey

1939–

About the Author and the Author's Writing

Edna Buchanan has seen enough of society's underbelly to last her a lifetime—or at least as long as she wants to write murder thrillers. She began her writing career on a major city newspaper's crime beat. "Nobody loves a police reporter," she said on her Web site. "The job can be lonely and arduous. I have been threatened with arrest, threatened physically, had rocks thrown at me. I've gotten threatening letters, subpoenas, and obscene phone calls, some of them from my editors. It is tiring, haunting, and truly wonderful."

The author was born in 1939 in Paterson, New Jersey. Her father worked in a factory and later ran a tavern. Her mother was a respiratory therapist. Edna knew at a very early age—four, she says on her Web site—that she wanted to write professionally. She worked for Western Electric in New Jersey. She took creative writing classes at Montclair State Teachers College before she moved to Florida, where she joined the newsroom of the *Miami Beach Daily Sun* in the late 1960s. "That was my real education," she says in Contemporary Authors Online, "on-the-job training…. I have often felt that maybe I could have done better had I had a college degree or studied journalism. But I guess I've done OK."

In 1970, she began her professional writing career as a general assignment reporter for the *Miami Herald* with crime as a specialty. In 1973, when she took on the police beat, she found she had no shortage of stories, because the international drug trade had taken hold of the city. She received a Pulitzer Prize in 1986 for general reporting. Two years later, she left the newspaper. She described her journalistic years in two memoirs, *The Corpse Had a Familiar Face* (1987) and *Never Let Them See You Cry* (1992).

Buchanan's first crime novel, a police procedural called *Nobody Lives Forever* (1990), garnered an Edgar Award nomination. The next book began her long-running <u>Britt Montero</u> series, *Contents under Pressure* (1992). The heroine has a lot in common with the author: she is a reporter who goes all out to secure a story. The daughter of a Cuban freedom fighter, Montero also mirrored Miami's societal and political complexities.

On her Web site, the author says she has found crime fiction very satisfying because, often starting with a real case, she can bend and shape it and actually give it a
satisfactory resolution that is not always available in reality or in true-crime writing.

"The genre is an escape, a sanctuary, in an increasingly chaotic world overtaken
by unresponsive government agencies, rush hour traffic, voice mail, and other unspeakable torments," she told MysteryNet.com. "Mystery novels offer intellectual
challenge, structure, and triumph of logic and order in a world where such comforts are
increasingly rare."

Critics have seen Buchanan's fiction blossom. "Montero becomes a more tex-
tured, deeper character with each entry in the series," *Booklist* reviewer Wes
Lukowsky said of *Love Kills* (2007), "and the personal revelations here are as riveting
as the crimes being investigated."

Buchanan is fond of her characters. "I spend more time with these characters than
with my own friends," she told Bookreporter. "Each is flawed, with his and her own
ghosts and personal problems. They clash, often with each other, yet work as a team to
accomplish what seems impossible. They are funny, brave, loyal and very human."

Ideas come easily to Buchanan. She once interviewed a convicted murderer, a
woman who admitted to her sexual excitement in stabbing her victim repeatedly. The
author used that shocking personality for the character of Keppie Travis in *Garden of
Evil* (1999). Travis kidnaps Britt Montero and takes her on a wild shooting spree. The
author's familiarity with Miami's detectives assigned to review unsolved crimes similarly inspired a new series that began with *Cold Case Squad* (2004). "There's so little
true justice in the world, and we all yearn for justice. It's a thrill when the ghost of
some murdered person can finally rest because someone is out there following up on
forgotten cases to bring the truth to light," she told *Publishers Weekly*.

Works by the Author

Nobody Lives Forever (1990)
Legally Dead (2008)

Britt Montero Series

Contents under Pressure (1992)
Miami, It's Murder (1994)
Suitable for Framing (1995)
Act of Betrayal (1996)
Margin of Error (1997)
Garden of Evil (1999)
You Only Die Twice (2001)
The Ice Maiden (2002)
Love Kills (2007)

Cold Case Series

Cold Case Squad (2004)
Shadows (2005)

Contributor

Naked Came the Manatee, with Brian Antoni, Dave Barry, Tananarive Due, James W. Hall, Vicki Hendricks, Carl Hiaasen, Elmore Leonard, Paul Levine, and Evelyn W. Mayerson (1996)

Nonfiction

Carr: Five Years of Rape and Murder (1979)

The Corpse Had a Familiar Face: Covering Miami, America's Hottest Beat (1991)

Never Let Them See You Cry: More from Miami, America's Hottest Beat (1992)

Vice: Life and Death on the Streets of Miami (1992)

For Further Information

Edna Buchanan interview, Bookreporter, 2004. http://www.bookreporter.com/authors/au-buchanan-edna.asp (viewed February 21, 2008).

"Edna Buchanan on Writing Mysteries," MysteryNet.com. http://www.mysterynet.com/books/testimony/ghosts.shtml (viewed February 21, 2008).

Edna Buchanan profile, Contemporary Authors. Reproduced in Biography Resource Center. Farmington Hills, MI: Gale, 2008. http://galenet.galegroup.com/servlet/BioRC (viewed February 21, 2008).

Edna Buchanan Web site. http://www.ednabuchanan.com/ (viewed November 8, 2008).

"Footloose in Florida," Salon.com. http://archive.aslon/com/books/feature/2000/01/28/mysteries/index1.html (viewed February 21, 2008).

Howell, Kevin, "New Technology Solves Old Cases and Writes New Books." *Publishers Weekly*, April 19, 2004.

Lukowsky, Wes, *Love Kills* review. *Booklist*, May 1, 2007.

Lee Child

Adventure; Crime; Thrillers: Military, Political

Benchmark Series: <u>Jack Reacher</u>

Coventry, England
1954

Photo credit: Sigrid Estrada

About the Author and the Author's Writing

Jack Reacher is about as footloose as you can be. He has no family. He owns no home, no automobile, no clothing except what he's wearing. Well, he does have a fold-up toothbrush. In the novel *Bad Luck and Trouble* (2007), when his motel room is severely trashed, what really troubles him? They threw his toothbrush on the floor and crushed it underfoot. "Bastards," Reacher says. That really made him mad.

Lee Child's series character Jack Reacher, "the Paul Bunyan of the thriller world, is a driver who's known to travel so lightly that his toothbrush, passport and meager funds are his only baggage," marveled Janet Maslin in a review in the *New York Times*. The charismatic ex-military MP has steadily worked his way onto the best-seller lists.

Child was born in Coventry, England, in 1954. He was educated in a middle-class environment in Birmingham. Growing up, he read Enid Blyton's <u>Secret Seven Society</u> stories, Captain W. E. Johns's <u>Gimlet</u> books, and Alistair MacLean's adventures. He earned a law degree, with honors, from University of Sheffield in 1977 but never practiced. "I would recommend doing a law degree but not doing it as a career," he told interviewer David Henry of Manchester Online. "It gives you an insight into how the world works, but you are not worried about your marks, so you can do other things." Child met his future wife, American-born Jane, at university. They have one child and now live in the United States.

For two decades, Child worked for Granada Television in Manchester, England, as a presentation director and shop steward involved with such programs as *Jewel in the Crown, Prime Suspect*, and *Brideshead Revisited*. After a downsizing in the late 1990s, he decided to write a thriller. "To me there is only one genre: suspense/mystery/crime," he said in a *Publishers Weekly* interview in 2004. "Right from the cave

38

man days, we had stories that involved danger and peril, and eventually safety and resolution."

Child had no writing experience, but he'd seen what worked in television if one aimed high. He had come to enjoy Robert B. Parker's <u>Spenser</u> novels and John D. MacDonald's <u>Travis McGee</u> stories. He set out to create his own solid series character.

"The plot is like a rental car, it's got to work for a week and then you forget about it…. But it's the character that endures in people's imagination," he said in a TWBooks interview.

With a low tolerance for depressed, dysfunctional, alcoholic heroes, he created normal, decent, totally unadorned Reacher, albeit a man with no home or personal ties. "I was determined to avoid the hero-as-self-aware-damaged-person paradigm," he said in a WritersWrite interview. "I'm afraid as a reader I got sick of all the depressed and miserable alcoholics that increasingly people the genre. I wanted a happy-go-lucky guy. He has quirks and problems, but the thing is, he doesn't know he's got them."

In one respect, Reacher is Child. Reacher was demoted to captain and drummed out of the service. "And cast adrift," said Child in *Mystery Scene*. "Which is why I started writing, I suddenly needed a new career after 18 years of being a TV director."

Child's series hero is disciplined and skilled. Overseas for so long, he's only now had the opportunity to explore his home country, the United States. He's unconnected. He pays no Social Security, he receives no mail. That's part of a dream for his readers, who are about evenly split between genders. "For men, as they get bogged down with responsibilities, commitments, bureaucracy, it is a fantasy just to think of shedding everything literally…. For women, there's a kind of fantasy that such a man might conceivably knock on her door. Mainly because he wouldn't stick around," Child said in an interview with *Time*'s Andrea Sachs. Reacher's personability, and his optimal sense of survival, strike a chord with readers.

Child shuns villains of the James Bond/Dr. No mold. "In a sense I do wish to have banal baddies, and explore the issue that evil is often banal," he commented in a SHOTSmag interview. He added, however, that if Reacher is a David, he needs a Goliath, and "Goliath has to be someone who is very fearsome, to balance and retain a level of suspense."

To start a novel, Child needs only a "thing," a hook, something that lets Reacher find his way. He does research as necessary, although for *Without Fail*, which looks closely at Secret Service methods of protecting the vice president, the author had no cooperation. So he made a good guess. "The thing that haunts the Secret Service is the JFK assassination," he said in a BookPage conversation. Thus its actions are all based on never letting that happen again.

Child says he writes quickly and generally completes a manuscript in six months. "Mostly I write very instinctively, but the one rule I trust is that the first line is the most important line, the first paragraph, the first page," he told interviewer Jeff Abbott. "You've got to start with action, or a question, or the promise of something imminent."

And that's how *Gone Tomorrow* (2009) starts: Reacher is riding on a New York subway when he sees a woman who exhibits all the traits of a suicide bomber.

Works by the Author

Jack Reacher Series

The Killing Floor (1997)
Die Trying (1998)
Tripwire (1999)
Running Blind (2000), in United Kingdom retitled *The Visitor*
Echo Burning (2001)
Without Fail (2002)
Persuader (2003)
The Enemy (2004)
One Shot (2005)
The Hard Way (2006)
Bad Luck and Trouble (2007)
Nothing to Lose (2008)
Gone Tomorrow (2009)

Contributor

Fresh Blood 3, edited by Maxim Jakubowski and Mike Ripley (1999), includes "James Penney's New Identity"

Like a Charm, edited by Karin Slaughter (2004), includes "The Snake Eater by the Numbers"

The Cocaine Chronicles, edited by Gary Phillips and Jervey Tervalon (2005), includes "Ten Keys"

Death Do Us Part, edited by Harlan Coben (2006), includes "Safe Enough"

Bloodlines, edited by Jason Starr and Maggie Estep (2006), includes "The .50 Solution"

Greatest Hits: Original Stories of Hitmen, Hired Guns, and Private Eyes, edited by Robert J. Randisi (2006), includes "The Greatest Trick of All

The Chopin Manuscript, with David Corbett, Jeffery Deaver, Joseph Finder, Jim Fusilli, John Gilstrap, James Grady, David Hewson, John Ramsey Miller, P. J. Parrish, Ralph Pezullo, S. J. Rozan, Lisa Scottoline, Peter Spiegelman, and Erica Spindler (2007)

Editor

Killer Year: Stories to Die For … from the Hottest New Crime Writers (2007)

For Further Information

"A Reacher Moment… or Two," TW Books. http://www.twbooks.co/uk/crimescene/leechildinterview.htm (viewed February 21, 2008).

Abbott, Jeff, "A Conversation with Lee Child," Writer2Writer. http://www.jeffabbott.com/writer_child.html (viewed January 31, 2008).

Donahue, Dick, "Late to the crime scene," *Publishers Weekly*, May 31, 2004.

Grollman, Michael S., "Lee Child's Knight Errant," BookPage. http://www.bookpage.com/0205bp/lee_child.html (viewed February 21, 2008).

Henry, David, "The Thrill of Success," Manchester Online, 2004. http://www.manchesteronline.co.uk/entertgainment/arts/literature/s/87/87264_the_thrill_of_success.html (viewed October 17, 2004).

Jack Reacher Web site. http://www.jackreacher.co.uk/ (viewed February 21, 2008).

Karim, Ali, "Shooting the Breeze with Lee Child," SHOTSmag.com, 2005. http://www.shotsmag.co/uk/interviews2005/lee_child.html (viewed February 21, 2008).

Lee Child Web site. http://www.leechild.com (viewed February 21, 2008).

Maslin, Janet, "He's Taut of Style and Light of Foot." *New York Times*, May 14, 2007.

Ott, Bill, "Roughing Up His Readers." *American Libraries*, February 2007.

Sachs, Andrea, "Q&A: Author Lee Child." *Time*, June 11, 2007.

Smith, Kevin Burton, "This Man's Army." *Mystery Scene*, Summer 2004.

White, Claire E., "A Conversation with Lee Child," Writers Write. http://www.writerswrite.com/journal/aug01/child.htm (viewed September 9, 2004).

Lincoln Child and David Preston

Adventure: Survival/Disaster, Paranormal; Espionage; Christian Fiction

Benchmark Title: *The Relic*

Lincoln Child
Westport, Connecticut
1957–
Douglas Preston
Cambridge, Massachusetts
1956–

Lincoln Child, photo by Chris Pedota

About the Authors and the Authors' Writing

Although they also write separately, their prose written together has soared onto the best-seller lists. When Lincoln Child worked as an editor at St. Martin's Press in New York in the mid-1980s, he wanted someone to write a book about the American Museum of Natural History. Doug Preston worked for the museum and wrote for the institution's magazine. The two met, hit it off, and inked a contract. Preston wrote and Child edited the nonfiction *Dinosaurs in the Attic*.

David Preston, photo by Fred J. Field/
Boston Globe

Then Preston had a new idea, a murder mystery. Child thought it might do better as a techno-thriller. Why not set it in a natural history museum? Why not write it together?

"I was in the process of leaving the publishing industry by that time and my own nascent writing interests—which had more or less dried up while working so closely with other people's manuscripts—had begun to reassert themselves," Child said in a conversation with New Mystery Reader. "That was how *Relic* got started."

"I think that book writing partnerships are often extremely difficult and fraught with problems," Preston said in an Absolute Write interview. "But Lincoln and I, we both have similarly twisted minds. We both see the world in the same way, and have absolute faith and trust in each other's judgment."

Their first effort—about murders in the New York Museum of Natural History and autopsy evidence that the killer was not a human—was made into a motion picture in 1997, and their continued collaboration has yielded a dozen best-selling novels, with the authors promising that there are more to come.

Lincoln Child was born in Westport, Connecticut, in 1957. He majored in English at Carleton College in Northfield, Minnesota. Following graduation, he went to work for St. Martin's as an editorial assistant in 1979, and within five years, he had moved up to full editor. He worked on books by James Herriot and M. M. Kaye, among others. He established the company's mass-market horror division in 1987 and edited a handful of horror anthologies, but soon after, he left to become a systems analyst for Metropolitan Life Insurance. When his partnership with Preston blossomed, Child became a full-time writer. Now a New Jersey resident, he has written several solo novels, including *Utopia*. He and his wife, Luz, have one child.

Douglas Preston was born in Cambridge, Massachusetts, in 1956. After graduating from Pomona College in California with a bachelor of arts degree in 1978, he joined the staff of the American Museum of Natural History in New York, where he managed and wrote for its publications section. He also wrote for periodicals such as *Atlantic Monthly* and *Smithsonian* and penned nonfiction books about the American Southwest—among them, *Cities of Gold*. In 1985, he was managing editor of the journal *Curator*. The next year, he moved to New Mexico and became a full-time writer. Preston and his wife, Christine, have three children.

There's give-and-take when these writers team up. First they hash out a plot, by phone, fax, or e-mail. Child creates an outline, and they bat it back and forth until both are satisfied. Preston writes a draft. Child edits it. Preston polishes it. With time, the two have become more comfortable with each other's thinking, each other's way of writing, so the steps have gone more smoothly.

Do they disagree? "Of course we do!" Preston told interviewer Hallie Ephron. "Sometimes, we argue like an old married couple…. The finished books are much better as a result of our always questioning each other's work, trying to find the best possible way in which to write the story."

The authors live at different ends of the country, and they have different writing inclinations outside their partnership. "Linc is more attracted to high-tech stories, I'm more attracted to adventure stories," Preston told Bookreporter.com. "Our joint novels seem to swing back and forth between these extremes, but when we go off on our own, we have our own areas of interest." For example, Child initially proposed *Utopia* as a joint novel, Preston demurred. So Child wrote it on his own and achieved popular success.

Sometimes readers have an expectation that each new book will be bigger and better than the last. "I would hope that, if you people your story with characters the reader can identify and empathize with, if you place them in an interesting setting, and present them with an interesting problem, you won't need to rely on special effects or overblown devices," Child said in an interview on the Hatchette Book Group Web site.

In a Meet the Writers interview, Child offered advice to would-be writers: "Be patient, and have fun—it sounds like a truism, but the act of writing should be, in part, its own reward. Doug and I tried to have fun while we wrote *Relic*, and we also tried hard to make it the kind of book that we ourselves would like to read."

Works by Lincoln Child and Douglas Preston

The Relic (1995)
Mount Dragon (1996)
Reliquary (1997)
Riptide (1998)
Thunderhead (1999)
The Ice Limit (2000)
The Cabinet of Curiosities (2002)
Still Life with Crows (2003)
*Brimston*e (2004)
Dance of Death (2005)
The Book of the Dead (2006)
The Wheel of Darkness (2007)
Cemetery Dance (2009)

Anthology

Thriller: Stories to Keep You Up All Night, edited by James Patterson (2006), includes "Gone Fishing"

Works by Lincoln Child

Utopia (2002)
Death Match (2004)
Deep Storm (2007)
Terminal Freeze (2009)

Editor (Lincoln Child)

Dark Company: The Ten Greatest Ghost Stories (1984)
Dark Banquet: A Feast of Twelve Great Ghost Stories (1985)
Tales of the Dark (1987)
Tales of the Dark 2 (1987)
Tales of the Dark 3 (1988)

Works by Douglas Preston

Jennie (1994)
The Codex (2004)
Tyrannosaur Canyon (2005)
Blasphemy (2008)

Nonfiction (Douglas Preston)

Dinosaurs in the Attic: An Excursion into the American Museum of Natural History (1986)

Talking to the Ground: One Family's Journey on Horseback across the Sacred Land of the Navajo (1996)

Royal Road: El Camino Real from Mexico City to Santa Fe (1996)

Cities of Gold: A Journey across the American Southwest (1999)

Ribbons of Time: The Dalquest Research Site (2006)

The Monster of Florence, with Mario Spezi (2008)

Adaptations in Other Media

The Relic (1997), motion picture based on the novel

For Further Information

Douglas Preston and Lincoln Child interview, May 2005, bloggingauthors.com. http://www.bloggingauthors.com/2006/05/05/interview-douglas-preston-lincoln-child-new-york-times-bestsellers/ (viewed November 3, 2007) (Page no longer active).

Douglas Preston interview, Absolute Write. http://www.absolutewrite.com/novels/douglas_preston.htm (viewed November 3, 2007).

Douglas Preston interview, Bookreporter. http://www.bookreporter.com/ authors/au-preston-douglas.asp (viewed November 3, 2007).

Ephron, Hallie, "Interview: Douglas Preston & Lincoln Child, New York Times Bestsellers," Bloggingauthors.com. http://www.bloggingauthors.com/2006/05/05/interview-douglas-preston-lincoln-child-new-york-times-bestsellers/ (viewed November 9, 2007).

Gulli, Andrew F., "Interview: Douglas Preston." *Strand Magazine*, October 2008.

Lincoln Child and Douglas Preston interview, Meet the Writers, Barnes & Noble. http://www.barnesandnoble.com/writers/writerdetails.asp?z=y&cid=1021830#interview (viewed November 15, 2007).

Lincoln Child and Douglas Preston Web site. http://www.prestonchild.com/ (viewed November 8, 2008).

Lincoln Child interview, Hatchettebookgroup.com http://www.hachettebookgroupusa.com/authors/3/1290/interview10524.html (viewed November 3, 2007).

Lincoln Child interview, New Mystery Reader. http://www.newmysteryreader.com/lincoln_child.htm (viewed November 3, 2007).

Tom Clancy

Adventure; Espionage; Thrillers: Mercenary, Techno; True Adventure

Benchmark Series: <u>Tom Ryan</u>

Baltimore, Maryland

1947–

About the Author and the Author's Writing

Tom Clancy has dominated the techno and espionage thriller genres for two decades. He has also generated several hugely popular video games such as Ghost Recon and EndWar. The games in turn have yielded more books. At the highest echelon of success for American fiction writers, he's in a cycle only to be envied.

"The cornerstone of the Rainbow Six product line—the game—is a classic piece of Clancyana, a geopolitical action thriller in which the player leads a counterterrorism task force," J. C. Herz explained in the *New York Times* when the first Clancy game came out in 1998.

A decade—and several games—later, Splinter Cell, in which veteran agent Sam Fisher must infiltrate a vicious terrorist group to stem a planned attack, offered video game freaks a new challenge. "Kill too many criminals and you'll blow your cover," explained a Newswire story. "Hesitate too long and millions will die. Do whatever it takes to complete your mission, but get out alive." Cool stuff.

Clancy was born in 1947 in Baltimore, Maryland, the son of a mail carrier and a credit employer. In 1969, he graduated from Loyola College with a degree in English. That same year, he failed a military physical and also married Wanda Thomas, manager of an insurance agency. The couple has four children. Clancy quit his job as an insurance agent to write his first novel, *The Hunt for Red October*—the gripping story of efforts by naval leaders in America and the USSR to find a Soviet submarine whose captain wants to defect. He hoped the book would find a publisher; he never dreamed it would become a best seller.

Clancy's novels are packed with details of armaments and operations—it's not surprising Naval Institute Press was his first choice as publisher. But he disdains the label "techno thriller": "I've never written the same book twice," he asserted in a Quill Academy interview.

A major inspiration in his writing, Clancy told Verbosity, was Frederick Forsyth's *The Day of the Jackal*. "The book is perhaps the best thriller ever done—and more than that, it redefined the thriller novel, converting it into a highly respectable genre. Then I asked myself, 'Why are all the good thriller writers Brits? Why can't an American do it?' So I did, and I guess it worked."

The series character Jack Ryan, the author concedes, is largely a fictional version of himself. Clancy wants his characters to be humans, not superheroes, he said, with human issues to deal with, human virtues, and human flaws.

Not all reviewers find humanity in Clancy's characters. "There is something very creepy about Clancy's protagonists," Bill Bell said in a review of *The Teeth of the Tiger*. "All are developmentally arrested, all are obsessed with manliness and machinery, and all are posturing frat boy conversationalists."

Clancy continually researches for his books, and has been welcomed by military personnel to, among other facilities, the National Training Center in Fort Irwin, California, to witness Army war games. He has never, however, been privy to classified documents; and he has no security clearance. What he writes about is based on material openly available. He interviewed Edward L. Beach, a World War II submarine captain, and Arkady Shevchenko, a Soviet defector, for firsthand details (never having been aboard a submarine before drafting *The Hunt for Red October* or inside a Politburo meeting before writing *Red Storm*).

Clancy's writing has been uncannily prescient. In his novel *Debt of Honor*, a character named Sato flies an airplane into the U.S. Capitol, killing most of the government leaders. However, touring Ground Zero in New York after September 11, 2001, Clancy is quoted in *The Writer* as saying, "You can't keep up with reality right now. Nobody has a big enough imagination."

Besides his own two series featuring CIA operatives Ryan and John Clark (a darker but more humorous variation on Ryan), and his nonfiction works, Clancy, with Martin H. Greenberg, has created the concept and universe for the <u>Power Plays</u> series; with Steve Pieczenik, he has shaped the <u>Net Force</u> and <u>Net Force Explorers</u> series for young adults and the <u>Op Center</u> series, all written by other authors.

Clancy's enormous popularity has given him a soapbox to air his political views. Following the 2001 terrorist attacks, he bemoaned in the *Wall Street Journal* the country's lack of confidence in the CIA, which with better resources and support might have prevented the hijackings: "The loss of so many lives in New York and Washington is now called an 'intelligence failure,' mostly by those who crippled the CIA in the first place, and by those who celebrated the loss of its invaluable capabilities."

Clancy told *Publishers Weekly*'s Jeff Zaleski that his readers are "people who want to know how the world really works. My covenant with my readers is that I tell them the way things really are. If I say it, it's real."

Is the writing life all fun and games? Clancy told Lev Grossman for *Time*, "I guess it is for the first one or two, but after that it just becomes miserable work, like digging in the dirt with a shovel. But it's something you have to do. You can't not do it."

 # Works by the Author

Fiction

Red Storm Rising, with Larry Bond (1986)
The Teeth of the Tiger (2003)

Jack Ryan Series

The Hunt for Red October (1984)
Patriot Games (1987)
Cardinal of the Kremlin (1988)
Clear and Present Danger (1989)
The Sum of All Fears (1991)
Debt of Honor (1994)
Executive Orders (1996)
The Bear and the Dragon (2000)
Red Rabbit (2002)

Jack Ryan Jr. Series

The Teeth of the Tiger (2003)

John Kelly/John Clark Series

Without Remorse (1993)
Rainbow Six (1998)

Tom Clancy's EndWar Series

EndWar, by David Michaels (2008)

Net Force Series, Created by Tom Clancy and Steve Pieczenik

Net Force, by Steve Perry and Steve Pieczenik (1998)
Hidden Agendas, by Steve Pieczenik (1999)
Night Moves, by Steve Pieczenik (1999)
Breaking Point, by Steve Perry and Steve Pieczenik (2000)
Point of Impact, by Steve Perry and Steve Pieczenik (2001)
Cybernation, by Steve Perry and Steve Pieczenik (2001)
State of War, by Steve Perry (2003)
Changing of the Guard, by Steve Perry and Larry Segriff (2003)
Springboard, with Steve Perry and Larry Segriff (2005)
The Archimedes Effect, with Steve Perry and Larry Segriff (2006)

Net Force Explorers Series (for Young Adults), Created by Tom Clancy and Steve Pieczenik

Virtual Vandals, by Diane Duane (1998)
The Deadliest Game, by Bill McCay (1998)
End Game, by Diane Duane (1998)
One Is the Loneliest Number, by Diane Duane, Steve Perry, and Steve Pieczenik (1999)

The Ultimate Escape (1999)
Cyberspy, by Bill McCay (1999)
The Great Race, with Bill McCay (1999)
Shadow of Honor, by Mel Odom (2000)
Private Lives, by Bill McCay (2000)
Safe House, by Diane Duane (2000)
Gameprey, by Mel Odom (2000)
Duel Identity, by Bill McCay (2000)
Deathworld, by Diane Duane (2000)
High Wire, by Mel Odom (2001)
Cold Case, by Bill McCay (2001)
Runaways, by Diane Duane (2001)
Cloak and Dagger (2002)
Own Goal (2002), published in the United States as *Death Match* (2003)

Power Plays Series, Created by Tom Clancy and Martin H. Greenberg

Politika (1997)
Ruthless.com (1998)
Shadow Watch (1999)
Bio-Strike (2000)
Cold War, by Jerome Preisler (2001)
Cutting Edge, by Jerome Preisler (2002)
Zero Hour, by Jerome Preisler (2003)
Wild Card, by Jerome Preisler (2004)

Tom Clancy's Ghost Recon

Ghost Recon (2008) by David Michaels

Tom Clancy's Op-Center Series, Created by Tom Clancy and Steve Pieczenik

Op-Center, by Steve Pieczenik (1995)
Mirror Image, by Steve Pieczenik and Jeff Rovin (1995)
Games of State, by Steve Pieczenik (1996)
Acts of War, by Steve Pieczenik (1996)
Balance of Power, by Steve Pieczenik (1998)
State of Siege, by Steve Pieczenik and Jeff Rovin (1999)
Divide and Conquer, by Steve Pieczenik and Jeff Rovin (2000)
Line of Control, by Jeff Rovin (2001)
Mission of Honor, by Jeff Rovin (2002)

Sea of Fire, by Jeff Rovin (2003)
Call to Treason, by Steve Pieczenik and Jeff Rovin (2004)
War of Eagles, by Steve Pieczenik and Jeff Rovin (2005)

Tom Clancy's Splinter Cell

Splinter Cell, by Raymond Benson writing as David Michaels (2004)
Operation Barracuda, by Raymond Benson writing as David Michaels (2005)
Checkmate, by David Michaels (2006)
Fallout, by David Michaels (2007)

Video Games

Red Storm Rising (1990)
SSN (inspired book of same title)
Shadow Watch (based on Power Play)
Rainbow Six Series (1998–2008)
Ghost Recon Series (2001–2007)
Splinter Cell Series (2002–2008)
EndWar Series (2008–)
Air Combat Series (2008–)

Nonfiction

Submarine: A Guided Tour inside a Nuclear Warship (1993)
Armored Cav: A Guided Tour of an Armored Cavalry Regiment (1994)
Fighter Wing: A Guided Tour of an Air Force Combat Wing (1995)
SSN: Strategies of Submarine Warfare (1996)
Marine: A Guided Tour of a Marine Expeditionary Unit (1996)
Airborne: A Guided Tour of an Airborne Task Force (1997)
Carrier: A Guided Tour of an Aircraft Carrier (1999)
Special Ops (2000)
War in Boats: My World War II Submarine Battle, with William J. Ruhe (2004)

Commander Series

Into the Storm: A Study in Command, with General Fred Franks (1997)
Every Man a Tiger, with General Charles Horner (1999)
Shadow Warriors, with General Carl Stiner (2002)
Battle Ready, with General Tony Zinni (2004)

Adaptations in Other Media

The Hunt for Red October (1990), motion picture
Patriot Games (1992), motion picture

Clear and Present Danger (1994), motion picture
Net Force (1998), television production
Op-Center (1999), television production
The Sum of All Fears (2002), motion picture

For Further Information

Bell, Bill, "It's Clancy Fun in the Son." *New York Daily News,* August 13, 2003.

Clancy, Tom, "First We Crippled the CIA. Then We Blamed It." *Wall Street Journal,* September 18, 2001.

Cowley, Jason, "He Is the Most Popular Novelist on Earth, Whose Images of Catastrophe Animate the Modern American Psyche," *New Statesman,* September 24, 2001.

Donnelly, John, Tom Clancy interview, Salon.com. http://www.salon.com/june97.clancy970604.html (viewed April 7, 2003).

Garson, Helen S. *Tom Clancy: A Critical Companion.* Westport, CT: Greenwood Press, 1996.

Goldstein, Bill, "Some Best-Seller Old Reliables Have String of Unreliable Sales," *New York Times,* January 20, 2003.

Grossman, Lev, "10 Questions for Tom Clancy." *Time,* July 29, 2002.

Herz, J. C., "For Clancyland, a Game-to-Novel Pipeline." *New York Times*, July 30, 1998.

Hormann, Richard, "Secret Agent Men: Web Spooks Dig Deep for Intelligence on Thriller Writer Tom Clancy." *Entertainment Weekly* (June 7, 2002).

"Is There a Clear and Future Danger? An Interview with Tom Clancy, Intellectual Capital, June 26, 1997. http://hem.passagen.se/clancy/interv9.htm (viewed June 5, 2003).

Jones, David, and John D. Jorgenson, eds., Tom Clancy entry. *Contemporary Authors New Revision Series,* volume 62. Detroit: Gale Research, 1998.

Kornbluth, Jesse, Tom Clancy interview, Book Report. http://hem/passagen.se/clancy.interv3.htm (viewed June 5, 2003).

Maryles, Daisy, "Clancy's Lucky 13th." *Publishers Weekly,* August 25, 2003.

Moire, Allen, "Tom Clancy's Timing Remarkable." *The Writer,* May 2002.

"Nivea for Men: Partners with Unisoft to Integrate Products into Tom Clancy's Splinter Cell Double Agent." PR Newswire, November 14, 2006.

Stern, Carol Simpson, Tom Clancy entry. *St. James Guide to Crime & Mystery Writers,* fourth edition, Jay P. Pederson, ed. Detroit, MI: St. James Press, 1996.

Tom Clancy interview, Quill Academy. http://hem/.passagen.se/clancy.interv10.htm (viewed June 5, 2003).

Tom Clancy interview, Verbosity. http://hem.passagen.se/clancy./interv6.htm (viewed June 5, 2003).

Tom Clancy Web site. http://www.penguinputnam.com (viewed April 7, 2003).

Tom Clancy Web site. http://www.clancyfaq.com/books/htm#books (viewed April 7, 2003).

Vinciguerra, Thomas, "Word for Word: The Clancy Effect; Quick! Man the F56 Kryton Hydro Thermal-Sensitive Torpedoes!" *New York Times,* August 18, 2002.

Zaleski, Jeff, "The Hunt for Tom Clancy." *Publishers Weekly,* July 13, 1996.

Harlan Coben

Crime; Sports; Thrillers

Benchmark Title: *Tell No One*

Newark, New Jersey
1962–

Photo credit: Beatrice Grand

About the Author and the Author's Writing

Myron Bolitar, the hero of Harlan Coben's long-running crime series, is a sports agent. That doesn't mean his books are about athletics or that the author is a red-blooded sports enthusiast. "I never watch it on TV…. What I like about the sports world is the potential for conflict and even murders," he said in an interview with Partners in Crime. "And it doesn't drive the books. The sports world is a super-intense, high-stakes microcosm. Every emotion is fervently raised to the tenth power."

And that's how Coben has garnered mystery writing's top honors, including the Anthony, Edgar, Nevermore, and Shamus awards.

Harlan Coben was born in Newark, New Jersey, in 1962. He is married to Anne Armstrong, a pediatrician whom he met at Amherst College. They were both members of Psi U fraternity. They have four children and live in New Jersey. Intending to pursue a law degree, Coben earned a bachelor of arts degree in political science from Amherst in 1984. But he'd already begun to write fiction. He never sent his first manuscript to a publisher. Based on experiences in Spain (his grandfather owned a travel company), Coben found his first work too self-absorbed to print. So he tried something else.

Coben developed a fascination with the crime genre by reading the current generation of mystery writers, Robert B. Parker, Mary Higgins Clark, Sue Grafton, and Lawrence Block. He took the mystery form as a springboard. "I always wanted to write 'novels of immersion,'" he told *Amherst* magazine interviewer Karen C. Fox. "The kind of book you take on vacation, and then you can't leave your room."

He wrote two paperback originals with sports settings, one in the romantic suspense vein about a Celtics star who fakes his own death, another about an AIDS researcher who is killed. (Both books are now out of print.) His third book, *Deal Breaker*

(1995), introduced Bolitar, a sharp-tongued hustler who still lives in his parents' basement and chums with "Win" Lockwood, a WASPish fan of sex movies. With his office manager, a bisexual former professional wrestler named Esperanza Diaz, he operates MB SportsReps. Coben has said the Bolitar character is loosely based on himself—in a wishful-thinking way.

Calling Coben's prose refreshing, Kevin Burton Smith in a review of *Darkest Fear* commended the "off-the-wall but always human characters—it all just feels right and comfortable, like slipping on a beloved old pair of running shoes. Better yet, the author has something to *say*."

Among themes found in Coben's novels is misunderstood past. "I love old secrets," the author said in a Mystery One Bookstore conversation. "I love family bonds that can strangle or soothe. I love terrible misfortune and impossible redemption."

Coben is a stay-at-home dad. Once the kids are off to school or daycare, he goes to a coffee shop or library and writes on a legal pad. He works from a rough outline. He later transfers, fleshes out, and edits the chapters in a word processing program. Often he experiences a rush of creative energy as he nears the end of a book.

"I settle on the crime ahead of time, but the other character stuff—will Myron and Win stay friends, for example—I'll decide what happens as I go along. I'll usually have an idea by the time I'm started for an early twist, but the rest of the twists come as I'm writing," he told *Atlantic Monthly*.

He is known for sharp turns and unexpected conclusions in his books. "I love those hands-out-of-the-graves moments where everything changes at the end," he admitted to fellow thriller author Jeff Abbott. "This is just the way my mind works…. I'm going to try to fool you."

After seven books, Coben left Bolitar for a while to write stand-alone novels. "I've never had an interest in writing a series like Hercule Poirot or Sherlock Holmes, where the character never ages or changes," the author said in an interview in *The Writer*. "I don't want Myron to just solve a case; I wanted it to be personal. The problem is: How many catharses can a man go through before he's unrealistic and no longer fun to write about?" (Bolitar returned in the 2006 novel *Promise Me*.)

Fortunately, Coben had plenty of non-Bolitar ideas. *Tell No One*, for example, is about pediatrician David Beck's pursuit of his wife's murderer—eight years later, when he receives an anonymous e-mail. The book sold better than the earlier crime series, probably because non-sports-fan readers gave it a try. The author had some reticence about how its suburban setting would fit with international conspiracy blockbusters. But he wrote what he was comfortable with. "That was the challenge: could I write about an ordinary man, with family bonds and ties, and still make that book big enough to work?" Coben explained to Dick Lochte for *Mystery Scene*. The book went back to press nine times in the first weeks it was on sale, proof enough of his success.

Ideas aren't that hard to come by, Coben says on his Web site. "The hard part is recognizing which ideas will work and developing that idea into a workable story. An idea is not a plot. An idea is not a novel. Turning it into a story … that's where the real work comes in."

Works by the Author

Play Dead (1990)

Miracle Cure (1991)

Tell No One (2001)

Gone for Good (2002)

No Second Chance (2003)

Just One Look (2004)

Three Great Novels (2004), omnibus includes *Tell No One, Gone for Good*, and *Darkest Fear*

The Innocent (2005)

The Woods (2007)

Hold Tight (2008)

Tell No One and Gone for Good (2008), omnibus

Myron Bolitar Mysteries

Deal Breaker (1995)

Drop Shot (1996)

Fade Away (1996)

Back Spin (1997)

One False Move (1997)

The Final Detail (2000)

Darkest Fear (2000)

Deal Breaker and Drop Shot (2006), omnibus

Promise Me (2006)

Long Lost (2009)

Contributor

Malice Domestic 7, edited by Sharyn McCrumb (1998), includes "A Simple Philosophy"

Opening Shots Volume 2: More Great Mystery and Crime Writers Share Their First Published Stories, edited by Lawrence Block (2001), includes "Entrapped"

Editor

Mystery Writers of America Presents Death Do Us Part: New Stories about Love, Lust, and Murder (2006), includes "Entrapped"

Adaptations in Other Media

Ne le dis a personne (2006), motion picture based on *Tell No One*

Deal Breaker (announced), motion picture based on the novel

For Further Information

Ayers, Jeff, *The Woods* review. *Library Journal*, March 15, 2007.

Fletcher, Connie, *Promise Me* review. *Booklist*, April 1, 2006.

Fox, Karen C., "The Subtle Art of the Suburban Page-Turner." *Amherst Magazine*, Spring 2005.

Harlan Coben interview, Partners & Crime. http://www.crimepays.com/coben.htm (viewed January 31, 2008).

Harlan Coben Web site. http://www.harlancoben.com/ (viewed January 31, 2008).

"Interview with Harlan Coben," Mystery One Bookstore. http://www.mysteryone.com/HarlanCobenInterview.htm (viewed January 31, 2008).

Konigsberg, Eric, "Paperback Writer." *Atlantic Monthly*, July–August 2007.

Lochte, Dick, "Mr. Coben's Neighborhood." *Mystery Scene*, Spring 2004.

Pfaff, Leslie Garisto, "In the Gray Zone with Harlan Coben." *The Writer*, September 2006.

Smith, Kevin Burton, *Darkest Fear* review, January magazine, August 2000. http://januarymagazine.com/crfiction/darkestfear.html (viewed February 8, 2008).

Swilley, Stephanie, "Harlan Coben Tells All," BookPage. http://www.bookpage.com/0107bp/harlan_coben.html (viewed January 31, 2008).

Margaret Coel

Crime

Benchmark Series: <u>Wind River Reservation</u>

Denver, Colorado
1937–

About the Author and the Author's Writing

Her experience as a journalist gave Margaret Coel a keen news sense. Her experience writing a history book gave her a mound of good information about the Arapahos in Colorado. Her attendance at a public talk by Tony Hillerman gave her a desire to write fiction. Her Roman Catholic background gave her an outlook for her mystery series character Father O'Malley. And her desire to depict the Native American world intelligently gave her the personality of character Vicky Holden.

All Coel needed was a plot, which she came up with quickly enough, and she was ready to write a successful crime-suspense novel—the first of many.

The author was born Margaret Speas in Denver, Colorado, in 1937. Her father was a railroad engineer. In 1960, she graduated from Holy Family High School and later from Marquette University, where she received a bachelor of arts degree. After completing graduate studies at the University of Colorado, she attended Oxford University. In 1962, she married dentist George W. Coel, and they had three children.

Margaret Coel worked as a reporter for the *Westminster* (Colorado) *Journal* in 1960 and 1961 and as a feature writer with the *Boulder Daily Camera* from 1972 to 1975. From 1985 to 1990, she taught writing at the University of Colorado in Boulder. She worked as a freelance writer from 1972 to 1990, and from 1995 on.

Coel's first book, published in 1981, was a nonfiction work that required four years of research, *Chief Left Hand: Southern Arapaho.* "That's what took me into the Arapaho world," the author said in an interview for *Rocky Mountain News* in 2008. "The government happened to send them to a reservation in central Wyoming, so when I decided to write mystery novels, I thought, 'I'll set the novels on the reservation.'"

Coel might never have latched onto the Native American theme in her fiction but for her attendance at a conference in 1985 at which mystery writer Hillerman described the challenges of writing novels that incorporated Navajo culture and lore. Coel knew she could do the same with the Arapaho.

As she settled into her research for what became the <u>Wind River Reservation</u> series of crime thrillers, she made several visits to speak with and observe the Arapaho. Trust came slowly. She related the experience, one day, of being outside the Blue Sky Hall and Wind River when a golden eagle circled overhead. One woman was startled, and took it as an ill omen. But the next day, the woman was visibly relieved. "They had consulted one of the elders who reminded them that whenever the eagle comes," Coel said in a Fresh Fiction interview, "it is a good sign. 'This white woman,' he said, 'will write the truth about our people.'"

"Conflict and suspense are, in my opinion, essential to any piece of writing with pretenses to being a novel," the author said in an interview with an Arapahoe Library District staff member. Personal conflict between the main characters exists in all of the author's Wind River Reservation novels. The conflict is Jesuit priest John O'Malley's continuing struggle to avoid alcohol and his newfound struggle to avoid romantic involvement with tribal lawyer Vicky Holden. And that's not to mention the conflict that arises from each new mystery. In *The Girl with Braided Hair* (2007), for example, the two become deeply involved in a decades old murder, and barely keep a few steps ahead of a very-much-alive killer who doesn't want his secrets revealed.

Coel didn't write her first novel until she had settled on her heroes. "In my opinion, the best mystery novels are character-driven," the author said in a Bookreporter interview. "Plots are fun and I certainly want a strong plot in a mystery novel, but the novels that resonate are those with great characters—the kind who get under your skin and seem like real people."

She settled on a Catholic hero to reflect her own religious background. O'Malley works at the reservation and has a strong knowledge of native lore. But he's forever an outsider. Holden is little better. She is apathetic to her native religion but is becoming increasingly appreciative of the elders and the cultural bonds of their spiritualism.

"They are people who live at the edge of two cultures," Coel said in an interview in *Mystery Scene* in 2006. "John is white, and has to learn about the Arapaho. Vicky is an Arapaho who has gone to the white culture and returned. I look at them as bridge people, people who have to understand both cultures."

The author traces her interest in Western history to her ancestors four generations ago who settled a year after the Sand Creek Massacre of 1864. As a result of the bloody episode, Arapahos and Cheyennes were forced out of Colorado Territory. Today the Arapaho and Shoshone share the Wind River Indian Reservation in Wyoming.

The Sand Creek Massacre figures in Coel's latest novel, *Blood Memory*, in which investigative reporter Catherine McLeod, already grappling with her unknown connections to the Arapaho killed during the warfare, has to elude a modern-day killer who doesn't want her to probe too deeply into the past.

Coel's work day begins at about 8:30 in the morning, she says. She writes fiction until about 2 in the afternoon, then deals with mail and e-mail and business matters. Research often takes her to outdoor sites or to library shelves.

She has written short stories featuring O'Malley, Holden, and the Arapahos for limited, signed hardcover publication. Each story is based on one of the ten Arapaho commandments.

Coel admits to a degree of serendipity in her writing success. "The Arapahos have a saying," she said in a *Mystery News* interview with Lynn Kaczmarek. "They say that stories exist in the universe and every once in a while they decide to be told and when they decide to be told, they choose the storyteller."

And with Margaret Coel, they've chosen well.

Works by the Author

Blood Memory (2008)

Ten Commandment Limited Edition Series

Dead End (1997)
Hole in the Wall (1998)
Honor (1999)
Stolen Smoke (2000)
The Woman Who Climbed to the Sky (2001)
My Last Goodbye (2002)
Bad Heart (2004)
Day of Rest (2005)
Nobody's Going to Cry (2006)
Whirlwind Woman (2007)

Wind River Reservation Series

The Eagle Catcher (1995)
The Ghost Walker (1996)
The Dream Stalker (1997)
The Story Teller (1997)
The Lost Bird (1999)
The Spirit Woman (2000)
The Thunder Keeper (2001)
The Shadow Dancer (2002)
Killing Raven (2003)
Wife of Moon (2004)
Eye of the Wolf (2005)
The Drowning Man (2006)
The Girl with Braided Hair (2007)

Anthologies

More Murder, They Wrote, edited by Elizabeth Foxwell and Martin H. Greenberg (1999), includes "The Man in Her Dream"

Crime through Time III, edited by Sharan Newman (2000), includes "Murder on the Denver Express"

Women before the Bench, edited by Carolyn Wheat (2001), includes "A Well Respected Man"

The World's Finest Mystery and Crime Stories: Third Annual Collection, edited by Ed Gorman and Martin H. Greenberg (2002), includes "A Well-Respected Man"

Wild Crimes, edited by Dana Stabenow (2004), includes "The Man Who Thought He Was a Deer"

Contributor

The Sunken Sailor, with Simon Brett, Jan Burke, Dorothy Cannell, Deborah Crombie, Eileen Dreyer, Carolyn Hart, Edward Marston, Francine Mathews, Sharan Newman, Alexandra Ripley, Walter Satterthwait, Sarah Smith, and Carolyn Wheat, edited by Elizabeth Foxwell (2004)

Nonfiction

Chief Left Hand: Southern Arapaho (1981)
Goin' Railroading, with Sam Speas (1985)

For Further Information

Blood Memory review, *Publishers Weekly*, July 21, 2008.

Cogdill, Oline, "At the Edge of Two Worlds." *Mystery Scene*, Fall 2006.

Kaczmarek, Lynn, Margaret Coel interview, Mystery News. http://www.blackravenpress.com/Author%20pages/mcoel.htm (viewed November 12, 2008).

Margaret Coel interview, Arapahoe Library District. http://arapahoelibraries.org/go2.cfm?pid=11739&p1=11404 (viewed November 12, 2008).

Margaret Coel interview, Bookreporter, September 9, 2003. http://www.bookreporter.com/authors/au-coel-margaret.asp (viewed November 12, 2008).

Margaret Coel interview, Fresh Fiction. http://freshfiction.com/author.php?id=152 (viewed November 13, 2008).

Margaret Coel Web site. http://www.margaretcoel.com/ (viewed November 12, 2008).

Rowan, John, *The Girl with Braided Hair* review. *Booklist*, August 2007.

Thorn, Patti, "Interview with Author Margaret Coel," *Rocky Mountain News*, August 29, 2008.

Michael Connelly

**Crime-Suspense; Thrillers:
Legal, Serial Killers**

Benchmark Series: <u>Harry Bosch</u>

Philadelphia, Pennsylvania

1956–

Photo credit: Robert Azmitia

About the Author and the Author's Writing

The Hieronymus Bosch we know little about was a fifteenth-century Dutch painter. The Harry Bosch we know quite a lot about, thanks to Michael Connelly's popular fiction series, is a twenty-first-century crime novel hero. Both Bosches lived in worlds of moral turpitude, violence, and sin. And Connelly won't be disappointed if his readers make a connection between painter and policeman.

Right out of the gate, Connelly, a Florida and California journalist, won the 1992 Mystery Writers of America Edgar Award for Best First Novel for *The Black Echo*. The book introduces Bosch, a veteran homicide detective with the Los Angeles Police Department. With a background as surreal as his historical namesake, Harry Bosch was the son of a defense attorney and a Hollywood prostitute. He grew up an orphan, joined the Army, was a "tunnel rat" in Vietnam, joined the cops when he returned, weathered an internal affairs probe into his killing of a suspect while with the robbery division, and ended up in homicide. As the series progresses, Bosch (in *Lost Light*) retires from the department, holds a private eye's ticket for a couple of years, then re-ups with the Robbery and Homicide Division's Homicide Special Unit (after *The Narrows*).

In the character's first appearance, he is assigned the case of a Vietnam vet—a fellow tunnel rat—whose body was found in a drainage pipe, dead of an apparent drug overdose. Bosch quickly gets his teeth in the puzzle. The reader only thinks he knows how it will turn out. "You start off seeing the light at the end of the tunnel," Connelly told Janet Maslin of the *New York Times*. "But all sorts of things can happen in the tunnel."

Harry Bosch "is more than just a cop—he's a man with a mission, a mission to, in his own words, 'speak for the dead,'" observe Kelty Levender and Dale Stoyer in a Harry Bosch page on ThrillingDetective.com, adding that resolution is "often at great personal and professional cost to Harry."

So who is the creator of this compelling character? Connelly was born in Philadelphia in 1956. In 1980, he earned a bachelor of arts degree in journalism from the University of Florida. He worked as a reporter with newspapers in Daytona Beach and Fort Lauderdale and was nominated for a Pulitzer Prize (with two fellow journalists) in 1986 for a South Florida *Sun-Sentinel* piece about survivors of an airline crash. He abandoned the Sunshine State for the Golden State, where he became a crime reporter for the *Los Angeles Times*.

While in college, Connelly discovered Raymond Chandler's crime prose and, interestingly, was able to channel his hero when he rented an apartment in L.A. that Chandler had once lived in. Connelly describes the place in *Echo Park*. In 2003 and 2004, he served as president of the Mystery Writers of America. Now a full-time novelist, he again lives in Florida.

Connelly has also swung some of the characters from the Bosch books into their own novels. Terry McCaleb, an FBI profiler in the Bosch books, takes center stage in *Blood Work* (1998), in which he recuperates from a heart transplant operation and ends up solving the murder of his donor. (Clint Eastwood played the role in the movie.) Rachel Walling, another FBI agent in *The Narrows* (2004), *Echo Park* (2006), and *The Overlook* (2006), first showed up in the stand-alone title *The Poet* (1996), along with tabloid reporter Jack McEvoy. In a slight departure, the heroine of *Void Moon* (2000) is cat burglar Cassie Black.

And in yet another departure, Connelly wrote a novel about a lawyer. Bosch's half-brother Mickey Haller is protagonist of *The Lincoln Lawyer* (2005). "It was certainly a switch since many of the detectives I know really despise criminal defense attorneys. But as I got into the writing, I realized that my character, Mickey Haller, was just as smart at what he does as Harry Bosch. He is just as resilient and relentless, too." Haller and Bosch are together in *The Brass Verdict* (2008).

Connelly is attuned to police procedure and has enjoyed a strong relationship with present and former detectives. "I always wanted to write about the spirit of what that job is like, the quiet nobility of it. It's thankless if you do it right, and all the cameras come out if you do it wrong," he told interviewer Colette Bancroft of the *St. Petersburg Times*.

Connelly can be described as a controlled writer. He appreciates that some authors let their characters direct the course, but he doesn't. "I don't even understand that," he said in an interview for Consumer HelpWeb. "To me, writing is a craft and I work at it. So when I compose my stories no characters—let alone the main character—do things I don't expect. They do what I tell them—through the writing—to do."

In a *Publishers Weekly* conversation with Jeff Zeleski, Connelly stated, "I do believe in evil." He explained further that most policemen he knows are less concerned with whether that evil is nature or nurture. They just want to squash it. "And that is more interesting to me as a writer, because it's very hard to do that, and it's very hard to do that without costing yourself something."

Works by the Author

The Poet (1996)

Blood Work (1998)

Void Moon (2000)

Three Great Novels 2: The Thrillers: The Poet, Blood Work, Void Moon (2002), omnibus

Chasing the Dime (2002)

The Lincoln Lawyer (2005)

Harry Bosch Series

The Black Echo (1992)

The Black Ice (1993)

The Concrete Blonde (1994)

The Last Coyote (1995)

Trunk Music (1997)

Angels Flight (1999)

The Harry Bosch Novels: Black Echo, Black Ice, Concrete Blonde (2000), omnibus

A Darkness More than Night (2001)

Three Great Novels: The Last Coyote, Trunk Music, Angels Flight (2001), omnibus

City of Bones (2002)

Lost Light (2003)

The Harry Bosch Novels: The Last Coyote, Trunk Music, Angels Flight (2003), omnibus

The Narrows (2004), sequel to *The Poet*

Three Great Novels 3: A Darkness More than Night, City of Bones, Lost Light (2004), omnibus

Two Great Novels: The Black Echo and The Black Ice (2004), omnibus

The Closers (2005)

Echo Park (2006)

The Overlook (2007), paperback edition includes bonus Chapter 23, which originally appeared on Connelly's Web site

The Brass Verdict (2008), also a sequel to *The Lincoln Lawyer*

Editor

The Best American Mystery Stories 2003, with Otto Penzler (2003)

Murder in Vegas: New Crime Tales of Gambling and Desperation (2005)

The Blue Religion: New Stories about Cops, Criminals, and the Chase (2008), includes "Father's Day"

Anthologies

Murderers' Row, edited by Otto Penzler (2003), includes "Two-Bagger"

The Best American Mystery Stories 2002, edited by James Ellroy and Otto Penzler (2002), includes "Two-Bagger"

Men from Boys, edited by John Harvey (2003), includes "After Midnight"

Murder ... and All That Jazz, edited by Robert J. Randisi (2004), includes the Harry Bosch story "Christmas Even"

Dangerous Women, edited by Otto Penzler (2005), includes "Cielo Azul"

The Secret Society of Demolition Writers, edited by Marc Parent (2005), anonymous story

Plots with Guns, edited by Anthony Neil Smith (2005), includes "Angle of Investigation"

The Penguin Book of Crime Stories, edited by Peter Robinson (2007), includes "Angle of Investigation"

Los Angeles Noir, edited by Denise Hamilton (2007), includes "Mulholland Drive"

Hollywood and Crime: Original Crime Stories Set during the History of Hollywood, edited by Robert Randisi (2007), includes "Suicide Run"

Dead Man's Hand: Crime Fiction at the Poker Table, edited by Otto Penzler (2007), includes "One Dollar Jackpot"

A Prisoner of Memory and 24 of the Year's Finest Crime and Mystery Stories, edited by Ed Gorman and Martin H. Greenberg (2008), includes "Mulholland Drive"

Nonfiction

Crime Beat (2006)

Adaptations in Other Media

Blood Work (2002), motion picture

For Further Information

Aldrich, Chris, Michael Connelly interview, *Mystery News,* October–November 2005.

Ayers, Jeff, "Connelly Finds Writing Short Is Not So Sweet," Seattle PI. http://seattlepi.nwsource.com/books/318417_connelly05.html (viewed October 28, 2007).

Ayers, Jeff, "Michael Connelly Q&A." *Library Journal,* October 1, 2005.

Bancroft, Colette, "For Author Michael Connelly, Crime Pays." *St. Petersburg Times,* October 25, 2007.

Fulford, Robert, "Forget Skirts and Spinach, This Gumshoe Works for the Badge." *National Post,* July 4, 2006.

Levender, Kelty, and Dale Stoyer, "Double-Barrelled Blast: Harry Bosch," Thrilling Detective. http://www.thrillilngdetective.com/eyes/bosch.html (viewed January 24, 2008).

Maslin, Janet, "The Crimes They Are A-Changin'." *New York Times*, May 13, 2002.

Michael Connelly interview, Book Help Web. http://book.consumerhelpweb. com/authors/connelly/interview.htm (viewed October 28, 2007.

Michael Connelly Web site. http://www.michaelconnelly.com (viewed March 25, 2008).

Zaleski, Jeff, "Writing Toward Justice." *Publishers Weekly*, April 12, 2004.

Robin Cook

Adventure; Thrillers: Medical, Bio, Business/Finance

Benchmark Title: *Coma*

New York, New York

1940–

Photo credit: John Earle

About the Author and the Author's Writing

Robin Cook started out in a *Coma*, overcame *Fever, Outbreak*, and *Mutation*, only to take a *Fatal Cure*. It was an *Acceptable Risk*, if not a major *Shock*, for the best-selling author. That's all to have a little fun with the writer who is widely credited with having created the modern medical thriller.

Cook was born in Woodside, Queens, New York, in 1940, the son of an artist father. In 1962, he graduated from Wesleyan University with a bachelor of arts degree. In the early 1960s, he worked as a laboratory assistant to oceanographer Jacques Cousteau. He earned his medical credentials from Columbia University in 1966 and did postgraduate study at Harvard University. He served in the U.S. Navy from 1969 to 1971 as an aquanaut and was discharged as a lieutenant commander. He has been twice married. He has homes in Boston and Florida.

After residencies at Queen's Hospital in Honolulu (1966–1968) and Massachusetts Eye and Ear Infirmary in Boston (1971–1975), Cook joined the latter facility's staff in 1975 as an ophthalmic surgeon. Still on staff, he has ended his private practice. Beginning in 1972, the year he wrote the nonfiction book *The Year of the Intern,* he was also a clinical instructor at Harvard Medical School. Sales of that book were a disappointment, but Cook wanted to write more. He turned to fiction for his next book.

"What I really wanted to do was make sure the book got published," he told reporter Judy Klemesrud. Thus, the thriller was set in hospital corridors. But more than a thriller, *Coma* afforded Cook the opportunity to examine women in medicine and unseemly practices in the marketing of organs. He needed to do only cursory research into anesthesiology and to speak with women physicians "to try to understand what it's like."

Coma immerses us in the already scary (at least to most of us) world of medicine as Susan Wheeler begins her internship at Boston Memorial. She becomes suspicious when she sees so many patients, admitted for what should be routine surgery, become comatose in the operating room and sent for long-term care at a nearby facility. After that, well … "Her search thrusts her into an escalating cycle of terrifying events that keeps the action moving," said *New York Times* reviewer Mel Watkins. With its compelling story and breakneck pacing, the book rocketed onto best-seller lists.

As his career took off—and sales of his books to Hollywood producers set records—Cook explored in vitro fertilization, managed care, and pharmaceuticals research in his novels. Each advance in medicine gives him a new angle. *Shock*, his novel about stem cell research, was in print before the topic became a hot one in American politics.

"Besides entertaining readers, my main goal is to get people interested in some of these issues," Cook said in a BookPage interview, "because it's the public that ultimately really should decide which way we ought to go in something as ethically questioning as stem cell research."

The public doesn't mind the educational value, as long as the action flows. *Critical* reviewer Barbara Lipkien Gershenbaum pointed out that Cook's work has "a lot of dialogue that drives the plot along at a breakneck pace and an interesting story played out by characters who fit their roles beautifully."

Cook is comfortable with his niche. His medical novels "capture everything a thriller should have—all the mystery, the gothic elements," he told *People Weekly*. "I could write about World War II or spies or great white sharks—but we are all patients. If you read scary medical stories in the newspapers, you know you are at risk."

 # Works by the Author

The Year of the Intern (1972)

Coma (1977)

Sphinx (1979)

Brain (1981)

Fever (1982)

Godplayer (1983)

Mindbend (1985)

Outbreak (1987)

Mortal Fear (1988)

Mutation (1989)

Vital Signs (1990)

Harmful Intent (1990)

Blindsight (1991)

Terminal (1992)

Fatal Cure (1993)

Acceptable Risk (1994)

Contagion (1995)

Chromosome 6 (1997)

Invasion (1997)
Toxin (1997)
Abduction (1999)
Vector (1999)
Shock (2000)
Seizure (2003)
Marker (2005)
Crisis (2006)
Critical (2007)
Foreign Body (2008)

Adaptations in Other Media

Coma (1978), motion picture based on novel
Sphinx (1981), motion picture based on novel
Mutation (1990), motion picture based on novel
Harmful Intent (CBS, 1993), television production based on the novel
Mortal Fear (NBC, 1994), television production based on novel
Robin Cook's Virus (NBC, 1995), television production based on *Outbreak*
Outbreak (1995), licensed title, but not based on the novel
Terminal (NBC, 1996), television production based on novel
Robin Cook's Invasion (USA, 1997), television production
Robin Cook's Acceptable Risk (TBS, 2001), television production
Foreign Body (2008), motion picture based on novel

For Further Information

Critical review, Bookreporter. http://www.bookreporter.com/reviews2/039915423X.asp (viewed December 17, 2007).

Gershenbaum, Barbara Lipkien, *Critical* review, Bookreporter. http://www.bookreporter.com/reviews2/039915423X.asp (viewed December 17, 2008).

Klemesrud, Judy, "Robin Cook." *New York Times*, November 6, 1977.

McDonald, Jay, "What a Shock: Robin Cook Fuses Stem Cells with a Suspenseful Tale," BookPage, September 2001. http://www.bookpage.com/0109bp/robin_cook.html (viewed December 27, 2007).

Newlove , Donald, *Coma* review. *New York Times Book Review*, May 8, 1977.

Robin Cook entry, Contemporary Authors Online, reproduced in Biography Resource Center. Farmington Hills, MI: Thomson Gale, 2007. http://galenet.galegroup.com/servlet/BioRC (viewed December 17, 2007).

Sales, Nancy Jo, "The Doctor Is In." *People Weekly*, February 12, 1996.

Watkins, Mel, *Coma* review. *New York Times*, May 14, 1977.

Stephen Coonts

Adventure; Espionage; Thrillers: Military, Techno

Benchmark Title: *Flight of the Intruder*

Morgantown, West Virginia

1946–

Photo courtesy of the author

About the Author and the Author's Writing

With the same determination and diligence that made him a top combat pilot during the Vietnam War, Stephen Coonts has learned and polished his writing craft. His novel *Flight of the Intruder* soared onto the best-seller lists in 1986, as have a dozen sequels.

Stephen Paul Coonts was born in 1946 in Morgantown, West Virginia, and grew up in the nearby coal mining town of Buckhannon. He graduated from West Virginia University in 1968 with an A.B. degree in political science. Immediately commissioned as an ensign in the U.S. Navy, he undertook flight training on the A-6 Intruder. He made two combat cruises with the Attack Squadron 196 on the USS *Enterprise*. After the war, he was a flight trainer on the A-6 for two years. He served as an assistant catapult and arresting gear officer on the USS *Nimitz* before leaving active duty in 1977.

After working briefly as a policeman and taxi driver, he enrolled at the University of Colorado School of Law, from which he received his law degree in 1979. He practiced in West Virginia for two years, then returned to Colorado in 1981 and worked as staff attorney for an oil company. A divorce from his first wife in 1984 and a layoff from his job spurred Coonts to do something he'd long thought of doing.

"It was a tough time," Coonts told Claire E. White of Writers Write. "But there's always life waiting at the end of the road. You have to make up your mind that you're going to do something about your troubles. Take action. So I decided to write a book."

Thirty-four editors strafed *Flight of the Intruder* before Naval Institute Press—which had had success with Tom Clancy's submarine thriller—offered a

$5,000 advance and published the book. It spent twenty-eight weeks on the *New York Times* best-seller list and was the basis for a 1991 motion picture.

One hot book was no guarantee of continued success. The publisher rejected his idea for a second novel because it was more about nuclear politics than flying. But Doubleday was glad to publish *Final Flight* and the Jake Grafton series was off the ground. Coonts paid attention to secondary characters in the Grafton books, and one of them, Tommy Carmellini, took the lead in two later adventures.

Coonts believes he has grown with each book. "You learn the craft by reading," he said in an interview with Jenna Glatzer for Absolute Write. "If you don't have time to learn the craft, you are doomed before you start and had better find other past-times."

The author starts each novel with a concept (which his editor has accepted), but he does not outline his books before he writes. The lack of specificity may slow his writing pace (he's had to throw away 100 pages on occasion), but he believes it makes for an edgier, more appealing work for readers. Likewise, although he is known for techno thrillers, he is careful to keep his military lingo and technology within the grasp of the average reader.

The technology presented in his books results from vigorous research, judicious interviews with experts, and sometimes just good guesses at what's brewing in the military-industrial world. "The problem is that if you just make it a military-action adventure," he told Tim Warren of *Publishers Weekly*, "it becomes very hard to sell to the general public. I also get a lot of mail from women who say they like reading a book with no political ax to grind, which treats women as real people." In that spirit, the author's second wife, Deborah Buell, reads and comments on his manuscripts, ensuring violence and sex levels that are comfortable for women readers.

Because fans also appreciate a mature hero, Jake Grafton gets a little older, a little wiser with each book. "He has evolved into an action-adventure hero through the years.... What I have tried to write is a believable action-adventure guy, a person that readers can readily identify with. He is not James Bond or Dirk Pitt, though his creator would gladly trade royalty checks with the creators of either of those two studs," Coonts said in a Bookreporter interview. In *Liberty* (2002), written after the September 11 attacks on America, Grafton, now a rear admiral, goes after a network of terrorists that wants to get its hands on a nuclear weapon.

Coonts has owned as many as four airplanes in private life, and his forty-eight-state journey in the early 1990s with his son, flying a vintage Stearman, inspired the nonfiction book *The Cannibal Queen*.

With Martin H. Greenberg of TeknoBooks, Coonts created the Deep Black paperback series featuring National Security Agency operative Charlie Dean, a former Marine sniper who now battles cyber threats around the world. Jim DeFelice cowrites the books, which will run at least six volumes with St. Martin's Press. Coonts has written two Saucer books and a change-of-pace love-and-understanding story that his early publisher Pocket Books didn't want in 1994, but that St. Martin's liked and brought out under a penname, Eve Adams, in 2006.

With wars in Iraq and Afghanistan, with the U.S. military equipped and trained as never before, Coonts has tapped a vibrant market.

Works by the Author

Fortunes of War (1998)
The 17th Day (1999)
The Garden of Eden (2006), written as Eve Adams
The Assassin (2008)

Deep Black Series, created with Martin H. Greenberg, written with Jim DeFelice

Deep Black (2003)
Biowar (2004)
Dark Zone (2004)
Payback (2005)
Jihad (2007)
Conspiracy (2008)
Arctic Gold (2009)

Jake Grafton Series

Flight of the Intruder (1986)
Final Flight (1986)
The Minotaur (1989)
Under Siege (1990)
Red Horseman (1993)
The Intruders (1994)
Cuba (1999)
Hong Kong (2000)
America (2001)
Liberty (2003)
The Assassin (2008), also features Tommy Carmellini

Saucer Series

Saucer (2002)
The Conquest (2004)

Tommy Carmellini Series

Liars and Thieves (2004), in United Kingdom as *Wages of Sin*
The Traitor (2006)

Editor

Combat (2001)
On Glorious Wings: The Best Flying Stories of the Century (2003)
Victory (2003)

Nonfiction

The Cannibal Queen: A Flight into the Heart of America (1992)

War in the Air: True Accounts of the 20th Century's Most Dramatic Air Battles, by the Men Who Fought Them (1996)

Adaptations in Other Media

Flight of the Intruder (1991), motion picture

For Further Information

Cohen, George, *Liberty* review. *Booklist*, December 1, 2002.

Glatzer, Jenna, "Interview with Stephen Coonts," Absolute Write. http://www.absolutewrite.com/novels/stephen_coonts.htm (viewed November 11, 2007).

Hartlaub, Joe, Stephen Coonts interview, Bookreporter. http://www.bookreporter.com/authors/au-coonts-stephen.asp (viewed November 11, 2007).

Stephen Coonts Web site. http://www.coonts.com/ (viewed November 11, 2007).

Warren, Tim, "Stephen Coonts: Ace of Suspense." *Publishers Weekly*, August 9, 1999.

White, Claire E., "A Conversation with Stephen Coonts," Writers Write, January 2000. http://www.writerswrite.com/journal/jan00/coonts.htm (viewed November 11, 2007).

Robert Crais

Crime; Thrillers

Benchmark Series: <u>Elvis Cole and Joe Pike</u>

Baton Rouge, Louisiana

1954–

About the Author and the Author's Writing

The glib Elvis Cole, who appeared in Robert Crais's initial crime novel *The Monkey's Raincoat* in 1987, seemed at first more a variation on Richard S. Prather's wise-cracking Shell Scott than Ross Macdonald's psychologically insightful Lew Archer. Time proved otherwise as the Cole books have merged power, pace, and character to offer a solid hero and attract a huge following.

Robert Crais was born in Baton Rouge, Louisiana, in 1954. Many in the Crais family were police officers or worked for an oil refinery. Crais studied mechanical engineering in college. He abandoned that potential career to attend the Clarion Writers' Workshop in Michigan in 1975 and study with science fiction writers Gene Wolfe and Samuel R. Delaney. He moved to Los Angeles in 1976 and soon had an agent and steady work scripting action television shows. His first story to appear in print was "With Crooked Hands" in the anthology *Clarion SF* in 1977.

The author found scriptwriting a competitive and heart-wrenching field. His manuscripts seldom survived intact. He wanted to write books. And the death of his father spurred him to write one. While Crais couldn't control things happening in his own life, he found that he could manipulate his characters in a book.

Crais's hip Los Angeles private eye Cole and the silent, menacing, ex-cop, seen-only-when-needed partner Joe Pike are both veterans of the Vietnam War. The experience shaped their characters in perhaps unexpected ways. "Elvis and Joe believe something that most people want to believe, namely, that everyone matters," Crais said in a Mystery Ink interview. "Not just the rich or the famous; each of us has depth, and that depth deserves respect."

The mysteries' "subversive pleasure is seeing an 'every-Angeleno'—a man who plots his routes around favorite takeout and waits for a whiff of eucalyptus after rain—pit his cockiness against a series of Goliaths. In the course of his career, he has triumphed over the yakuza, the Mafia, corrupt cops, and the Russian mob," Ariel Swartley wrote in *Los Angeles Magazine*.

Crais took some guidance from his youthful reading of Stan Lee's Marvel comics, which often featured troubled, flawed teen heroes, and the science fiction of Robert Heinlein, in which young male characters often overcame their dismal pasts. His Elvis Cole voice appears to owe something to Rex Stout's Archie Goodwin, of whom he wrote adoringly in the introduction to a 1993 edition of *Before Midnight*. "Rex Stout has given the narrator a clean appealing voice, just enough attitude to show that he's nobody's chump, and a wit like [Raymond Chandler's Philip Marlowe] on a day when all the bio-rhythms are up."

Where do his characters come from? "To write honestly and well, you have to invest yourself—even in the bad guys. So yeah, I'm the heroes, Elvis and Joe Pike, but I'm also the bad guys, the self-serving detective, the homeless guy, even the serial killer. It's all me in some way or another," Crais ventured in a *Cincinnati Enquirer* interview.

In a change of direction, Crais's *Demolition Angel* features Carol Starkey of the LAPD bomb squad, and *Hostage* is about suburban police chief Jeff Talley. *The Two-Minute Rule* stars ex-con Max Holman, who is forced to team with ex-FBI agent Katherine Pollard to solve his son's murder.

Cole and Pike in *Indigo Slam* help three children find their father; in *Free Fall*, they help Jennifer Sheridan's boyfriend. Families and relationships are important to Cole, a theme the author explores further in *The Last Detective*. In that book, Crais takes a few risks with point of view—sometimes observing things as Pike or Ben Chenier, Cole's girlfriend's son—and with genre—it is a suspense novel and police procedural, as well as a mystery.

Crais has also begun to probe his female characters more. "It's liberating in that it allows me to explore an area of life that, normally, I haven't in my books. I'm serious about my writing. I don't want to write the same story over and over and over again. I want my work to grow, to be a better writer," he said in a *January* magazine interview with Kevin Burton Smith.

There's little permanent in life for Crais's characters. Cole has had to make tough choices, as the series progresses, including abandoning his relationship with Louisiana lawyer Lucy Chenier. "*The Forgotten Man* furthers the journey that began in *The Last Detective* as Elvis continues the search up-river for his own 'heart of darkness,'" Crais said in his e-mail newsletter.

In *L.A. Requiem*, Pike is featured more prominently, and he had a strong role in *The Watchman*, in which he develops a sympathetic relationship with scatterbrained heiress Larkin Blakley. Pike recognizes that, deep down, they have a common thread, a common yearning.

Crais wanted to know what made Pike tick. "That is, why is he pulled so tight, why is he so internal? And to reveal that, I knew I needed a character [Blakley] who could reach him, who could touch those deep places. I wanted to bring the character to a place where I knew he was moved," Crais told Scott Timberg of the *Los Angeles Times*.

In addition to writing novels, Crais has scripted a variety of crime action television programs—from *Baretta; Quincy, M.E.; and Hill Street Blues* (for which he received an Emmy nomination) to *Cagney & Lacy, L.A. Law, Miami Vice*, and *JAG*. He's sold film rights to his own novels, such as *Hostage*, to Hollywood producers for a Bruce Willis film. But he's protective of Cole and Pike. He wants readers to imagine the rugged characters in their own minds.

"I am insane," he admitted in a *San Diego Union-Tribune* interview. "Elvis and Joe exist for me and my readers. I have no wish to have Hollywood improve on my creations.... Once there's that actor up there, I'm worried that the collaboration with readers will be forever damaged."

Works by the Author

Demolition Angel (2000)

Hostage (2001)

The Two-Minute Rule (2006)

Elvis Cole Series

The Monkey's Raincoat (1987)

Stalking the Angel (1989)

Lullaby Town (1992)

Free Fall (1993)

Voodoo River (1995)

Sunset Express (1996)

Indigo Slam (1997)

L.A. Requiem (1998)

The Last Detective (2003)

The Forgotten Man (2004)

The Watchman (2007)

Chasing Darkness (2008)

Anthologies

Clarion SF, edited by Kate Wilhelm (1977), includes "With Crooked Hands"

2076: The American Tricentennial, edited by Edward Bryant (1977), includes "The Dust of Evening"

Raymond Chandler's Philip Marlowe: A Centennial Celebration, edited by Byron Preiss (1988), includes "The Man Who Knew Dick Bong"

Absolute Disaster: Fiction from Los Angeles, edited by Lee Montgomery (1996), includes "The Man Who Knew Dick Bong," with character Philip Marlowe changed to Deets Boedecker

Introduction

The Private Eye Writers of America Presents Mystery Street, edited by Loren D. Estleman (2001)

Teleplays and Screenplays

Baretta (TV series, 1977–1978), episodes "Make the Sun Shine," "It Goes with the Job," and "Woman Trouble"

Quincy, M.E. (TV series, 1978–1981), episodes "Death by Good Intention," "No Way to Treat a Body," "A Question of Death," "The Depth of Beauty," "Dark Angel," "Semper Fidelis," "An Ounce of Prevention," "The Eye of the Needle," "Hot Ice," "Murder by S.O.P.," and "By Death of a Child."

Joe Dancer (TV series, 1980–1981), episodes "A Clear Cut Case of Murder" and "The Monkey Mission"

Riker (TV series, 1981), episode "Sisters"

The Second Family Tree (TV series), episode "Triangles"

Hill Street Blues (TV series, 1981), episodes "The Last White Man on East Ferry Avenue," "The Second Oldest Profession," and "Cranky Streets"

Cassie and Company (TV series, 1982), episode "Anything for a Friend"

Cagney & Lacey (TV series, 1982), episodes "Witness to an Incident," "Beauty Burglars," "One of Our Own," and "I'll Be Home for Christmas"

The Mississippi (TV series, 1983), as Jerry Gret Samouche, episode "There Is a Tiger in the Town"

Twilight Zone (TV series, 1986), episode "Monsters

Miami Vice (TV series, 1986), episodes "Payback" and, as Elvis Cole, "Borrasca"

In Self Defense (TV movie of week, 1987)

The Equalizer (TV series, 1988), episodes "Last Call" and "Regrets Only"

Cross of Fire (TV miniseries, 1989)

L.A. Law (TV series, 1992), episode "Love in Bloom"

Men (TV series), episodes "When the Wind Blows" and "Brave Men"

Earth II (TV series, 1995), episode "All about Eve"

JAG (TV series, 1995), as Elvis Cole, episode "Desert Son"

Also unproduced teleplays for *Vega$, Baretta, Joe Dancer, Partners in Crime, and Futuretales;* unproduced TV pilots *Molly's Place, M.V.P., The Kidd Brothers, Guardians, Spider-Man, Bloodhouse, Achangel, Cruisers, Endless Summer, Dr. Strange, Chameleon, Mr. Lyle, Storm City, Dr. Rick, Sheroes, The Heat, Florida Straits, Decoy, Invisible Man,* and *Crooks;* and TV movies *Night Chills* and *Victims of Pan Am Flight 103.*

For Further Information

Batten, Jack, "Deadly Sleuths Good to Go." *Toronto Star*, April 20, 2003.

Crais, Robert, "Archie and Me," introduction, *Before Midnight*. New York: Bantam, 1993.

"Forgotten Man," Robert Crais.com e-mail newsletter, September/October 2003.

Knippenberg, Jim, "Robert Crais Talks about His Life of Crime." *Cincinnati Enquirer*, June 22, 1999.

Peacock, Scot, ed., Robert Crais entry. *Contemporary Authors*, volume 187. Detroit, MI: Gale Research, 2000.

Robert Crais interview, Mystery Ink. http://www.mysterinkonline.com/interviewrcrais.htm (viewed July 26, 2003).

Robert Crais Web site. http://www.robertcrais.com (viewed January 24, 2008).

Salm, Arthur, "Author Robert Crais Puts Joe Pike Front and Center in 'The Watchman'—and 'A Force of Nature' Rips through LA." *San Diego Union-Tribune*, March 25, 2007.

Smith, Kevin Burton, "The Explosive Talents of Robert Crais," January maga-
    zine. http://www.januarymagazine.com/profiles/rcrais.html (viewed July
    26, 2003).

Swartley, Ariel, "Elvis Is Back." *Los Angeles Magazine*, March 2003.

Timberg, Scott, "Latest Twist from L.A.'s Crais: Sidekick as Star." *Los Angeles
    Times*, February 21, 2007.

Michael Crichton

Adventure; Historical Fiction; Science Fiction; Thrillers: Techno, Bio

Benchmark Title: *Jurassic Park*

Chicago, Illinois

1942–2008

About the Author and the Author's Writing

A favorite theme in Michael Crichton's books, such as *The Andromeda Strain* (1969) and *Jurassic Park* (1990), is technology gone awry. The author sees his task as a popular fiction author going beyond sensationalism in drawing attention to an issue. "The problem is to be able to deal with both sides at once," he said in a HarperCollins interview. "We are, as a society, tremendously dependent on science and technology…. [But] the creators of technology often do not seem to be concerned about the effects of their work as outsiders think they ought to be." Scientists won't listen, he argues, if the critics, even in fiction, don't know what they're talking about.

His scientific caution was apparent in *State of Fear* (2004), in which Crichton refused to jump on the global-warming bandwagon. "The global changes in temperature that everyone is so excited about is one-third of a degree…," he told interviewer Jasper Gerard in 2005. "Does the world face a drought of fossil fuels? It has held that fear since 1860," the author scoffed. "Talking about resources ignores human ingenuity."

John Michael Crichton was born in 1942 in Chicago, Illinois, and grew up in Roslyn, New York. In 1964, he received his A.B. from Harvard University summa cum laude, Phi Beta Kappa. He was a Henry Russell Shaw Traveling Fellow 1964–1965 and visiting lecturer in anthropology at Cambridge University in England in 1965. A 1969 graduate of Harvard Medical School, he served a year as a postdoctoral fellow at California's Salk Institute for Biological Sciences. By that time, he had already written a handful of novels under pennames to help pay his way through school (e.g., *A Case of Need*, about a Chinese American obstetrician accused of performing an illegal abortion) and *The Andromeda Strain*. A career change was inevitable.

Crichton innovated the "bio-thriller," science-based suspense novels such as *The Andromeda Strain*, in which a satellite crash lands on Earth bearing a life-threatening bacteria. In *The Terminal Man*, the author explored the effects of a computer implanted in character Harry Benson's brain, ostensibly to control his psychomotor epilepsy, but instead creates in him an enormous fear of machines and turns him into a killer.

Crichton watched others turn his best-selling novels into popular films and began to script and direct films himself, beginning with the television movie *Binary* in 1972 and the theatrical film *Westworld* the next year. Long interested in computers, Crichton's software firm FastTrack pioneered in special effects work that won him an Academy of Motion Pictures Arts and Sciences Technical Achievement Award in 1992. Other awards range from an Emmy and a Peabody (for *ER*) and Mystery Writers of America Edgar Allan Poe Awards (for *A Case of Need* and *The Great Train Robbery*). A newly discovered species of dinosaur was named for him in 2000, the *Bienosaurus crichtoni*. Five times married and four times divorced, with one daughter, he lived in Los Angeles and had homes in New York and Hawaii.

Crichton has said his plots are generally triggered by concepts that interest him, such as nanotechnology (in *Prey*), the science of extreme miniaturization of machines that could lead to vastly smaller computers or medical breakthroughs such as treatment for cancer. Most of Crichton's books were long in gestation, from concept to print: *The Great Train Robbery* took three years; *Jurassic Park*, eight years; *Sphere*, twenty. *Prey*, on the other hand, took nine months. He usually plans his novels carefully, because they are plot-, rather than character-, driven.

The author did his research largely through reading. "I start with journals and reviews—symposiums on artificial life and things like that," he told interviewer Benjamin Svetkey. "The goal is to find the state of knowledge in a particular field. For example, with *Prey* I had to figure out what a nanotechological assembly line would look like. I struggled with it and was never satisfied. Then I read in a journal that somebody had figured it out."

Deviating slightly from his standard theme of technology, in *Rising Sun,* he wrote of crime and political intrigue, and in *Disclosure* of corporate sexual politics. The author said he anticipated the latter, in which a male was the victim, would stir a reaction among feminists, but he was caught by surprise to be accused of racism in his depiction of ruthless Japanese businessmen in the former. For *Jurassic Park*, Crichton was accused of being antiscience, to which he countered the book and film helped trigger a renewed interest in the dinosaur age at natural history museums.

Crichton found good points and bad in his double-faceted career. Book writing provided greater control of the end product, but it was a solitary endeavor. Filmmaking and television were collaborative efforts in which the end product seldom reflected a single artistic vision. Yet each could be enormously satisfying—for him, and for his fans.

Crichton died in 2008. In an appraisal, Charles McGrath in the *New York Times* said, "Very few readers who started a Crichton novel ever put it down." What more could a thriller writer ask for?

 # Works by the Author

Fiction

The Andromeda Strain (1969)
The Terminal Man (1972)
The Great Train Robbery (1973)
Westworld (1974)

Eaters of the Dead (1976), also titled *The 13th Warrior*
Congo (1980)
Sphere (1987)
Jurassic Park (1990)
Rising Sun (1991)
Disclosure (1993)
Michael Crichton: A New Collection of Three Complete Novels (1994), includes *Cargo, Sphere,* and *Eaters of the Dead*
Airframe (1996)
Twister (1996), with Ann-Marie Martin
Timeline (1998)
Michael Crichton Collection (2000), includes *Jurassic Park, The Lost World,* and *The Andromeda Strain*
Prey (2002)
State of Fear (2004)
Next (2006)

Jurassic Park Series

Jurassic Park (1980)
The Lost World (1995)

Writing as Jeffrey Hudson

A Case of Need (1968), reissued as by Michael Crichton

Writing as John Lange

Odds On (1966)
Scratch One (1967)
Easy Go (1968) retitled, *The Last Tomb* (1974)
Zero Cool (1969)
The Venom Business (1969)
Drug of Choice (1970)
Grave Descent (1970)
Binary (1972)

Writing as Michael Douglas, with Douglas Crichton

Dealing: Or, the Berkeley-to-Boston Forty-Brick Lost-Bag Blues (1970)

Nonfiction

Five Patients: The Hospital Explained (1970)
Jasper Johns (1977), revised (1994)
Electronic Life: How to Think about Computers (1983)
Travels (1988)

Adaptations in Other Media

The Andromeda Strain (1971), motion picture

Carey Treatment (1972), motion picture based on *A Case of Need*

Dealing: Or, the Berkeley-to-Boston Forty-Brick Lost-Bag Blues (1972), motion picture

Pursuit (television movie, 1972), Crichton screenplay, based on *Binary*

Extreme Close-up (1973), Crichton screenplay

Westworld (1973), Crichton screenplay based on his novel

Terminal Man (1974), motion picture

Coma (1977), Crichton screenplay, based on Robin Cook novel

Great American Train Robbery (1978), Crichton screenplay based on his novel

Looker (1981), Crichton screenplay

Runaway (1984), Crichton screenplay

Physical Evidence (1989), Crichton screenplay

Rising Sun (1993), motion picture, Crichton cowriter

Jurassic Park (1994), motion picture

Disclosure (1994), motion picture

ER (television series, 1994–2009), Crichton creator and writer

Congo (1995), motion picture

Twister (1996), Crichton cowriter

Lost World: Jurassic Park II (1997), motion picture

Sphere (1998), motion picture

13th Warrior (1999), motion picture based on *Eaters of the Dead*

Jurassic Park III (2001), motion picture

Timeline (2003), motion picture

For Further Information

"Conversation with Michael Crichton," HarperCollins. http://www.harpercollins.com/author/authorExtra.aspx?authorID=24395&isbn13=97800 61015724&displayType=bookinterview (viewed October 29, 2007).

Gerard, Jasper, Michael Crichton interview, January 2, 2005. *Sunday Times*. http://www.timesonline.co.uk/tol/news/article407531.ece (viewed November 4, 2007).

Grimes, William, "Michal Crichton, Author of 'Jurassic Park' and Other Thrillers, Dies at 66." *New York Times*, November 6, 2008.

McGrath, Charles, "Builder of Windup Realms That Thrillingly Run Amok." *New York Times*, November 6, 2008.

Michael Crichton interview, ReadersRead. http://www.readersread.com/features/michaelcrichton.htm (viewed June 3, 2003).

Michael Crichton Web site. http://www.michaelcrichton.net (viewed October 29, 2007).

Rezek, John, and David Sheff, Michael Crichton interview. *Playboy,* January 1999.

Svetkey, Benjamin, "Michael Crichton Gets Small." *Entertainment Weekly,* November 29, 2002.

Zibart, Eve, "Is Michael Crichton a Jap-Basher? Xenophobic? Worried? No. No. Sort of," BookPage (March 1992). http://www.bookpage.com/BPinterview/crichton392.html (viewed June 3, 2003).

Clive Cussler

Photo credit: Rob Greer

Adventure: Military, Spy; Crime; Thrillers: Techno, Nazis

Benchmark Series: Dirk Pitt

Aurora, Illinois

1931–

About the Author and the Author's Writing

Clive Cussler is best known for his ongoing adventure novels about Dirk Pitt. But with three fiction series chugging along strongly in the hands of cowriters, in 2007 Cussler dove into the twilight of the historical American West. *The Chase* tells the story of "the Budget Bandit," who robs banks, kills witnesses, and abruptly disappears. Ace outlaw hunter Isaac Bell has his hands full—and never anticipates the locomotive pursuit to come!

A dramatic change of pace, perhaps. But pure Cussler.

Clive Eric Cussler was born in 1931 in Aurora, Illinois, and grew up in Alhambra, California. From 1949 to 1950 he attended Pasadena City College. In the service during the Korean War, he was an aircraft mechanic and flight engineer in the Military Air Transport Service. After his discharge, he went to Orange Coast College in California. He married Barbara Knight in 1955. She died in 2003.

In 1961, Cussler started Bestgen & Cussler Advertising in Newport Beach, California. He left in 1965 to become creative director for Darcy Advertising in Hollywood, a position he held for three years. From 1970 to 1975, he was vice president and creative director of broadcast for Mefford, Wolff and Weir Advertising in Denver, Colorado, winning numerous international awards for radio and television commercials. He then joined the sales staff of Aquatic Marine Dive Equipment in Newport Beach.

In 1965, Cussler began writing. When his wife took an evening job for the local police department, he found himself with extra time after their three children went to bed. "That was when I thought it would be fun to write a little. I only had in mind a little paperback series, so I just started writing evenings and weekends," he said in a

Readers Room conversation. After four years, he had two manuscripts. An agent found a hardcover publisher.

The author borrowed his son Dirk's bedroom to use as an office to write. So it was only fair that he also borrowed his son's name for his series hero, Dirk Pitt. To make his character and story different from all the others out there, the author, a longtime SCUBA diver, decided to use a maritime setting.

Sales were modest until 1976, when *Raise the Titanic!* made the best-seller lists.

Cussler sought to make Pitt a little different sort of hero, he said in *St. James Guide to Crime & Mystery Writers*. "One who wasn't a secret agent, police detective, or a private investigator. Someone with rough edges, yet a degree of style, who felt equally at ease entertaining a gorgeous woman … or downing a beer with the boys…. A congenial kind of guy with a tinge of mystery about him."

Cussler generally starts his Pitt adventures with an episode from history. He knows how the adventure will end, but the middle comes only in the writing. "It's all in my head," he told Bookreporter in a 1999 interview, "the only thing I put down in notes is who's got green eyes and red hair, things like that."

The history in Cussler's books is well researched. And sometimes he anticipates the future, as in *Valhalla Rising*, in which he describes an attempt to ram the World Trade Center foundation with a propane gas-loaded tanker ship.

Cussler created the fictional National Underwater & Marine Agency (NUMA), which, with the help of writer Paul Kemprecos, is the focus of its own series of books featuring Kurt Austin and Joe Zavala. NUMA is the organization that employs Pitt and other running characters. A recognized authority on shipwrecks, Cussler did underwater exploration at his own expense and decided to establish a nonprofit foundation. He used the NUMA name. Cussler serves as founder and chairman of NUMA and provides most of the financing. The organization has discovered more than sixty sunken ruin sites including that of the CSS *Hunley*, the Civil War submarine. A recent NUMA find was the *Carpathia*, the ship that sailed to the rescue of *Titanic* survivors.

Cussler is a fellow of the Explorers Club of New York and the Royal Geographic Society of London. Maritime College, State University of New York, awarded the author a doctor of letters degree in May 1997, in honor of his nonfiction book *The Sea Hunters*. Cussler owns some eighty-five vintage automobiles including a Stutz, Pierce-Arrow, and Allard. He has homes in Colorado and Arizona.

It took Cussler about nine months to write the early Pitt books; these days, it's more apt to be fourteen or fifteen months. More and more he relies on a coauthor, such as Craig Dirgo on the new Oregon Files books, to help. His son, Dirk Cussler, has started to cowrite the Pitt tales.

Cussler wrote himself into one of his novels, *Atlantis Found*. Pitt is at a classic car meet and introduces himself to an older, gray-bearded gent. Cussler had vowed never to sell film rights, since he was so disappointed with a 1980 film version of *Raise the Titanic!* He changed his mind but was disappointed a second time with the 2005 motion picture based on *Sahara*.

In his judgment, Dirk Pitt can only be pictured in words.

Works by the Author

White Death (2003)
The Chase (2007)

Dirk Pitt Series

The Mediterranean Caper (1973), retitled *Mayday!*
Iceberg (1975)
Raise the Titanic! (1976)
Vixen 03 (1978)
Night Probe! (1981)
Pacific Vortex! (1983)
Deep Six (1984)
Cyclops (1986)
Clive Cussler; Iceberg, Dragon, Deep Six (1988), omnibus
Treasure (1988)
Dragon (1990)
Sahara (1992)
Inca Gold (1994)
The Mediterranean Caper and Iceberg (1995), omnibus
Shock Wave (1996)
Clive Cussler Gift Set: Treasure, Dragon and Sahara (1996), omnibus
Flood Tide (1997)
Atlantis Found (1999)
Flood Tide and Cyclops (2001), omnibus
Valhalla Rising, with Paul Kemprecos (2001)
Clive Cussler: Two Novels (2001), includes *Flood Tide* and *Cyclops*
Trojan Odyssey (2003)
Black Wind, with Dirk Cussler (2004)
The Treasure of Khan, with Dirk Cussler (2006)
Arctic Drift (2008)

NUMA Files Series with Paul Kemprecos

Serpent (1999)
Blue Gold (2000)
Fire Ice (2002)
The NUMA Files Collection (2002), omnibus
White Death (2003)
Lost City (2004)
Polar Shift (2005)

Navigator (2007)
Medusa (2009)

Oregon Files

Golden Buddha, with Craig Dirgo (2003)
Sacred Stone, with Craig Dirgo (2004)
Dark Watch, with Jack DuBrul (2005)
Skeleton Coast, with Jack DuBrul (2006)
Golden Buddha/Sacred Stone (2006), omnibus
Plague Ship, with Jack DuBrul (2008)
Corsair, with Jack DuBrul (2009)

Nonfiction with Craig Dirgo

The Sea Hunters (1996)
Clive Cussler and Dirk Pitt Revealed (1998)
The Sea Hunters II: Diving the World's Seas for Famous Shipwrecks (2002)

Juvenile Fiction

Adventures of Vin Fiz (2006)

Adaptations in Other Media

Raise the Titanic! (1980), motion picture
Sunk on Christmas Eve (2001), motion picture
Sea Hunters (2002), motion picture
Sahara (2005), motion picture

For Further Information

Ayers, Jeff, *The Chase* interview. *Library Journal*, September 1, 2007.

"Clive Cussler: An Exaggerated Adventure Story." *Maclean's*, June 4, 2007.

Clive Cussler interview, Coffee with Kate. http://www.readersroom.com/coffee14.html (viewed October 29, 2007).

Clive Cussler interviews, Bookreporter (Septtember 11, 2001, and November 6, 1999). http://www.bookreporter.com/authors/au-cussler-clive.asp (viewed May 30, 2003).

Clive Cussler Web page. http://www.bradland.com/cussler/clive/index.html (viewed May 30, 2003).

Clive Cussler Web page. http://www.penguinputnam.com/static/packages/us/clivecussler/ (viewed May 30, 2003).

Golden Buddha review. *Publishers Weekly,* August 25, 2003.

Hinckley, Karen, Clive Cussler entry. *St. James Guide to Crime & Mystery Writers*, 4th ed. Jay P. Pederson, ed. Detroit, MI: St. James Press, 1996.

Hitchcock, J. A., "Clive Cussler May Very Well Be the Best Author You're Probably Not Reading." *Mothership,* April 17, 2000.

Levesque, Marc, "An Interview with Dr. Clive Cussler," Time2watch.net. http://www.time2watch.net/cusslerinterview.htm (viewed May 30, 2003).

National Underwater & Marine Agency Web page. http://www.numa/net (viewed November 12, 2008).

Peacock, Scot, ed., Clive Cussler entry. *Contemporary Authors New Revision Series*, volume 91. Detroit, MI: Gale Research, 2000.

Valero, Wayne. *The Collector's Guide to Clive Cussler*. 2000. (Self-published)

Jeffery Deaver

Crime-Suspense; Thrillers: Legal, Cyber, Serial Killers, Nazis

Benchmark Series: <u>Lincoln Rhyme</u>

Glen Ellyn, Illinois

1950–

Photo credit: Charles Harris/Corbis

About the Author and the Author's Writing

Jeffery Deaver has a mission: To entertain his readers with "the most exciting roller coaster ride of a suspense story I can possibly think of," he told Mystery News interviewer Reed Andrus in 2002. This means, he went on, a "strong (though possibly flawed) hero, sick and twisted bad guys, deadlines every few chapters, a short time frame for the entire story, lots of surprising plot twists and turns and plenty of cliffhangers."

Born in Glen Ellyn, Illinois, not far form Chicago, in 1950, Deaver long knew he wanted to be a writer. But to muster material for his fiction, he pursued a different career. After earning his bachelor's degree from the University of Missouri and his law degree from Fordham University, he practiced law on Wall Street. Avocationally, he became a folk musician and amateur cook. He lives in Virginia and California.

"Authors of fiction I believe need to have lived life," he told Ali Karim for SHOTS: The Crime & Mystery Magazine, "and so I cast about looking for various outlets for my writing in my twenties, but I didn't really seriously pursue it until I'd been a journalist, until I'd traveled around the world."

Deaver's first writing was a nonfiction guide to law school. He wrote two quickie novels under the name Jeffery Wilds Deaver. His craft coalesced with *The Bone Collector*, a book he never intended to launch a series. The protagonist, Lincoln Rhyme, is a quadraplegic, able to move only one finger. He is the brains. His arms and legs are Amelia Sachs, his policewoman love interest.

"I wanted to write a very cerebral, Holmesian character who combats crime with his thought processes more than fast car chases and shooting," the author said in an interview with John Connolly. He pictured the ultimate thrilling climax: a main character already trapped in a motionless body, further ensnared by his foe.

Rhyme and the multiple plot twists and turns of the story struck a chord with readers; and Deaver didn't mind bringing him back for further books. As he added in the interview with Connolly, "Sometimes I do need to take a deep breath and back off, but I am addicted to them."

As his career progressed, Deaver's writing changed. "When I decided to try writing less of that [character digressions] and adding more intricate plots and additional twists … readers seemed to enjoy the books more. So I've made that my niche," he said in a Bookreporter interview.

The author says he typically spends two-thirds of a year researching and composing an outline for a novel. The outline can run upwards of 250 pages and specifies every bend and turn of the story. He keeps his plots otherwise stripped bare. If it doesn't advance the story, it doesn't go down on paper once he begins the actual writing. From there, it is often only a couple of months until he has a manuscript.

Although his books are plot driven, that doesn't mean he ignores character. He makes sure they are believable and offers enough detail to give them distinct personalities.

As his career kicked into gear, Deaver turned out more books than his publisher could handle in a year. Thus the William Jefferies byline appeared for a second series, the John Pellham books about a Hollywood location scout. These and the Rhyme crime puzzles joined Deaver's Rune Trilogy, about a New York television personality, and stand-alones such as *The Lesson of Her Death* (1993), about a serial killer, and *Garden of Beasts*, which is set in Berlin in 1936.

"I love magic and illusion," the author said in a *Telegraph* interview in 2006. "In my novel *The Vanished Man*, my villain is an illusionist, a sort of David Blaine, who uses the techniques of magic and sleight of hand. It's also about me. About how I construct my books. Watch the left hand, and the right hand is doing something different."

Works by the Author

Voodoo (1988), as Jeffery Wilds Deaver

Always a Thief (1988), as Jeffery Wilds Deaver

Mistress of Justice (1992)

The Lesson of Her Death (1993)

Praying for Sleep (1994)

The Maiden's Grave (1995)

Devil's Teardrop: A Novel of the Last Night of the Century (1999)

Speaking in Tongues (2000)

The Lesson of Her Death/Speaking in Tongues (2000), omnibus

Praying for Sleep/Maiden's Grave (2001), omnibus

Blue Nowhere (2001)

Twisted: The Collected Short Stories of Jeffery Deaver (2003)

Praying for Sleep/The Bone Collector (2003), omnibus

Garden of Beasts (2004)

Dish Served Cold (2006), novella

More Twisted: Collected Stories (2006)
A Dish Served Cold (2007), Amazon Short digital story
The Bodies Left Behind (2008)

Kathryn Dance Series

The Sleeping Doll (2007)

Lincoln Rhyme Series

The Bone Collector (1997)
Coffin Dancer (1998)
Empty Chair (2000)
Stone Monkey (2002)
The Vanished Man (2003)
Twelfth Card (2005)
Cold Moon (2006)
The Broken Window (2008)

Location Scout Series as William Jefferies

Shallow Graves (1992)
Bloody River Blues (1993)
Hell's Kitchen (2001)

Rune Trilogy

Manhattan Is My Beat (1988)
Death of a Blue Movie Star (1990)
Hard News (1991)

Contributor

Transgressions Series
Death's Betrayal, with Sharyn McCrumb (2005)

Editor

A Century of Great Suspense Stories (2001), includes "The Weekender"
A Hot and Sultry Night for Crime (2003), includes "Ninety-eight Point Six"

Anthologies

Crimes of the Heart, edited by Carolyn Hart (1995), includes "Together"
Best of the Best (Crimes and Misdemeanors), edited by Elaine Koster and Joseph Pittman (1997), includes "Wrong Time, Wrong Place"
The Best American Mystery Stories 1997, edited by Robert B. Parker (1997), includes "The Weekender"

Law and Order, edited by Cynthia Manson (1997), includes "Interrogation"

Year's 25 Finest Crime and Mystery Stories, edited by Ed Gorman and Martin H. Greenberg (1998), includes "The Kneeling Soldier"

The Best American Mystery Stories 1999, edited by Ed McBain (1999), includes "Wrong Time, Wrong Place"

Irreconcilable Differences, edited by Lia Matera (1999), includes "Eye to Eye"

Blue Lightning, edited by John Harvey (1999), includes "Nocturne"

A Confederacy of Crime, edited by Sarah Shankman (2000), includes "The Widow of Pine Creek"

World's Finest Mystery and Crime Stories, edited by Ed Gorman (2000), includes "Beautiful"

Créme de la Crime, edited by Janet Hutchings (2000), includes "Triangle"

Best American Mystery Stories 2000, edited by Donald E. Westlake (2000), includes "For Services Rendered"

Opening Shots, volume 2, edited by Lawrence Block (2001), includes "Together"

Much Ado About Murder, edited by Anne Perry (2002), includes "All the World's a Stage"

World's Finest Mystery and Crime Stories, volume 3, edited by Ed Gorman and Martin H. Greenberg (2002), includes "Surveillance"

Men from Boys, edited by John Harvey (2003), includes "The Poker Lesson"

World's Finest Mystery and Crime Stories, volume 4, edited by Ed Gorman and Martin H. Greenberg (2003)

The Adventure of the Missing Detective, edited by Ed Gorman and Martin H. Greenberg (2005), includes "The Westphalian Ring"

Greatest Hits, edited by Robert J. Randisi (2005), includes "Chapter and Verse"

A New Omnibus of Crime, edited by Tony Hillerman and Rosemary Herbert (2005), includes "CopyCat"

Transgressions, edited by Ed McBain (2005), includes "Forever"

Dangerous Women, edited by Otto Penzler (2005), includes "Born Bad"

Deadly Bride and 21 of the Year's Finest Crime and Mystery Stories, volume 2, edited by Ed Gorman (2006), includes "Born Bad"

The Best American Mystery Stories 2006, edited by Scott Turow and Otto Penzler (2006), includes "Born Bad"

A Merry Band of Murderers, edited by Claudia Bishop and Don Bruns (2006), includes "The Fan"

Manhattan Noir, edited by Lawrence Block (2006), includes "A Nice Place to Visit"

Murder at the Foul Line, edited by Otto Penzler (2006), includes "Nothing but Net"

Dead Man's Hand, edited by Otto Penzler (2007), includes "Bump"

A Prisoner of Memory and 24 of the Year's Finest Crime and Mystery Stories, edited by Ed Gorman and Martin H. Greenberg (2008), includes "Making Amends"

Nonfiction

Complete Law School Companion (1984)

Adaptations in Other Media

Dead Silence (1997), television film based on *A Maiden's Grave*
The Bone Collector (1999), motion picture

For Further Information

Andrus, Reed, "Jeffery Deaver: His Gift Is His Song," Mystery News, April/May 2002. http://www.blackravenpress.com/Author%20pages/deaver.htm (viewed November 26, 2007).

Ayers, Jeff, *The Vanished Man* review. *Library Journal*, March 1, 2003.

Connolly, John, Jeffery Deaver interview, John Connolly Books. http://www.johnconnollybooks.com/int_deaver.html (viewed October 28, 2007).

DeAngelo, Carol, *The Empty Chair* review. *School Library Journal*, December 2000.

Jeffery Deaver interview, Bookreporter. http://www.bookreporter.com/authors/au-deaver-jeffery.asp (viewed October 26, 2007).

Jeffery Deaver Web site. http://www.jeffreydeaver.com/ (viewed October 26, 2007).

Karim, Ali, "The Pressure Cooker World of Jeffrey Deaver." SHOTS: The Crime & Mystery Magazine. http://www.shotsmag.co.uk/Jeffrey%20Deaver%20Interview.htm (viewed October 28, 2007).

Standaert, Michael, "Deaver Meaning." *Carmel Magazine*, December 2006.

"Writer's Life: Jeffery Deaver," *London Telegraph*. http://www.telegraph.co.uk/arts/main.jhtml;jsessionid=ROWX5NWIGORBRQFIQMFSFFWAVCBQ0IV0?xml=/arts/2006/07/09/bodeaver.xml&sSheet=/arts/2006/07/09/bomain.html (viewed October 28, 2007).

Nelson DeMille

Adventure; Espionage;
Crime; Thrillers: Military,
Legal, Techno

Benchmark Title: *Plum Island*

New York, New York

1943–

Photo credit: Sandy DeMille

About the Author and the Author's Writing

Nelson DeMille isn't particularly old-fashioned. Except when it comes to writing his frantic-paced blockbusters. He scrawls them out by hand. "Writing longhand has many advantages, especially for someone like me who can't type," he said in an interview with Kacey Kowars in 2004. "I really think there's a more direct connection between the brain, eye, and hand if you're writing with pen or pencil, looking down at what you've written."

DeMille prefers to do his own research, to experience things firsthand. "Usually, I begin by reading about a subject until I have enough knowledge to interview people who are in that profession or occupation that I'm writing," he said on his Web site—anyone from FBI agents to laboratory technicians. "Then I go to the locations where my novels are set." After visiting places such as Moscow, for *The Charm School*, or Ohio, for *Spencerville*, he can provide details he might have missed otherwise.

DeMille was born in New York City in 1943. The family moved to Long Island, where his father was a builder and his mother a medical technician. He attended Hofstra University for three years before serving in the U.S. Army beginning in 1966. As a first lieutenant, he was an infantry platoon leader with the First Cavalry in Vietnam and was awarded an Air Medal, Bronze Star, and Vietnamese Cross of Gallantry. Upon his discharge in 1969, he completed his studies at Hofstra, earning his bachelor's degree in political science and history. He has since received Doctor of Humane Letters degrees from Hofstra and Dowling College, and a Doctor of Literature from Long Island University. He has three children from his first two marriages.

Fresh out of the Army, DeMille began his writing career penning police crime novels for $1,500 a shot while he worked as a carpenter, house painter, deckhand, art dealer, and editorial assistant. He wrote paperback original novels, moonlighting while working as an insurance investigator. He took a gamble with the manuscript *By the Rivers of Babylon*: in 1978, he told his agent it had to sell for a good price. And it did, in the six figures. That novel kicked the author's writing career into high gear. It's about a commercial aircraft headed for a United Nations peace conference; the plane is forced to land, and its crew and passengers are captured by Palestinian terrorists.

DeMille's later novels have been set against backdrops of the Vietnam War (the <u>Paul Brenner</u> books), Long Island society (*Plum Island*), and small-town Ohio (*Spencerville*).

Because of DeMille's research tenacity, his methodical way of writing, and the need sometimes to write as many as four drafts, it can take a year and a half to two years to finish a book. His longer thrillers require considerable discipline to write. He spends more time shaping an outline before he starts. "I'm outlining more," he said in a Bookreporter interview, "but a good writer should not be confined by his or her own outline. You need to see opportunities that arise during the writing and stray from the outline as you'd stray from a road map if you saw something interesting."

DeMille's favorite authors range from Graham Greene and John Steinbeck to Ernest Hemingway, Agatha Christie, and Edith Wharton. He says Ayn Rand's *Atlas Shrugged* had the greatest impact on his literary tastes. "I read this book in college, as many of my generation did, and I was surprised to discover that it said things about our world and our society that I thought only I had been thinking about," he said on the Barnes & Noble Meet the Writers Web site. He referred specifically to what he sees as a rise in mediocrity in our culture.

A man without serious hobbies, DeMille enjoys meals with friends. He travels the world, but home is where he's found most of the time—a 10,000-square-foot Tudor-style home on Long Island that he designed himself and that took four years to build. He shares it with his fiancée, Sandy Dillingham, and their son.

Several recent novels have featured homicide detective John Corey and, as the series progressed, the character's wife, FBI agent Kate Mayfield. DeMille said he was surprised to find that Corey has a wide following of women readers. "That surprised me, because he is the antithesis, I thought, of what women want," he told Bethanne Kelley Patrick for *Publishers Weekly*. "I guess I tapped into something, though, because most of my fan mail on these books is from women."

DeMille admits the lure of the writing life is great. The investment can seem to be as simple as a desk and word processor. But it also takes a thoughtful mind and talent. "When someone tells me they want to write novels," he jokingly told interviewer Paula Gordon, "I suggest they take two aspirin and go to bed."

 Works by the Author

By the Rivers of Babylon (1978)
Mayday, with Thomas H. Block (1979)
Cathedral (1981)
Talbot Odyssey (1984)
Word of Honor (1985)

The Charm School (1988)
Gold Coast (1990)
Nelson Demille Omnibus (1992)
Spencerville (1994)
The Gate House (2008), sequel to *Gold Coast*

John Corey Series

Plum Island (1997)
Lion's Game (2000)
Night Fall (2004)
Wild Fire (2006)

Paul Brenner Series

The General's Daughter (1992)
Up Country (2002)

Contributor

Plot Thickens, edited by Mary Higgins Clark (1997), includes "Revenge and Rebellion," with Lauren DeMille
Dangerous Women, edited by Otto Penzler (2005), includes "Rendezvous"

Editor

The Best American Mystery Stories 2004, with Otto Penzler (2004)

Writing as Brad Matthews

Killer Sharks: The Real Story (1977)

Writing as Jack Cannon

Joe Ryker Series
Sniper (1989)
Hammer of God (1989)
Smack Man (1989)
Cannibal (1989)
Night of the Phoenix (1989)
Death Squad (1989)

Writing as Kurt Ladner

Hitler's Children (1976)

Nonfiction

Five Million Dollar Woman: Barbara Walters (1976), written as Ellen Kay

Take Off!: How Long Island Inspired America to Fly (2000), written as Nelson DeMille

Adaptations in Other Media

The General's Daughter (1999), motion picture
Word of Honor (TNT, 2003), television film
Mayday (CBS-TV, 2005), television film

For Further Information

Bellafante, Ginia, "At Home with Nelson DeMille: Dark Plots Conceived in a Tudor Setting." *New York Times*, November 9, 2006.

Kowars, Kacey, Nelson DeMille interview. http://www.nelsondemille.net/author/interview.asp (viewed November 3, 2007).

Nelson DeMille interview, Bookreporter. http://www.bookreporter.com/authors/au-demille-nelson.asp (viewed November 1, 2007).

Nelson DeMille interview, Meet the Writers, Barnes & Noble. http://www.barnesandnoble.com/writers/writerdetails.asp?cid=881694 (viewed November 1, 2007).

Nelson DeMille interview, Paula Gordon Show. http://www.paulagordon.com/shows/demille/ (viewed November 3, 2007).

Nelson DeMille Web site. http://www.nelsondemille.net/ (viewed November 1, 2007).

Patrick, Bethanne Kelly, "DeMille, Close Up." *Publishers Weekly*, September 18, 2006.

Richards, Linda, "Nelson DeMille Inteview," January magazine. http://www.januarymagazine.com/profiles/demille.html (viewed October 29, 2007).

Jack DuBrul

Adventure; Espionage; Crime; Thrillers: Global, Bio

Benchmark Series: <u>Geologist Philip Mercer</u>

Burlington, Vermont

1968–

About the Author and the Author's Writing

The fictional hero Philip Mercer is a globe-trotting, ex-commando geologist who saves the world from human and natural disasters. His over-the-top personality belies that of his creator, Jack DuBrul, once a carpenter, later an apartment complex manager who, nevertheless, entertains a growing legion of fans with each new book.

DuBrul conceived Mercer and the general plot of his first published novel, *Vulcan's Forge*, in 1988, two years before he graduated from George Washington University in Washington, D.C., with a bachelor of arts degree in international relations, and a special interest in the Middle East and Africa. He tucked the first pages of the manuscript in a drawer—alongside an earlier, 600-page manuscript that he believes is unpublishable. He retrieved the *Vulcan's Forge* notes a few years later, when he was living in Florida and working as a builder and bartender. He reworked his original KGB-CIA plotline, completed the book working evenings, and submitted it through a relative to an agent. The agent placed it with Tor/Forge. And DuBrul's career was off.

After the third title in the series had been published, DuBrul quit the hammer-and-nail trade and moved to Vermont to become a full-time writer. He also took over management of family real estate holdings after his parents' deaths. DuBrul, a Vermont native, was born in Burlington in 1968. He grew up an avid reader, a World War II buff, and a fan of the original *Star Trek* television drama. He went to the private school Westminster School in Simsbury, Connecticut.

On his Web site, DuBrul apologizes for not having had more dramatic life experiences before he began writing. "I get a little discouraged when I read the biographies of other thriller writers," he said. "Many of them are ex-military, retired special ops soldiers, clandestine agents with impressive records of defending the righteous…. Mine is more like a collection of anecdotes because all I've ever wanted to be is a thriller writer."

So what has DuBrul done? He has taken flying lessons; and he's skydived and tried SCUBA. And he's traveled to a couple dozen countries, several that are off the usual tourist itinerary, such as Greenland as well as Eritrea, and other parts of Africa. But mostly he peppers his books with facts gleaned from solid research and an active imagination. An idea came to him for *Deep Fire Rising* after he watched a Discovery Channel program about volcanos. What, he wondered, if the Cumbre Vieja volcano in the Canary Islands erupted, sending a major tsunami toward the Caribbean and Florida? Who would know about, and profit from, such a storm? And how could Mercer prevent it?

DuBrul has honed his craft since the first book. He has become more adept at personalities. His running characters, he has said, are partially based on people he knows. Take his brother, Dave DuBrul—spell it backward and you have the name of a thug, Evad Lurbud, in *Vulcan's Forge*. Mercer's buddy, the eighty-plus-year-old Harry White, is a cleaned up variation on a homeless man who once lived in the boiler room of DuBrul's father's commercial building. Mercer's love interests in the books come from various sources. DuBrul himself is pleased having a relationship with only one woman. He married another Vermonter, Debbie Saunders, in 2001.

Critics have given DuBrul a strong welcome. "DuBrul's writing is a fusion of [Clive] Cussler and Tom Clancy, without overdoing the arcane technology as Clancy often does," Nancy Pearl wrote in *Library Journal*. The comparison is interesting, because within a year, DuBrul became coauthor of the third in Cussler's <u>Oregon Files</u> series of the seagoing adventures of Juan Cabrillo and the crew of a clandestine spy ship.

DuBrul is in no hurry to abandon his Mercer books, though. "It's difficult to build a 'brand name' in publishing," the author said in an interview on the Jack DuBrul Fan Page, "and at this stage it wouldn't be a good move to put out a Jack DuBrul book about alien invaders or a courtroom drama. I think readers are beginning to equate my books with fast-paced adventure and I love to give them what they want."

 ## Works by the Author

Geologist Philip Mercer Series

Vulcan's Forge (1998)
Charon's Landing (1999)
The Medusa Stone (2000)
Pandora's Curse (2001)
River of Ruin (2002)
Deep Fire Rising (2003)
Havoc (2005)

Oregon Files with Clive Cussler

Dark Watch (2005)
Skeleton Coast (2006)
Plague Ship (2008)
Corsair (2009)

For Further Information

Medusa Stone review. *Publishers Weekly*, April 17, 2000.
Vulcan's Forge review. *Publishers Weekly*, December 8, 1997.

Jack DuBrul interviews, Jack DuBrul Fan Page. http://www.geocities.com/
mynamejean/interview.html and http://www.geocities.com/mynamejean/
interview2.html (viewed October 8, 2007).

Jack DuBrul Web site. http://www.jackdubrulbooks.com/ (viewed November
12, 2008).

Pearl, Nancy, "Macho Heroes! Evil Villains!! Adventure!!!" *Library Journal*,
February 15, 2004.

Barry Eisler

Crime; Espionage; Thrillers: Global, Techno

Benchmark Series: <u>John Rain</u>

New Jersey

1964–

Photo credit: Naomi Brookner

About the Author and the Author's Writing

Barry Eisler chose his hero's name purposely. John Rain is deceptively soft sounding. Sleet might have been more appropriate for the hard-as-nails, can't-quite-retire, Japanese American assassin who first appeared in *Rain Fall* in 2002.

Rain is a powerful opponent. "I caught the gun in my left hand and used my right foot to blast his legs out from under him in *deashibarai*, a side foot sweep that I had performed tens of thousands of times in my quarter century at the Kodokan," he says in the sequel, *Rain Storm* (2004).

Rain, as should be apparent, is a master martial artist in a sinister world of intrigue. A Vietnam War veteran, he became a paid assassin, his specialty causing deaths that authorities have no reason to think are other than natural or accidental. But he's come to regret his career choice and is only lured back into service in an extreme circumstance, such as when his friend Dox is being held captive in *Requiem for an Assassin* (2007).

Eisler writes from what he knows: he's been a covert operative for the Central Intelligence Agency and is proficient in hand-to-hand combat. He has trained in wrestling, boxing, karate, judo, and Brazilian jujitsu. "Mostly they trained me at the SOTC— Special Operations Training Course. Where else can you learn how to pilot small watercraft, conduct airdrops, fire off M-79 grenade launchers, and make improvised explosive devices? And get paid for it?" Eisler said in an interview with *Mystery Scene*.

The author's attention to detail in fight scenes has brought him a wide following from the martial arts realm. In an interview for Mixed Martial Arts Coverage Web site, he described for Mike Alan his favorite move: "It starts with a modified side control … and then transitions into an arm bar…. In the latter, you sort of slither across the other guy's body as though you might be transitioning to the mount, but instead you just gradually take up the guy's opposite arm and bar it from above." Novices needn't understand the language to appreciate the aura and skills of martial artists.

Eisler was born in New Jersey in 1964. In 1986, he received a bachelor of arts degree from Cornell University and a juris doctorate from the same school in 1989. He worked for Hamada & Matsumoto in Tokyo, Japan, as an attorney; then was in-house counsel for Matsushita Electric and Industrial Co. in Osaka before joining the U.S. State Department for three years. As a covert agent with the CIA's Directorate of Operations, he trained in long and small arms, improvised explosives, surveillance, and counterterrorism. Later he worked briefly for a Silicon Valley tech startup.

Eisler's earliest interest in writing was as a teenager, when he wrote short stories. During his years at law school, he produced a regular newspaper column about foreign policy. After he left federal employ, he wrote his first novel. Fifty rejections later, his book found a home. Although the long road to publication was discouraging, Eisler has said he kept faith by knowing he had done the best he could with his manuscript.

"The most critical asset that any intelligence officer can bring to bear professionally, and also that any citizen can bring to bear in keeping safe, is awareness of your surroundings," Eisler told *Publishers Weekly*'s Robert C. Hahn.

Eisler had a natural subject for *Rain Fall*. "Working with the agency was a hugely valuable experience," he said in an interview with Jonathan Maberry and Janice Gable Bashman. "In addition to exposure to tools and tactics that have influenced my writing, I came away with an insider's view of how intelligence really works—how it functions and dis-functions, how decisions filter down to the field."

He described his character in an Onthemat.com interview: "John Rain is a guy who was raised in two countries but accepted in neither. Also, he had some unpleasant experiences in Vietnam as a member of U.S. Special Forces. All of which has served to forge a highly cynical persona."

Eisler's books exploit the Japanese setting. The author is enormously taken with the country's cities, its population densities, its geographic variety, and its people.

"I like to create fiction that's an extension of actual events—the kind of fiction that makes you wonder," he told Mystery One Bookstore. He researches extensively through reading and interviews. "Most of all, I use on-site investigations, making sure to literally walk in John Rain's footsteps to ensure that what I'm describing is accurate and also conveyed, I hope, with some immediate emotional impact."

Eisler offers his ideas on craftsmanship on his Web site, Barryeisler.com. "All good writing conveys necessary information while simultaneously feeding a hunger for more information," he said. "Engage all the senses—not just visual. If you're describing a place, what are the ambient sounds? What does it smell like? Temperature?"

Although the thriller genre allows little room for lengthy characterization, Eisler's John Rain has slowly emerged and evolved as a hero. "The main trick is to get inside the character's head and to try to present him as fully human," he said in a Mystery Ink conversation. "No one looks in the mirror and sees a bad guy; we all have our justifications and rationalizations. By presenting some of Rain's, I hope to bring about a degree of empathy."

Works by the Author

Fault Line (2009)

John Rain Series

Rain Fall (2002)
Hard Rain (2003), in United Kingdom as *Blood from Blood*
Rain Storm (2004), in United Kingdom as *Choke Point*
Killing Rain (2005), in United Kingdom as *One Last Kill*
The Last Assassin (2006)
Requiem for an Assassin (2007)

Adaptations in Other Media

Rain Fall (2009), motion pictured based on the novel

For Further Information

Alan, Mike, "Interview: Ground Fighting Novelist Barry Eisler," MMAFighting.com, September 3, 2004. http://mmafighting.com/articles/interviews/barryeisler.html (viewed October 11, 2007).

Barry Eisler interview, OntheMat.com, December 31, 2002. http://onthemat.com/articles/Barry_Eisler_Interview_01_01_2003.html (viewed October 11, 2007).

Barry Eisler Web site, http://www.barryeisler.com/ (viewed November 12, 2008).

Fletcher, Connie, *Rain Fall* review. *Booklist,* May 16, 2002.

Hahn, Robert C., "Paying a Horrible Price: PW Talks with Barry Eisler." *Publishers Weekly*, May 1, 2006.

"Interview with Barry Eisler, Mystery One Bookstore, September 2002. http://www.mysteryone.com/BarryEislerInterview.htm (viewed October 11, 2007).

Mayberry, Jonathan, and Janice Gable Bashman, "An Interview with Barry Eisler." *Wild River Review,* October 2007.

Montgomery, David J., "10 Questions with Barry Eisler," Mystery Ink, July 2005. http://www.myseryinkonline.com/2005/07/10_questions_wi.html (viewed October 11, 2007).

Requiem for an Assassin review. *Publishers Weekly*, April 30, 2007.

Smith, Kevin Burton, "The Barry Eisler Files." *Mystery Scene*, Summer 2007.

Linda Fairstein

Photo credit: Peter Simon

Crime: Legal

Benchmark Series: <u>Alexandra Cooper</u>

Mount Vernon, New York

1947–

About the Author and the Author's Writing

When a famed dancer disappears during a Lincoln Center performance, New York City prosecutor Alexandra Cooper and NYPD investigators Mercer Wallace and Mike Chapman quickly encounter a menacing physician whom they suspect preys on women. Welcome to Linda Fairstein's novel *Death Dance* (2005). "This thriller is chock-full of authentic detail, showcasing Fairstein's extensive knowledge of legal and forensic issues," said *Library Journal* reviewer Rebecca Stankowski.

Fairstein certainly has the credentials. From 1972 to 2002, she worked on the staff of the New York County District Attorney's office, all but the first two years as chief of the sex crimes prosecution unit. From 1981 to 2002, she was deputy chief of the trial division. This was no light workload. Nevertheless, the Mount Vernon, New York, native found time to write one nonfiction book and four novels. Since she retired, Fairstein has written another half dozen novels, and counting. At the same time, she has consulted with national media and is a frequent public speaker.

Fairstein, who was born in 1947, comes from a medical family. Her father was an anesthesiologist, her mother a registered nurse. Her early reading included Sherlock Holmes and the Hardy Boys, works by Louisa May Alcott and Robert Louis Stevenson, Dostoevsky's *Crime and Punishment* and Dickens's *Bleak House*. In recent years, she has read works by contemporaries such as P. D. James, Ruth Rendell, Lisa Scottoline, Carl Hiaasen, Elmore Leonard, and John le Carré.

After receiving an A.B. degree in nineteenth-century British literature from Vassar College in 1969, she earned a J.D. from the University of Virginia School of Law in 1972. In 1987, she married lawyer Justin N. Feldman, who often appears in cameo bits in her novels. He has three children by an earlier marriage. The family has homes in New York and Martha's Vineyard, Massachusetts.

103

Fairstein recalls that her first two years with the New York DA's office were a challenge, as then-DA Frank Hogan was not keen on women prosecutors, she told *Publishers Weekly.* In 1974, Hogan's successor, Robert Morgenthau, assigned her to the then-formed sex crimes unit. "There were great changes in the laws governing prosecution of sex crimes," she told *PW,* "and I became deeply involved in an area that hadn't really existed when I started out." Among high-profile cases she was involved in were the "Preppie Murder" of Jennifer Levin and the rape of the Central Park jogger.

Her experiences provided rich material for a nonfiction book, and publishers inquired of Fairstein about engaging a ghostwriter. But she wanted to write the book herself. The result was *Sexual Violence: Our War against Rape,* published in 1993. "I turned to writing novels to soften the hard facts of what I do in this field," she said in a conversation made available by Simon & Schuster. "I was determined to create a character and a series based on real cases and actual crimes—to inform as well as to entertain."

In summer 1994, the author's agent, Esther Newberg, brought best-selling novelist Patricia Cornwell to lunch with Fairstein just before Fairstein was to go on vacation—and start writing a novel. That was just the inspiration she needed.

Her running series character, Alexandra Cooper, of course, personifies the author. Cooper also comes from a medical family, although she's younger, thinner, and blonder, Fairstein has said. Because her heroine so closely mirrors herself, Fairstein has scoffed at ever becoming bored with Alex Cooper. Cooper has a sense of humor—necessary in the grim world of crime, particularly sex crime.

While she has kept up on the latest in scientific advances in forensics, Fairstein has found that some things never change. "One hundred percent honesty is rare [in witnesses]," she said in an interview with the *University of Virginia Archives Magazine.* "And while most flaws in human nature prompt my empathy, in the criminal justice system there's nothing worse than the lie. A single simple lie about a critical fact in a case can forever change lives."

Fairstein says she outlines her novels only as much as is necessary to satisfy her publisher. "I start out with the idea for a story, do a loose plotting and timeline before I begin, and generally find that by the fifth or sixth chapter, I've changed direction already…. As the characters develop more fully, they start to take me places I never dreamed of going when I started out," she said in a Page One interview.

Dense plots, and opportunities to research and share information about, say, the world of museum politics or the waterfront appeal to the author. "Although the murders and plot lines in my novels are fictitious, the procedural aspects of Alex Cooper's prosecutorial life are absolutely drawn from my own experience and meant to reflect that pretty accurately," she said in a Bookreporter interview.

 Works by the Author

Alexandra Cooper Series

Final Jeopardy (1996)
Likely to Die (1997)
Cold Hit (1999)
The Deadhouse (2001)

The Bone Vault (2003)
The Kills (2004)
Entombed (2005)
Death Dance (2006)
Bad Blood (2007)
Killer Heat (2008)
Lethal Legacy (2009)

Nonfiction

Sexual Violence: Our War against Rape (1993)

Editor

The Best American Crime Reporting 2007 (2007)

Adaptations in Other Media

Final Jeopardy (ABC-TV, 2001), television film based on the novel

For Further Information

"Conversation with Linda Fairstein," Simon & Schuster, June 1997. http://www.ishipress.com/convfair.htm (viewed February 8, 2008).

Evans, Paul, "Murder, She Writes." *University of Virginia Archives Magazine*, Fall 2007.

Linda Fairstein interview, Bookreporter, 2004. http://www.bookreporter.com/authors/au-fairstein-linda.asp (viewed January 8, 2008).

Linda Fairstein interview, Page One. http://www.pageonelit.com/interviews/LindaF.html (viewed February 8, 2008).

Picker, Leonard, "PW Talks with Linda Fairstein: From Prosecutor to Author." *Publishers Weekly*, November 13, 2006.

Stankowski, Rebecca House, *Death Dance* review. *Library Journal*, November 15, 2005.

Zvirin, Stephanie, *Killer Heat* review. *Booklist*, November 15, 2007.

Christine Feehan

Fantasy; Horror; Romance: Paranormal; Vampires

Benchmark Series: <u>Carpathians</u>

California

Birth date not disclosed

Photo credit: Cassandra Young

About the Author and the Author's Writing

Even form-altering, plasma-slurping Carpathians need love. Of an ancient race, living among human beings, the Carpathians are nearly extinct. What few children they bear tend to be sons, and they often die before their first birthdays. No daughter has been born for five centuries. (Carpathians live a long time.) Lifemates give the males much-needed emotion, direction, and distraction from the urge to kill. Once a male has killed, he becomes a ruthless, soulless vampire. That's just how it is in the universe author Christine Feehan has shaped for her <u>Dark Series</u> of paranormal novels.

With four active series, in contemporary as well as preternatural romances, the author brims with ideas. Born Christine King, in a family of ten sisters and three brothers, the California native long yearned to write. When she was in high school, she one day injudiciously scrawled a love scene in her notebook during math class. The teacher confiscated the paper and read it to the class—to the mortification of instructor and student.

Professional writing was a delayed career, however. The author, who holds a third-degree dan black belt in Tang So Do Muk Duk Kwan, taught that Korean martial art and other self-defense techniques for two decades. Many of her eleven children (from a "hers, his, ours, and adopted" marriage to Richard Feehan) were out of the house by the time she acceded to the urgings of family and friends and submitted a manuscript to a publisher. Dorchester Publishing accepted *Dark Prince* for its Love Spell imprint in 1999. Over the next decade, Feehan wrote another eighteen stories in the <u>Dark Series</u>, started three other series, and delved occasionally into straightforward romance.

In an interview with Clair E. White for Writers Write, Feehan explained why she drifted to the "dark side" in her writing: "I was in a very dark place in my life. We had suffered a terrible loss in our family and I found it had robbed me of my ability to write, which was like breathing to me. I created the Carpathian world out of that darkness." The Carpathians, as we have seen, live in a bleak world of emptiness and yearning.

Strong sellers in paperback, Feehan's <u>Dark Series</u> began to come out in hardcover with the 2006 publication of *Dark Celebration*, which, despite its Christmas setting, *Booklist* reviewer Diana Tixier Herald explained, still bubbled with "vampire attacks, deadly danger from a mage, and steamy sex between the telepathic, shape-shifting Carpathians." On the brighter side, the book also included holiday recipes sent in by fans.

Feehan writes from an office in her home. Having grown up in a chaotic household with numerous siblings, the author had little trouble putting words to paper even as her children swarmed around her. She only insists on being alone to write her steamy love scenes. Her large family gave her no end of relationship experiences to draw on in her writing. And her years of martial arts training provided the spiritual as well as physical stability necessary to turn out great amounts of marketable fiction on deadline. She edits the previous day's words before beginning a new chapter each day. Her husband reads and comments on each manuscript.

Feehan's <u>Dark Series</u> focuses on different characters within the same universe. She writes them from a male point of view and offers heroes who are rugged, focused, and monogamous. She begins each book with a general plot but lets the characters take the lead.

"My characters dictate to me exactly how they act," she said in a Writerspace interview, "what they think and how they respond."

The author's books have a firm sense of place. Feehan says she reads and researches her settings firsthand. She traveled to New Orleans so she could better write about that city in one book. At an editor's request, she began writing gothic romances. Gothics by nature emphasize the heroine. Although she misses the male point of view, Feehan says this affords a welcome change.

"I can't write two books from the same series in a row," she said on her Web site, "in order to keep my writing fresh, I have to spread things out a bit." Despite the time needed to research books and edit manuscripts, she manages to produce three or four books a year.

Feehan's <u>Drake Sisters</u> series is about modern-day witches. The <u>Ghost Walker</u> books are about soldiers whose latent psychic abilities have been enormously enhanced by the secret work of Dr. Peter Whitney. The Leopard People, an exotic race, is featured in another, sensual series of novels that began with Wild Rain.

"I like to be able to use my imagination and the power of the paranormal to expand creativity," Feehan said in a Sensual Romances interview. "I like the use of dark and light and good and evil. It's plain fun to create stories of this nature. That and I may be a trifle twisted."

 # Works by the Author

The Scarlatti Curse (2001)

Lair of the Lion (2002)

Fantasy, with Sabrina Jeffries, Emma Holly, and Elda Minger (2002), includes "Awakening"

Lover Beware, with Katherine Sutcliffe, Eileen Wilks, and Fiona Brand (2003), includes *Dark Symphony*

Wild Rain (2004), sequel to "Awakening"

Fever (2006), includes *Wild Rain* and "Awakening"
Dark Dreamers, with Marjorie M. Liu (2006)

Carpathians or Dark Series

1. *Dark Prince* (1999)
2. *Dark Desire* (1999)
3. *Dark Gold* (2000)
4. *Dark Magic* (2000)
5. *Dark Challenge* (2000)
6. *Dark Fire* (2001)
7. *Dark Dream* (2001)
8. *Dark Legend* (2002)
9. *Dark Guardian* (2002)
10. *Dark Symphony* (2003)
11. *Dark Descent* (2003)
12. *Dark Melody* (2003)
13. *Dark Destiny* (2004)
14. *Hot Blooded*, with Maggie Shayne, Emma Holly, and Angela Knight (2005), includes "Dark Hunger"
15. *Dark Secret* (2005)
16. *Dark Demon* (2006)
17. *Dark Celebration* (2006)
Dark Hunger (2007), manga comic based on story from "Hot Blooded"
18. *Dark Possession* (2007)
19. *Dark Curse* (2008)

Christmas Stories Series

A Very Gothic Christmas, with Melanie George (2001), includes *After the Music*
The Twilight before Christmas (2003)
The Wicked and the Wondrous (2004), includes *The Twilight before Christmas* and *After the Music*
The Shadows of Christmas Past, with Susan Sizemore (2004), includes *Rocky Mountain Miracle*
A Christine Feehan Holiday Treasury (2007), includes *After the Music, The Twilight before Christmas*, and *Rocky Mountain Miracle*

Drake Sisters Series

Magic in the Wind (2003)
Oceans of Fire (2005)
Dangerous Tides (2006)
Safe Harbor (2007)
The Turbulent Sea (2008)

Ghost Walker Series

Shadow Game (2003)
Mind Game (2004)
Night Game (2005)
Conspiracy Game (2006)
Deadly Game (2007)
Predatory Game (2008)
Murder Game (2009)

For Further Information

Christine Feehan entry, Contemporary Authors Online, reproduced in Biography Resource Center. Farmington Hills, MI: Thomson Gale, 2007. http://galenet.galegroup.com/servlet/BioRC (viewed December 17, 2007).

Christine Feehan interview, Writerspace. http://www.writerspace.clom/interviews/feehan403/html (viewed December 17, 2007).

Christine Feehan Web site. http://www.christinefeehan.com/ (viewed December 17, 2007).

Herald, Diana Tixier, *Dark Celebration* review, *Booklist*, September 1, 2001.

"Interview with Christine Feehan," Sensual Romance. http://sensualromance.writerspace.com/cfeehaninterview.html (viewed December 17, 2007).

White, Claire E., "A Conversation with Christine Feehan," Writers Write, March 2002. http://www.writerswrite.com/journal/mar02/feehan.htm (viewed December 17, 2007).

Joseph Finder

Adventure; Espionage, Paranormal; Thrillers: Business/Finance

Benchmark Title: *High Crimes*

Chicago, Illinois

1958–

Photo credit: Jason Grow

About the Author and the Author's Writing

Thriller author Joseph Finder is all business—monkey business, that is, in the corporate universe. His early novels portray traditional governmental espionage. With *Paranoia* (2004), he began to explore betrayals, secret plots, idea thefts, and other shenanigans in global industry.

Finder was born in Chicago in 1958, the son of two college professors. He gained an early taste for unusual climes when his family moved to Afghanistan, The Philippines, Washington state and, eventually, Albany, New York, where he went to high school. In 1980, he received a bachelor of arts degree, summa cum laude, from Yale University, and a master's from Harvard University's Russian Research Center in 1984. While at Yale, he sang with a musical group called the Whiffenpoofs. He has written for *Atlantic Monthly, Harper's,* the *New York Times,* the *Washington Post*, and *Publishers Weekly*, among others.

A specialist in international affairs and espionage, he completed his first book, the nonfiction *Red Carpet*, in 1983, when he was a teaching fellow at Harvard. It explores the involvement of prominent American businessmen such as David Rockefeller, Armand Hammer, Cyrus Eaton, Averell Harriman, and Donald Kendall with the politics of the Soviet Union. The work was based on interviews and documents, some obtained through the Freedom of Information Act. Hammer took exception to the book and threatened a lawsuit. When the Soviet Union fell apart, documentation emerged that verified Finder's writing.

Finder felt there was more to the story, and he moved to fiction for *The Moscow Club* (1990), a book about an American operative's efforts to foil a secret plan to bring Communists back to power in Russia.

The novel was not an immediate sale; it took three years. "Instead of writing a manuscript, getting it rejected, and then moving on to the next, I wrote a book, had it turned down by several agents, listened to their reasons why it didn't work, and then revised. Over and over again," the author said on his Web site. However, with the sale of that book, first to a British publisher in 1989, then to Viking in the United States, the author quit his teaching position at Harvard.

The author continued to write about international espionage with *Extraordinary Powers*, which starts out with the possible murder of the director of the CIA and the likelihood of a Soviet mole within the ranks of a spy agency. He explains on his Web site that he begins each book with an idea, however skimpy, perhaps from a newspaper article, maybe information from someone with whom he has spoken. He researches his idea by reading and traveling, and he slowly builds a plot and creates his characters. He starts writing without always knowing everything that's going to happen but with a general idea of the ending.

"My plots tend to be fairly complex machines, but I never want the reader to *experience* them as complex," he said in an interview *The Writer*'s Jeff Ayers. "I think of them like good Swiss watches: There are an awful lot of tiny moving parts inside, but all the reader should know or care about is that the thing runs smoothly."

The idea for *Killer Instinct*, his novel about international electronics manufacturers, came to him after he decided he wanted a flat-panel television in 2004 so he could watch the Boston Red Sox. He knew very little about flat-panel TVs, but he learned. "I wanted a breakthrough technology to be in the book," the author said in an interview with Electronic House. "So I made up this technology that was like an LCD screen that you could roll up, and then I found a guy at MIT who is developing this [using OED]. I found out that the technology is feasible, but it's not out there yet." That was the background. The treachery was all Finder's imagination.

By now, Finder had found his niche—the business world. The transition to corporate dirty tricks, whether in aero-tech or furniture making, wasn't a far stretch from international intrigue. "A lot of intelligence officers now work as in-house security officers for major corporations," the author told *The Economist*, "and I'd ask them, 'What could a bad guy do inside a company?'"

Finder took out a membership in a shooting range and interviewed former Special Forces personnel so he could better depict the hero in *Killer Instinct*—salesman Jason Steadman, who buys a weapon for protection—and the villain—Kurt Semko, a veteran of the Iraq war who has an unusual way of helping Steadman increase sales.

Corporate intrigue doesn't mean characters are locked in a board room. *Power Play* takes place mostly at a Canadian hunting lodge, for example, where the entire administration of a troubled aerospace firm is held captive for ransom and only the middling exec Jake Landry has the skills to save them.

The author says he enjoys finding out more about an industry, whether it is aviation or furniture: "people will tell me things, as a novelist, that they'd never tell a journalist. I love passing the insider stuff on to my readers in the form of page-turning entertainment," he told Bookreporter.

Works by the Author

The Moscow Club (1990)

Extraordinary Powers (1994)

The Zero Hour (1996)

High Crimes (1998)

Paranoia (2004)

Company Man (2005), in the United Kingdom as *No Hiding Place* (2005)

Killer Instinct (2006)

Power Play (2007)

The Chopin Manuscript, with Lee Child, David Corbett, Jeffery Deaver, Jim Fusilli, John Gilstrap, James Grady, David Hewson, John Ramsey Miller, P. J. Parrish, Ralph Pezullo, S. J. Rozan, Lisa Scottoline, Peter Spiegelman, and Erica Spindler (2007)

Vanished (2009)

Nonfiction

Red Carpet: The Connection between the Kremlin and America's Most Powerful Businessmen (1983)

Adaptations in Other Media

High Crimes (2002), based on the novel

For Further Information

Ayers, Jeff, "Joseph Finder: The Art of Suspense." *The Writer*, March 2007.

Castle, Steve, "Thriller Set in Electronics World," Electronic House, March 5, 2007. http://www.electronichouse.com/article/fictional_thriller_set_in_electronics_ world/C1255/ (viewed December 26, 2007).

"Chief Fiction Officer." *The Economist*, August 25, 2007.

Donahue, Deirdre, "Joseph Finder Hits Pay Dirt with Thriller 'Company Man.'" *USA Today*, April 26, 2005.

Halpern, Jake, "Reality Writes." *Boston Globe*, May 14, 2006.

Joseph Finder interview, Bookreporter. http://www.bookreporter.com/authors/au-finder-joseph.asp (viewed December 26, 2007).

Joseph Finder Web site. http://www.josephfinder.com (viewed November 12, 2008).

Sachs, Andrea, "Chapters for the CEO Set." *Time*, May 28, 2006.

Ian Fleming

Adventure; Espionage; Thrillers

Benchmark Series: <u>James Bond</u>

London, England

1908–1964

About the Author and the Author's Writing

More than a half century since the British secret agent 007 appeared in Ian Fleming's *Casino Royale*, James Bond remains a popular culture phenomenon. Blockbuster motion pictures appear regularly. (The latest at this writing, *Quantum of Solace*, had opening-weekend ticket sales of $67.5 million, a record for the franchise.) Graphic novels capture the spirit of the original writing, while new authors bring out contemporary prose adventures featuring the suave spymaster.

One might consider Ian Fleming a relic of the Cold War. But critic Christopher Hitchens suggests otherwise in the introduction to a reissue of *From Russia with Love*: "By some latent intuition, Fleming was able to peer beyond the Cold War limitations of mere spy fiction and to anticipate the emerging milieu of the Colombian cartels, Osama bin-Laden and indeed the Russian mafia—as well as the nightmarish idea that some such fanatical freelance megalomaniac would eventually collar some weapons-grade plutonium."

Fleming was born in 1908, the son of Conservative Member of Parliament Valentine Fleming. Before Ian turned nine, his father died in combat in World War I. His mother, Eve Fleming, sent him to Durnford School, where he read the adventure novels of Sapper, John Buchan, Sax Rohmer, and Robert Louis Stevenson, and then to Eton, where his main interest was sports. After a scandal over a prostitute ended his studies at Royal Military College at Sandhurst, he completed his education in Switzerland, Munich, and Geneva. In 1929, he joined the Reuters news agency. "He went to work in its Moscow bureau, and in 1933 covered the trial of six British engineers from the Metropolitan-Vickers Company charged with spying and plotting against the Soviets—widely believed to have been a sham," according to BBC News. All fodder for the future fiction writer: a Russian secretary implicated in the Vickers case was the inspiration for Tatiana, the Bond seducer in *From Russia with Love*.

After two years, Fleming refused a transfer to the Far East. He quit journalism to become a stockbroker. Standing 6 feet 2 inches, with black hair and penetrating blue eyes, he developed a fondness for alcohol and tobacco and a hedonistic lifestyle, all of which flourished when, in 1939, he took a post as personal assistant to the British director of Naval Intelligence, Admiral John Godfrey. Ranked a lieutenant commander, he traveled around the world. He established an intelligence unit that saw action during the invasion of Germany. He helped develop a never-triggered plan should the Nazis decide to invade France and established an intelligence unit that saw action on D-day. Following the war, Fleming handled a network of reporters for the *Sunday Times*. In 1952, he married Ann Rothermere, a divorcee with whom he had had an affair. They had one child.

Fleming had a beach house retreat called Goldeneye in Jamaica, and he began to write novels there each winter. "The scent and smoke and sweat of a Casino are nauseating at three in the morning," he began *Casino Royale*. "James Bond suddenly knew that he was tired." The story was filmed for American television in 1954, by which time Fleming had two more novels in bookstores.

Fleming's books are marked by a flamboyant, cultured hero who drives a 1933 4.5 litre Bentley (and later an Aston Martin); drinks his dry martinis shaken, not stirred; smokes blended Morland cigarettes; and carries a concealed .25 Beretta. A mark of Fleming's prose that differentiated him from Sapper and other early adventure writers was his attention to detail, his mention of specific brands, his careful crafting of a refined character.

Fleming continued to work part of the year for the *Sunday Times*, as the columnist called Atticus, until 1959. His novels did modestly well, although some reviewers charged they were elitist and sexist. In 1961 the author suffered a heart attack. When motion picture versions of *Doctor No*, *Goldfinger*, and *From Russia with Love*, featuring the Scottish actor Sean Connery as Bond, were released and President John F. Kennedy revealed his pleasure in reading the spy tales, Fleming's work gained even greater popularity.

However, Fleming didn't live to see the decades-long Bond phenomenon rise to its current dizzying heights. He died in 1964 at age fifty-six. "Ian Fleming had been born with everything except money," *Time* magazine said. "The creation of James Bond made up for that lack. It returned him an estimated million dollars a year over the past decade and permitted the luxury of a London town house just across the road from Buckingham Palace."

"He had not set out to be a writer. He did not, in fact, write his first book, *Casino Royale*, until he was forty-three. But he had always loved writing and he had always loved books," niece Kate Fleming states on the Ian Fleming Centre Web site.

In a *Playboy* interview conducted shortly before his passing, Fleming described his hero: "He's sort of an amalgam of romantic tough guys, dressed in 20th century clothes, using 20th century language. More true to the type of commands and secret service men than to the heroes of ancient thrillers."

Certainly Bond was overblown. There was no "00" designation, meaning a license to kill. "He readily admitted his plots were fantastic," Paul Davis wrote in a half-century tribute to Fleming, "yet he said they were often based on the real world of intelligence. He noted that on occasion a news story would 'lift a corner of the veil' and reveal the real world of spies and commandoes."

But as some have asked, were Ernest Blofield or Doctor No really that far removed from Manuel Noriega or Saddam Hussein?

 # Works by the Author

Diamond Smugglers (1957)

James Bond Series

Casino Royale (1954), retitled *You Asked for It* (1955)

Live and Let Die (1954)

Moonraker (1955), retitled *Too Hot to Handle* (1957)

Diamonds Are Forever (1956)

From Russia with Love (1957)

Doctor No (1958)

Goldfinger (1959)

For Your Eyes Only: Five Secret Exploits of James Bond (1960), in the United Kingdom as *For Your Eyes Only: Five Secret Occasions in the Life of James Bond* (1960)

Thunderball (1961)

The Spy Who Loved Me (1962)

On Her Majesty's Secret Service (1963)

You Only Live Twice (1964)

Bonded Fleming (1965), includes *Thunderball, For Your Eyes Only,* and *The Spy Who Loved Me*

The Man with the Golden Gun (1965)

More Gilt-Edged Bonds (1965), includes *Live and Let Die, Moonraker,* and *Diamonds Are Forever*

Octopussy (1965), in the United Kingdom as *Octopussy and The Living Daylights* (1966)

Quantum of Solace: The Complete James Bond Stories (2008)

James Bond Novels by Other Writers

Colonel Sun, by Robert Markham (Kingsley Amis) (1968)

James Bond: The Authorized Biography, by John Pearson (1973)

James Bond, the Spy Who Loved Me, by Christopher Wood (1977), movie novelization

James Bond and Moonraker, by Christopher Wood (1979), movie novelization

License Renewed, by John Gardner (1981)

For Special Services, by John Gardner (1982)

Ice Breaker, by John Gardner (1983)

Role of Honour, by John Gardner (1984)

James Bond in Win, Place, or Die, by R. L. Stine (1985),

Find Your Fate Series

Berlin Escape: The Last Great Adventures of James Bond (1985)

Nobody Lives Forever, by John Gardner (1986)

No Deals, Mr. Bond, by John Gardner (1987)

Scorpion, by John Gardner (1988)

Win, Lose or Die, by John Gardner (1989)

Brokenclaw, by John Gardner (1991)

Death Is Forever, by John Gardner (1992)

James Bond Quartet (1992), includes *Casino Royale, Live and Let Die, Moonraker,* and *From Russia with Love*

Never Send Flowers, by John Gardner (1993)

Seafire, by John Gardner (1994)

Essential James Bond (1994), includes *Thunderball, On Her Majesty's Secret Service, You Only Live Twice, The Man with the Golden Gun, Octopussy,* and *The Living Daylights*

Ian Fleming's James Bond (1994), includes *Moonraker, From Russia with Love, Doctor No, Goldfinger, Thunderball,* and *On Her Majesty's Secret Service*

License to Kill, by John Gardner (1995), movie novelization

Goldeneye, by John Gardner (1995), movie novelization

Cold, by John Gardner (1996), in United States as *Cold Fall*

James Bond Omnibus (1997), includes *Thunderball, On Her Majesty's Secret Service,* and *You Only Live Twice*

James Bond Omnibus (1997), includes *From Russia with Love, Doctor No,* and *Goldfinger*

Zero Minus Ten, by Raymond Benson (1997)

Tomorrow Never Dies, by Raymond Benson (1997), movie novelization

Facts of Death, by Raymond Benson (1998)

High Time to Kill, by Raymond Benson (1999)

The World Is Not Enough, by Raymond Benson (1999), movie novelization

Doubleshot, by Raymond Benson (2000)

Never Dream of Dying, by Raymond Benson (2001)

Man with the Red Tattoo, by Raymond Benson (2002)

Die Another Day, by Raymond Benson (2003), movie novelization

Moneypenny Diaries: Guardian Angel, edited by Dr. Kate Westbrook (2005)

Devil May Care, by Sebastian Faulks (2008)

Graphic Novels

James Bond 007: Serpent's Tooth, by Doug Moench (1995)

James Bond: Goldfinger, by Ian Fleming, Henry Gammidge, and John McClusky (2004)

James Bond: The Man with the Golden Gun, by Ian Fleming, Jim Lawrence, and Yaroslav Horak (2004)

James Bond: Octopussy, by Ian Fleming and Jim Lawrence (2004)

James Bond: On Her Majesty's Secret Service, by John McClusky and Henry Gammidge (2004)

James Bond: Casino Royale, by Ian Fleming, Anthony Hern, Henry Gammidge, and John McClusky (2005)

James Bond: Dr. No, by Ian Fleming, Henry Gammidge, and John McClusky (2005)

James Bond: Colonel Sun, by Kingsley Amis, Jim Lawrence, and Yaroslav Horak (2005)

James Bond: The Spy Who Loved Me, by Ian Fleming, Jim Lawrence, and Yaroslav Horak (2005)

James Bond: Golden Ghost, by Jim Lawrence and Yaroslav Horak (2006)

James Bond: Death Wing, by Ian Fleming, Jim Lawrence, and Yaroslav Horak (2007)

James Bond: Phoenix Project, by Jim Lawrence and Yaroslav Horak (2007)

James Bond: Trouble Spot, by Jim Lawrence and Yaroslav Horak (2007)

James Bond: Shark Bait, by Ian Fleming, Jim Lawrence, Yaroslav Horak, and Harry North (2008)

Juvenile Fiction

Chitty-Chitty-Bang-Bang: The Magical Car (1964)

Young Bond Series by Charlie Higson

SilverFin (2005)

Blood Fever (2006)

Double or Die (2007)

Nonfiction

Thrilling Cities (1965)

Contributor

Fleming Introduces Jamaica, edited by Morris Cargill (1965)

Adaptations in Other Media

Casino Royale (1954), television production

Doctor No (1962), motion picture

From Russia with Love (1963), motion picture

Goldfinger (1964), motion picture

Thunderball (1965), motion picture

You Only Live Twice (1967), motion picture

Casino Royale (1967), motion picture

Chitty-Chitty, Bang-Bang (1968), motion picture

On Her Majesty's Secret Service (1969), motion picture

Diamonds Are Forever (1971), motion picture

Live and Let Die (1973), motion picture

The Man with the Golden Gun (1974), motion picture

The Spy Who Loved Me (1977), motion picture

Moonraker (1979), motion picture

For Your Eyes Only (1981), motion picture

Octopussy (1983), motion picture

Never Say Never Again (1983), motion picture

A View to a Kill (1985), motion picture

Living Daylights (1987), motion picture

License to Kill (1989), motion picture

GoldenEye (1995), motion picture

GoldenEye: The Secret Life of Ian Fleming—The Real James Bond (1989), television documentary

Spymaker: The Secret Life of Ian Fleming (1990), documentary

James Bond Jr. (1991), television series

Tomorrow Never Dies (1997), motion picture

The World Is Not Enough (1999), motion picture

Die Another Day (2002), motion picture

Casino Royale (2006), motion picture

Quantum of Solace (2008), motion picture

For Further Information

Benson, Raymond. *James Bond Bedside Companion*. New York: Galahad Books, 1986.

Cathcart, Brian, "The Man with the Golden Typewriter, Taittinger Champagne, Rolex Watches, Beluga Caviar and Sea Island Underpants: Ian Fleming's Bond Novels Anticipated Our Fascination with Brands." *New Statesman*, November 13, 2006.

Chancellor, Henry. *James Bond: The Man and His World—The Official Companion to Ian Fleming's Creation*. London: John Murray, 2005.

Cork, John, "Ian Fleming: A Literary Style & Legacy, Name's Bond, James Bond Web site. http://www.klast.net/bond/flem_leg.html (viewed October 5, 2007).

Davis, Paul, "HappyAnniversary, Mr. Bond," Crime Beat, 2002. http://www.orchardpressmysteries.com/happy_anniversary_mr_bond.html (viewed November 11, 2007).

Hitchens, Christopher, "Bottoms Up: Ian Fleming, the Man behind James Bond, Was a Sadist, a Narcissist, and an All-Around Repressed Pervert. But He Also Saw Past the Confines of the Cold War." *Atlantic Monthly*, April 2006.

Hitchens, Christopher, introduction. *From Russia with Love*. New York: Penguin Classics, 2002.

Ian Fleming interview. *Playboy*, December 1964.

Ian Fleming Web site. http://www.ianflemingcentre.com/ (viewed October 5, 2007).

"Man Behind Bond," BBC News, November 19, 1999. http://news.bbc.co.uk/1/hi/special_report/1999/11/99/shaken_not_stirred/525010.stm (viewed October 5, 2007).

"Man with the Golden Bond." *Time*, August 21, 1964.

"Real James Bond," Channel 4 Real Lives. http://www.channel4.com/history/microsites/R/real_lives/james_bond.html (viewed October 5, 2007).

Winder, Simon. *The Man Who Saved Britain: A Personal Journey into the Disturbing World of James Bond*. New York: Farrar, Straus & Giroux, 2006.

Vince Flynn

Espionage; Thrillers: Political, Global

Benchmark Series: <u>Mitch Rapp</u>

St. Paul, Minnesota

1966–

About the Author and the Author's Writing

"Rapp hit the landing with a thud, grabbed the railing, and started down the next flight. He couldn't get the vision of the burning white Toyota SUV out of his head…. He needed to get out there and help them."

It's two-thirds of the way through Vince Flynn's *Protect and Defend* (2007), and his counterterrorism operative Mitch Rapp is deep in Iran, and deep in trouble. And that's just the way fans like it. Except for his debut novel, Flynn has only written about agent Rapp, embroiling the character in up-to-the-moment Middle East intrigue.

Vincent Flynn was born in 1966 in St. Paul, Minnesota. He earned a degree in economics from the University of St. Thomas in 1988. After working in sales and marketing with Kraft General Foods, he joined the United States Marine Corps in 1990. He was disqualified from the flight program at Officers Candidate School because of a medical history of childhood convulsions. Even though he had been diagnosed as dyslexic in grammar school, he felt the urge to write, but instead he joined United Properties in the Twin Cities and sold commercial real estate. The writing bug never left him. He quit his job, moved to Colorado, and wrote the manuscript for *Term Limits*. Flynn lists as influences Ernest Hemingway, Robert Ludlum, Tom Clancy, and J. R. R. Tolkien, among others.

Over the next five years, sixty publishers rejected *Term Limits,* but Flynn still had faith in the book. He self-published it, and regional sales were sufficient to attract both an agent and a two-book contract with Pocket Books. When the book appeared in paperback in 1997, it became a best seller; and his subsequent novels have never failed to find a large audience.

Transfer of Power (1999) introduced Rapp. Terrorists have taken over the White House and slaughtered dozens of people. The Secret Service has whisked President Robert Hayes to a secret hideout, so he is not among the hundreds held hostage. The CIA's top terrorism expert, Rapp, has to navigate the corridors of Washington's power brokers as well as negotiate with the extremists to resolve the crisis. Rapp prefers to work alone—and when you don't know who to trust, that may be the best way.

"Flynn delivers a riveting espionage thriller that will satisfy action fans … but won't alienate readers who want a little nuance with their suspense," said *Booklist* reviewer Mary Frances Wilkens.

Explaining the series hero's genesis (before September 11) on the Fox News program *The O'Reilly Factor*, Flynn said, "These people [radical Islamic fundamentalists] are saying death to America. Osama bin Laden had already attacked us once. He said he's going to do it again. And I felt that we should be out there taking these guys on, not waiting and playing defense. I created the Mitch Rapp character."

The Third Option, the first sequel, found Rapp going after a European arms dealer with ties to Saddam Hussein. (It came out in 2000, before the Iraq War.) He meets with betrayals on his own side. "These are people in high places trying to discredit the CIA in order to further their own political futures," said *Library Journal*'s Patrick Wall, "and they make the mistake of having Rapp for an enemy and eventually pay the price." The reviewer noted the author "has toned down the right-wing rhetoric a bit from the earlier works."

Only temporarily, it turns out. In an interview with a *Washington Times* reporter in November 2007, during the heat of the primary campaign when United States policy on torture was a hot topic, Flynn said he thought it was acceptable to use the extreme technique of waterboarding with Islamic terrorists. "I think it should be done in the rarest of situations," he qualified. "Anybody who says torture doesn't work hasn't studied the history of torture. Torture, or aggressive interrogation, is only as good as the interrogators. Take Khalid Sheikh Mohammed, for instance. He got waterboarded and he sang like a canary." The statements, as one might expect, drew considerable response.

Living with his wife and three children in Minnesota and having won a new publishing pact with Atria, Flynn had to pass up an offer to join the writing staff for the Fox television series *24* for its fifth season. Instead, he and the show's producers set about developing a different series, which has yet to appear.

Pleased with his best-seller success, Flynn's goals in life aren't that complex: "Keep doing what I love and stay faithful to my wife and kids," he says on his Web site.

Works by the Author

Term Limits (1997)

Mitch Rapp Series

Transfer of Power (1999)
The Third Option (2000)
Separation of Power (2001)
Executive Power (2002)
Memorial Day (2004)
Consent to Kill (2005)
Act of Treason (2006)
Protect and Defend (2007)
Extreme Measures (2008)

For Further Information

Eisler, Barry, "Vince Flynn, Left-Winger?" Eisler blog. http://www.barryeisler.com/2007/11/vince-flynn-left-winger.html (viewed December 27, 2007).

Hudson, Audrey, "A Page from His Book." *Washington Times*, November 16, 2007.

Protect and Defend review. *Publishers Weekly*, September 24, 2007.

Vince Flynn entry, Contemporary Authors Online, reproduced in Biography Resource Center. Farmington Hills, MI: Thomson Gale, 2007. http://galenet.galegroup.com/servlet/BioRC (viewed December 17, 2007).

Vince Flynn interview, The O'Reilly Factor, October 18, 2005. http://www.foxnews.com/story/0,2933,172748,00.html (viewed December 27, 2007).

Vince Flynn Web site. http://www.vinceflynn.com (viewed November 12, 2008).

Wall, Patrick, *The Third Option* review. *Library Journal*, October 15, 2000.

Wilkens, Mary Frances, *Transfer of Power* review. *Booklist,* May 15, 1999.

Ken Follett

Adventure; Espionage; Historical Fiction; Suspense

Benchmark Title: *Eye of the Needle*

Cardiff, Wales

1949–

Photo courtesy of Ken Follett

About the Author and the Author's Writing

When Oprah Winfrey selected Ken Follett's *The Pillars of the Earth* for her book club, the epic story set in the twelfth century had already been in print for eighteen years. Still, the publisher New American Library printed another 612,000 copies for a special book club edition. Such was the power of the television personality—although Follett hasn't done so badly on his own.

Ken Follett was born in Cardiff, Wales, in 1949, the son of a tax inspector and his wife. He became an avid reader at a young age, in part because his born-again Christian parents would not allow him to watch television or go to movies. When he was ten, the family moved to London, and he attended public schools. In 1970, he received a bachelor of arts degree in philosophy, with honors, from University College in London.

While in college, Follett played guitar and was drawn to Bob Dylan's songs. He is still an active amateur musician. He credits his interest in philosophy with helping him develop as a writer. "When you study philosophy," he said on his Web site, "you have to have an off-the-wall imagination. It's the same with fiction, which is all about imagining situations that are different from the real world." Follett began to write during the Vietnam War era, when he had plenty of political, as well as philosophical, food for thought. He later became active in the Labour Party.

From 1970 to 1973, Follett was a newspaper reporter for the *South Wales Echo*. He worked for the *London Evening News* until 1974. As a journalist, he covered breaking news events and occasionally interviewed musicians. He began to write novels in part to pay for a car repair and because he heard through a friend that it was easy to get a book advance. Under the penname of Symon Myles, he wrote three books featuring Apples Carstairs, a sexy and violent hero whom the author now considers far short of his standard. At the time, he was trying to emulate Ian Fleming.

From 1974 to 1977, Follett worked for a publisher, Everest Books, first as a deputy managing director, then as editorial director. His *The Shakeout* and *The Bear Raid* featuring Piers Roper, an industrial spy, came out during these years. Later becoming dissatisfied with these and the Carstairs books, Follett let them lapse out of print. He hastily wrote on commission *Amok: King of Legend*, a King Kong-ish adventure, and *Capricorn One*, the novelization of a screenplay about a faked space flight to the moon. He wrote mystery and science fiction for younger readers, under his own name and as Martin Martinsen.

Follett credits his American agent, Al Zuckerman, with helping him improve his writing by fleshing out characters. Some readers found his villains too empathetic, but Follett said in an Amazon.com interview, "The problem is that when the villain is a point-of-view character, you as the reader are going to spend a lot of time in his company. So he has to be interesting, and he has to be kind of likable, otherwise you're going to put the book down."

Working as a full-time writer beginning in 1977, Follett caught fire with his eleventh book, the suspenseful *Eye of the Needle* (1978), a work with a strong female protagonist. It spent thirty weeks on the *New York Times* best-seller list and earned its author a Mystery Writers of America Edgar Award. It was also made into a popular motion picture. Follett continued to write thrillers—*The Key to Rebecca* and *Lie Down with Lions* among them—but has also given readers a few surprises such as *The Pillars of the Earth*, which is set against the construction of a Middle Ages cathedral.

Follett told the Oprah Book Club audience that the idea for the 973-page book came after he became interested in the cityscapes around him and visited an Anglican cathedral in Peterborough. "I knew the story of humankind's attempts to build ever taller and more beautiful churches. I understood the place of this building in history, my history. I was enraptured by the Peterborough Cathedral."

The author's nonfiction includes *On Wings of Eagles*, an account of the rescue from Iran of two employees of Ross Perot during the 1979 revolution.

Follett comes up with plots at the edge of the news, whether terrorist blackmail or, in *The Third Twin*, secret experiments in genetic engineering. He has delved into history with *Code to Zero*, which is about the Cold War space race, and *Jackdaws*, which is set during World War II.

"Follett's forte—in fiction and nonfiction—is the variation upon history," observed Anne Janette Johnson. "Every human relationship is somehow blighted or molded by the complexities of world politics, and all the emotional and sexual entanglements are played out against a backdrop of historical events."

Believing accurate details give the reader a strong feeling of authenticity in a story, Follett uses a professional researcher in New York, Dan Starr, to dig up books and articles and track down professionals. He does his own interviews, and he never bases characters on real people, because that would be limiting. "The characters have to do what I need them to do to make the plot go," he told *USA Today*'s Jeffrey Stinson.

To satisfy readers of *The Pillars of the Earth*, the author in 2007 released *World Without End*, a 1,024-page sequel set in the same fictional town of Kingsbridge, two centuries later. Descendants of Tom Builder, Aliena, and other characters from the first book come upon a dark secret. He waited so long, Follett said in a Bookreporter.com interview, because he wanted a grand theme. "When finally I thought of a story based around the Black Death and the birth of modern medicine, I felt I had at last come up with a big enough theme."

Follett has two children by his first wife, Mary Emma Ruth Elson. His second wife is Barbara Broer Follett, a member of Parliament from Stevenage, Hertfordshire, where they have a home. The Folletts also have places in London—where Follett, an enthusiast of the Bard, frequently attends performances of Royal Shakespeare Company—and in Antigua.

Works by the Author

The Shakeout (1975)
The Bear Raid (1976), sequel to *The Shakeout*
Eye of the Needle (1978)
Triple (1979)
The Key to Rebecca (1980)
The Man from St. Petersburg (1982)
Lie Down with Lions (1986)
The Pillars of the Earth (1989), retitled *Pillars of the Almighty* (1994)
Night over Water (1991)
Under the Streets of Nice (1991)
A Dangerous Fortune (1993)
A Place Called Freedom (1995)
The Third Twin (1996)
The Hammer of Eden (1998)
Code to Zero (2000)
Jackdaws (2001)
Hornet Flight (2002)
Whiteout (2004)
World Without End (2007), sequel to *The Pillars of the Earth*

Juvenile Fiction

The Secret of Kellerman's Studio (1976), retitled *Mystery Hideout* (1990)
The Power Twins and the Worm Puzzle: A Science Fantasy for Young People (1991), published as by Martin Martinsen; as *The Power Twins* (1991) by Ken Follett

Screenplays

Fringe Banking (1978)
A Football Star (1979), with John Sealey
Lie Down with Lions (1988)

Nonfiction

The Heist of the Century, with Rene Louis Maurice (1978), as *The Gentlemen of 16 July* (1980); revised as *Under the Streets of Nice: The Bank Heist of the Century* (1986)

On Wings of Eagles (1983)

The Art of Suspense: A Lecture on the History of the Thriller (DVD, 2007)

Written as Bernard L. Ross

Amok: King of Legend (1976)

Capricorn One (1978)

Written as Simon Myles

Apples Carstairs Series

The Big Needle (1994), retitled *The Big Apple* (1975) as by Ken Follett (1986)

The Big Black (1974)

The Big Hit (1975)

Written as Zachary Stone

The Modigliani Scandal (1976), published as by Ken Follett (1985)

Paper Money (1977), as by Ken Follett (1987)

Adaptations in Other Media

Eye of the Needle (1981), motion picture

The Key to Rebecca (1985), motion picture

On Wings of Eagles (1985), motion picture

Lie Down with Lions (1994), motion picture

The Third Twin (1997), motion picture

For Further Information

Bowman, David, "The Salon Interview; Ken Follett," Salon.com. http://dir.salon.com/books/int/1998/12/cov_02intc.html (viewed July 5, 2003).

Johnson, Anne Janette, Ken Follett entry, *Contemporary Authors New Revision Series*, volume 54. Jeff Chapman and John D. Jorgenson, eds. Detroit, MI: Gale Research, 1997.

Ken Follett entry, *Authors and Artists for Young Adults*, volume 50. Detroit, MI: Gale Group, 2003.

Ken Follett interview, Amazon.com. http://www.amazon.com/exec/obidos/tg/feature/-/115584/ref=ed_cp_2_3_b/102-8920117-1500149 (viewed July 5, 2003).

Ken Follett interview, Bookreporter. http://www.bookreporter.com/authors/au-follett-ken.asp (viewed January 4, 2008).

Ken Follett Web site. http://www.ken-follett.com/ (viewed November 12, 2008).

"Oprah Picks 'Pillars of the Earth.'" *Publishers Weekly*, November 19, 2007.

Stinson, Jeffrey, "Follett Follow Through to 'End.'" *USA Today*, October 9, 2007.

"Top Author Talks about Reading." http://www.huyton-today.merseyside.org/issue6/kenfollettinterview.html (viewed July 5, 2003).

Frederick Forsyth

Adventure; Espionage; Suspense; Thrillers

Benchmark Title: *The Day of the Jackal*

Ashford, Kent, England

1938–

About the Author and the Author's Writing

Frederick Forsyth's novel *The Afghan* is about British and American intelligence, in anticipation of another al-Qaeda-style attack, placing agent Mike Martin in deep cover with the terrorist group. "Forsyth writes with a bare-bones, reportorial style that makes his stories feel as realistic as anything one might read in the daily newspaper," said reviewer David Pitt in *Booklist*. "No one else has managed to make the very flatness of the documentarian's style an effective instrument for generating tension."

Some readers mistake Forsyth's objectivity for disdain, but Forsyth explains it differently: "I regard it as a journalist's perspective. I was taught: Keep the adjectives out. I'm saying: This is what a sniper does, and that's the way they do it. If you want to be shocked—fine. If you want to be intrigued—fine. If you want to be full of admiration—fine," Forsyth told *Spiegel*'s' reporter Malte Herwig.

The author's gripping fiction debut, *The Day of the Jackal*, released in 1971, "practically invented the political assassination subgenre," says a writer in MysteryGuide.com. After that success, Forsyth went on to write *The Odessa File, The Dogs of War,* and, in 2003, *The Avenger*—in which Osama bin Laden is a real-life character—novels that established him as a keen political observer and purveyor of top-notch thrillers.

Born in 1938 in Ashford, in rural East Kent, England, Forsyth attended Tonbridge School and Granada University in Spain. He joined the Royal Air Force, where he served from 1956 to 1958, becoming one of its youngest pilots at age nineteen. When he left military service, he became a reporter for *Eastern Daily Press* in Norfolk. In 1961, as a Reuters correspondent in Paris, Germany, and Czechoslovakia, he gained a deep knowledge of national and international politics. He worked for the British Broadcasting Corporation in the mid-1960s but left after a disagreement over coverage of the Biafra-Nigeria war in 1967. Knowing he had a good story, he wrote the nonfiction *Biafra*.

Forsyth wrote for the *Daily Express* and *Time* magazine, but in extra time wrote a draft of *The Day of the Jackal*. "It was my first attempt at fiction," he said in a Books at Transworld interview. "I had little idea I could even tell a story, but I had to give it a try because I was flat broke!" The gist of his plot grew from an incident in Paris in the early 1960s when OAS agents tried six times to kill Charles de Gaulle because of his support for an independent Algeria. The manuscript circulated among several editors' desks before it found a home. It went on to win the Mystery Writers of America Edgar Allan Poe Award for best novel.

After a time, Forsyth found writing thrillers limiting. The author told Larry King on CNN he felt shackled to the spy genre. "I had done mercenaries, assassins, Nazis, murderers, terrorists, special forces soldiers, fighter pilots, you name it, and I got to thinking, could I actually write about the human heart, and I'm vain enough to think, maybe I could."

Following a dinner conversation with friend and theater impresario Andrew Lloyd Webber, he decided to write a sequel to *The Phantom of the Opera,* called *The Phantom of Manhattan,* which was released in 1999.

He returned to his thriller hallmark with *Avenger*, in which the hero, a former Vietnam War tunnel rat, has dedicated himself to making things right ever since his daughter was kidnapped and murdered and his wife committed suicide. Believing himself retired, Colin Dexter reluctantly hires out to find and bring back a young man who is being held captive by a Serbian warlord.

The old spark shone bright. "Forsyth's extraordinary care with detail, his solid voice, and his exquisite pacing make this a totally engrossing thriller," wrote Connie Fletcher for *Booklist*.

Critic Andrew F. Macdonald summed it up, saying the author's "'docudrama' genre, interweaving truth and fiction, was not Forsyth's invention—numerous writers have practiced it as well—but he is certainly its most prolific exponent."

Twice married and with two sons, the author in leisure time is an avid fisherman. He has a country estate in Hertfordshire.

Works by the Author

The Day of the Jackal (1971)
The Odessa File (1972)
The Dogs of War (1974)
The Shepherd (1976)
The Devil's Alternative (1979)
The Fourth Protocol (1984)
The Negotiator (1989)
The Deceiver (1991)
The Fist of God (1994)
Icon (1996)
The Phantom of Manhattan (1999), sequel to Gaston Leroux's *The Phantom of the Opera*
Quintet (2000), electronic book
Avenger (2003)
The Afghan (2006)

Collections

No Comebacks: Collected Short Stories (1972)
The Veteran: Five Heart-Stopping Stories (2001)

Screenplay

The Fourth Protocol (1987)

Editor

Great Flying Stories (1991), includes "The Shepherd"

Nonfiction

The Biafra Story (1969)
Emeka (1982)
I Remember: Reflections on Fishing in Childhood (1995)

Adaptations in Other Media

The Day of the Jackal (1973), motion picture
The Odessa File (1974), motion picture
The Dogs of War (1981), motion picture
The Fourth Protocol (1987), motion picture
Jackal (1997), motion picture

For Further Information

Avenger review, Bookfinder. http://www.bookfinder.us/review1/031319517.html (viewed June 17, 2004).

Bedell, Geraldine, "Ready, Freddie, Go." *Observer* (May 12, 2002).

Brown, Derek, "Frederick Forsyth." *Guardian,* September 18, 2000. http://www.guardian.co.uk/netnotes/article/0,6729,370388,00.html (viewed June 17, 2004).

Cabell, Craig. *Frederick Forsyth: A Matter of Protocol: The Authorized Biography.* London: Robson Books, 2003.

Clark, Judy, *Avenger* review, Mostly Fiction. http://mostlyfiction.com/spy-thriller/forsyth.htm (viewed June 14, 2004).

Day of the Jackal review, Mystery Guide. http://www.mysteryguide.com/bkForsythJackal.html (viewed June 17, 2004).

Farndale, Nigel, "Looking for Other Icons." *Sunday Times,* August 31, 1997.

Frederick Forsyth entry. *Contemporary Novelists,* 7th ed. Detroit, MI: St. James Press, 2001.

Frederick Forsyth entry, *Contemporary Popular Writers.* Detroit, MI: St. James Press, 1996.

Frederick Forsyth entry, *St. James Encyclopedia of Popular Culture.* Detroit, MI: St. James Press, 2000.

Frederick Forsyth interview, Books at Transworld. http://www.booksattransworld.co.uk/catalog/interview.htm?command=search&db-twmain.txt&eqisbndata=0593050932 (viewed June 14, 2004).

Herwig, Malte, "They Take the Mind, and What Emerges Is Just Tapioca Pudding." *Spiegel Online*. December 29, 2006. http://www.spiegel.de/international/spiegel/0.1518.457074.00.html (viewed January 14, 2008).

Jerome, Helen M., "Return to Formula: Frederick Forsyth Is Back in Business." *Book,* November/December 2001.

Larry King Live Weekend transcript, April 15, 2000. http://www.cnn.com/TRANSCRIPTS/0004/15/lklw.00.html (viewed June 17, 2004).

Macdonald, Andrew F., Frederick Forsyth entry. *St. James Guide to Crime & Mystery Writers*, 4th ed. Jay P. Pederson, ed. Detroit, MI: St. James Press, 1996.

Pitt, David, *The Afghan* review. *Booklist*, August 1, 2006.

Veteran review. *Publishers Weekly*, November 20, 2000.

Stephen Frey

Crime; Thrillers: Political, Business/Finance

Benchmark Title: *The Takeover*

Birthplace not identified
1960–

About the Author and the Author's Writing

Meteoric rises. Precipitous drops. Enormous windfalls. Calamitous losses. Welcome to Wall Street. Is it any wonder investors—and readers of Stephen Frey's thrillers—are paranoid? Feel outpaced? Afraid they're being manipulated by unseen hands?

Consider *The Fourth Order* (2007), which tells the story of Michael Rose. The chief financial officer for the energy giant Trafalgar Industries wants to diversify through acquisition of a global information technology business. He expects resistance from the company, CIS Technologies. But from members of his own board of directors? Until now an expert at the big business game, Rose has no clue how small a chip he is. He is about to come up against the international machinations of the secret Order.

Welcome to the world of Stephen Frey.

Details of Frey's personal life are as tightly held as the secretive power-mongers that people his stories. We do know that he was born in 1960. He received his B.A. and M.B.A. from the University of Virginia at Charlottesville, the latter from the Darden School in 1987. He has held executive positions with Westdeutsche Landesbank, J.P. Morgan, and Irving Trust, all in New York, and Albion Investors in Virginia. He has held an interest in a soft drink distributorship. He now lives in Florida, where he is managing director of a private equity firm by day and a thriller writer by night. He and his wife have two daughters.

Frey's first book, *The Takeover* (1995), tells how a secret society of graduates of Harvard Business School have joined together with the goal of replacing a liberal U.S. president. Andrew Falcon, a young specialist in mergers, is a small cog in their great machine. As he comes to realize what's going on, he races against time to thwart their plans. "John Grisham meets Robert Ludlum on Wall Street in this fast-paced novel," praised *USA Today* reviewer John H. Healy. Frey enjoyed the praise, as he has said Grisham's *The Firm* and other books were early inspirations for his writing.

Frey's novels have included some, such as *Silent Partner* and *The Inner Sanctum*, with vibrant female characters. When the plot warrants, when he wants counterpoint to another character, or when he wants romance, he's always pleased to include strong female voices.

The author takes pains to describe the inner workings of America's financial centers as painlessly as possible. His wife is his first reader, and the first to point out when he goes on too long, he has said.

Working from an outline—both a publisher's requirement and a useful tool to navigate the zigzag plots—"The book still takes twists and turns that I never imagined," he said in a Bookreporter interview. "In fact, that's how I actually start writing, I make the outline more and more detailed until I realize I might as well be writing."

With major financial catastrophe in the late 2000s, Frey's to-the-point thrillers are even more keenly anticipated by his readers.

Works by the Author

The Takeover (1995)
The Inner Sanctum (1997)
The Vulture Fund (1997)
The Legacy (1998)
The Insider (1999)
Trust Fund (2001)
The Day Trader (2002)
Silent Partner (2003)
Shadow Account (2004)
The Fourth Order (2007)
Forced Out (2008)
Hell's Gate (2009)

Christian Gillette Series

The Chairman (2005)
The Protégé (2005)
The Power Broker (2006)
The Successor (2007)

Anthology

The Best of the Best: Celebrating Fifty Years of Signet Authors, edited by Elaine Koster and Joseph Pittman (1998), includes "Paranoia"

For Further Information

Healy, John H., *The Takeover* review. *USA Today*, August 30, 1995.

Melton, Emily, *The Vulture Fund* review. *Booklist*, July 1996.

Slater, John, "Stephen Frey—Noted Author and Private Equity Dealmaker," DealCast, 2007. http://www.mergers.com/stephen-frey-noted-author-and-private-equity-dealmaker/ (viewed February 7, 2008).

Stephen Frey biography, Random House. http://www.randomhouse.com/rhpg/catalog/display.pperl?isbn=9780345500250 (viewed February 7, 2008).

Stephen Frey interview, Bookreporter, 2003. http://www.bookreporter.com/authors/au-frey-stephen.asp (viewed February 7, 2008).

Alan Furst

Adventure; Espionage; Thrillers: Historical, Nazis

Benchmark Title: *The Polish Officer*

New York, New York

1941–

About the Author and the Author's Writing

A Manhattan-born grandson of Jewish immigrants, Furst has long been drawn to the Old World, both as a journalist and as a novelist. With his gripping spy tales set on the eve of World War II, Alan Furst has shaped his own niche in the world of espionage novels. "I never wanted to be a Cold War novelist," Furst told Chauncey Mabe for the *South Florida Sun-Sentinel*. "For John le Carré, it was always who's betraying who, the hall-of-mirrors kind of thing. When you go back to the '30s, it's a case of good vs. evil, and no kidding."

"Furst's novels work, and satisfy on a very high level, because the real character is Europe itself, a sprawling yet controlled and familiar landscape being subjected to the indignities of war and occupation," said Martin Walker, writing in *The National Interest* about the writer's fiction set during World War II.

Furst graduated from Oberlin College at age twenty-one, in 1962, and received a master of arts degree from Pennsylvania State University four years later. As a Fulbright teaching fellow at the Faculte des Lettres at the University of Montpellier, he lived in southern France. He moved to Washington when he became an employee of the Seattle Arts Commission.

He wrote four mystery novels. He became a staff writer for *Esquire* and a columnist for the *International Herald Tribune* and a travel writer for *Islands* magazine. He lived in Paris and Spain, where he began work on *Night Soldiers* (1988), his first novel.

Reared on the spy novels of Ian Fleming and Eric Ambler, Furst decided to root his ventures very firmly in the past. "I'm just fascinated by the period, and by the incredible courage … endless ingenuity and courageous passion people had to fight against evil," he explained to Todd Leopold of CNN.com. "I am constitutionally incapable of coming up with a plot. My plots come from history. You'll never find a bad guy fighting with a good guy at the edge of a cliff."

"How would he react in the same situation?" he asked himself as he shaped his books. He experienced an epiphany in 1983, he told interviewer Jay MacDonald for BookPage, when he sought to visit his ancestral home in the Soviet Union and encountered enormous and manipulative bureaucracy. He couldn't go where he wanted.

"It really hit me like a wind and it wasn't subtle at all," Furst said. "During World War II, everyone, in Europe at least, thought this might be it, that this was about as much life as they were going to have, and that changes things, especially romantic relationships."

Furst takes great care in his delineation of characters, recalling an experience from drama club in high school when a character on stage made one simple motion that changed the audience's whole perception of that character. "That's the story I use to remind myself that you can lose an audience immediately if you do the wrong thing with a main character," he told Elfrieda Abbe in *The Writer* in 2003. "You don't have a long time to have the main character be liked by the reader, therefore, it's best to show him when he's at his best in a situation with some tension in it."

Furst cedes that his writing has many influences, from black-and-white cinema, to music, to his absorption with European culture. "I really can project myself into thinking like a Frenchman in 1940," he told Crime Time interviewer Woody Haut, "hoping the axe wasn't going to fall. Then, after it did, hoping it wasn't going to be too bad."

The author enjoys digging into history, and peppers his plots with obscure facts. *Dark Voyage*, for instance, is about Eric DeHaan, the captain of a merchant commandeered by the British to carry valuable cargo through Nazi mines in the Baltic Sea. How plausible was it that a freighter could dodge the Germans? Furst knew the Nazis had limited radar capabilities. "The big radars they had didn't go that far out to sea. The level of surveillance was nothing like it is now," he said in a conversation with Grant Howard for Book Passage. "What has changed the world now is the satellite, which can see anything. But that wasn't true then." When he wrote *Night Soldiers*, he knew the OSS went to Ellis Island to buy tattered clothing from arriving immigrants, so their agents would look authentic when they went abroad.

How does he secure this information? "I will even sit down by the fireplace on a cold winter night and curl up around a diplomatic history of Rumania. For some reason I'm just strange for this," he told Identity Theory writer Robert Birnbaum.

His emphasis on the past, interestingly, resonates with a post–September 11 readership, B. R. Myers wrote in *Atlantic Monthly*, due in part to a growing "aversion to globalization. His characters are constantly moving across militarized borders, showcasing the colorful checkerboard of distinct politics that Europe used to be."

Works by the Author

Your Day in the Barrel (1976)
Paris Drop (1980)
Caribbean Account (1981)
Shadow Trade (1983)
Night Soldiers (1988)
Dark Star (1991)
The Polish Officer (1995)
Kingdom of Shadows (2000)
Blood of Victory (2002)

Dark Voyage (2004)

Foreign Correspondent (2006)

The Spies of Warsaw (2008)

Jean Casson Series

World at Night (1996)

Red Gold (1999)

Editor

Book of Spies: An Anthology of Literary Espionage (2002)

Nonfiction

One Smart Cookie: How a Housewife's Chocolate Chip Recipe Turned into a Multimillion-Dollar Business—The Story of Mrs. Field's Cookies, with Debbi Fields (1987)

For Further Information

Abbe, Elfrieda, "Master of Intrigue," *The Writer*, May 2003.

Alan Furst Web site, http://www.alanfurst.net/ (viewed October 18, 2007).

Birnbaum, Robert, Alan Furst interview, identitytheory.com. http://www.identitytheory.com/people/birnbaum9.html (viewed October 8, 2007).

Haut, Woody, "Writing for the Maverick Reader: Alan Furst," *Crime Time*, October 8, 2007. http://www.crimetime.co.uk/interviews/alanfurst.php (viewed October 8, 2007).

Howard, Grant, "Alan Furst Discusses His Novel *Dark Voyage*, a Story of Courage and Intrigue in 1941," Book Passage. http://www.bookpassage.com/content.php?id=180 (viewed October 8, 2007).

Leopold, Todd, "Spy Novelist Alan Furst: "I Love the Gray Areas,'" CNN.com. http://archives.cnn.com/2001/SHOWBIZ/books/12/04/alan.furst/ (viewed October 8, 2007).

Mabe, Chauncey, "Espionage Courting History." *South Florida Sun-Sentinel*, July 27, 2008.

MacDonald, Jay, "A Journalist Turns Spy in Alan Furst's Latest WWII Novel." *BookPage*, June 2006.

Myers, B. R., "A Man of Action." *Atlantic Monthly*, June 2006.

Walker, Martin, "Night and Fog: Alan Furst and the Literature of Espionage." *National Interest*, Winter 2004.

Lisa Gardner

Crime-Suspense; Romance; Thrillers: Serial Killers

Benchmark Title: *The Survivors Club*

Oregon

Birth date not disclosed

About the Author and the Author's Writing

When romantic suspense author Lisa Gardner began to work in earnest on her novel *The Killing Hour*, she had a pretty good idea of the characters—FBI agent-in-training Kimberly Quincy, daughter of former FBI profiler Pierce Quincy, and Michael "Mac" McCormack, a Georgia Bureau of Investigations special agent. She also knew the setting—the FBI Academy at Quantico, Virginia. But she didn't quite have a handle on the villain.

"I spent the spring researching crimes," she said in a Bookreporter interview with Stephen White. "I read books, watched TV, dug into history, and then ran across a creepy little story that clicked everything together in my mind, courtesy of the French." She crafted an eco-killer who works with two victims at a time, and she set her heroine after a fresh kidnap victim to save. Gardner was off.

"Mac and Kimberly make a good investigative team whose strengths, when combined, make them an unbeatable force out in the field," commented reviewer Harriet Klausner. "They also are able to lean on one another in times of stress and it is fascinating to watch their relationship evolve throughout the story and behind closed doors." This is a *romantic* suspense novel, after all.

Lisa Gardner grew up in Oregon in what she described on her Web site as a normal suburban home with two accountant parents. "I've always loved to read and I've always loved to write," she states. "At eighteen I got the bright idea to write a romance novel. I needed something to do during the day before I went to my summer job as a waitress." A favorite writer at the time was M. M. Kaye, author of *The Far Pavilions*, with its extraordinary blend of history and setting.

Things couldn't have worked out better if she'd written her own storyline. That summer manuscript, by the time she was in her junior year of college, sold to Silhouette Intimate Moments. The book appeared under the name Alicia Scott. The only disappointment was the payment: $3,000. It was enough for a new computer, and a determination on Gardner's part to find a real job. After she graduated from the University of Pennsylvania with a degree in international relations, she became a management consultant in something called process reengineering.

Gardner continued to write and even sold a book to CBS for a made-for-television movie in 1995, *At the Midnight Hour*. But she itched to try something else. An avid reader of true crime, she also devoured the prose of Stephen King, John Saul, and V. C. Andrews. She had already tested the crime field with her romance *The One Who Almost Got Away*, featuring FBI Agent Regina O'Doul and a thief called "The Highwayman." So she wrote an all-out suspense novel. *The Perfect Husband* was the result—the story of a woman who slowly realizes her marriage partner isn't all he seems.

The suspense book and successors, issued under her own name, found a broad audience for the New Hampshire resident. Real-life murders continue to inspire the author. *The Other Daughter*, she said on her Web site, is based on the Ted Bundy story. *The Third Victim*, she said, "is based on the string of school shootings we've had in the United States. That research was very sad for me, but I also needed to do it. Like most Americans, I wanted to understand what would drive kids to perform such heinous acts. Many of the answers surprised me."

To ensure the accuracy of her law enforcement details, she routinely consults friends in the field or interviews new sources such as ATF and FBI agents, even a professional sniper. For *The Survivors Club*, she pumped members of the Rhode Island State Police about their training and their ways of investigating crimes.

The author shapes most of her novels as she did *The Killing Hour*, first with a character in mind, then built a series of crimes around her. She discussed *Alone* on publisher Orion's Web site: "I then came up with two plausible endings—one that convicted her, one that exonerated her. Then I started writing to see which ending would prevail. It was neat to work on a project that at any time could go either way." Her publisher at Bantam was taken with Gardner's new book and decided to get behind the author as much as it had gotten behind another romance-turned-suspense author, Tami Hoag.

Gardner has also written several books about Pierce Quincy. "I enjoy writing books with continuing characters," she said in a 2003 Bookreporter interview, "for the same reason readers enjoy reading them—I genuinely miss the people and want to catch up on their lives."

Works by the Author

The Other Daughter (1999)

The Survivors Club (2002)

Two Great Novels: The Other Daughter, The Perfect Husband (2003)

Three Great Novels—The Thrillers: The Perfect Husband, The Other Daughter, The Third Victim (2003), omnibus

Three Great Novels 2: The Next Accident, The Survivor's Club, The Killing Hour (2004), omnibus

I'd Kill for That, with Rita Mae Brown, Jennifer Crusie, Linda Fairstein, Heather Graham, Kay Hooper, Katherine Neville, Anne Perry, Kathy Reichs, Julie Smith, and Tina Wainscott (2004)

Hide (2007)

Say Goodbye (2008)

The Neighbor (2009)

Pierce Quincy and Rainie Conner Series

The Perfect Husband (1997)
The Third Victim (2001)
The Next Accident (2001)
The Killing Hour (2003)
Gone (2006)

Written as Alicia Scott

Waking Nightmare (1994)
The One Who Almost Got Away (1997)
At the Midnight Hour (1997)
Hiding Jessica (1997)
The One Worth Waiting For (1997)
The Quiet One (1997), sequel to *The One Worth Waiting For*
Shadow's Flame (1999)
Walking After Midnight (1999)
Marrying Mike ... Again (2000)

Maximillian's Children

Brandon's Bride (1998)
MacNamara's Woman (1998)
Maggie's Man (1998)

36 Hours Series

Partners in Crime (1998)

Adaptations in Other Media

At the Midnight Hour (1995), television film
The Survivors Club (2004), television film
Instinct to Kill (2005), based on *The Perfect Husband*, television film

For Further Information

"Art of Suspense," Boookreporter. http://www.bookreporter.com/suspense_
thriller/gardner_white_interview.asp (viewed January 13, 2008).
"Cultivating Gardner." *Publishers Weekly*, August 11, 1997.
Klausner, Harriet, *Killing Hour* review, *The Best Reviews*. http://
thebestreviews.com/review13168 (viewed January 21, 2008).
Lisa Gardner interview, Bookreporter. http://www.bookreporter.com/authors/
au-gardner-lisa.asp#view030718 (viewed January 13, 2008)

Lisa Gardner interview, Orion Publishing Group. http://www.orionbooks. co/uk/AandA.aspx?id=4976&catID=1 (viewed January 13, 2008).

Lisa Gardner Web site. http://www.lisagardner.com/ (viewed November 12, 2008).

One Who Almost Got Away review. *Library Journal*, May 15, 1996.

Tess Gerritsen

Romantic Suspense; Thrillers: Medical, Techno, Serial Killers

Benchmark Series: Jane Rizzoli

San Diego, California

1953–

Photo credit: Jacob W. Gerritsen

About the Author and the Author's Writing

Her delicate features belie her volatile temperament. Her readers accuse her of writing grisly, gripping novels. "But you never see the violence," the author countered in a *Boston Globe* interview. "You see people doing their jobs: The cop, the medical examiner, looking at the spattered blood and saying, 'this is what happened in this room.'"

Tess Gerritsen trained as a physician and practiced for several years in Hawaii, until her writing career took off. She is comfortable with graphic descriptions of body parts and mayhem.

The author was born in San Diego, California, in 1953, the daughter of a Chinese immigrant mother and a second-generation Chinese American father. As teens, she and her brother went to a lot of fright movies, an experience that helped her appreciate that terror could, in fact, be entertaining. She received her bachelor's degree from Stanford University in 1975 and her medical degree from the University of California at San Francisco in 1979. After she completed her internal medicine residency, she and her husband Jacob Gerritsen (since 1977) settled in Hawaii. Gerritsen and her husband eventually relocated to coastal Maine, where he is in private practice and she writes full time. She is also an amateur violinist and avid gardener.

As a child, Gerritsen was an avid reader of Nancy Drew mysteries, J. R. R. Tolkien fantasy, and Ray Bradbury science fiction. She wrote a short story that won a state fiction contest and was published in *Honolulu Magazine*. She began to write romantic suspense novels in 1987. It was a genre she had become comfortable with while she attended med school.

"My most vivid memories of medical training were of exhaustion. I was so busy cramming in facts that by the end of each day, I'd feel my head was bursting. For comfort, I turned to books," she said in an interview with Ali Karm for SHOTS Crime & Mystery Magazine.

After nine Harlequin and Harper romance books, she wrote her first medical thriller, *Harvest* (1996). It was her first book to make the *New York Times* best-seller list. The inspiration for the book, she said, came from a conversation with a policeman-turned-security agent for American businesspeople traveling abroad. He told her the eerie story of street orphans in Russia being kidnapped by the Russian mafia and sold as organ donors.

An unexpected conversation with a third-grade teacher who wanted to read about sex and killers inspired her to write *The Surgeon* (2001), in which the serial murderer is knowledgeable in human anatomy and knows how to inflict the most pain in his victims.

With *The Surgeon*, she also began a series featuring Boston police detective Jane Rizzoli and medical examiner Maura Isles.

Gerritsen is not the only author to specialize in medical thrillers. But her background, she suggests, gives her an edge both in the ability to convey details and in characterization. "Medical training was a window into the most personal aspects of peoples' lives," she said in a Writers Write interview. "I've seen the most heartbreaking tragedies, and watched families at their very best—and worst. I think it's the insight into human nature that makes medicine such intense preparation for any writing."

The author does her own research. "I learned how important this is, back when I wrote my thriller *Gravity*, which was set aboard the International Space Station," she told Bookreporter. A NASA engineer she had hoped to engage as a researcher persuaded her to do her own digging, "that the only way to really understand a subject is to make the discoveries yourself. And while doing the research, I discover facts that often become new and unexpected plot twists."

Gerritsen lets her characters tell their own stories. "I've learned to just relax and let the characters take form all by themselves. I don't do character outlines. Often, I know only the barest details about their lives. Getting to know a character is like getting to know real people," she said in an interview for Writing Forums. She aspires to have conflict in every chapter. If characters don't get along with each other, all the better.

Without a detailed outline, she creates unforgettable stories. "I sit down and let the story take me where it will," she explained on her Web site. "I enjoy being surprised by how a story evolves, and I think it preserves the surprise for my readers as well."

Works by the Author

Adventure's Mistress (1985)

Love's Masquerade (1986)

Under the Knife (1990)

Call after Midnight (1991)

Never Say Die (1992)

Whistleblower (1992)

Three Complete Novels: Presumed Guilty, Whistleblower, and Never Say Die (1992)

Presumed Guilty (1993)

In Their Footsteps (1994)

Peggy Sue Got Murdered (1994)

Thief of Hearts (1995)

Keeper of the Bride (1996)

Harvest (1996)

Life Support (1997)

Bloodstream (1998)

Gravity (1999)

Perfect Timing (2001)

Harvest/Life Support (2005), omnibus

Under the Knife/Whistleblower (2005), omnibus

Call after Midnight/Under the Knife (2006), omnibus

Murder and Mayhem (2006), omnibus, includes *In Their Footsteps, Under the Knife*, and *Call after Midnight*

Never Say Die/Whistleblower (2007), omnibus

The Bone Garden (2007)

Jane Rizzoli and Maura Isles Series

The Surgeon (2001)

The Apprentice (2002)

The Sinner (2003)

Body Double (2004)

Vanish (2005)

The Mephisto Club (2006)

The Keepsake (2008), in United Kingdom as *Keeping the Dead*

Anthologies

Heatwave, with Barbara Delinsky and Linda Lael Miller (1998), includes *Under the Knife*

Something to Hide, with Lynn Erickson (1999), includes *Thief of Hearts*

Take 5, volume 4, with Mary Lynn Baxter and Annette Broadrick (2001)

Stolen Memories, with Jayne Ann Krentz and Stella Cameron (2002), includes *Thief of Hearts*

Unveiled, with Stella Cameron and Amanda Stevens (2002), includes *Whistleblower*

Double Impact, with Debra Webb (2003), includes *Never Say Die*

Family Passions, with Barbara Delinsky and Jayne Ann Krentz (2004), includes *Presumed Guilty*

Screenplay

Adrift (CBS 1993), television film

For Further Information

Anable, Steve, "PW Talks with Tess Gerritsen: I'm No Angel." *Publishers Weekly*, August 7, 2006.

Bone Garden review. *Publishers Weekly*, August 13, 2007.

Dunn, Adam, "Thriller Writer Utilizes Hands-on Experience." *Publishers Weekly*, July 14, 2003.

Ephron, Hallie, "Chilled to the Bone." *The Writer*, September 2008.

Karm, Ali, Tess Gerritsen interview, SHOTS: The Crime & Mystery Magazine. http://shotsmag.co.uk/SHOTS%2017/Tess%Gerritsen/gerritsen.htm (viewed October 1, 2007).

Mehegan, David, "Death Becomes Her: Author's Grisly Novels Thrill Women." *Boston Globe*, September 2, 2006.

Tess Gerritsen interview, Bookreporter.com, September 15, 2006. http://www.bookreporter.com/authors/au-gerritsen-tess.asp (viewed October 1, 2007).

Tess Gerritsen interview, Writing Forums. http://www.writingforums.org/showthread.php?p=5148 (viewed October 1, 2007).

Tess Gerritsen Web site. http://www.tessgerritsen.com/ (viewed November 13, 2008).

White, Claire E., "A Conversation with Tess Gerritsen," Writers Write, October-November 2001. http://www.writerswrite.com/journal/nov01/gerritsen/jt (viewed October 1, 2007).

W. E. B. Griffin
(William E. Butterworth III)

Adventure: Military, Global; Crime

Benchmark Series: Brotherhood of War

Newark, New Jersey

1929–

About the Author and the Author's Writing

William Edmund Butterworth III's aliases appear on his books more often than his real name, in virtually every genre, from military, sports, history, mystery, aviation, and auto racing to romance and suspense. He is best known to today's reading public as W. E. B. Griffin, author of the Brotherhood of War and Badge of Honor thrillers. His newest series features Charley Castillo, special agent to the president of the United States in the post–September 11 era. In *The Hunters* (2007), Castillo runs into professional jealousy from the director of National Intelligence, as his investigation team goes to Uruguay in quest of the killer of an American diplomat.

Born in 1929 in Newark, New Jersey, the author grew up in New York City and Wallingford, a suburb of Philadelphia. He has been married twice and has three children.

In 1946, he enlisted in the U.S. Army, trained in counterintelligence, and was assigned to the Army of Occupation in Germany. He later became a member of the staff of Major General I. D. White, who held command of the U.S. Constabulary. After discharge, he attended Phillips University in Germany but was recalled to active duty, again under White, serving at Fort Knox and in Korea. He was a combat correspondent and information officer and received the Expert Combat Infantryman's Badge. Upon his discharge in 1953, he became chief of the U.S. Army Signal Aviation Test and Support Activity's Publications Division at Fort Rucker, Alabama.

In the 1960s the author wrote car racing and athletics stories for young adults. He also wrote nonfiction books about astronomy and automobiles. He coauthored humorous Korean War books in the M*A*S*H series with creator Richard Hooker.

Butterworth took on his W. E. B. Griffin penname in 1982 for an adult series, the Brotherhood of War. Spanning the years from World War II to Vietnam, the books have been praised for their historical and technical accuracy. As that series was underway, he began others: The Corps, depicting the valor of members of the U.S. Marine Corps from World War II to Korea; Honor Bound, about Office for Strategic Services operatives working against pro-Nazi Perón in Argentina during World War II; and Badge of Honor, about members of the Philadelphia Police Department. Men at War

146

novels, about members of Colonel William "Wild Bill" Donovan's Office of Strategic Services during the Second World War, were originally published under the byline Alex Baldwin and were later revised and reissued under the Griffin byline. The newest entries are by Griffin with his son, William E. Butterworth IV.6

Griffin says it often takes nine months to research and write a new book. <u>Badge of Honor</u> books, he said on his Web page, are based on real cases investigated by Philadelphia police. His fictional characters often interact with historical figures. *Double Agents* (2007), in the <u>Men at War</u> series, for example, finds author Ian Fleming and actors David Niven and Peter Ustinov (all of whom were in the British service during World War II) assisting the OSS.

"You have to really think about how an actual person would behave in a given circumstance," Griffin said in an interview with Barnes & Noble. "I've been very lucky all along in either (rarely) knowing the character myself, or being with people who knew them intimately, and have been willing to tell me about them, and their behavior, in private."

Griffin, who has homes in Alabama and in Buenos Aires, has won numerous awards including the Brigadier General Robert L. Dening Memorial Distinguished Service Award of the U.S. Marine Corps Combat Correspondents Association. He has also received an honorary doctor of philosophy in military fiction degree from Norwich University. He holds honorary memberships in the Special Forces Association, the Marine Corps Combat Correspondents Association and the U.S. Army Otter and Caribou Association.

"Nothing honors me more than a serviceman, veteran, or cop telling me he enjoys reading my books," the author said on his Web page.

 # Works by the Author

Written as W. E. B. Griffin

<u>Badge of Honor Series</u>

Men in Blue (1988)

Special Operations (1989), originally written as by John Kevin Dugan

The Victim (1990)

The Witness (1991)

The Assassin (1992)

The Murderers (1995)

The Investigators (1998)

Final Justice (2003)

<u>Brotherhood of War Series</u>

The Lieutenants (1982)

The Captains (1982)

The Majors (1983)

The Colonels (1983)

The Berets (1985)

The Generals (1986)

The New Breed (1987)
The Aviators (1988)
Special Ops (2001)
The Corps Series
Semper Fi (1986)
Call to Arms (1987)
Counterattack (1990)
Battleground (1991)
Line of Fire (1992)
Behind the Lines (1995)
Close Combat (1995)
In Danger's Path (1999)
Under Fire (2002)
Retreat, Hell! (2004)
Honor Bound Series
Honor Bound (1993)
Blood and Honor (1997)
Secret Honor (2000)
Death and Honor, with William E. Butterworth IV (2008)
Men at War Series
The Last Heroes (1985), originally issued as by Alex Baldwin
The Secret Warriors (1985), originally issued as by Alex Baldwin
The Soldier Spies (1986), originally issued as by Alex Baldwin
The Fighting Agents (1987), originally issued as by Alex Baldwin
Saboteurs, with William E. Butterworth IV (2006)
Double Agents, with William E. Butterworth IV (2007)
Traffickers, with William E. Butterworth IV (2009)
Presidential Agent Series
By Order of the President (2004)
The Hostage (2005)
The Hunters (2006)
The Shooters (2008)
Black Ops (2008)

Written as Allison Mitchell

Wild Harvest (1984)
Wild Heritage (1985)

Written as Eden Hughes

The Wiltons (1981)
The Selkirks (1983)

Written as Edmund O. Scholefield

Tiger Rookie (1966)
L'il Wildcat (1967)
Bryan's Dog (1967)
Maverick on the Mound (1968)
Yankee Boy (1971)

Written as Jack Dugan

The Deep Kill (1984)

Written as James McM. Douglas

Hunger for Racing (1967)
Racing to Glory (1969)
The Twelve-Cylinder Screamer (1970)
Drag Race Driver (1971)
A Long Ride on a Cycle (1972)

Written as Patrick J. Williams

Fastest Funny Car (1967)
Grand Prix Racing (1968)
Up to the Quarterdeck (1969)
The Green Ghost (1969)
Racing Mechanic (1969)

Written as Walker E. Blake

The Level and the Lost (1962)
Heartbreak Ridge (1962)
Once More with Passion (1964)
Doing What Comes Naturally (1965)

Written as W. E. Butterworth

M*A*S*H Series with Richard Hooker
*M*A*S*H Goes to Maine* (1972)
*M*A*S*H Goes to Paris* (1974)
*M*A*S*H Goes to New Orleans* (1975)
*M*A*S*H Goes to Morocco* (1975)
*M*A*S*H Goes to London* (1976)
*M*A*S*H Goes to Las Vegas* (1976)
*M*A*S*H Goes to Hollywood* (1976)
*M*A*S*H Goes to Vienna* (1976)
*M*A*S*H Goes to Miami* (1976)

M*A*S*H Goes to San Francisco (1976)
M*A*S*H Goes to Texas (1977)
M*A*S*H Goes to Montreal (1977)
M*A*S*H Goes to Moscow (1978)

Juvenile Fiction written as W. E. Butterworth

Comfort Me with Love (1961)
Hot Seat (1961)
Where We Go from Here (1962)
The Court-Martial (1962)
The Love-Go-Round (1962)
Hell on Wheels (1962)
The Girl in the Black Bikini (1962)
Le Falot (1963)
Fast Green Car (1963)
Stock Car Racer (1966)
Helicopter Pilot (1967)
Road Racer (1967)
Air Evac (1967)
Orders to Vietnam (1968)
Redline 7100 (1968)
Stop and Search (1969)
Wheel of a Fast Car (1969)
Grand Prix Driver (1969)
Steve Bellamy (1970)
Marty and the Micro Midgets (1970)
Fast and Smart (1970)
Susan and Her Classic Convertible (1970)
Moving West on 122 (1970)
Crazy to Race (1971)
My Father's Quite a Guy (1971)
Return to Racing (1971)
Team Racer (1971)
The Race Driver (1971)
The Narc (1972)
Dateline: Talladega (1972)
Sky-jacked! (1972)
Race Car Team (1973)
Yankee Driver (1973)
Flying Army (1973)
Dave White and the Electric Wonder Car (1974)
Stop Thief! (1974)
Return to Daytona (1974)
The Roper Brothers and Their Magnificent Steam Automobile (1976)

Christina's Passion (1977)
Net Stop Earth (1978)
Tank Driver (1978)
The Air Freight Mystery (1978)
Under the Influence (1979)
LeRoy and the Old Man (1980)

Nonfiction

The Wonders of Rockets and Missiles (1964)
The Wonders of Astronomy (1964)
Soldiers on Horseback: The Story of the United States Cavalry (1966)
The Image Makers (1967)
Flying Army: The Modern Air Arm of the U.S. Army (1971)
Wheels and Pistons: The Story of the Automobile (1971)
The High Wind: The Story of NASCAR Racing (1972)
Tires and Other Things: Some Heroes of Automotive Evolution (1974)
Black Gold: The Story of Oil (1975)
Mighty Minicycles (1976)
Careers in the Service (1976)
An Album of Automobile Racing (1977)
Hi-Fi: From Edison's Phonograph to Quadraphonic Sound (1977)

Nonfiction Written as Webb Beech

No French Leave (1960)
Article 92: Murder-Rape (1965)
Warrior's Way (1965)
Make War in Madness (1966)

For Further Information

Hall, Elizabeth, "Tell It of the Marines." *Pages*, March/April 2004.

Hunters review, Bookreporter. http://www.bookreporter.com/reviews2/0399153799.asp (viewed November 2, 2007).

Jones, Daniel, and John D. Jorgenson, eds., W. E. Butterworth entry, *Contemporary Authors New Revision Series*, volume 64. Detroit, MI: Gale Research, 1998.

Official W. E. B. Griffin Web site. http://www.nmark.com/webgriffin.author.html (viewed June 30, 2003).

W. E. B. Griffin biography, Barnes & Noble. http://www.barnesandnoble.com/writers/writerdetails/.asp?userid-0H4KV3ZHTM&cid=883328#bio (viewed June 30, 2003).

W. E. B. Griffin Web site. http://www.webgriffin.com (viewed November 13, 2008).

James Grippando

Crime: Suspense; Thrillers: Legal, Political

Benchmark Series: Jack Swyteck

Waukegan, Illinois

1958–

Photo credit: Annie Huebsch

About the Author and the Author's Writing

Trial lawyers are skilled at shaping stories. They try to impress upon a jury a certain perspective on events, while a district attorney promotes another version of the facts. Juries seldom have all the details at hand; they have to make decisions based on what they're told.

It's a lot like fiction writing. The author carefully lays out a persuasive scenario, not telling the reader too much at first, drawing out the suspense. For example, James Grippando's first novel, *The Pardon* (1994), gets into the thick of things right off. Jack Swyteck's client has a date with the Florida electric chair. Swyteck's father, Governor Harry Swyteck, refuses to issue a pardon. Unknown to either, the execution triggers a psychopath, bent on revenge on both father and son. "Between the chilling opening scene of the hours before an inmate's execution and the climactic meeting between Jack and his nemesis, author Grippando, a Miami attorney, ratchets the tension up every few pages," said reviewer Thomas Gaughan in *Booklist*.

Grippando was born in 1958 in Waukegan, Illinois. His father was a printer, his mother a college instructor and author of a textbook on nursing. He attended the University of Illinois for a year then moved with his family to Florida, where he earned a bachelor's degree with honors from the University of Florida in 1980. In 1982, he completed requirements for his juris doctorate from the same institution, again with honors. After serving as executive editor of the *University of Florida Law Review,* Grippando was inducted into the Order of the Coif. He clerked for the Honorable Thomas Clark of the U.S. Court of Appeals in Atlanta. He was a trial lawyer in Miami from 1984 to 1996 and once spent seven years as lead counsel in a case involving chicken farmers in the state. Now a full-time writer, Grippando is a cyclist, inline skater, golfer, and sailor by avocation. He and his wife, Tiffany, live in Florida.

The author has said he is in awe of the Pulitzer Prize–winning play *A Man for All Seasons*, whose subject, the brilliant lawyer Sir Thomas More, believed in the sanctity of the oath. (More was beheaded for refusing to swear approval of the marriage of King Henry VIII to Ann Boleyn.) Grippando said he was appalled at how often witnesses lie on the stand. It reinforced his philosophy as a writer: be true to your readers.

As a trial lawyer, Grippando says on his Web site, he sees all facets of humanity, including courageous victims facing and testifying against their aggressors. "Just as courageous, you see people with no personal stake in the case come forward ... simply to make sure that justice is done," he said. "On the other hand, you deal with the snakes who can't give an honest answer to a simple question."

Pleased enough with his first hero, the author has brought the wise-cracking law dog back (along with his over-the-edge ex-con bar owner associate Theo Knight and romantic interest and/or foe FBI agent Andie Henning), for six more novels involving kidnappers, serial killers, and murder.

South Florida is as much a character in the books as the humans are. "I can't underestimate the impact Miami—the city in which I live—has had on my writing. Miami evokes all the right buzz words—smart and sexy, young and beautiful—but it also has a self-destructive quality that triggers the kind of fascination we have with a reckless youth," Grippando said in a Barnes & Noble interview.

A 2001 novel finds another Miami lawyer, Nick Rey, trying to ransom his businessman father, who has been kidnapped in Colombia. Grippando interviewed victims and families as background for his novel. "No single victim or family experienced all of the horrible things that Nick and his father experience in *A King's Ransom*, but that is not to say that the dangers are overstated in my novel. Some victims suffered far worse," the author said in a Bookreporter conversation.

Grippando's first young adult novel, *Leapholes*, was also a first publishing effort for the American Bar Association. The group brought the book out in 2006, marking a possible new direction for the writer.

Works by the Author

The Informant (1996)
The Abduction (1998)
Found Money (1999)
Under Cover of Darkness (2000)
A King's Ransom (2001)
The Pardon/Beyond Suspicion (2006), omnibus
Lying with Strangers (2007)

Jack Swyteck Series

The Pardon (1994)
Beyond Suspicion (2002)
Last to Die (2003)
Hear No Evil (2004)
Got the Look (2006)
When Darkness Falls (2007)

Last Call (2008)
Born to Run (2008)

Anthologies

Thriller: Stories to Keep You Up All Night, edited by James Patterson (2006)

For Young Adults

Leapholes (2006)

For Further Information

Gaughan, Thomas, *The Pardon* review. *Booklist*, September 1, 1994.

James Grippando interview, Barnes & Noble. http://search.barnesandnoble.com/booksearch/isbninquiry.asp?ean=9780060831165#TABS (viewed January 14, 2008).

James Grippando interview, Bookreporter. http://www.bookreporter.com/authors/au-grippando-james.asp (viewed January 13, 2008).

James Grippando Web site. http://www.jamesgrippando.com (viewed November 13, 2008).

John Grisham

Crime; Thrillers: Legal, Political

Benchmark Title: *The Firm*

Jonesboro, Arkansas

1955–

About the Author and the Author's Writing

John Grisham's courtroom novel *The Firm* spent forty-six weeks on the best-seller list, according to *Publishers Weekly*; *The Runaway Jury* and other successors averaged twenty-five weeks at the top. His popularity put Grisham into a comfort zone to write what he wanted to write—novels with a sports twist and nonfiction.

Success, however, has not changed the author's writing habits—still the same August to November each year, the same table and chair and computer—still the same drive for excellence. Much of November is devoted to rigorous editing. "The editor, who is also my agent, looks at the second draft and makes extensive notes. Then I do the third draft, and the fourth and the fifth. The mistake that many big authors make is to get lazy and shy away from careful editing. You can usually tell it in their work," he said in a 2006 SlushPile.net interview.

John Grisham was born in 1955 in Jonesboro, Arkansas, the son of a construction worker and his homemaker wife. Early on, he hoped to become a professional baseball player. Growing up he read the usual books and authors popular with young people of the day: Dr. Seuss, the Hardy Boys, Chip Hilton, Mark Twain, and Charles Dickens. He says John Steinbeck's *Tortilla Flat* made an impression on him.

Grisham received a bachelor of science degree in accounting from Mississippi State University and a juris doctorate from the University of Mississippi. He married Renee Jones, and they have two children. They have a farm in Mississippi and a plantation in Virginia.

Admitted to the bar in Mississippi in 1981, Grisham began private practice in Southaven, Mississippi, and for a decade, put in sixty to seventy hours a week in criminal defense and personal injury litigation cases. From 1984 to 1990, he served in the Mississippi House of Representatives. Inspired by an account he heard from a twelve-year-old rape victim, he wrote *A Time to Kill* (1989), which quickly went out of print.

Then he started a new novel, according to the author's Web site, "the story of a hotshot young attorney lured to an apparently perfect law firm that was not what it appeared. When he sold the film rights to *The Firm* to Paramount Pictures for $600,000, Grisham suddenly became a hot property among publishers, and book rights were bought by Doubleday."

Not all critics were impressed. "Sustaining momentum, not building character, is Grisham's specialty," *Entertainment Weekly*'s Gregory Kirschling said in a review of the author's later *The King of Torts*.

In the meantime, Grisham quit his law practice to concentrate on writing, returning to the courtroom only once, in 1996 to fulfill an old promise to represent the family of a brakeman who was killed when pinned between two rail cars.

Grisham likes to support the underdog, and he is fascinated with fugitives, he told interviewer Ellen Kanner. "It's not as difficult as it may seem, to disappear. I always wonder why people would voluntarily show up in court and go to jail for ten years. Some people have absolutely nothing to lose if they disappear."

Wife Renee Grisham is an important part of the family writing machine, before a manuscript goes to the editor/agent. "I constantly inundate Renee with all sorts of story ideas, and it's her job to tell me to shut up and keep searching," the author told Jesse Kornbluth of Book Report. "She has an uncanny ability to spot a good story; I tend to think that almost anything will work. Once I start writing, she is merciless as the chapters pour forth."

At his wife's instigation, Grisham lightened up considerably for *The Brethren*, he said in an interview with *Entertainment Weekly*'s Benjamin Svetkey. " I tried to write the funniest thing I could think of without going into all-out comedy. But, you know, all the books I've ever written have had a lot of jokes in them, a lot of one-liners. I just always end up cutting them out."

Further outside chambers is *A Painted House* from 2001, a family story related by seven-year-old Luke Chandler of growing up on a cotton farm in rural Arkansas Delta country in 1952. It was a very personal book. "The stories have been around forever, ever since I was a little kid," the author told Jennifer Harden of *USA Today*. "A lot of the stories were just old family tales, handed down from a father and grandfather, both with a great sense of exaggeration. So I don't know what's true and what's not."

Grisham has satisfied his fascination with sports heroes with two books: *Bleachers* (2003) is the story of a former high school quarterback who goes to see his old dying coach, and *Playing for Pizza* (2007) is about a Cleveland Browns third-string quarterback who so blows an opportunity to score, he is relegated to playing for a team called the Panthers, in Parma, Italy. Grisham was back in court for 2008's *The Appeal*, which goes to show, even if you win a big settlement, it isn't over until the appeal's been dragged out for years and years.

In his nonfiction book *The Innocent Man: Murder and Injustice in a Small Town* (2006), Grisham took a straightforward journalistic approach. It relates the wrongful conviction of baseball player Ron Williamson of Oklahoma, sent to Death Row for a rape and murder. The case opened Grisham's eyes, the author said. "Exonerations seem to be happening weekly. And with each one of them, the question is asked—how can an innocent man be convicted and kept in prison for 20 years? My book is the story of only one man, but it is a good example of how things can go terribly wrong with our judicial system," Grisham said in a 20 Second Interview on Amazon.com.

Grisham has made further impact outside his writing through, for example, his support of endowed scholarships and writer residencies at the University of Mississippi. The university maintains a John Grisham Room of archival materials from his political and writing careers.

Works by the Author

A Time to Kill (1989)
The Firm (1991)
The Pelican Brief (1992)
The Client (1993)
The Chamber (1994)
The Rainmaker (1995)
The Runaway Jury (1996)
The Partner (1997)
The Street Lawyer (1998)
The Testament (1999)
The Brethren (2000)
A Painted House (2001)
Skipping Christmas (2001)
The Summons (2002)
The King of Torts (2003)
Bleachers (2003)
The Last Juror (2004)
The Broker (2005)
Playing for Pizza (2007)
The Appeal (2008)
The Associate (2009)

Collection

John Grisham (1993)

Anthology

Legal Briefs, edited by William Bernhardt (1998)

Nonfiction

The Innocent Man: Murder and Injustice in a Small Town (2006)

Screenplays

The Gingerbread Man, original screenplay written as Al Hayes (2002)
Mickey (2005)

Adaptations in Other Media

The Firm (1993), motion picture
The Pelican Brief (1994), motion picture

The Client (1994), motion picture

The Chamber (1996), motion picture

A Time to Kill (1996), motion picture

The Rainmaker (1997), motion picture

A Painted House (2003), television film

The Runaway Jury (2003), motion picture

Christmas with the Kranks (2004), motion picture based on *Skipping Christmas*

For Further Information

"Author Profile: John Grisham," Collect Books. http://collectbooks.about.com/library/weekly/aa011903a.htm (viewed July 4, 2003).

Donahue, Dick, "Tasty Top 'Torts.'" *Publishers Weekly*, February 17, 2003.

"18 Hits in 15 Years." *Publishers Weekly*, January 24, 2005.

"Few Words with John Grisham," Amazon.com. http://www.amazon.com/Innocent-Man-Murder-Injustice-Small/dp/0739340484 (viewed October 22, 2007).

Harden, Jennifer, "'Painted House' Freshens the Past." *USA Today* (April 17, 2003).

"Interview: John Grisham, Author," Slushpile. http://www.slushpile.net/index.php/2006/03/01/interview-john-grisham-author/ (viewed October 22, 2007).

John Grisham interview, Academy of Achievement (June 2, 1995). http://www.achievement.org/autodoc/page/gri0int-1 (viewed July 4, 2003).

John Grisham Web site. http://www.randomhouse.com/features/grisham/author.html (viewed July 4, 2003).

Johnson, Ted, "Home Again." *TV Guide* (April 26, 2003).

Kanner, Ellen, John Grisham interview, Bookpage. http://www.bookpage.com/BPinterviews/grisham392.html (viewed July 4, 2003).

Kennedy, Dean, "The Jury Is In." *Entertainment Weekly*, June 7, 1996.

Kirshling, Gregory, "Laws of Motion." *Entertainment Weekly* (February 14, 2003).

Kornbluth, Jesse, John Grisham interview, Bookreporter, May 1997. http://www.bookreporter.com/authors/att-grisham-john.asp (viewed July 4, 2003).

Reese, Jennifer, "Incomplete Pass: John Grisham Tackles a Gridiron Novel with *Bleachers* but Fumbles the Ball." *Entertainment Weekly*, September 12, 2003.

Syken, Bill, "Gridiron Grisham: The Best-Selling Author Winningly Draws on His Quarterback Days." *Sports Illustrated*, September 1, 2003.

Zaleski, Jeff, "The Grisham Business." *Publishers Weekly*, January 19, 1998.

Michael Gruber

Crime-Suspense; Thrillers: Legal, Paranormal

Benchmark Title: *The Book of Air and Shadows*

Brooklyn, New York

1940–

Photo credit: Nina Subin

About the Author and the Author's Writing

One way to make a big first impression as a thriller writer is to polish your craft ghostwriting fifteen best sellers for your better-known cousin. That's what Michael Gruber did, until he tired of the constraints and anonymity. Of course, not everyone has a cousin who has made a name for himself as a homicide detective, district attorney, Beverly Hills mayor, Congressional investigator, special council, and deputy chief counsel for the Congressional committee that investigated the Kennedy and King assassinations.

Robert K. Tanenbaum, who has a reputation for never having lost a felony case, responded in the mid-1980s to a request from the publisher Franklin Watts to write a novel. Tanenbaum wrote 100 pages then sought the guidance of his cousin, Gruber, who had recently been a speechwriter. Gruber suggested that he could rewrite the book and negotiated a contract to split the advance and royalties evenly. *No Lesser Plea* came out in 1987 and had fourteen sequels, all with a strong following. The books follow New York County Chief Assistant District Attorney Butch Karp and various family members including his dog-raising wife, Marlene Ciampi; his resourceful daughter, Lucy; and his young son, Giancarlo. In *Library Journal,* Jo Ann Vicarel praised a later entry, *Absolute Rage*, as "Expertly combining his prodigious knowledge of the legal system with the usual social concerns," believing it was written solely by Tanenbaum. Tanenbaum gave interviews and signed books, never letting on that he had employed a ghostwriter.

"Gruber's credit was limited to a thank you on the acknowledgements page," according to a Gruber profile on the HarperCollins Web site. "Eventually the relationship dissolved." Gruber struck out on his own, years of experience under his belt.

Michael Gruber was born in 1940 in Brooklyn, New York. He received bachelor of arts degrees from Columbia University and City College of New York. A new interest in marine biology prompted him to enroll at the University of Miami, where he earned a doctorate in 1973. From 1968 to 1969, he was a U.S. Army medic. He now lives in Seattle, Washington, with his wife. They have three children.

Although he holds a Ph.D. in marine biology, Gruber primarily worked in other fields after graduating. He worked as a cook. He was an analyst and later planning director for human resources in Dade County, Florida. Beginning in 1977, during the Jimmy Carter administration, he worked in the Office of Science and Technology Policy in Washington. He was a policy analyst and speechwriter for the Environmental Protection Agency's head, William Ruckelshaus.

"In 1986, I was promoted to the Senior Executive Service of the U.S., the highest level of the federal civil service," the author said on his Web site. "That same year, Robert K. Tanenbaum contacted me and asked me to write a courtroom thriller to be published under his name." Gruber contractually could not reveal the relationship, but he vented frustrations over the years in an Internet chatroom.

"At first it was a lark," Gruber said in a *Pacific Northwest* magazine interview. "I got into it and started developing the characters, and the characters started coming alive. The Tanenbaum books were domestic comedies wrapped up in a legal-thriller box. They were funny and witty and sad in a way that real novels are."

In 1988, Gruber moved to Washington to work as a speechwriter and environmental expert for the state land commission. The Karp novels were sufficiently successful, even with shared royalties, that two years later he became a full-time writer.

Gruber's first book under his own name, a juvenile title called *The Witch's Boy*, didn't immediately find a publisher. So he developed a trilogy of paranormal thrillers featuring a Cuban police detective in Miami, Jimmy Paz.

Was it a stretch for a white writer to have a black hero? Gruber in a Bookreporter interview said he wrote about Paz "by invention, imagination and sympathy, the same way male authors can invent real female characters and female writers can invent real male ones. It's absurd to think that we can only make characters out of personal experience." Ken Bolton, in reviewing *Valley of Bones* for *Library Journal*, noted the novel featuring Paz and psychologist Lorna Wise "mixes spiritualism with a pinch of intellectualism, taking the story to a depth rarely seen in the crime fiction genre. Vivid characterizations and sapient cultural analysis confirm that Gruber is an author to watch."

Gruber's *The Book of Air and Shadows* (2007) is a literary pursuit often compared to Dan Brown's *The Da Vinci Code*. In a BookBrowse interview, Gruber said he conceived the idea one day while in his lawyer's office. "The issue at hand, which I won't get into, was essentially about the value of an oral anecdote with respect to a work of fiction based on the same." The book's plot revolves around a missing Shakespeare document, the Bracegirdle Manuscript.

Gruber pulled off a complex plot like the pro he is. "What Michael Gruber has omitted in car chases and shootouts (and rest easy, these elements aren't completely erased), he's more than made up for with a rich cast of characters who are difficult to leave when the final pages are turned," approved Robin Vidimos in the *Denver Post*.

Gruber has shown great skill in pushing the boundaries of genre fiction while at the same time thoroughly entertaining his audience.

Works by the Author

The Book of Air and Shadows (2007)
The Forgery of Venus (2008)

Butch Karp and Marlene Ciampi Legal novels, ghostwritten for Robert K. Tanenbaum

No Lesser Plea (1987)
Depraved Indifference (1989)
Immoral Certainty (1991)
Reversible Error (1992)
Material Witness (1993)
Justice Denied (1994)
Corruption of Blood (1995)
Falsely Accused (1996)
Irresistible Impulse (1997)
Act of Revenge (1999)
Reckless Endangerment (1999)
True Justice (2000)
Enemy Within (2001)
Absolute Rage (2002)
Resolved (2003)

Jimmy Paz Trilogy

Tropic of Night (2003)
Valley of Bones (2005)
Night of the Jaguar (2006)

Juvenile

The Witch's Boy (2005)

For Further Information

Bolton, Ken, *Valley of Bones* review. *Library Journal*, January 1, 2005.

Gwinn, Mary Ann, "Michael Gruber: The Ghost Who Came Out of the Shadows." *Pacific Northwest/Seattle Times Magazine,* March 28, 2005.

Michael Gruber interview, BookBrowse. http://www.bookbrowse.com/author/interviews/full/index.cfm?author_number=876 (viewed January 28, 2008).

Michael Gruber interview, Bookreporter. http://www.bookreporter.com/authors/au-gruber-michael.asp (viewed January 28, 2008).

Michael Gruber Web page, HarperCollins. http://www.harpercollins.co/.uk/authors/default.aspx?id=6582 (viewed January 28, 2008).

Michael Gruber entry, Contemporary Authors Online. Reproduced in Biography Resource Center. Farmington Hills, Mich.: Thomson Gale, 2008. http://galenet.galegroup.com/serviet/BioRC (viewed January 28, 2008).

Michael Gruber Web site. http://www.michaelgruberbooks.com/ (viewed January 28, 2008).

Robert K. Tanenbaum entry, Contemporary Authors Online. Reproduced in Biography Resource Center. Farmington Hills, MI: Thomson Gale, 2008. http://galenet.galegroup.com/serviet/BioRC (viewed January 28, 2008).

Simon, Clea, "Witty Thriller Plays on Past and Present." *Boston Globe*, March 24, 2007.

Vicarel, Jo Ann, *Absolute Rage* review. *Library Journal*, August 2002.

Vidimos, Robin, "Car Chases, Shootouts and ... Old Books?" *Denver Post*, April 6, 2007.

Woo, Adam, "A Lost Shakespeare Play? Let the Intrigue Begin," *Seattle Times*, April 6, 2007.

Laurell K. Hamilton

Fantasy; Horror:
Psychological; Romance:
Paranormal; Vampires

Benchmark Series: Vampire Hunter

Heber Springs, Arkansas

1963–

Photo credit: Richard Nichols

About the Author and the Author's Writing

Tough as nails and with an attitude to boot, Anita Blake works at night for the city of St. Louis. A certified necromancer, she reanimates vampires, zombies, and shape-shifters long enough to question them and complete her paperwork. That's her routine side. More dangerous is her sideline as a licensed vampire hunter and federal marshal. She tracks and slays vampires who have taken human lives. And she looks into paranormal crimes on contract with the Regional Preternatural Investigation Team. Never heard of such professions? Or such menaces? They exist—in Laurell K. Hamilton's alternate world of her best-selling series of novels.

Hamilton often heard stories of the bizarre from her grandmother, Laura Gentry. As a young teen, she read Robert E. Howard's fantasy and horror collection *Pigeons from Hell*. It sparked her interest in writing.

The author was born Laurell Kline in a family she has described as Scotch-Irish hill people in Heber Springs, Arkansas, in 1963. Her mother died in a car accident when she was six; and her grandmother raised her in Sims, Indiana. She began to write stories when she was nearly thirteen, some in the Howard vein, some in the style of Louisa May Alcott, and some both. She devoured *The Writer* and began to submit her stories to periodicals. Deciding she needed a college degree if she was going to conquer the literary world, she attended Indiana Wesleyan University (formerly Marion University) and earned degrees in English and biology. While working as an art editor, she continued to polish the manuscript that became *Nightseer*, her first published novel. She sold her first story to fantasy author Marion Zimmer Bradley for an anthology.

Hamilton created Anita Blake's world from her interest in British monster films of the 1960s. "The old Hammer films left an indelible impression on me as a child. Once I had the idea for Anita's world I planned for longevity. Not just one book, but volumes. I don't think I've ever had a stand alone book idea in my life," she said in an All About Romance conversation.

Besides being suspenseful, the books that feature Blake, Jean Claude Variant, and other continuing characters are very sensuous. This accounts, to a degree, for their popularity with romance fans. "I want a kiss to be so believable it gives the reader shivers," the author said on her Web site. "Two things I do well are sex and violence, but I don't want gratuitous sex or violence. The sex and violence is only as graphic as need be."

She wrote books for the existing <u>Star Trek</u> and <u>Ravenloft</u> series. When she needed a break from Blake, Hamilton began the <u>Meredith Gentry</u> series, stronger on romance and politics, set in the old French court. The heroine is a fairy princess who has the ability to change her appearance, which comes in handy when she moonlights as a private detective. Having read a lot of hardboiled detective fiction, particularly Robert B. Parker's <u>Spenser</u> novels, Hamilton shaped Gentry accordingly. "I wanted a heroine who would be as tough as the men or tougher … and I wanted to strike a blow for equality. I may have gone a little far in that direction," she said in a Missouri Center of the Book conversation.

Her series characters have different personalities. "With Merry I wanted someone who argued with me less," the author said in an SF Site interview. "Anita is very middle America while Merry is not…. [Merry's] culture is totally different from Anita's. For Merry I read a lot of old folklore and oral tales that had been written to get her attitude and voice."

"I write, in part, to make sense of things," the author said in a Powells.com interview. "To make sense of my inability to organize domestic arrangements … to make sense of my fear of water and my nearly seductive attraction to it … to explore a world where shifting shape can lead to new discoveries."

Hamilton and her second husband, Jonathan Green, and her daughter live in St. Louis County, Missouri. Green, a comic book fan, urged Hamilton to adapt the <u>Blake</u> books for a graphic novel series from Marvel Comics. One thing she insisted on was that her heroine look like a real woman, and in her view, artist Brett Booth came through. Hamilton referred to Blake as her "sulky girl" in a *Publishers Weekly* interview. "She spends the whole first book just pissed off. If she meets a man, she will be angrier the more attracted she is to him. I've been writing this character for over a decade, yet I didn't realize this about her until I saw the comic art." The publication immediately sold out its first printings.

Hamilton is gratified at her character's endurance. Genre fads come and go. "A lot of writers think, This genre is hot, so I'll write this. But what they don't realize is in three to four years that can change," Hamilton told *Writer's Digest*. "In the late '80s, I had a short story about Anita Blake. Everyone loved it, but nobody would buy it."

The author says she has no plans to abandon category fiction. "I love genre," Hamilton said in a *Locus* magazine interview in 2000. "Now that I'm being very successful, publishers are trying to mainstream me, but I'm unabashedly genre. It's what I like to read, which I like to write."

Works by the Author

Nightseer (1992)
Strange Candy (2006), short stories

Anita Blake, Vampire Hunter Series

Guilty Pleasures (1993)
The Laughing Corpse (1994)
Circus of the Damned (1995)
The Lunatic Café (1996)
Bloody Bones (1996)
Club Vampyre (1997), includes first three novels
The Midnight Café (1997), includes second three novels
The Killing Dance (1997)
Burnt Offerings (1998)
Blue Moon (1998)
Black Moon Inn (1998), includes seventh and eighth novels
Obsidian Butterfly (2000)
Narcissus in Chains (2001)
Cerulean Sins (2003)
Incubus Dreams (2004)
Nightshade Tavern (2005), includes ninth and tenth novels
Micah (2006)
Danse Macabre (2006)
The Harlequin (2007)
Micah and Strange Candy (2007), omnibus
The First Death, with Jonathan Green (2007), adapted by Stacie M. Richie and
    Jess Ruffner-Booth, graphic novel based on *Guilty Pleasures*
Blood Noir (2008)
Skin Trade (2009)

Meredith Gentry Series

A Kiss of Shadows (2000)
A Caress of Twilight (2002)
Seduced by Moonlight (2004)
A Stroke of Midnight (2005)
Mistral's Kiss (2006)
A Lick of Frost (2007)
Swallowing Darkness (2008)
Divine Misdemeanors (2009)

Ravenloft Series

11. *Death of a Darklord* (1995)

Star Trek: The Next Generation Series

24. *Nightshade* (1992)

Anthologies

Spells of Wonder, edited by Marion Zimmer Bradley (1989), includes "Stealing Souls"

Memories and Visions, edited by Susanna J. Sturgis (1989), includes "A Token for Celandine"

Sword and Sorceress No. 7, edited by Marion Zimmer Bradley (1990), includes "Winterkill"

Sword and Sorceress No. 8, edited by Marion Zimmer Bradley (1990), includes "Geese"

Superheroes, edited by John Varley and Ricia Mainhardt (1995), includes "A Clean Sweep"

Out of This World, with Susan Krinard, J. D. Robb, and Maggie Shayne (2001), includes 100 pages of *Narcissus in Chains*

Cravings, with MaryJanice Davidson, Eileen Wilks, and Rebecca York (2004)

Bite, with MaryJanice Davidson, Charlaine Harris, Angela Knight, and Vickie Taylor (2004)

Adaptations in Other Media

Laurell K. Hamilton's Anita Blake: Vampire Hunter (announced for 2010), IFC television series

For Further Information

"Conversation with Laurell K. Hamilton," SF Site. http://www.sfsite.com/11a/lh187.htm (viewed January 21, 2008).

Hamilton, Laurell K., "Rejection: A Beginning," Powells. http://www.powells.com/essays/laurellkhamilton.html (viewed January 21, 2008).

"Laurell K. Hamilton: Death & Sex," Locus, September 2000. http://www.locusmag.com/2000/Issues/09/Hamilton.html (viewed January 21, 2008).

"Laurel K. Hamilton: Kiss-Ass Author," All About Romance, January 12, 2002. http://www.likesbooks.com/lhk.html (viewed January 21, 2008).

Laurell K. Hamilton Web page. http://www.randomhouse.com/features/lkhamilton/author.html (viewed January 21, 2008).

Laurell K. Hamilton Web site. www.laurellkhamilton.org/ (viewed January 21, 2008).

Maury, Laurel, "Anita Blake Stakes Out Comics." *Publishers Weekly*, July 10, 2007.

Schneider, Maria, "Genre Bender." *Writer's Digest*, April 2008.

Tiedemann, Mark W., Laurell K. Hamilton interview, Missouri Center for the Book, October 2003. http://books.missouri.org/eviews/october.html (viewed January 28, 2008).

Thomas Harris

Crime; Horror: Psychological; Thrillers: Serial Killers

Benchmark Title: *The Silence of the Lambs*

Jackson, Tennessee

1940–

About the Author and the Author's Writing

"A census taker tried to quantify me once," the prisoner told FBI agent Clarice Starling in *The Silence of the Lambs*. "I ate his liver with some fava beans and a big Amarone. Go back to school, little Starling."

Other writers may craft serial killers and cannibals truer to the real thing, but none is more vivid in readers' minds than the erudite, psychotic psychiatrist Hannibal Lecter in Thomas Harris's series of thrillers that began with *Red Dragon* in 1981. Although critics generally consider *Lambs* Harris's best Lecter work, the author has continued to probe the character's life, and each new book has become a major motion picture.

Born in Jackson, Tennessee, in 1940, Harris was the son of an electrical engineer. He grew up in Rich, Mississippi, reportedly in an isolated childhood, and was a voracious reader. After graduating from Baylor University in Texas with a bachelor of arts degree in English in 1964, he covered the night police beat for the *Waco Tribune-Herald* until 1968, when he went to work for Associated Press in New York City. He married but later divorced, and has a daughter.

Harris found a plot thread in the killing of Israeli athletes at the 1972 Munich Olympics. His first novel, *Black Sunday* (1975), is about terrorists who commandeer a blimp, rig it with a shrapnel bomb, and maneuver it to explode over the Super Bowl in Miami—with the president of the United States in the audience.

Hannibal Lecter had only a small part in Harris's next book, *Red Dragon* (1981), which is about FBI Agent Will Graham's quest for a murderer. But "Hannibal the Cannibal," as he was nicknamed, was too good a character to ignore, and he came center stage in Harris's third book. In *The Silence of the Lambs*, the FBI's Starling recruits Lecter to help profile another serial killer. Lecter's on-and-off charm as he plays cat-and-mouse with the agent made the book a best seller (duplicated when filmed with Anthony Hopkins and Jodie Foster in 1991). "Mr. Harris doesn't fool around or settle for trite effects," said *New York Times* reviewer Christopher Lehmann-Haupt. "He goes straight for the viscera." The book won Anthony, World Fantasy, and Bram Stoker awards, and the movie brought home five Academy Awards. Lecter and Starling were featured again in *Hannibal*, but *Hannibal Rising* swung back to the villain's youth and the death of family members during World War II to explain the origins of the cultured doctor's extreme cruelty.

Harris is a slow writer, both because of the level of his exhaustive research (he went to the FBI headquarters in Quantico, Virginia, to gather information for *Lambs*) and his care in crafting the story. "His books never really need any editing," Harris's agent Mort Janklow told Guardian Unlimited. "What he delivers has the quality of a precisely cut gem."

In 1999, *Newsweek* unearthed a few details about Harris from friends: "He's a guy who loves to cook and to eat. A big man with graying hair, Harris ... is soft-spoken, twinkly-eyed and unfailingly polite. Not a true recluse, he entertains friends with both his dinners and his Southern-style storytelling."

Harris and his partner, Pace Barnes, live in South Florida and Sag Harbor, Long Island. Although he owns a Jaguar and a Porsche, he lives a relatively modest lifestyle. He often visits Paris and other cities in Europe. He gives no interviews and makes no publicity tours, although he did once say of Hannibal Lecter, "He's immensely amusing company. I work in this little office and I'm always glad when he shows up."

Works by the Author

Black Sunday (1974)

Hannibal Lecter Series

Red Dragon (1981)
The Silence of the Lambs (1988)
The Silence of the Lambs/Red Dragon (1991), omnibus
Hannibal (1999)
Hannibal Lecter Omnibus (2002)
Hannibal Rising (2006)
Red Dragon/Silence of the Lambs (2007), omnibus

Adaptations in Other Media

Black Sunday (1977), motion picture
Manhunter (1986), motion picture, retitled *Red Dragon: The Curse of Hannibal Lecter* and *Red Dragon: The Pursuit of Hannibal Lecter*
The Silence of the Lambs (1991), motion picture
Hannibal (2001), motion picture
Red Dragon (2002), motion picture
Hannibal Rising (2007), motion picture

For Further Information

Cathleen McGuigan, Devin Gordon, and Ray Sawhill, "Second Helping." *Newsweek*, June 7, 1999.

Cowley, Jason, "Creator of a Monstrous Hit," Guardian Unlimited. http://www.guardian.co.uk/books/2006/nov/19/fiction.thomasharris (viewed April 4, 2009).

Lehmann-Haupt, Christopher, *The Silence of the Lambs* review. *New York Times*, August 15, 1988.

Ray, Alice, "Fine Young Hannibal," BookPage. http://www.bookpage.com/0702bp/thomas_harris.html (viewed November 12, 2008).

Thomas Harris Web site, http://www.randomhouse.com/features/thomasharris (viewed November 12, 2007).

Jack Higgins (Harry Patterson)

Adventure; Crime; Espionage; Military: Historical

Benchmark Title: *The Eagle Has Landed*

Newcastle Upon Tyne, England

1929–

About the Author and the Author's Writing

The laudatory blurbs span the generations. "Unsurpassed by any adventure story in recent years," said best-selling 1970s adventure author Alistair MacLean of Jack Higgins's *The Eagle Has Landed* (1975). "Higgins is the master of adventure and I could not put this down," said 2000s best-selling techno author Tom Clancy of *Eye of the Storm* (1992).

Higgins has gone through several phases in his writing career and shows no sign of letting up. Born in Newcastle Upon Tyne, England, in 1929, the author Harry Patterson (his real name) moved with his mother to Belfast, Northern Ireland, after his parents split. He retains dual citizenship. As a youth, he spent a lot of time at the library and read voraciously. He particularly enjoyed the works of Graham Greene, F. Scott Fitzgerald, and Alistair Maclean. He began to write short stories as a teenager, although he did not sell a book until he was twenty-nine.

From 1947 to 1949, he served with the Royal Horse Guards unit of the British Army, assigned to the East German border, where he demonstrated great skill at intelligence and sharpshooting—characteristics that would distinguish his later fictional creations. He worked in civil service postings from 1950 to 1955. He was certified as an educator at Leeds Training College for Teachers in 1958 and in 1962 earned a bachelor of science degree in sociology from the University of London. From 1958 to 1964, he taught history at Allerton Grange Comprehensive School in Leeds then lectured in liberal studies at Leeds College of Commerce for four years. He was James Graham College's senior lecturer in education from 1968 to 1970. He has twice been married, to Amy Margaret Hewitt (1958–1984) and to Denise Lesley Anne Palmer (since 1985); he has four children from his first marriage.

When his writing gained prominence, Higgins left teaching. Success was not instant, however.

"I was a struggling schoolmaster. I was struggling very much to make some kind of living by writing," he told *New York Times* reporter Edwin McDowell, "but I couldn't because the return on each book was so small. That meant I had to publish books one after the other, so I used several names." He has been Harry Patterson (for Nick Miller stories), Martin Fallon (for Paul Chavasse novels), Hugh Marlowe, James Graham, and Jack Higgins.

Higgins's *The Eagle Has Landed* was the breakthrough. A seminal World War II thriller, the title was on the best-seller lists for thirty-six weeks and sold upward of 50 million copies. Revenues prompted Patterson to move to the tax-advantageous Jersey, one of the Channel Islands.

The Eagle Has Landed had all the solid elements needed for thriller success: a dark, credible Northern Irish hero, Liam Devlin; sinister villains, Himmler and other Nazis; and a reasonably credible premise, the kidnapping of Prime Minister Winston Churchill. Michael Caine, Donald Sutherland, and Robert Duvall played these roles in the movie.

The idea for the book was not a new one. Higgins told interviewer Emma Wells he'd conceived the plot while in the army. "The book was different—the first serious attempt to show 'the good German.' It involved months of research, though it took me only eight weeks to write. I would work all night. I set up a camp bed in the corner of the dining room so I didn't disturb the family."

Devlin is one of Higgins's most popular characters, but it was a Devlin protégé, Sean Dillon, who carried on the thriller legacy beginning with *Eye of the Storm* (1992). Another angry IRA member, Dillon wants revenge when his father is killed in a Belfast confrontation with the British. Known as "The Man of 1000 Faces," Dillon eventually sours on the cause and takes mercenary assignments with the PLO, the Israelis, and the KGB.

Higgins says he nearly killed Dillon off in that first book. He was a villain, after all. But his wife's better sense prevailed; the author rewrote the final chapter, and the character evolved. "The result was, that when I was doing another book, I hadn't intended using Dillon; it was the book about Martin Bormann's U-boat being found on the reef in the Virgin Islands. The U-boat that Bormann had, supposedly, escaped in," the author said on the HarperCollins Crimes & Thrillers Web site. Dillon had the requisite flying and diving talents, so Higgins recruited him for the book. Government insiders cleaned Dillon's record and set him to new tasks. A new series was born.

Higgins's strength as a writer has proved to be his nurturing of interesting plots and his faith in well-rounded characters. "The idea of what the book should be about is the important thing, and you can say that to yourself in two or three sentences, then the rest of it is a development of real people, just like real life," he explained to a BBC reporter in 2008.

Works by the Author

Published as by Harry Patterson in Great Britain, as by Jack Higgins in the United States

Sad Wind from the Sea (1959)

Cry of the Hunter (1960)

The Thousand Faces of Night (1961)

Comes the Dark Stranger (1962)

Hell Is Too Crowded (1962)

The Dark Side of the Island (1963)

Pay the Devil (1963)

Thunder at Noon (1964), also titled *Dillinger* (1983)

A Phoenix in the Blood (1964)
Wrath of the Lion (1964)
Passage by Night (1964)
The Iron Tiger (1966)
Toll for the Brave (1971)
To Catch a King (1979), also titled *The Judas Gate*

Nick Miller Series

The Graveyard Shift (1965)
Brought in Dead (1967)
Hell Is Always Today (1968)

Dramas

Walking Wounded (1987), for stage
The Island City (1987), for radio
Dead of Night (1990), for radio

Published as by Hugh Marlowe

Seven Pillars to Hell (1963), rewritten as *Sheba* (1994)
Passage by Night (1964)
A Candle for the Dead (1966), rewritten as *The Violent Enemy* (1969)

Published as by Jack Higgins

East of Desolation (1968)
In the Hour before Midnight (1969), also titled *The Sicilian Heritage* (1970)
Night Judgement at Sinos (1970)
The Savage Day (1972)
A Prayer for the Dying (1973)
Storm Warning (1976)
The Valhalla Exchange (1976)
Day of Judgment (1978), prequel to *The Savage Day*
Solo (1980), also titled *The Cretan Lover*
Luciano's Luck (1981)
Exocet (1983)
A Season in Hell (1988)
Memoirs of a Dance Hall Romeo (1989)
Sure Fire (2006)
Death Run (2007), sequel to *Sure Fire*
Rough Justice (2008)
A Darker Place (2009)

Brigadier Dougal Munro and Captain Jack Carter Series

Night of the Fox (1986)
Cold Harbor (1989)
Flight of Eagles (1998)

Liam Devlin Series

The Eagle Has Landed (1975)
Touch the Devil (1982)
Confessional (1985)
The Eagle Has Flown (1990), sequel to *The Eagle Has Landed*

Sean Dillon Series

Eye of the Storm (1992), also titled *Midnight Man*
Thunder Point (1993)
On Dangerous Ground (1994)
Angel of Death (1995)
Drink with the Devil (1996)
The President's Daughter (1997)
The White House Connection (1998)
Day of Reckoning (2000)
Edge of Danger (2001)
Midnight Runner (2002)
Bad Company (2003)
Dark Justice (2004)
Without Mercy (2005)
The Killing Ground (2007)

Published as by James Graham

A Game for Heroes (1970)
The Wrath of God (1971)
The Khufra Run (1972)
The Run to Morning (1974)

Published as by Martin Fallon

Paul Chavasse Series
The Testament of Caspar Schultz (1962), also titled *The Bornmann Testament*
Year of the Tiger (1963), rewritten (1996)
The Keys of Hell (1965)
Midnight Never Comes (1966)
The Dark Side of the Street (1967)
A Fine Night for Dying (1969)

Young Adult Novel

Sure Fire, with Justin Richards (2008)

Adaptations in Other Media

The Violent Enemy (1968), motion picture based on *A Candle for the Dead*
The Wrath of God (1972), motion picture based on the novel
The Eagle Has Landed (1977), motion picture based on the novel
To Catch a King (1984), television production based on the novel
A Prayer for the Dying (1987), motion picture based on the novel
Confessional (1989), television production based on the novel
Night of the Fox (1990), television production based on the novel
On Dangerous Ground (1995), television production based on the novel
Midnight Man (1995), television production based on *Eye of the Storm*
Thunderpoint (1996), television production based on the novel
Windsor Protocol (1996), television production based on the novel

For Further Information

Harry Patterson entry, Contemporary Authors Online. Reproduced in Biography Resource Center. Farmington Hills, MI: Gale, 2008. http://galenet.galegroup.com/servlet/BioRC (viewed February 15, 2008).

Jack Higgins entry, George Kelley. In *St. James Guide to Crime & Mystery Writers*, 4th ed. Jay P. Pederson, ed. Detroit, MI: St. James Press, 1996.

Jack Higgins entry, Internet Movie Database. http://www.imdb.com/name/nm0383396 (viewed February 15, 2008).

Jack Higgins interview, BBC. http://www.bbc.co.uk/jersey/content/articles/2006/03/01/jack_higgins_interview_ss_feature.shtml (viewed February 15, 2008).

Jack Higgins interview, HarperCollins Crime & Thrillers. http://www.collins-crime.co.uk/Authors/interview.aspx?id=253&aid=2627 (viewed February 15, 2008).

McDowell, Edwin, "Higgins Odyssey: Potboiler to Best Seller." *New York Times*, July 28, 1982.

Morning, Todd, *Sure Fire* review. *Booklist*, October 1, 2007.

Wells, Emma, "Time and Place: Jack Higgins." *Sunday Times*, December 16, 2007.

Patricia Highsmith

Crime-Suspense; Thrillers: Serial Killers

Benchmark Title: *The Talented Mr. Ripley*

Fort Worth, Texas

1921–1995

Photo credit: Simone Sassen

About the Author and the Author's Writing

Patricia Highsmith led a life nearly as troubled as that of her character Mr. Ripley, although at least her murders were always on paper. Her following in America was sporadic in her lifetime, despite a Crime Writers Association Silver Dagger award in 1964, and despite her influence on other writers. However, the longtime expatriate in Europe, where her perceived misanthropy, fluctuating sexuality, and brash plots were generally accepted, was awarded the Grand Priz de Littérature Policière in 1957. Recognition has accelerated considerably since the late 1990s, as her books have returned to print and several television and theatrical films have been made based on her works.

Born Mary Patricia Plantman in Fort Worth, Texas, in 1921, the author never knew her father. Her parents broke up before she was born. Her relationship with her mother was strained. Mary Coates Plangman Highsmith once told her daughter she had consumed turpentine in a failed attempt at abortion before Patricia was born. Patricia took the last name of her stepfather and first met her birth father when she was twelve. She spent some of her childhood with her grandmother.

"As a child and in her youth Highsmith showed talents in arts—she painted and remained a talented sculptor, but she had determined to be a writer," according to a Books and Writers profile.

In 1942, she received a bachelor of arts degree from Barnard College in New York. After several inconsequential jobs, including one in retail and another in providing plots to comic book script writers, she met Truman Capote, who arranged for her to go to the Yaddo arts colony in New York state, and there she wrote a novel, *Strangers on a Train*. Its publication and the film by Alfred Hitchcock in 1951 brought her instant recognition. The book set the tone for her later stories, which appeared over a forty-year period. Neither police nor detective stories, they were criminous works in which villains were sympathetic, and innocent people sinned.

"This reluctance to judge or to help readers easily allocate sympathy or animosity to characters makes her writing approach the condition of black comedy at times," suggests Ian A. Bell in *Crime & Mystery Writers*.

Her "novels and stories are, at their extreme, macabre expeditions into fear, more horror than crime, like Roald Dahl's *Tales of the Unexpected*. Even her less extreme works are bleak and unremitting, pushing the acceptable boundaries of suspense," Mike Ashley said in *The Mammoth Encyclopedia of Modern Crime Fiction*.

Highsmith first visited Europe in 1949 but only moved there permanently in 1963, to live in France, Italy, and Switzerland. Her wanders in the United States were often fruitful to her research. In *Plotting and Writing Suspense Fiction*, she described a leisurely sojourn in the Massachusetts resort town Lenox, where she rented rooms from a local undertaker. The man was "very voluble about his profession, though he drew the line at permitting me to visit his establishment and see the tree-shaped incision he made in the chest before stuffing the corpse." Learning the mortician filled cadavers with sawdust, she adjusted a planned plot device for her novel-in-progress, *The Talented Mr. Ripley*.

Her best realized, and only serial, character, Tom Ripley, is a con artist who, on the lam, accepts a convenient plea from a millionaire to go to Europe to check on the man's son, Dickie Greenleaf. Ripley ends up killing the son and assuming his good life—with all the travails (and occasional future murders) that brings.

"Ripley leaves a trail of unsuspecting dupes, outwitted nemeses and dead bodies. Ripley always charms—and always gets away with murder. He was a character with whom Highsmith came to identify quite closely," David Bowman wrote in *Book* magazine.

Ripley's personality is both complex and puzzling. "I don't think Ripley is gay," Highsmith told interviewer Gerald Peary in 1987, in answer to a frequent question. "He appreciates good looks in other men, that's true. But he's married in later books. I'm not saying he's very strong in the sex department. But he makes it in bed with his wife."

Highsmith's own sexuality was mixed. She had relationships with men (among them novelist Marc Brandel) and women (notably with writer Marijane Meaker, who wrote under the name M. E. Kerr, and who wrote a tell-all memoir years later). Highsmith used the penname Claire Morgan for *The Price of Salt* (1952), her second book, a love story couched in the pulpish prose of the era, but with her own twists and turns in plot. As Terry Castle noted in Slate, "Highsmith has to be one of the boldest plotters in the history of the modern novel, a maker of gambits that shouldn't work but nonetheless do."

Andrew Wilson, who had access to Highsmith's diaries when he wrote *Beautiful Shadow*, a biography, observed, "After the collapse of each of her brief, but intense, relationships, she felt so depressed that she sometimes felt incapable of writing. Her melancholy was so deep, her spirit so paralyzed, she felt she could not even summon up enough energy to commit suicide."

Highsmith, as temperamental and moody as she could be, nevertheless wrote compelling prose. "At its chilling, deadpan best, Patricia Highsmith's writing is wicked in the old-fashioned, very scary sense of the word. It puts a spell on you, after which you feel altered and even tainted," Mark Harris suggests in *Entertainment Weekly*.

Works by the Author

Strangers on a Train (1950)

The Blunderer (1954), in the United Kingdom as *Lament for a Lover* (1956)

Deep Water (1957)

A Game for the Living (1958)

This Sweet Sickness (1960)

The Cry of the Owl (1962)

The Two Faces of January (1964)

The Glass Cell (1964)

The Story-Teller (1965) in the United Kingdom as *A Suspension of Mercy* (1965)

Those Who Walk Away (1967)

The Tremor of Forgery (1969)

A Dog's Ransom (1972)

Edith's Diary (1977)

People Who Knock on the Door (1983)

Found in the Street (1986)

Small g: A Summer Idyll (1995)

Mr. Ripley Series

The Talented Mr. Ripley (1955)

Ripley Under Ground (1970)

Ripley's Game (1974)

The Boy Who Followed Ripley (1980)

The Mysterious Mr. Ripley (1985), includes *The Talented Mr. Ripley, Ripley Under Ground*, and *Ripley's Game*

Ripley Under Water (1991)

The Talented Mr. Ripley, Ripley Under Ground, Ripley's Game (1999), omnibus

Collections

The Snail Watchers, and Other Stories (1970), in the United Kingdom as *Eleven: Short Stories* (1970)

Little Tales of Misogyny (1977)

Slowly, Slowly in the Wind (1979)

The Black House (1981)

Mermaids on a Golf Course (1988)

The Selected Stories of Patricia Highsmith (2001)

Nothing That Meets the Eye: The Uncollected Stories of Patricia Highsmith (2002)

Plays

Strangers on a Train, by Craig Warner (2003), based on the novel

For Juvenile and Young Adult Readers

Miranda the Panda Is on the Veranda, with Doris Sanders (1958)
The Animal-Lover's Book of Beastly Murder (1975)

Published as by Claire Morgan

The Price of Salt (1952), retitled *Carol* (1984)

Nonfiction

Plotting and Writing Suspense Fiction (1966)
Tales of Natural and Unnatural Catastrophe (1987)

Adaptations in Other Media

Strangers on a Train (1951), based on the novel
Studio One (1956), television episode: "The Talented Mr. Ripley"
Jane Wyman Presents The Fireside Theatre (1957), television episode: "The Perfect Alibi"
77 Sunset Strip (1958), television episode: "One False Step"
Purple Noon (Plein Soleil) (1960), motion picture based on *The Talented Mr. Ripley*
The Alfred Hitchcock Hour (1962), television episode: "Annabel"
Le Meurtrier (1963), motion picture based on *The Blunderer*
The Wednesday Thriller (1965), television episode: "The Cellar"
Enough Rope (1966), based on *The Blunderer*
Once You Kiss a Stranger (1969), motion picture based on *Strangers on a Train*
Tell Her That I Love Her (Dites-Lui Que Je l'Aime) (1977), motion picture based on *This Sweet Sickness*
The American Friend (Der Amerikanische Freund) (1977), motion picture based on *Ripley's Game*
Die Glaeserne Zelle (1978), motion picture based on *The Glass Cell*
Eaux Profondes (1981), motion picture based on *Deep Water*
The South Bank Show (1982), television episode: "Patricia Highsmith: A Gift for Murder"
Tief Wasser (1983), television production
Ediths Tagebuch (1983), motion picture
Tales of the Unexpected (1984), television episode: "Sauce for the Goose"
The Two Faces of January (Die Zwei Gersichter Des Januar) (1986), motion picture based on the novel
The Cry of the Owl (Le Cri du Hibou) (1987), motion picture based on the novel
Der Geschichtenerzähler (1989), motion picture based on *The Cry of the Owl*
The Day of Reckoning (Le Jour du Châtiment) (1990), television episode
Chillers (1990), television production
The Stuff of Madness (1990), television production

Patricia Highsmith's Tales (Les Cadavres Exquis de Patricia Highsmith) (1990), television episode

Trip Nach Tunis (1993), motion picture based on *The Tremor of Forgery*

La Rançon du Chien (1996), television production

Once You Meet a Stranger (1996), television production based on *Strangers on a Train*

The Talented Mr. Ripley (1999), motion picture based on the novel

Ripley's Game (2002), motion picture based on the novel

Found in the Street (2004), motion picture based on the novel

Ripley Under Ground (2005), motion picture based on the novel

For Further Information

Ashley, Mike. *The Mammoth Encyclopedia of Modern Crime Fiction.* New York: Carroll & Graf, 2002.

Bell, Ian A., Patricia Highsmith entry, *St. James Guide to Crime & Mystery Writers*, 4th ed. Jay P. Pederson, ed. Detroit, MI: St. James Press, 1996.

Bowman, David, "Femme Fatale: What Was It That Drove Patricia Highsmith to Create a Killer as Intriguing as Tom Ripley? We May Never Know." *Book*, March-April 2003.

Castle, Terry, "Pulp Valentine," Slate, May 23, 2006. http://www.slate.com/toolbar.aspx?action=print&id=2142254 (viewed December 26, 2007).

Graham, Don, "Accentuate the Negative: It's Time Patricia Highsmith Got the Respect She Deserves in Her Native Texas. After All, It Was the Breeding Ground of Her Trademark Misanthropy." *Texas Monthly*, November 2004.

Harris, Mark, "Strange Magic: Patricia Highsmith's Complex Yet Entrancing Crime Thrillers Find New Life Six Years after Her Death." *Entertainment Weekly*, August 24, 2001.

Meaker, Marijane. *Highsmith: A Romance of the 1950s.* San Francisco: Cleis, 2003.

Patricia Highsmith filmography, Internet Movie Database. http://www.imdb.com/name/nm0383604/ (viewed December 27, 2007).

Patricia Highsmith profile, Books and Writers. http://www.kirjastso.sci.fi/highsm.htm (viewed December 26, 2007).

Peary, Gerald, Patricia Highsmith interview. http://www.geraldpeary.com/interviews/gh/highsmith/html (viewed December 26, 2007).

Riddell, Mary, "Murder in Mind: Patricia Highsmith Wrote Gripping—and Disturbing—Thrillers Such As the Mr. Ripley Stories. But the Author's Own Life Holds Vital Clues to the Dark Plots She Hatched." *Daily Mail*, June 12, 2004.

Sallis, James, *The Selected Stories of Patricia Highsmith* review, Boston Review. http://bostonreview.net/BR26.5/sallism.html (viewed December 26, 2007).

Wilson, Andrew. *Beautiful Shadow: A Life of Patricia Highsmith.* New York: Bloomsbury, 2004.

Tami Hoag

Crime-Suspense; Romantic Suspense; Romance: Paranormal; Thrillers: Legal

Benchmark Title: *Night Sins*

Cresco, Iowa

1959–

About the Author and the Author's Writing

Tami Hoag had a comfortable career writing romance novels. But her fascination with the writing of thriller authors Ken Follett and Jack Higgins nudged her into a different direction. With *A Thin Dark Line* in 1997, she worked her plot from a true case of a Minnesota woman who was stalked by one of her coworkers.

"It seems a big leap, since I started [out] writing romantic comedy," she told *Publishers Weekly* interviewer Bridget Kinsella. "I had become increasingly frustrated writing category romance, because there just isn't enough room to maneuver." With thrillers, Hoag found that she could bring out a few dead bodies and introduce criminal or political, as well as romantic, suspense.

Tami Mikkelson was born in Cresco, Iowa, in 1959 and grew up in Minnesota. Her father was an insurance salesman. She married her high school boyfriend, computer programmer Daniel Hoag. The marriage has since ended. She has lived in New York, Virginia, and California. She worked as a saleswoman, as a circulation manager for a newspaper, as a typist and clerk, and as a horse trainer before becoming a writer. To kill time one day while waiting for a tow truck, she read a light romance novel. She was taken with how easy it might be to write one. She shaped a manuscript particularly to one of Bantam's romance lines, it was accepted, and *The Trouble with J. J.* appeared in 1988. She wrote a stream of novels for the publisher, some appearing in trilogies. She has resisted series characters with her thrillers, however, only infrequently bringing back favorite characters in follow-up stories.

"While I don't have the temperament to write a series in the traditional book after book sense, I'm always open to returning to characters—if they have a story to tell. I won't take characters and force a story on them, which is one of the pitfalls of being locked into a series," she said in a Bookreporter conversation.

Hoag's breakout novel was *Night Sins* (1995), which was made into a television miniseries. It is about the impact of a child's kidnapping on a small town. A second novel, *Guilty as Sin*, featured the same heroine. Another returning character is Elena Estes, whom readers met in *Dark Horse* (2002) as a policewoman who had left the force in the aftermath of her partner's death. Estes had taken refuge on a friend's

Florida ranch. A young teen came to her for help in finding a missing older sister. The novel is set against a world of dressage and professional horsemanship—Hoag herself is a professional rider—and a sequel, *The Alibi Man* (2007), finds Estes tracking the killer of a young groom into the higher levels of society.

At her publisher's urging, Hoag lightly rewrote some earlier romantic suspense novels, giving them a harder edge to appeal to her new readers. But crime novels aren't that dissimilar from romances, the author told reporter Jay MacDonald. "The intensity of the emotion is very similar. If you're writing a romance, you want a high level of emotional tension and to take people on a roller-coaster ride through that relationship, and of course that's what you want to do in crime fiction as well."

A man in Minneapolis killed several prostitutes and set their bodies on fire. The general public seemed unconcerned, because of who the victims were. What if?, Hoag wondered, before she wrote *Ashes to Ashes*. "What if suddenly one of the victims wasn't a prostitute. Then what? You don't know any more about that person. It's all in your perception and the stereotypes that you've held about this victim," she said in a January magazine interview.

Hoag says she prefers to write in the afternoon. She writes on the computer, revising her pages as she goes, rather than editing the entire draft manuscript at once.

Because thrillers require more attention, and more involved plots than most romances, Hoag approaches a new novel having worked out her characters in detail and having settled on and researched a plot angle or background. She says she takes ideas from the headlines.

The author researches law and investigation procedures from her own library. And she interviews knowledgeable people. She creates a general plan for the book but begins writing and lets the characters take certain control of how things work out.

"I don't work from an outline because I prefer to be free from any imagined boundaries," the author said on her Web site. "I want the story to happen; I want to be as surprised and shocked as I hope readers will be."

Works by the Author

The Trouble with J. J. (1988)
McKnight in Shining Armor (1988)
Mismatch (1989)
Straight from the Heart (1989)
Magic (1990), sequel to *The Trouble with J. J.*
Sarah's Sin (1991)
Heart of Dixie (1991)
Still Waters (1992)
Taken by Storm (1992)
Last White Knight (1992)
Dark Paradise (1994)
Night Sins (1995)
Guilty as Sin (1996), sequel to *Night Sins*
A Thin Dark Line (1997)

The Tami Hoag Omnibus (2001), includes *Magic, Lucky's Lady*, and *Cry Wolf*

Three Great Novels (2001), omnibus includes *Guilty as Sin, Night Sins*, and *A Thin Dark Line*

Dark Horse (2002)

Two Great Novels (2003), omnibus includes *Night Sins* and *Guilty as Sin*

Three Great Novels—The Thrillers (2003), includes *Ashes to Ashes, Dust to Dust,* and *Dark Horse*

Killing the Messenger (2004)

The Alibi Man (2007), sequel to *Dark Horse*

Tempestuous/Restless Heart (2007), omnibus

Person of Interest (2008)

Night Sins/Guilty as Sin (2008), omnibus

Deeper Than Dead (2008)

Doucette Series

The Restless Heart (1991)

Lucky's Lady (1992)

Cry Wolf (1993)

Kovac/Liska Series

Ashes to Ashes (1999)

Dust to Dust (2000)

Prior Bad Acts (2006), also titled *Dead Sky*

Quaid Horses Series

Rumor Has It (1988)

Man of Her Dreams (1989)

Tempestuous (1990)

Rainbow Chasers Series

Heart of Gold (1990)

Keeping Company (1990)

Reilly's Return (1990)

Contributor

The Putt at the End of the World, with Lee K. Abbott, Dave Barry, Richard Bausch, James Crumley, James W. Hall, Tim O'Brien, Ridley Pearson, and Les Standiford (2000)

Adaptations in Other Media

Night Sins (CBS, 1997), television film

For Further Information

Dark Horse review. *Publishers Weekly*, July 29, 2002.

Engleman, Patty, *The Alibi Man* review. *Booklist*, March 1, 2007.

Fitzgerald, Carol, Joe Hartlaub, and Wiley Saichek, Tami Hoag interview, Bookreporter, 2004. http://www.bookreporter.com/authors/au-hoag-tami.asp (viewed March 2, 2008).

Kinsella, Bridget, "Tami Hoag: The Road from Romance to Suspense." *Publishers Weekly*, April 21, 1997.

Lynn, Allison, and Joanne Fowler, "Making Crime Pay: Moving from the Sensual to the Sinister Put Tami Hoag on the Bestseller List." *People Weekly*, February 24, 1997.

MacDonald, Jay, "Fame & Fortune: Author Tami Hoag," Bankrate. http://www.bankrate.com/brm/news/investing/20060808b1.asp?prodtype=invest (viewed March 2, 2008).

Richards, Linda, Tami Hoag interview, January magazine. http://www.januarymagazine.com/profiles/hoag.html (viewed March 2, 2008).

Tami Hoag entry, Contemporary Authors Online, Gale, 2008. Reproduced in Biography Resource Center. Farmington Hills, MI: Gale, 2008. http://galenet.galegroup.com/servlet/BioRC (viewed March 2, 2008).

Tami Hoag Q&A, Random House. http://www.randomhouse.com/bantamdell/tamihoag/qa.html (viewed March 2, 2008).

Kay Hooper

Crime; Romantic Suspense; Thrillers: Paranormal, Serial Killers

Benchmark Series: <u>Hagen</u>

Atwater, California

1957–

Photo credit: Sigrid Estrada

About the Author and the Author's Writing

Writing is 99 percent perspiration. But once in a while, sheer inspiration strikes, as it did with suspense author Kay Hooper when she wrote *Hiding in the Shadows* (2000), an entry in her paranormal "thrillogy" featuring FBI profiler Noah Bishop and his Special Crimes unit. "It's such a rare occurrence, one of the magical 'possibilities' that keep me writing because, when it happens, it makes working a pure joy—at least for that wonderful moment," the author said on a Random House Web page.

Hooper was born in Atwater, California, in 1957, at the military base where her father was stationed. The family soon moved to North Carolina. She entered Isothermal Community College for its business classes, but quickly switched her focus to literature and history.

"I wrote bad poetry as a teenager," Hooper once told *Contemporary Authors*, "read voraciously and continually marveled at the (to me) mysterious abilities of the people who strung words together.... Now that I have written many books myself, I know that writing is difficult, frustrating, exhilarating, and a lovely business altogether."

Dell purchased Hooper's first Regency romance, *Lady Thief*, and published it in 1980. Hooper wrote numerous romances for that publisher and, along with authors Iris Johansen and Fayrene Preston, contributed several entries to a collective Delaney romance series.

In 1988, Hooper also wrote a science fiction romance, *Summer of the Unicorn*. Critic Barbara E. Kemp said of Hooper's writing, "She writes with humor and passion, develops her characters well and is adept at creating intriguing plots." Hooper's interest in suspense novels grew with the Hagen series, featuring a group of undercover agents. Having ultimately broken away from formulaic romance fiction—she found

184

the rules confining—she enjoys the freedom of experimentation and examination of a variety of topics and settings.

Hooper became intrigued with the paranormal and has written several trilogies within the framework of the Special Crimes Unit. *Touching Evil* (2001), for example, brings together two seers, an empath, and a ghost to hunt a monster in Seattle. *Blood Dreams* (2007) finds the psychics in Georgia in search of a serial killer. The challenge? He may also be a psychic.

A fan of the classic mysteries of Agatha Christie and Dorothy L. Sayers, Hooper eventually shunned the cozy for the bloody crime story. In a Bookreporter interview, Hooper said she has long been drawn to the outsider. "I think it was a gradual evolution, really to put those interests and elements together. Psychic investigators made sense to me; I was able to see the possible, if not probable, scientific basis for the abilities, and matching that with criminal investigation also made sense."

Often asked the source of her ideas, the author said on her Web site that her imagination is at work every minute she's awake, and experience enables her to identify quickly what will work in a novel and what will not. She tosses an idea around for a while before she sits at her computer to begin writing. She uses snips of conversation, character traits, and plot angles she's collected. When she wrote category romance, a book might come together in a month. With suspense novels, the process takes a little longer.

Her advice to young writers, found on her Web site, includes disciplining oneself to think like a writer. "Mentally ask yourself 'what if …' and begin spinning a story whenever you encounter an interesting situation or person."

Works by the Author

Lady Thief (1981)

Mask of Passion (1982)

Return Engagement (1982)

Breathless Surrender (1982)

Taken by Storm (1983)

On Wings of Magic (1983)

Elusive Dawn (1983)

Kissed by Magic (1983)

CJ's Fate (1984)

Moonlight Rhapsody (1984)

Something Different (1984)

Pepper's Way (1984)

If There Be Dragons (1984)

Illegal Possession (1985)

Eye of the Beholder (1985)

Rebel Waltz (1986)

Belonging to Taylor (1986)

Larger Than Life (1986), available only through Loveswept book club

Time after Time (1986)

On Her Doorstep (1986)
Summer of the Unicorn (1988)
Enemy Mine (1989)
Crime of Passion (1991)
The Haviland Touch (1991)
House of Cards (1991)
The Wizard of Seattle (1993)
Masquerade (1994)
The Haunting of Josie (1994)
Amanda (1996)
After Caroline (1997)
Finding Laura (1998)
Haunting Rachel (1999)
Once a Thief (2002)
Always a Thief (2002), sequel to *Once a Thief*
Enchanted (2003), omnibus includes *Kissed by Magic, Belonging to Taylor*, and *Eye of the Beholder*
Elusive (2004), omnibus includes *Elusive Dawn, On Her Doorstep*, and *Return Engagement*
The Real Thing (2004), omnibus includes *Enemy Mine* and *The Haviland Touch*
Amanda/Haunting Rachel (2006), omnibus
Something Different/Pepper's Way (2007), omnibus

Bishop/Special Crimes Unit Series

Stealing Shadows (2000)
Hiding in the Shadows (2000)
Out of the Shadows (2000)
Touching Evil (2001)
Whisper of Evil (2002)
Sense of Evil (2003)
Hunting Fear (2004)
Chill of Fear (2005)
Sleeping with Fear (2006)
Blood Dreams (2007)
Blood Sins (2008)

Delaneys of Killaroo Series

Adelaide, the Enchantress (1987)

Delaney Historicals

Golden Flames (1988)
Velvet Lightning (1988)

Hagen Series

In Serena's Web (1987)
Raven on the Wing (1987)
Rafferty's Wife (1987)
Zach's Law (1987)
The Fall of Lucas Kendrick (1988)
Unmasking Kelsey (1988)
Outlaw Derek (1988)
Shades of Gray (1988)
Captain's Paradise (1988)
It Takes a Thief (1989)
Aces High (1989)

Men of Mysteries Past Series

The Touch of Max (1993)
Hunting the Wolfe (1993)
The Trouble with Jared (1993)
All for Quinn (1993)

Once Upon a Time Series

Golden Threads (1989)
The Glass Shoe (1989)
What Dreams May Come (1990)
Through the Looking Glass (1990)
The Lady and the Lion (1990)
Star-Crossed Lovers (1990)
The Matchmaker (1991)
The Shamrock Trinity (contributor)
Rafe, the Maverick (1986)

Contributor

Christmas Love Stories (1991), includes "Holiday Spirit"
The Delaney Christmas Carol (1992), includes "Christmas Future"
My Guardian Angel (1995), includes "Almost an Angel"
Yours 2 Keep (1999), includes "Arts Magica"

For Further Information

Chelton, Mary K., *Blood Dreams* review. *Booklist*, December 1, 2007.
Kay Hooper bibliography, Wikipedia. http://en.wikipedia.org/wiki/Kay_Hooper (viewed March 2, 2008).

Kay Hooper entry, Contemporary Authors Online, Gale, 2008. Reproduced in Biography Resource Center. Farmington Hills, MI: Gale, 2008. http://galenet.galegroup.com/servlet/BioRC (viewed March 2, 2008).

Kay Hooper interview, Random House. http://www.randomhouse.com/catalog/display.pperl?isbn=9780553576924&view=auqa (viewed March 11, 2008).

Kay Hooper Web site. http://www.kayhooper.com/ (viewed March 2, 2008).

Kemp, Barbara, Kay Hooper entry, *Twentieth-Century Romance and Historical Writers*, 2nd ed. Lesley Henderson, ed. Chicago: St. James Press, 1990.

Touching Evil review. *Publishers Weekly*, June 18, 2001.

Linda Howard

Crime: Assassins; Espionage; Historical Fiction; Romance; Romantic Suspense: Paranormal

Benchmark Title: *Strangers in the Night*

Gadsden, Alabama

1950–

About the Author and the Author's Writing

Daisy Minor is thirty-four and feels frumpy. She despairs of ever finding a date, much less a dream date. What if she makes herself over? What if she becomes a party girl? She throws her practical pajamas into the wastebasket. "She had the wild thought of sleeping naked tonight," we read in Linda Howard's 2002 novel *Open Season*. "A little thrill ran through her. That was something a party girl would do, wasn't it? And there was nothing wrong with sleeping naked. She had never heard Reverend Bridges say anything at all about what one wore, or didn't wear, to bed."

Daisy Minor moves out of her folks' home, rents an apartment, and buys a new wardrobe. She never imagines her transformation into a free spirit will invite a stalking white slaver—or bring her into the protection of Police Chief Jack Russo, a former SWAT team member from a big city who has been transplanted to the same small Alabama town where Daisy works as librarian.

"*Open Season* is Linda Howard at the top of her game," said Romance Reader reviewer Cathy Sova. "All of her trademarks are here: wise guy alpha hero, smart heroine with a bit of sass, a relationship that sizzles, intriguing secondary characters, and a thread of suspense to tie them all together."

With an initial 192,000 copy print run, the book leapt onto the *Publishers Weekly* best-seller list.

The author said she had no particular model for her spunky heroine. "The characters are just themselves," she said on the Mystery Guild Web site. "I'm sure there are people in the world who know someone like Daisy, or think they themselves are like Daisy, but to me she's just herself."

Howard has had great success with Daisy Minor and other accessible characters —including some in recent books who encounter the paranormal.

The author was born in Gadsden, Alabama, in 1950. She began to write fiction for her own enjoyment when she was nine. Early favorite authors were Margaret Mitchell and Robert Ruark. Twenty years later, still writing, and working for a trucking company, she met her husband, Gary F. Howington. He has three adult children from an earlier marriage. They have a rural home in Alabama that they share with two golden retrievers.

As secretary to the terminal manager, she said on a Fantastic Fiction Web page, "I worked in every phase of the transportation business, but my main duties were payroll, insurance, and the efficiency and production reports." She yearned to write something more satisfying, more creative. She decided it was time to submit a manuscript, and did. She sold it to Silhouette, and they published the romance in 1982. Several of the author's first books appeared under her real name before she adopted the Linda Howard penname. In 1981, she became a charter member of Romance Writers of America and has served as a regional director. Her husband, whom she met at the trucking company, is now a professional Bassmasters competitor—and when she tags along, it's an opportunity to experience unusual places that sometimes end up in her books.

Mr. Perfect, for example, is set in Warren, Michigan. "My husband had a bass tournament there last summer and we stayed at the Studio Plus that was almost directly across from the police station. And I couldn't pass up the opportunity when I had that many cops in reach. I just couldn't," she said in a Writerspace chat. *Mr. Perfect* also afforded the author a rare opportunity to lighten her prose with humor. Malvina Yock commented on the book's "snappy, sexy, fast-paced interactions between the hero and heroine.... I should mention they both have a car fetish. In a particularly raunchy kissing scene, set outside in full view of the entire neighborhood, the desperately aroused hero begs the heroine to come inside to finish what they've started. She counters by asking to see his fabled red truck." There's more than romantic suspense in the book, as the hero, undercover policeman Sam Donovan, is soon looking after Jaine Bright professionally—when a killer has slain one of her close friends and apparently is after her as well.

Howard has written straight romance, historicals, and crime novels—and variations within those genres. *A Lady of the West* is about a Southern belle, Victoria Waverly, whose sensibilities are jarred when she marries New Mexico cattle baron Frank McLain and becomes embroiled in a fight with the revenge-seeking Starrett brothers, who hold a major grudge against McLain. *Kiss Me While I Sleep* is a modern-day espionage thriller in which contract assassin Lily Mansfield pursues a personal vendetta when a girl she once saved from the streets, along with her surrogate parents, are killed. Her revenge opens the gates to pursuit by the killer's family and by CIA Agent Lucas Swain. *After the Night,* a gothic Louisiana tale of murder and retribution, pits the Devins against the Rouillards. *Raintree Inferno* introduces paranormal elements as the modern-day descendants of the Ansara wizards, long isolated on a Caribbean island but now dispersed into the modern business world, take revenge on the Raintree clan that defeated them.

Although sometimes accused of having super-alpha heroes in her books, the author has responded simply that a strong female character needs a strong male. She has also said that once she's in a writing mode, she feels she has little control over her characters. They bring her the stories. "I can't decide I'm going to do a certain type book, plot it, then sit down and write it.... A particular story has to grab me by the throat, shake me, and not let me go until I've written it," she said in an All About Romances conversation in 2004.

Whatever the subgenre, Howard is consistent in one respect: "I will always have a strong romantic relationship in my books because otherwise, I'm not really interested in writing the book," she told interviewer Laurie Gold for All About Romance in 2000.

 Works by the Author

As Linda S. Howington (reissued as by Linda Howard)

All That Glitters (1982)
An Independent Wife (1982)
Against the Rules (1983)
Lake of Dreams (1985)
Blue Moon (1999)

As Linda Howard

Come Lie with Me (1984)
Tears of the Renegade (1985)
The Cutting Edge (1985)
A Lady of the West (1990)
Duncan's Bride (1990)
Angel Creek (1991), sequel to *A Lady of the West*
The Way Home (1991)
The Touch of Fire (1992)
Linda Howard Collection: Midnight Rainbow/Diamond Bay (1992), omnibus
Overload (1993)
Heart of Fire (1993)
Loving Evangeline (1994), sequel to *Duncan's Bride*
Dream Man (1995)
After the Night (1995)
Shades of Twilight (1996)
White Out (1997)
Son of the Morning (1997)
Night Moves (1998), omnibus
Now You See Her (1998)
Dream Man/After the Night (1998), omnibus
Mr. Perfect (2000)
Open Season (2001)
Strangers in the Night (2001)
Lake of Dreams/Blue Moon/White Out (2001), omnibus
A Game of Chance (2001)
Dying to Please (2002)
Cry No More (2003)

To Die For (2004)
Killing Time (2005)
Shades of Twilight/Son of the Morning (2005), omnibus
Angel Creek/Lady of the West (2005), omnibus
Cover of Night (2006)
Drop Dead Gorgeous (2006), sequel to *To Die For*
Up Close and Dangerous (2007)
Death Angel (2008)
Loving Angeline (2008)
Burn (2009)

CIA Series

Kill and Tell (1998)
All the Queen's Men (1999)
Kiss Me While I Sleep (2004)

Mackenzie Series

Mackenzie's Mountain (1989)
Mackenzie's Mission (1992)
Mackenzie's Pleasures (1996)
Mackenzie's Magic (1996)
Mackenzie's Mountain/Mackenzie's Mission (1996), omnibus
The Mackenzie Family (1998), omnibus
A Game of Chance (2000)
Mackenzie's Legacy: Mackenzie's Mountain/Mackenzie's Mission (2005), omnibus
Mackenzie's Honor: Mackenzie's Pleasure/A Game of Chance (2005), omnibus

Raintree Series

Raintree Inferno (2007)

Rescues Series

Midnight Rainbow (1986)
Diamond Bay (1987)
Heartbreaker (1987)
White Lies (1988)

Sarah's Series

Sarah's Child (1985)
Almost Forever (1986)
Bluebird Winter (1987)

Contributor

Silhouette Christmas Stories, 1987, with Dixie Browning, Ginna Gray, and Diana Palmer (1987)

To Mother with Love, with Robyn Carr and Cheryl Reavis (1993)

Silhouette Summer Sizzlers '93, with Carole Buck and Suzanne Carey (1993)

Christmas Kisses, with Debbie Macomber and Linda Turner (1996)

Forever Yours, with Catherine Coulter and Barbara Delinsky (1997)

Harlequin, with Debbie Macomber and Diana Palmer (1997)

Upon a Midnight Clear, with Margaret Allison, Jude Deveraux, Stef Ann Holm, and Mariah Stewart (1997)

Heart's Desire, with Jayne Ann Krentz and Linda Lael Miller (1998)

Everlasting Love, with Jayne Ann Krentz, Kasey Michaels, Linda Lael Miller, and Carla Neggers (1998)

Heart and Soul, with Stella Cameron and Barbara Delinsky (1998)

Strangers in Paradise, with Heather Graham and Linda Lael Miller (1998)

Summer Sensations, with Heather Graham and Linda Lael Miller (1998)

Always and Forever, with Heather Graham and Linda Lael Miller (1998)

Through the Years, with Debbie Macomber and Fern Michaels (1999)

Under the Boardwalk, with Geralyn Dawson, Jillian Hunter, Miranda Jarrett, and Mariah Stewart (1999)

A Bouquet of Babies, with Stella Bagwell and Paula Detmer Riggs (2000)

Mackenzie's Pleasure/Defending His Own, with Beverly Barton (2001)

Come Lie with Me/Part of the Bargain/Yesterday's Love, with Linda Lael Miller and Sherryl Woods (2001)

Finding Home, with Elizabeth Lowell and Kasey Michaels (2001)

Summer Heat, with Lindsay McKenna and Ann Major (2001)

Unlikely Alliances, with Diana Palmer and Sharon Sala (2002)

Overload/If a Man Answers, with Merline Lovelace (2002)

Delivered by Christmas, with Joan Hohl and Sandra Steffen (2002)

What the Heart Can't Hide, with Ann Major and Susan Mallery (2003)

On His Terms, with Allison Leigh (2003)

100 Per Cent Hero, with Suzanne Brockmann (2003)

A Mother's Touch, with Emilie Richards and Sherryl Woods (2005)

Irresistible, with Diana Palmer (2005)

Way Home/Cowboy's Christmas Miracle/Because a Husband Is Forever, with Marie Ferrarella and Anne McAllister (2005)

For Further Information

A Lady of the West review. *Publishers Weekly*, August 10, 1990.

Baker, John F., "Howard Moves to Ballantine." *Publishers Weekly*, September 10, 2001.

Coleman, Sandy, Linda Howard interview, All About Romance, 2004. http://www.likesbooks.com/howard2004.html (viewed February 4, 2008).

Gold, Laurie, Linda Howard interview, All About Romance, 2000. http://www.likesbooks.com/lindahoward.html (viewed February 4, 2008).

Kiss Me While I Sleep review. *Publishers Weekly*, September 6, 2004.

Linda Howard bibliography, Fantastic Fiction. http://www.fantasticfiction.co/uk/h/linda-howard (viewed February 4, 2008).

Linda Howard chat, Writersspace. http://www.writerspace.com/chat/chat081300.html (viewed February 14, 2008).

Linda Howard entry, Contemporary Authors Online. Reproduced in Biography Resource Center. Farmington Hills, MI: Thomson Gale, 2008. http://galenet.galegroupcom/servlet/BioRC (viewed February 4, 2008).

Linda Howard interview, All About Romance, 2004. http://www.likesbooks.com/howard2004.html (viewed February 4, 2008).

Linda Howard interview, Mystery Guild. http://www.mysteryguild.com/doc/full_site_enrollment/author/fse_author_interview.jhtml?authorId=10030468 (viewed February 4, 2008).

Linda Howard profile, Fantastic Fiction. http://www.fantasticfiction.co/uk/linda-howard (viewed February 4, 2008).

Linda Howard Web page, Random House. http://www.randomhouse.com/author/results.pperl?authorid=35941 (viewed February 4, 2008).

Maryles, Daisy, "New in 'Season.'" *Publishers Weekly*, July 30, 2001.

Sova, Cathy, *Open Season* review, Romance Reader. http://www.theromancereader.com/howard-open.html (viewed February 14, 2008).

To Die For review. *Publishers Weekly*, December 6, 2004.

Yock, Malvina, "Humour in Romance Writing," Writing 4 Success. http://www.writing4success.com/romance_writing_hmour_yock.htm (viewed February 14, 2008).

Stephen Hunter

Adventure; Assassins; Espionage; Thrillers: Political

Benchmark Title: *Point of Impact*

Kansas City, Missouri

1946–

About the Author and the Author's Writing

Stephen Hunter has a dual career. Both sides involve words, but otherwise they have nothing in common. He reviews movies. And he shapes action novels, most featuring Bob Lee Swagger, a Vietnam War–era sniper.

Born in Kansas City, Missouri, Hunter grew up with his three siblings in suburban Chicago. His father taught linguistics at Northwestern University. His mother wrote children's books. Stephen knew by age seven that he would become a writer, he just didn't know yet what he would write about. Although guns were forbidden in the home, he developed a boy's fascination with them. After earning a bachelor of arts degree in journalism from Northwestern in 1968, he served for two years in the U.S. Army with the Third Infantry Regiment (Old Guard) in Washington, D.C. Later he wrote for a military publication, the *Pentagram News*.

In 1971, he joined the *Baltimore Sun* staff as a copyreader. From 1973 to 1982, he was the book review editor, then he became the paper's film critic. He moved to the *Washington Post* in 1997 and there earned an American Society of Newspaper Editors Distinguished Writing Award for criticism and a Pulitzer Prize in 2003 for film criticism. Now married to his second wife, he has two children and lives near Baltimore.

Hunter attends two or three film screenings a week and crafts his often vitriolic, always honest, reviews with great attention to language and nuance. One day Hunter went to see a movie—it was before he became a professional critic—and he picked up a gun magazine at a newsstand. It pictured a Smith & Wesson 745 on the cover, and he was hooked on firearms all over again. He purchased a Taurus PT-99; it was the beginning of his gun collection. At the same time, he began to think about a plot for a novel. Having seen a slew of World War II movies, he wondered about the Nazi snipers, often invisible in stories of Yanks overseas. He decided to write about a German marksman at war's end—and *The Master Sniper* came out in 1980.

Hunter wrote several more books, but he wasn't finished with the sniper theme. He read Charles Henderson's *Marine Sniper*, a biography of Sergent Carlos Hathcock, who had ninety-three confirmed career kills as a USMC shooter. What would it be like, after the war, for a man like Hathcock? Hunter wondered.

Creating his own sniper, Bob Lee Swagger, and changing the war to Vietnam, he wrote *Point of Impact* (1993), the first of a series of books about that character, or the character's father, Earl Swagger, a heroic World War II marksman who became a policeman. Earl died when Bob was young, shot by two punks. But their relationship endured.

Hunter's model for the younger Swagger "was Ty Cobb," the author told *American Handgunner* in 2003. "Cobb was a monster in some ways, but he had a father he adored who died when Cobb was young. Everything that Ty Cobb did was to prove himself to his father."

Hunter admits to personal quirks. He is forgetful. He forgets to obey the speed limit, for example, and racks up upwards of $2,000 in parking tickets a year, he said in an interview with *Washington Business Journal*. He eats alone. He disdains conversations with other reviewers. And when day is done, he heads home to write fiction—at least seventy-seven lines a day (from when he wrote longhand on a legal pad) on an antiquated word processor. He takes Prozac every day to knock the edge off.

"I empathize with what I call the 'difficult man,'" Hunter told the *Journal*. "He may be bitter, he may be angry, but there's something about him. He may also be heroic."

It took more than a decade, but Hunter's first Swagger book became the 2007 motion picture *Shooter,* starring Mark Wahlberg. (Another critic wrote the review for the *Post*.)

At the heart of Hunter's books are guns. Long an Ernest Hemingway fan (because of his manly prose and his love of weapons), Hunter also acknowledges Elmer Keith and a generation of gun writers.

"When I'm writing and when I'm shooting, I can get into a very deep level of concentration very quickly," the author told *Baltimore Sun* reporter Mary Carole McCauley. "It's not about power. It's not about sex, and it's not about ego. If anything, it's a sense of anti-self. When I'm in the zone, I'm sort of working on liberating my subconscious. It's a vacation from being Steve."

 # Works by the Author

The Master Sniper (1980)
The Second Saladin (1982)
The Spanish Gambit (1985), also issued as *Tapestry of Spies* (1997)
Target (1985)
The Day before Midnight (1989)
Dirty White Boys (1994)

Bob Lee Swagger Series

Point of Impact (1993)
Black Light (1996)
Time to Hunt (1998)
The 47th Samurai (2007)
Night of Thunder (2008)

Earl Swagger Series

Hot Springs (2000)
Pale Horse Coming (2001)
Havana (2003)

Nonfiction

Violent Screen: A Critic's 13 Years on the Front Lines of Movie Mayhem (1995)
American Gunfight: The Plot to Kill President Truman—and the Shoot-Out That Stopped It, with John Bainbridge Jr. (2005)
Now Playing at the Valencia: Pulitzer Prize-Winning Essays on Movies (2005)

Adaptations in Other Media

Shooter (2007), motion picture based on *Point of Impact*

For Further Information

American Gunfight review. *Publishers Weekly*, October 3, 2005.

Black Light review. *Publishers Weekly,* April 29, 1996.

Conroy, Robert, *The 47th Samurai* review. *Library Journal*, August 1, 2007.

Lohr, Greg A., "A 'Difficult Man.'" *Washington Business Journal*, September 28, 2001.

"Make Mine a Thompson!: *American Handgunner* Interview." *American Handgunner*, March 2003.

McCauley, Mary Carole, "Bullets in His Head." *Baltimore Sun*, March 11, 2007.

Stephen Hunter entry, Contemporary Authors Online, reproduced in Biography Resource Center, Farmington Hills, MI: Thomson Gale, 2007.

Unofficial Stephen Hunter Web site. http://www.stephenhunter.net (viewed November 14, 2008)

Greg Iles

Crime-Suspense; Espionage; Thrillers: Political, Serial Killers

Benchmark Title: *24 Hours*

Stuttgart, Germany

1960–

About the Author and the Author's Writing

Greg Iles abandoned his career as a rock guitarist and singer when his first thriller, *Spandau Phoenix*, found a publisher in 1992. But it wasn't until he was invited to play with Rock Bottom Remainders, the all-author band that includes Stephen King, Ridley Pearson, Amy Tan, Scott Turow, and others, several years later, that he knew he had made it as a writer.

Iles was born in West Germany in 1960, where his father was physician in charge of the medical clinic at the U.S. Embassy. When the family moved to Natchez, Mississippi, Iles became captain of the football team and joined the National Honor Society. In 1983, he graduated from the University of Mississippi. Iles still lives in that community with his dentist wife and their two daughters.

Once out of college, Iles worked as an X-ray and lab technician for his father before establishing the road band Frankly Scarlet, which toured extensively. Too extensively—upward of 50 weeks a year—to be conducive to married life. He quit and dove into writing a Nazi Germany novel, *Spandau Phoenix*, about how Hitler henchman Rudolf Hess placed a look-alike in Spandau Prison and escaped to South America to plot a new assault on Jews.

Iles found a ready audience for his alternate history novels, including *Black Cross*, about a secret Nazi weapon, but he soon stretched in other directions. "I would say that almost every book I've ever done has been a departure for me," he said in a BookPage interview with Jay Lee MacDonald. "The formula today is basically to re-write your last book. I just follow my nose; I write about what interests me each year. I don't put a governor on my imagination."

Mortal Fear (1997), for example, is about women who disappear from an online sex service. Chief suspect and techno-geek Harper Cole races to find the psychopathic killer. "In prose that is both articulate and literate, Iles is beguiling and suspenseful in this twisting, turning plot," said John B. Padgett on Mississippi Writers Page.

Iles has proven prescient; his *Mortal Fear* plot anticipated actual killings that grew out of chatroom exchanges, and two months after *Black Cross* came out, the gas Sarin that it describes was used in an attack in a Japanese subway.

198

24 Hours is a suspense tale about the abduction of a five-year-old girl with diabetes and the parents' race to find her before her insulin wears off. Iles wrote the first and third drafts of the screenplay, which was filmed as *Trapped*.

Sleep No More introduces a supernatural element to the story of a geologist who becomes obsessed with a woman he sees at his daughter's soccer game.

Recent Iles books are described as "southern Gothic," stories of small-town families stripped to reveal long-held secrets, violence, incest, and racism. "I deal with the human psychology and evil," the author told Paul Harris in Guardian Unlimited. "They are my twin issues."

Natchez prosecutor Penn Cage has appeared in two Iles novels, and the author has said on his Web site he has the plot for a third. Iles said that Natchez and environs has the feel, the authenticity he needed for *The Quiet Game* (1999), in which the main character seeks comfort after his wife's death. To his surprise, Cage enters a hornet's nest. His father is being blackmailed. The town harbors a dark secret involving the murder of a black Korean War veteran thirty years before. And there are things about his own past Cage doesn't know.

The second Cage book, *Turning Angel* (2005), may have come a little too close to telling stories about his own neighborhood. Or so Iles said on his Web site: "It's the Peyton Place phenomenon, in which a small town turns on the writer that it formerly embraced, for spilling what the town believes to be its darkest secrets." In this case, he suggested sexual abuse in leading families.

For *True Evil* (2006), Iles crafted the story of Dr. Chris Shepard, who is alerted by FBI agent Alexandra Morse that his wife may be plotting his demise.

"If Iles has a trademark, a single literary feature that identifies him, it's his intriguing, ordinary-people-in-extraordinary-situations premises that hook readers immediately, forcing us to read on," said *Booklist* reviewer David Pitt.

Iles's brand of Southern gothic thriller have been translated into a dozen languages and published in some twenty countries, and the latest, *Devil's Punchbowl* (2009), again featuring Penn Cage in a tale of double-cross and racial tension, can only find more fans.

Works by the Author

Spandau Phoenix (1992)
Black Cross (1995)
Mortal Fear (1996)
24 Hours (2000)
Dead Sleep (2001)
Sleep No More (2002)
Trapped (2002)
The Quiet Game/24 Hours/Dead Sleep (2003), omnibus
Footprints of God (2003)
Dark Matter (2004)
Blood Memory (2005)
True Evil (2006)
Third Degree (2007)

Penn Cage Series

The Quiet Game (1999)
Turning Angel (2005)
Devil's Punchbowl (2009)

Screenplays

Trapped (2002), motion picture based on *24 Hours*

For Further Information

Greg Iles profile, Meet the Writers, Barnes & Noble. http://www. barnesandnoble.com/writers/writeredetails.asp?z=y&cid=968057 (viewed October 13, 2007).

Greg Iles Web site. http://www.gregiles.com/ (viewed November 14, 2008).

Harris, Paul, "Evil under the Sun," Guardian Unlimited, March 13, 2005. http:// books.guardian.co/uk/departments/crime/story/0,6000,1436351,00,html (viewed October 13, 2007).

MacDonald, Jay Lee, "Greg Iles Strikes a New Chord: Former Rock Musician Crafts Haunting Suspense," BookPage. http://www.bookpage.com/0207bp/ greg_iles.html (viewed October 13, 2007).

Padgett, John B., "Greg Iles," Mississippi Writers Page. http://www.olemiss.edu/ depts/english/ms-writers/dir/iles_greg/ (viewed October 22, 2007).

Pitt, David, *True Evil* review. *Booklist*, December 15, 2006.

Jerry B. Jenkins

Photo credit: Mikel Healy Photography

Adventure; Crime; Fantasy; Christian Fiction; Science Fiction

Benchmark Series: <u>Left Behind</u>

Kalamazoo, Michigan

1949–

About the Author and the Author's Writing

When we first meet airline pilot Rayford Steele, in the novel *Left Behind*, he's mulling over his wife Irene's newfound interest in a small Christian congregation. It makes him uncomfortable. "Hers was not a church where people gave you the benefit of the doubt, assumed the best about you, and let you be," we read. "People there had actually asked him, to his face, what God was doing in his life."

Rayford would soon discover his relationship with God, in the course of more than a dozen rapid-paced adventures that tested his faith. These adventures formed the apocalyptic <u>Left Behind</u> series by Jerry B. Jenkins (who writes the books) and Tim LaHaye (who guides the biblical philosophy). After millions of people vanish during the Rapture, chaos reigns under the harsh dictator, Nicolae the antichrist. Christians struggle to survive until the arrival of the King of Kings. Rayford Steele is front and center in this series by Jenkins and LaHaye that transformed Christian fiction into a literature on steroids. They sold upwards of 65 million copies of their books and dominated the best-seller lists. They crafted offshoot series and series for juvenile readers.

"It's a thrill to be involved in fiction that not only entertains, but also changes lives," Jenkins says on the <u>Left Behind</u> Web page.

The writer's second agenda—entertaining readers had to come first—was to leave them with a strong Christian message. It is a message LaHaye, founder and president of Tim LaHaye Ministries, frequently preached: What will be the fate of Christians with the arrival of "end times" as predicted in the Book of Revelation? LaHaye's reputation, and his prophecy expertise, brought the <u>Left Behind</u> books to notice among both Christian and secular readers.

Jenkins was born in Kalamazoo, Michigan, in 1949. He attended Moody Bible Institute, Loop College, and William Rainey Harper College. In 1971, he married

201

Dianna Louise Whiteford. Because he suffered a sports-related injury in high school, Jenkins covered games for his school paper rather than pursuing sports himself, which led him eventually to became a journalist.

Sports writing, he said in an interview with C. J. Darlington for TitleTrakk.com, honed his ability "to work fast and get to the heart of the story in the first sentence. It was the pattern of the day to tell all the facts up front—the who, what, when, where, and why. I was taught to start with the why."

He became executive editor for *Moody Monthly* in 1973 and went on to become editor and then director of Moody Press. In 1985, he became vice president of Moody Bible Institute's Publishing Branch. In the meantime, he wrote articles for *Reader's Digest, Parade,* and Christian periodicals. He also wrote or cowrote a number of sports and other biographies and non-fiction books, including Dr. Billy Graham's memoirs. He wrote popular Christian fiction series including the Jennifer Grey mysteries and the Baker Street Sports Club books. Today he scripts the syndicated Gil Thorp daily newspaper comic strip and has a family production company that is actively turning his prose into live-action movies. In addition, he mentors an up-and-coming generation of Christian writers with his how-to book on writing.

Jenkins explains in an Amazon.com interview what he believes has helped make the Left Behind series so popular: "The cardinal rules of fiction call for appealing characters, a sense of tension and expectancy and a page-turning quality.... I do believe there is a hunger for God among the general population and a curiosity over what the Bible says and what some people believe is going to happen at the end of the world."

Jenkins has said he feels thousands of readers are looking over his shoulder as he works. While the Left Behind series has a biblical direction, Jenkins had no detailed outline as he wrote the individual books. Rather, he immersed himself in LaHaye's directions. "I write as a process of discovery," he said in *Insight on the News*, "so I write to see what happens. Sometimes I'm surprised and shocked when somebody ends up dead."

The series was originally envisioned as a single book. But as Jenkins began writing, it became obvious that there was more to be said. The book became six, then twelve books, with three more prequels and one sequel—sixteen in all.

Some critics condemned the series for what they saw as its intolerance. *Kingdom Come*, for example, finds the world's population gathered at Jesus' feet. Rayford is there, and he observes to an old man named Chaim that there are two groups. "Actually three," the old man said. "Those are the 'goats' over there, the followers of Antichrist who somehow survived to this point. You are among the 'sheep' on this side, but I represent the third group. I am part of Jesus' 'brethren,' the chosen people of God whom the sheep befriended. We are the Jews who will go into the Millennium as believers, because of people like you."

Gershom Gorenberg in *American Prospect* said the books "promote conspiracy theories; they demonize proponents of arms control, ecumenicalism, abortion rights and everyone else disliked by the Christian right; and they justify assassination as a political tool. Their anti-Jewishness is exceeded by their anti-Catholicism. Most basically, they reject the very idea of open, democratic debate."

Time writer John Cloud theorized "in this volatile moment [after September 11], many people are starting to read the Left Behind books not as novels but as tomorrow's newspapers. LaHaye believes that the Scriptures lay out a precise timetable for the end of the world, and the Left Behind books let us in on the chronology."

Michelle Goldberg at Salon.com found the books' politics troubling and says they provide "a narrative and a theological rationale for a whole host of perplexing conservative policies, from the White House's craven decision to cut off aid to the United Nations Family Planning Fund to America's surreally casual mobilization for an invasion of Baghdad—a city that is, in the <u>Left Behind</u> books, Satan's headquarters."

With the <u>Left Behind</u> series ended, Jenkins has found plenty of new projects, including new fictionalized biographies of the four Gospels, a political crime novel, *Riven*, and directorship of the Christian Writers Guild.

 Selected Works by the Author

Other books by the author may be found at his Web site: http://www.jerryjenkins.com.

The Operative (1987)

Rookie (1991)

The Deacon's Woman (1992), short stories

'Twas the Night Before (1997)

Though None Go with Me (2000)

Hometown Legend (2001)

American Leather (2001)

The Youngest Hero (2002)

Underground Zealot (2004)

Holding Heaven, with Ron DiCianni (2005)

Midnight Clear, with Dallas Jenkins (2007)

Riven (2008)

<u>Left Behind Series</u> with Tim LaHaye

Left Behind: A Novel of the Earth's Last Days (1995)

Tribulation Forces: The Continuing Drama of Those Left Behind (1996)

Nicolae: The Rise of Antichrist (1997)

Soul Harvest: The World Takes Sides (1998)

Apollyon: The Destroyer Is Unleashed (1999)

Assassins: Assignment Jerusalem, Target-Antichrist (1999)

The Indwelling: The Best Takes Possession (2000)

The Mark: The Beast Rules the World (2000)

The Desecration: Antichrist Takes the Throne (2001)

The Remnant: On the Brink of Armageddon (2002)

Armageddon: The Coming Battle of the Ages (2003)

Glorious Appearing: The End of Days (2004)

Prequel: The Rising (2005)

Prequel: The Regime (2005)

Prequel: The Rapture (2006)

Sequel: Kingdom Come: The Final Victory (2007)

There have also been five <u>Left Behind</u> graphic novels and five <u>Tribulation Force</u> graphic novels.

<u>Left Behind Political Series</u> by Neesa Hart

End of State (2003)
Impeachable Offense (2004)
Necessary Evils (2005)

<u>Left Behind Military Series</u> by Mel Odam

Apocalypse Dawn: The Earth's Last Days: The Battle Begins (2003)
Apocalypse Crucible (2004)
Apocalypse Burning (2004)

<u>Soon Series</u>

Soon: The Beginning of the End (2004)
Silenced: The Wrath of God Descends (2005)
Shadowed: Underground Zealot (2006)

Young Adult Fiction

<u>Left Behind: The Kids Series</u> with Tim LaHaye
The Vanishings (1998)
Second Chance (1998)
Through the Flames (1998)
Facing the Future (1998)
Nicolae High (1999)
The Underground (1999)
Busted (1999)
Death Strike (2000)
The Search (2000)
On the Run (2000)
Into the Storm (2000)
Earthquake! (2000)
The Showdown (2001)
Judgment Day (2001)
Battling the Commander (2001)
Fire from Heaven (2001)
Terror in the Stadium (2001)
Darkening Skies (2002)
The Attack of Appolyon (2002)
A Dangerous Plan (2002)
Secrets of New Babylon (2002)

Escape from New Babylon (2002)
Horsemen of Terror (2002)
Uplink from the Underground (2003)
Death at the Gala (2003)
The Beast Arises (2003)
Wildfire (2003)
The Mark of the Beast (2003)
Breakout (2003)
Murder in the Holy Place (2003)
Escape to Masada (2003)
War of the Dragon (2003)
Attack on Petra (2004)
Bounty Hunters (2004)
The Rise of False Messiahs (2004)
Ominous Choices (2004)
Heat Wave (2004)
The Perils of Love (2004)
The Road to War (2004)
Triumphant Return (2004)

<u>Worming Series</u> with Chris Fabry
The Book of the King (2007)
The Changeling (2007)
The Author's Blood (2008)
The Minions of Time (2008)
The Author's Rood (2009)

Motion Picture Adaptations

Left Behind: The Movie (2000), television film
American Leather (2002), television film
Hometown Legend (2002), television film
Midnight Clear (2007), television film

For Further Information

Cherry, Sheila, "Tour Guides to the Tribulation." *Insight on the News* (August 26, 2002).

Cloud, John, "Meet the Prophet: How an Evangelist and Conservative Activist Turned Prophecy into a Fiction Juggernaut." *Time,* July 1, 2002.

"Conversation with Jerry Jenkins & Tim LaHaye," FamilyChristian.com. http://www.familychristian.com/books/jenkins.lahaye.asp (viewed April 2, 2003).

Darlington, C.J., Jerry Jenkins interview, TitleTrakk. http://www.titletrakk.com/jerry_jenkins_interview.html (viewed Oct. 11, 2007)

"God in the End Times: An Interview with Jerry B. Jenkins," Amazon. http://www.amazon.com/exec/obidos/tg/feature/-/39251/104-3961905-2055953 (viewed April 2, 2003).

Goldberg, Michelle, "Fundamentally Unsound," Salon. http://dir.salon.com/story/books/feature/2002/07/29/left_behind/index1.html (viewed October 11, 2007)

Gorenberg, Gershom, "Intolerance: The Bestseller." *American Prospect,* September, 23, 2002.

Jerry B. Jenkins Web page. http://www.jerryjenkins.com (viewed November 14, 2008).

Left Behind Web page. http://www.leftbehind.com (viewed October 11, 2007).

Meet the Writers: Jerry B. Jenkins & Tim LaHaye, Barnes & Noble. http://www.barnesandnoble.com/writers/writerdetails.asp?userid=0H4KV3ZHMT&cid=968101#bio (viewed April 2, 2008).

Potter, Megan, "An Interview with Jerry B. Jenkins, Co-Author of the Left Behind Series of Books," Writing Corner. http://writingcorner.com/tips/writers-life/jerry_b_jenkins.htm (viewed April 20, 2003).

Iris Johansen

Adventure; Crime-Suspense; Romance; Romantic Suspense

Benchmark Series: Eve Duncan

Georgia

1938–

About the Author and the Author's Writing

Forensics sculptor Eve Duncan, heroine of Iris Johansen's best-selling crime series, grapples with her personal anxieties even as she strives to identify faceless victims. Eve was raised by a drug addict mother. Her marriage disintegrated, and her daughter, Bonnie, was murdered, although the body was never found. In the first book in this series, *The Killing Game* (1999), Eve has taken refuge on a Tahitian island, until her friend Detective Joe Quinn reports the discovery of a mass grave. One of the bodies may be Bonnie's. Then a stalker gives Eve more pressing worries.

Another Johansen heroine, Nell, survives the violent murder of her family and, only with the help of Nicholas, recovers her mental balance, undergoes reconstructive surgery to restore her appearance, and pursues the drug dealer villain.

The author was born in Georgia in 1938. She worked for a time for an airline. She is married and lives in Atlanta. Daughter Tamara Brooking is her research assistant. Son Roy is a screenwriter and novelist. She began writing paperback romance novels when her children left home for college. From the first Loveswept books, and entries in the Shamrock and Delaney series (some books are by other writers), she honed her craft. In 1991, she began to write historical romances, such as the Wind Dancer trilogy, books set in sixteenth-century Italy and France. Then she began to write romantic suspense. *The Ugly Duckling* (1996), her third hardcover, ratcheted her into a higher publishing echelon alongside Nora Roberts.

Johansen has a rigid writing regimen, beginning each morning by nine and not quitting until she has finished ten pages minimum. "It depends on the flow, the research, and the pace at which the characters are moving the story," she said in a Bookreporter interview in 2005. "There are times when the story is streaking like a bullet. Then I just hang on and stay with it."

Johansen makes each character distinct. Discussing her series heroine on her Web site, she said, "Eve's desire to identify and bring 'the lost ones' home was based on her background and character. Her love for her murdered daughter, Bonnie, and the knowledge that she had never found her was a constant torment and spurred Eve to help other parents in similar situations."

Johansen has plenty of fresh ideas and fresh characters. But she hates to give up a good one. She began to write the 2003 novel *Dead Aim* before the events of September 11, 2001, and quickly incorporated the national tragedy into the plot. The hero, Alex Graham, photographs disaster sites—natural and manmade—and stumbles on a sinister plot involving a revolution. The author incorporated other previous characters, Sarah Patrick (from *The Search*), handler of rescue dogs, and commando Judd Morgan (from *One to Trust*).

Johansen brought a young character from *The Killing Game*, Jane MacGuire, onto center stage in *Countdown* (2006). MacGuire, now the adopted daughter of Duncan and her husband Quinn, eludes a ruthless killer through her own devices.

Characters are important to Johansen. "I'm an author who has a great deal of difficulty outlining, knowing where the story's going—I have no idea," she said in an interview with Adam Dunn for *Publishers Weekly*. "I let the story tell itself. And when you're writing thrillers, that's a real challenge."

Which isn't to say the author doesn't enjoy her craft. Each book has its pleasures, she told BookBrowse. "Usually it is near the climax when everything is moving tornado-fast and I am carried along with it. However, there are times when I'm just as excited when I get some complicated bit of research right and fell I did a good job making that part of the story interesting."

 ## Works by the Author

The Lady and the Unicorn (1983)

No Red Roses (1984)

Return to Santa Flores (1984), sequel to *No Red Roses*

Blue Velvet (1985)

Forever Dream (1985)

White Satin (1985)

And the Desert Blooms (1986)

York the Renegade: Delaneys, the Shamrock Trinity (1986)

Til the End of Time (1986)

Golden Valkyrie/Trustworthy Redhead (1986), omnibus

Matilda, the Adventuress: Delaneys of Killaroo (1987)

Spellbinder (1987)

Star Light, Star Bright (1987)

This Fierce Splendor: Delaneys of Killaroo (1988)

One Touch of Topaz (1988)

Wicked Jake Darcy (1989)

Tender Savage (1990)

Unexpected Song (1990)

Bronzed Hawk (1990)

Reluctant Lark (1990)

Stormy Vows (1990)

Tempest at Sea (1990)

Winter Bride (1992)
Tiger Prince (1992)
The Delaney Christmas Carol, with Kay Hooper and Fayrene Preston (1992)
Star-Spangled Bride (1993)
Magnificent Rogue (1993)
Beloved Scoundrel (1994)
Midnight Warrior (1994)
Dark Rider (1995)
Lion's Bride (1996)
The Ugly Duckling (1996)
Long after Midnight (1997)
And Then You Die (1998)
The Search (2000)
Final Target (2001)
No One to Trust (2002)
Fatal Tide (2003)
Dead Aim (2003)
Firestorm (2004)
On the Run (2005)
Killer Dreams (2006)
Pandora's Daughter (2007)
Stormy Vows/Tempest at Sea (2007), omnibus
Quicksand (2008)
Silent Thunder (2008), with Roy Johansen
Dark Summer (2008)
The Treasure (2009), sequel to *Lion's Bride*

Clanad Series

Across the River of Yesterday (1987)
Last Bridge Home (1987)
Magnificent Folly (1989)
Tough Man to Tame (1991)

Delaneys: The Untamed Years Series

Golden Flames, with Kay Hooper (1988)
Satin Ice (1988)
Wild Silver (1988)

Eve Duncan Series

Face of Deception (1998)
The Killing Game (1999)

Body of Lies (2002)
Blind Alley (2004)
Countdown (2005)
Stalemate (2006)

Sedikhan Series

Capture the Rainbow (1984)
Golden Valkyrie (1984)
Touch the Horizon (1984)
Trustworthy Redhead (1984)
Summer Smile 1985)
Everlasting (1986)
Blue Skies and Shining Promises (1988)
Man from Half Moon Bay (1988)
Strong, Hot Winds (1988)
Notorious (1990)
Golden Barbarian (1991)

Wind Dancer Series

Wind Dancer (1991)
Storm Winds (1991)
Reap the Wind (1991)

For Further Information

Dunn, Adam, "Taking *Dead Aim*: Iris Johansen." *Publishers Weekly*, May 5, 2003.

Fitzgerald, Carol, Joe Hartlaub, and Wiley Saichek, Iris Johansen interview, Bookreporter. http://www.bookreporter.com/authors/au-johansen-iris.asp (viewed November 2, 2007).

Harris, Karen, *Killing Game* review, *Booklist*, August 2000.

Iris Johansen interview, BookBrowse. http://www.bookbrowse.com/author_interviews/full/index.cfm?author_number=369 viewed November 1, 2007).

Iris Johansen Web site. http://www.irisjohansen.com/ (viewed November 14, 2008).

Fitzgerald, Carol, Joe Hartlaub, and Wiley Saichek, Iris Johansen interview, Bookreporter.com. http://www.bookreporter.com/authors/au-johansen-iris.asp (viewed November 2, 2007).

Melnick, Sheri, *Stalemate* review. *Library Journal*, December 1, 2006.

William W. Johnstone

Adventure; Horror; Science Fiction; Western

Benchmark Series: <u>Ashes</u>

Missouri

1938–2004

Photo credit: Jo Johnstone Smith

About the Author and the Author's Writing

He's a retired soldier and mercenary now making his living as a writer. He's no friend to the government because of his hypercritical best-selling adventure novels.

For example, one of his characters, Ben Raines, learns of a terrorist plot to take over the country. At the same time, a deadly disease begins its relentless spread from city to city. Concerned about his family, not to mention the rest of mankind, Raines melds an unlikely "army" of bikers, isolationists, and militiamen—"Raines' Rebels"—to counter the dual plagues.

That's the gist of William W. Johnstone's thirty-four-book <u>Ashes Series</u> that began in 1983 and was reprinted beginning in 2008. The novels "are among the most realistic and disturbing … you need not concern yourself about running out of stimuli to rob you of a good night's sleep," said reviewer Richard Curtis.

When one crisis is averted, another arises. Raines—and the author—has little faith in the American government. As one character says in *Destiny in the Ashes* (2001), "'You don't repeal the laws of nature by passing man-made-laws, Anna. Man is an animal just like the lion or tiger in the jungle. When push comes to shove, he'll take what he can in whatever way he can in order to survive.'"

Author Johnstone is one of the last of the pulpish, gritty authors agile in several genres, a master of multiple series. He persevered when the dozens and dozens of action, secret agent, cowboy, and weird villains who reigned in paperback originals in the 1960s and 1970s succumbed to a more demanding audience. Johnstone, whose tradition is being carried on by J. A. Johnstone (a house name), offered pure escape, violence, action, gunplay, and a dose of conservative politics.

"The action scenes are well written," said Wes Lukowsky, discussing another series book, *Scream of Eagles*, for Booklist, "and there are actual historical figures scattered about, but ultimately this is the literary Western equivalent of the <u>Die Hard</u> films."

William Wallace Johnstone was born in 1938 in southern Missouri, the youngest of four children of a minister and a school teacher. He never finished high school. He attempted to join the French Foreign Legion, but was rejected for his age—fifteen. He worked in a carnival and was a deputy sheriff before he joined the U.S. Army in the late 1950s. In 1970, he began to write fiction, although his first book did not appear until a decade later. When *The Devil's Kiss* came out in 1980, Johnstone left radio broadcasting where he had worked for sixteen years and began to write books full time. Radio, he said, allowed him to nurture and shape his storytelling ability.

He wrote suspense and horror novels, apocalyptic thrillers, Westerns, even a romance—nearly two hundred books. All but two appeared under his name; he used William Mason for the others. Since his death in 2004 in Louisiana, his multiple series —and some new ones—have been carried on by Fred Austin and, now, J. A. Johnstone, a house name.

In a letter on his Web site, Johnstone expressed pride in his series heroes, from terrorist fighter John Barrone in the <u>Code Name</u> books to Ben Raines in the futuristic <u>Ashes</u> tales or Smoke Jensen in the <u>Mountain Man</u> sagas. "I try to create the kinds of believable characters that we can all identify with, real people who face tough challenges," he said. "When one of my creations blasts an enemy into the middle of next week, you can be damn sure he had a good reason."

 # Works by the Author

The Sanction (1981)

The Initiation (1982)

Bloodland (1986)

Death Master (1986)

Blood Valley (1988)

What the Heart Knows (1996)

Breakdown (1997)

Ordeal (1998)

Vengeance Is Mine (2005)

Doubtful, Wyoming (2006)

Lost Trails (2007)

Remember the Alamo, by J. A. Johnstone (2007)

<u>Ashes Series</u>

Out of the Ashes (1983)

Fire in the Ashes (1983)

Anarchy in the Ashes (1984)

Blood in the Ashes (1985)

Alone in the Ashes (1985)

Wind in the Ashes (1986)

Smoke from the Ashes (1987)

Danger in the Ashes (1988)

Valor in the Ashes (1988)
Trapped in the Ashes (1989)
Death in the Ashes (1990)
Survival in the Ashes (1990)
Fury in the Ashes (1991)
Courage in the Ashes (1991)
Terror in the Ashes (1992)
Vengeance in the Ashes (1993)
Battle in the Ashes (1993)
Flames from the Ashes (1993)
Treason in the Ashes (1994)
D-Day in the Ashes (1994)
Betrayal in the Ashes (1996)
Chaos in the Ashes (1996)
Slaughter in the Ashes (1997)
Judgment in the Ashes (1997)
Ambush in the Ashes (1998)
From the Ashes: America Reborn (1998)
Triumph in the Ashes (1998)
Hatred in the Ashes (1999)
Standoff in the Ashes (1999)
Crisis in the Ashes (2000)
Tyranny in the Ashes (2000)
Warriors from the Ashes (2001)
Destiny in the Ashes (2001)
Enemy in the Ashes (2002)
Escape from the Ashes (2003)

Black Ops Series

American Jihad, by Fred Austin (2006)

Blood Bond Series

Blood Bond (1989)
Brotherhood of the Gun (1990)
Gunsight Crossing (1991)
Gunsmoke and Gold (1992)
Devil Creek Crossfire (1992)
Shootout at Gold Creek (1993)
San Angelo Showdown (1994)
Death in Snake Creek (1994)
Slaughter Trail (2006)

The Hanging Road, by J. A. Johnstone (2007)
Texas Gundown, by J. A. Johnstone (2008)
Ride for Vengeance, by J. A. Johnstone (2008)

Blood Valley Series

Blood Valley, by J. A. Johnstone (2009)

Cat's Series

Cat's Cradle (1986)
Cat's Eye (1989)

Code Name Series

Payback (2000)
Survival (2000)
Death (2001)
Coldfire (2002)
Quickstrike (2003)
Extreme Prejudice (2004)
Kill Zone (2005)

Devil's Series

The Devil's Kiss (1980)
The Devil's Heart (1983)
The Devil's Touch (1985)
The Devil's Cat (1987)
The Devil's Laughter (1992)

Dog Team Series

The Last of the Dog Team (1980)
The Return of the Dog Team, by Fred Austin (2005)
Revenge of the Dog Team, by J. A. Johnstone (2009)

Eagles Series

Eyes of Eagles (1993)
Dreams of Eagles (1994)
Talons of Eagles (1996)
Scream of Eagles (1997)
Rage of Eagles (1998)
Song of Eagles (1999)
Cry of Eagles (1999)
Blood of Eagles (2000)

Destiny of Eagles (2004)
Revenge of Eagles (2005)
Pride of Eagles, by J. A. Johnstone (2006)
Crusade of Eagles, by J. A. Johnstone (2007)
Thunder of Eagles, by J. A. Johnstone (2008)

First Mountain Man (Preacher) Series

The First Mountain Man (1991)
Blood on the Divide (1992)
Absaroka Ambush (1993)
Forty Guns West (1993)
Cheyenne Challenge (1995)
Preacher and the Mt. Caesar (1995)
Blackfoot Messiah (1996)
Preacher (2002)
Preacher's Peace (2003)
Preacher's Justice (2004)
Preacher's Journey (2005)
Preacher's Fortune, by Fred Austin (2006)
Preacher's Quest, by J. A. Johnstone (2007)
Preacher's Showdown, by J. A. Johnstone (2008)
Preacher's Pursuit, by J. A. Johnstone (2009)

Fury Series

A Town Called Fury, by Fred Austin (2006)
Hard Country, by J. A. Johnstone (2007)
Judgment Day, by J. A. Johnstone (2007)

Invasion USA Series

Invasion USA, by Fred Austin (2006)
Border War, by J. A. Johnstone (2006)

Jacknife Series

Jacknife, by J. A. Johnstone (2008)

Last Gunfighter Series

The Drifter (2000)
Reprisal (2000)
Ghost Valley (2001)
The Forbidden (2001)
Showdown (2001)

Impostor (2002)
Rescue (2003)
The Burning (2003)
No Man's Land (2004)
Manhunt (2004)
Violent Sunday (2005)
Renegades (2005)
Savage Country (2006)
The Devil's Legion (2006)
Avenger, by J. A. Johnstone (2007)
Hell Town, by J. A. Johnstone (2007)
Ambush Alley, by J. A. Johnstone (2008)
Killing Ground, by J. A. Johnstone (2008)

Last Mountain Man (Smoke Jensen) Series

The Last Mountain Man (1985)
Return of the Mountain Man (1986)
Trail of the Mountain Man (1987)
Revenge of the Mountain Man (1988)
Journey of the Mountain Man (1989)
Law of the Mountain Man (1989)
War of the Mountain Man (1990)
Code of the Mountain Man (1991)
Pursuit of the Mountain Man (1991)
Courage of the Mountain Man (1992)
Blood of the Mountain Man (1992)
Fury of the Mountain Man (1993)
Rage of the Mountain Man (1994)
Cunning of the Mountain Man (1994)
Power of the Mountain Man (1995)
Spirit of the Mountain Man (1996)
Ordeal of the Mountain Man (1996)
Triumph of the Mountain Man (1997)
Vengeance of the Mountain Man (1997)
Honor of the Mountain Man (1998)
Battle of the Mountain Man (1998)
Pride of the Mountain Man (1998)
Creed of the Mountain Man (1999)
Guns of the Mountain Man (1999)
Heart of the Mountain Man (2000)
Justice of the Mountain Man (2000)

Valor of the Mountain Man (2001)
Warpath of the Mountain Man (2002)
Trek of the Mountain Man (2002)
Quest of the Mountain Man (2003)
Ambush of the Mountain Man (2003)
Wrath of the Mountain Man (2004)
Destiny of the Mountain Man, by Fred Austin (2005)
Betrayal of the Mountain Man, by J. A. Johnstone (2006)
Rampage of the Mountain Man, by J. A. Johnstone (2007)
Violence of the Mountain Man, by J. A. Johnstone (2008)

Last Rebel Series

Survivor (2004)

Mountain Man (Matt Jensen) Series

Matt Jensen, by J. A. Johnstone (2007)
Deadly Trail, by J. A. Johnstone (2008)
Purgatory, by J. A. Johnstone (2008)

Rig Warrior Series

Rig Warrior (1987)
Wheels of Death (1988)
Eighteen-Wheel Avenger (1988)

Satan Influenced Series

A Crying Shame (1983)
The Nursery (1985)
Rockinghorse (1986)
Jack-in-the-Box (1986)
Sweet Dreams (1986)
*Wolfsban*e (1987)
Baby Grand, with Joe Keene (1987)
Toy Cemetery (1987)
The Uninvited (1988)
Sandman (1988)
Carnival (1989)
Darkly the Thunder (1990)
Watchers in the Woods (1991)
Them (1992)
Bats (1993)
Night Mask (1994)

Hunted (1995)
Prey (1996)
Rockabilly Hell (1995)
Rockabilly Limbo (1996)
Blood Oath (1999)

Written as William Mason

Dagger (1984)
Eagle Down (1985)

Nonfiction Written as William W. Johnstone

From the Ashes: America Reborn—The Complete Guide to the Ashes Series and the Tri-State Manifesto (1998)

For Further Information

Curtis, Richard, "Ashes Series by William W. Johnstone," E-Reads. http://www.erreads.com/labels/Ashes.html (viewed January 17, 2008).

Lukowsky, Wes, *Scream of Eagles* review. *Booklist*, March 1, 1996.

William W. Johnstone entry, Wikipedia. http://en.wikipedia.org/wiki/William_W._Johnstone (viewed January 17, 2008).

William W. Johnstone Web site. http://www.williamjohnstone.net/ (viewed November 14, 2008).

Alex (Sharon) Kava

Crime-Suspense: Serial Killers

Benchmark Series: <u>Maggie O'Dell</u>

Silver Creek, Nebraska

Birth date not disclosed

Photo courtesy of the author

About the Author and the Author's Writing

Sharon M. Kava had just graduated from college and begun a job with a small-town Nebraska newspaper as a copy editor and graphic artist, in autumn 1983, when a dreadful crime struck the community. A boy disappeared. When his body was found, it was obviously murder. A second boy disappeared. Hunters soon discovered his body, not far from the Platte River. Authorities were convinced someone from the area had committed the crimes; more than three months later, an enlisted man at Offutt Air Force Base was arrested. He confessed to the two killings. By the time he was executed, in 1996, Kava had quit her full-time job and planned to write a novel. Having already lived through all the tension and fears of a thriller, she had an instant plot for *A Perfect Evil* (2001), the first book to feature FBI profiler Maggie O'Dell.

"I wanted to write a novel that recreated the terror and panic that surrounds crimes like these," the author said in an interview on her Web site, "[a] place like that, in a sense, is as naïve and innocent as the young boys who were murdered. In that respect, the community becomes a victim as well."

Born and reared in Silver Creek, Nebraska, the child of Polish immigrants, Kava had long thought of becoming a fiction writer. Her parents never encouraged her dream; instead, they pressed her to study hard. Her creativity prevailed in a small way. She wrote several short stories during her teenage years, hiding them from her folks. She attended the College of St. Mary on an art scholarship. To meet expenses, she worked at a hospital in Omaha, cleaning surgical instruments and equipment from the pathology department and morgue. In 1982, she graduated magna cum laude with a bachelor of arts degree in art and English.

After graduating, Kava worked for a newspaper, as well as in advertising and marketing. She established Square One, her own graphic design business, and produced packaging for national clients. She created greeting cards and directed commercials. In 1992, she became director of public relations at College of St. Mary. When she left in 1996, she returned part time to her graphics design work and refinanced her home to find the time to write.

She always knew how hard it would be to find a publisher. Several years earlier, she'd circulated a manuscript and collected some one hundred rejections from agents. But that experience just gave her greater focus and determination. The research was easy. She already knew the story would be based on the one she'd lived through. She fleshed out the details with newspaper files. Her main character quickly formed in her mind: a smart, tough, independent forensic psychologist. A woman.

Kava showed O'Dell little mercy. "When we are pushed to the edge, that's when we show our true character," she said in a *Publishers Weekly* interview. "That's where our values are, where our ideals are, what we believe in."

"This debut thriller pumps the suspense out smoothly … and Maggie is gutsy and appealing as an FBI agent facing constant danger," *Library Journal* reviewer Rebecca Stankowski said.

MIRA published the novel, the first in its new hardcover line. It appeared under the gender-blurred Alex Kava name. Doubleday Book Club picked it up. And her editor wanted a second book. *Split Second* (2001), the next O'Dell crime novel, forced Kava to write at a more brisk pace to meet deadline. There was also the pressure of meeting reader expectations following the success of the first book. This book grew from no particular case but rather from the general traits of many serial murderers. The heroine pursued a second serial killer, Albert Stucky, and came away from her encounter with the killer greatly shaken.

A member of Mystery Writers of America, Sisters in Crime and International Thriller Writers, Kava temporarily abandoned her O'Dell series to put a new heroine, scientist Sabina Galloway, in the sights of a hired killer in an eco-thriller, *Whitewash* (2007).

"I almost always know what my ending will be before I start," the author said in an interview with *Shots* magazine. "Now how I get there is a different journey each time…. I like the idea that my characters can surprise me. Hopefully, they'll surprise my readers, too."

 Works by the Author

One False Move (2004)
Whitewash (2007)

Maggie O'Dell Series

A Perfect Evil (2000)
Split Second (2001)
The Soul Catcher (2003)
At the Stroke of Madness (2003)
A Necessary Evil (2006)

Profile (2007), omnibus includes *Second Split, Soul Catcher,* and *At the Stroke of Madness*

Exposed (2008)

Anthology

Thriller: Stories to Keep You Up All Night, edited by James Patterson (2006), includes "Goodnight, Sweet Mother," an O'Dell story

For Further Information

Alex Kava interview, July 22, 2006. Murderati. http://murderati.typepad.com/murderati/2006/07/on_the_bubble_w_1.html (viewed November 2, 2007).

"Alex Kava Talks to Ali Karim of Shots Ezine." http://www.shotsmag.co.uk/interviews2006./a_kava/a_kava.html (viewed November 2, 2007).

Alex Kava Web site. http://www.alexkava.com/ (viewed November 14, 2008).

Hall, Melissa Mia, "PW Talks with Alex Kava." *Publishers Weekly*, April 23, 2007.

Stankowski, Rebecca House, *A Perfect Evil* review. *Library Journal*, July 2000.

Jonathan Kellerman

Crime-Suspense; Medical

Benchmark Series: <u>Alex Delaware Series</u>

New York, New York

1949–

Photo credit: Jonathan Exley

About the Author and the Author's Writing

Jonathan Kellerman's biggest struggle, as a best-selling author, was to get started—while nurturing a medical career and raising a family. "I won a literary award in college but for the next thirteen years I was a failed writer with a good day job—clinical psychologist/med school professor," he said in a Gather interview. "I believe the common thread between both of my jobs is a fascination with human behavior, in general, and the dark side, in specific."

Kellerman was born in 1949 in New York City, the son of an electrical engineer. He grew up in Los Angeles and in 1971 received a bachelor of arts degree from the University of California—Los Angeles. During his undergraduate years, he was a musician, cartoonist, and journalist. In 1973, he received a master's degree and then a Ph.D. in psychology the next year, both from UCLA. A specialist in child psychology, he interned at Children's Hospital of Los Angeles. Kellerman married Faye Marder in 1972. (Faye Kellerman is also a best-selling mystery writer.)

Kellerman established a medical practice and researched the psychological effects of extreme isolation on children for Children's Hospital. Although he published some nonfiction, his first <u>Alex Delaware</u> mystery, *When the Bough Breaks*, didn't come out until 1985. It won Edgar and Anthony awards for best first mystery novel. By then, he had a plethora of material from his practice to provide unusual background to his stories.

The Delaware leaf didn't fall too far from the Kellerman tree. "We're both psychologists, driven and curious and compulsive," he said on his Web site. "However, he's younger, leaner, more athletic, and better-looking. Being a single guy, he can get into the kind of trouble a long-married father of four must avoid. Perhaps he's my Walter Mitty fantasy."

Most of Kellerman's books have been in the Delaware series. To keep the character fresh, the author lets him grow. "I try to tell a great story and characterize well," he told *Publishers Weekly*'s Adam Dunn. "I prefer to write a character who evolves, who undergoes life changes, because it's more fun for me to write that, it's more interesting." Kellerman also nurtures one of the secondary characters, Detective Petra Connor, who first appeared in *Survival of the Fittest*, and brings her forward for more action in recent novels.

"It took me a while to learn to write dialogue," Kellerman said in a Bookpage interview, noting that his wife, Faye Kellerman, is more natural in that aspect.

"We tend to read each other's books in sizable chunks as they are written," he explained of their partnership to Crime Time. "I don't know that you could say we are ruthless with each other—in fact, I suppose we are very kind. There are ways to make suggestions which are not destructive."

The author does not shy from extreme violence in his novels. He said in a Tangled Web interview, "I deal with violence in a way that seems honest to me. I never aim to titillate, and in fact, I'm quite repulsed by explicit depictions of violence, particularly cinematic renditions. I'm simply struggling to deal with my own fear and anger—having dealt as a psychologist with real-life violence, I know it's not cute."

Kellerman has left his practice but continues to teach pediatrics and psychology at the University of Southern California Keck School of Medicine.

The Kellermans have collaborated on a book that pairs novellas (based on television scenarios that never sold). "It was a chance to create new characters and to travel," Jonathan Kellerman told journalist Judith Rosen. "Creating new characters is a great tonic for two writers who write series characters." That lasted one book. For their second joint effort, they wrote novellas featuring LAPD Detective Peter Decker (her series character) and Delaware (his).

Kellerman has found inspiration in the headlines; *Dr. Death*, for instance, features a character reminiscent of Dr. Jack Kevorkian, the advocate for assisted suicide. He acknowledged in a Bookreporter interview that many of his novels "tend to feature so-called 'social issues.' Probably because I like to wrestle with things that bother me. That probably also explains my choice of psychology as a profession. I'm also drawn to complex issues, such as assisted suicide, because I find questions much more interesting than answers."

As our times have grown ever more tumultuous, Kellerman is counting on an increasing number of readers taking refuge in escapist literature.

Works by the Author

The Butcher's Theater (1988)
Billy Straight (1998)
The Conspiracy Club (2003)
Twisted (2004), sequel to *Billy Straight*
Double Homicide, with Faye Kellerman (2005)

Alex Delaware Series

When the Bough Breaks (1985), in the United Kingdom as *Shrunken Heads* (1986)

Blood Test (1986)
Over the Edge (1987)
Silent Partner (1989)
Time Bomb (1990)
Blood Test/When the Bough Breaks/Over the Edge (1990), omnibus
Private Eyes (1992)
Devil's Waltz (1993)
Bad Love (1994)
Self-Defense (1995)
The Web (1996)
Jonathan Kellerman Omnibus (1996), includes *Bad Love* and *The Web*
The Clinic (1997)
Survival of the Fittest (1997)
Monster (1999)
Dr. Death (2000)
Flesh and Blood (2001)
The First Alex Delaware Omnibus (2001), includes *Blood Test* and *When the Bough Breaks*
The Murder Book (2002)
Devil's Waltz/Bad Love (2003), omnibus
A Cold Heart (2003)
Two Complete Alex Delaware Novels (2003), includes *Devil's Waltz* and *Bad Blood*
Therapy (2004)
Rage (2005)
Gone (2006)
Capital Crimes, with Faye Kellerman (2006), includes "Music City Breakdown"
Obsession (2007)
Compulsion (2008)
Bones (2008)
True Detectives (2009), features characters introduced in *Bones*

Anthologies

Murder for Love, edited by Otto Penzler (1996)
Law and Order (1997)
World's Finest Mystery and Crime Stories, edited by Ed Gorman (2000)

Editor

Diagnosis Dead: A Mystery Writers of America Anthology (1999), includes "Therapy"

Verse

Daddy, Daddy, Can You Touch the Sky? with Jesse Kellerman (1994)

Jonathan Kellerman's ABC of Weird Creatures (1996)

Nonfiction

Psychological Aspects of Childhood Cancer (1980)

Helping the Fearful Child: A Parent's Guide to Everyday and Problem Anxieties (1981)

Savage Spawn: Reflections on Violent Children (1999)

Editor

The Best American Crime Reporting 2008, with Thomas H. Cook and Otto Penzler (2008)

Adaptations in Other Media

When the Bough Breaks (1986), television production based on the novel

For Further Information

Carter, Dale, Jonathan Kellerman entry. *St. James Guide to Crime & Mystery Writers,* 4th ed., Jay P. Pederson, ed. Detroit, MI: St. James Press, 1996.

Dunn, Adam, "There Are Ways of Doing It." *Publishers Weekly*, April 14, 2003.

Farshaw, Barry, "Keeping It Fresh: Jonathan Kellerman," Crime Time. URL: http://www.crimetime.co.uk/interviews.jonathankellerman.html   (viewed June 13, 2003).

Fennel, Judi, "Jonathan Kellerman interview," Gather. http://www.gather.com/viewArticle.jsp?articleid=281474977229522 (viewed January 31, 2008).

Fletcher, Connie, *Capital Crimes* review. *Booklist*, November 1, 2006.

"Jonathan Kellerman Now Has 16 Consecutive Bestsellers to His Credit." *The Writer*, May 2003.

Jonathan and Faye Kellerman interview, Bookreporter, 2006. http://www.bookreporter.com/authors/au-kellerman-jonathan.asp (viewed January 31, 2008).

Jonathan Kellerman entry, *Authors and Artists for Young Adults*, volume 35. Detroit, MI: Gale Research, 2000.

Jonathan Kellerman interview, Crime Time, 2008. http://www.crimetime.co./uk/interviews/jonathankellerman.php (viewed January 31, 2008).

Jonathan Kellerman interview, Tangled Web. URL: http://www.twbooks.co.uk/authors/jkinterview.html (viewed June 13, 2003).

Jonathan Kellerman interviews, Bookreporter (November 24, 1997; January 22, 1997; December 10, 1999; December 15, 2000). http://www.bookreporter.com/authors/au-kellerman-jonathan.asp (viewed June 13, 2003).

Jonathan Kellerman Web site. http://www.jonathankellerman/com/ (viewed November 14, 2008).

Kellerman, Jonathan, "Private Eyes: A Therapist's Work Is Never Done." *Mystery Scene*, February 1992.

Maslin, Janet, "A Therapist Turned Sleuth Has Anger as His Weapon." *New York Times,* December 8, 2003.

Nelson, Catherine M., "A Criminal Mind" (Jonathan Kellerman interview). *The Armchair Detective,* Winter 1993.

Rosen, Judith, "Kellermans Double Up." *Publishers Weekly*, September 27, 2004.

Solimini, Cheryl, "Married They Write." *Mystery Scene*, Fall 2004.

Zvirin, Stephanie, *Compulsion* review. *Booklist*, January 1, 2008.

Zvirin, Stephanie, *Gone* review. *Booklist*, March 1, 2006.

Dean Koontz

Adventure; Crime-Suspense; Fantasy; Horror: Serial Killers; Thrillers: Paranormal

Benchmark Series: <u>Odd Thomas</u>

Everett, Pennsylvania

1945–

About the Author and the Author's Writing

While writing *The Face,* author Dean Koontz had an unsettling experience. Nearly 350 pages into the manuscript, absorbed in what he was writing, all of a sudden, two sentences snapped into his mind: "My name is Odd Thomas. I lead an unusual life." He began to write longhand, on a yellow-lined pad, and in no time had three pages and the start of a new book.

"When I wrote *Odd Thomas,* the title character came to me fully formed," Koontz said on his Web site, "as if he were a real person whom I had known all my life. No character in any of my previous novels led me through his story with such grace."

The author finished *The Face* and *Odd Thomas.* By then, he knew he would have to do more <u>Odd Thomas</u> books, to continue the story of the humble young man who sees ghosts and lesser spirits. *Odd Thomas* "is clearly and uniquely an original, a quietly haunting morality tale that beckons to be embraced and deserves to be studied," Joe Hartlaub wrote for Bookreporter. "Koontz salts Odd's narration with some wonderful zingers at the expense of cultural degeneracy and political folly," noted *Booklist* reviewer Ray Olson of *Brother Odd.*

Dean Ray Koontz has been a fixture on best-seller lists since the 1980s. He was born in 1945 in Everett, Pennsylvania. His family was not well off, and his father was an abusive alcoholic. Koontz nevertheless is relentlessly upbeat, and his novels frequently carry themes of transcendence, hope, and redemption. Good prevails.

The author paid his own way through college. *Atlantic Monthly* published a story he wrote for a college English class, "Kittens." In 1966, he received a bachelor of arts degree from Shippensburg State College. That same year, he married his high school girlfriend, Gerda Ann Cerra. He worked briefly in the Appalachian Poverty Title III Program and as a high school English teacher before turning to writing full time in 1969.

Often categorized as a horror writer, Koontz is more accurately a writer of suspense and has also given romances, supernatural stories, and science fiction a shot. ("Brian Coffey" wrote fast-paced novels, "Leigh Nichols" was known for intrigue, "Deanna Dwyer" swooned through gothics. These were all Koontz pennames.) Many of his books blend genres in a manner uniquely his, combining humor and romance with horror and science fiction. In *Oddkins*, for example, the traditional struggle of good against evil is fought by unusually animated stuffed toys.

"You can't coldly calculate and plan a new style. All you can do is determine what you hope to achieve, then create the mental environment that will let art happen on deeper levels of consciousness," he said in an interview with Stanley Waiter.

He labored with little recognition until *Midnight* stormed onto the best-seller lists in 1989. *The Key to Midnight* followed the next year. Lest his Leigh Nichols penname for *Key* become more popular than his own name, he soon abandoned all aliases. Many of his early works have come back into print, although, being a perfectionist, he has refused to reissue some and has rewritten others. When he set out to rewrite *Shattered*, it turned into a longer, new work, *Winter Moon*.

"Whether exploring the boundaries of identity (*Mr. Murder*), the vagaries of intelligence (*Watchers*), or the limits of re-engineering human response (*Strangers*), Koontz challenges his readers to reflect on their own experience, their relationship to the world, and their responsibility to 'make' their own lives," assert Nick Gillespi and Lisa Snell at Reason Online.

"The imagination comes from a lifetime of pumping bizarre fiction into myself as a reader," the author said in a Doorly.com interview. "And part of it is my skewed view of the world. If you keep your eyes open to the real world around us, there is nothing more bizarre than what happens around us on the street. Ninety percent of my books are just about that."

His favorite (and most influential) writer is John D. McDonald, although James M. Cain, Ray Bradbury, and Charles Dickens also had some sway. These days he says he reads Stephen King and Ed McBain, among others. That's if he has much time to read. The Southern California resident worked sixty- and seventy-hour weeks when writing *False Memory*. *Intensity* took six months, *Dark Rivers of the Heart* nearly twelve.

The Book of Counted Sorrows was a nonexistent book, an in-joke from which Koontz frequently quoted in his novels, until fan demand brought issuance of an actual *Book of Counted Sorrows* in 2001. Likewise, most of his books are stand-alones, but he wrote *Seize the Night* as a sequel to the Christopher Snow-Sasha Goodall story *Fear Nothing*. And, of course, the Odd books became a series.

"I think the world is a magical place," Koontz said in a *Pages* interview. "When I look at the world, I see a planet where a single butterfly flapping its wings can have a subtle impact around the globe. Many times, it's been molecular biology and quantum mechanics that have most directly bolstered my faith."

"Increasingly, his fictions confront the issues of individual responsibility in a world moving beyond the limits of reason and rationality," observed Michael R. Collings in *St. James Guide to Crime & Mystery Writers*. "His characters are increasingly isolated—'outsiders' in the classical sense—burdened with their own intricate psychological problems."

There are also big doses of humor in many of Koontz's books. *The Face*, in the view of Scott Brown, is pure self-parody: "The villain, for example, is one Vladimir 'Corky' Laputa, a bloodthirsty English professor-cum-anarchist who dabbles in every dastardly deed, from murder to graffiti to nontraditional approaches to literature. Corky plans to assault the Bel-Air manse of vapid superstar Channing 'The Face' Manheim."

With all the frightful situations he's put his characters through, is there anything that scares Koontz? "Not anything," he told *USA Today* in 2007, "except losing the people you love. As I get older, I feel there is less to be fearful about and more to take joy in."

 ## Works by the Author

Star Quest (1968)

The Fall of the Dream Machine (1969)

Fear That Man (1969)

Anti-Man (1970)

Beastchild (1970)

Dark of the Woods (1970)

The Dark Symphony (1970)

Dark of the Woods/Soft Come the Dragons (1970), omnibus

Hell's Gate (1970)

The Crimson Witch (1971)

A Darkness in My Soul (1972)

Starblood (1972)

Time Thieves (1972)

The Flesh in the Furnace (1972)

Warlock (1972)

Demon Seed (1973)

Hanging On (1973)

The Haunted Earth (1973)

A Werewolf among Us (1973)

After the Last Race (1974)

Nightmare Journey (1975)

Night Chills (1976)

Time Thieves (1977)

The Vision (1977)

Whispers (1980)

Darkness Comes (1983), published in United Kingdom as *Darkfall*

Phantoms (1983)

Twilight Eyes (1985)

The Voice of the Night (1985)

Strangers (1986)

Watchers (1987)

Lightning (1988)

Oddkins (1988)

The Shadow Sea (1988)

The Bad Place (1989)

Midnight (1989)

Relampagos (1989)

The Key to Midnight (1990)

Cold Fire (1991)

Hideaway (1991)

Three Complete Novels (1991), includes *Lightning, The Face of Fear,* and *The Vision*

Dragon Tears (1992)

Mr. Murder (1993)

Trapped, with Ed Gorman (1993), graphic novel

Winter Moon (1993)

Dark Rivers of the Heart (1994)

Three Complete Novels (1994), includes *Strangers, The Voice of the Night,* and *The Mask*

Intensity (1995)

Winter Moon/Icebound (1995), omnibus

Santa's Twin (1996)

Tick-Tock (1996)

Koontz I: The House of Thunder, Cold Fire, Dragon Tears (1996)

Koontz II: The Voice of the Night, Darkfall, Midnight (1996)

Koontz III: The Bad Place, Mr. Murder, Cold Fire (1996)

Demon Seed/Cold Fire/Dragon Tears/The House of Thunder/Lightning/Mr. Murder/The Servants of Twilight: Mixed (1997), omnibus

Sole Survivor (1997)

Fear Nothing (1998)

Key to Midnight/Shattered/House of Thunder (1998), omnibus

Seize the Night (1999), sequel to *Fear Nothing*

False Memory (1999)

Storm Front (1999)

From the Corner of His Eye (2000)

The Book of Counted Sorrows (2001)

Three Complete Novels: Cold Fire, Hideaway, The Key to Midnight (2001)

One Door Away from Heaven (2001)

By the Light of the Moon (2002)

The Face (2003)

The Taking (2004)

Velocity (2005)

The Husband (2006)

The Darkest Evening of the Year (2007)

The Good Guy (2007)

Your Heart Belongs to Me (2008)

Relentless (2009)

Dean Koontz's Frankenstein Series

Prodigal Son, with Kevin J. Anderson (2005)
City of Night, with Ed Gorman (2005)
Dead and Alive, with Ed Gorman (2008)

Odd Thomas Series

Odd Thomas (2003)
Forever Odd (2005)
Brother Odd (2006)
In Odd We Trust (2007), graphic novel
Odd Hours (2008)

Trixie the Dog Series

Life Is Good: Lessons in Joyful Living (2004)
Christmas Is Good (2005)
Bliss to You: Trixie's Guide to a Happy Life (2008)

Collections

Strange Highways (1991)
The Paper Doorway: Funny Verse and Nothing Worse (2001)
Every Day's a Holiday: Amusing Rhymes for Happy Times (2003)
The Book of Counted Sorrows (2003) verse

Anthologies

Again, Dangerous Visions 2, edited by Harlan Ellison (1972)
Time Thieves and Against Arcturus (1972)
The Edge of Never, edited by Robert Hoskins (1973)
Future City, edited by Roger Elwood (1973)
Final Stage, edited by Edward L. Ferman and Barry N. Malzberg (1974)
Criminal Justice Through Science Fiction, edited by Joseph D. Olander (1977)
Mystery Scene Reader, edited by Ed Gorman (1987)
Night Visions 4 (1987)
The Architecture of Fear, edited by Kathryn Cramer and Peter D. Pautz (1987)
Night Visions Hardshell, edited by Clive Barker (1987)
Between Time and Terror, edited by Stefan R. Dziemianowicz, Martin H. Greenberg, and Robert E. Weinberg (1990)
Under the Gun, edited by Ed Gorman (1990)
Predators, edited by Ed Gorman and Martin H. Greenberg (1993)
The Ultimate Witch, edited by John Gregory Betancourt and Byron Preiss (1993)
Cyber-Killers, edited by Ric Alexander (1997)

Written as Aaron Wolfe

Invasion (1975)

Written as Anthony North

Strike Deep (1974)

Written as Brian Coffey

The Face of Fear (1977)
The Voice of the Night (1980)

Tucker Series by Brian Coffey

Blood Risk (1973)
Surrounded (1974)
The Wall of Masks (1975)

Written as David Axton

Prisoner of Ice (1976), retitled *Icebound* (1995), as by Dean R. Koontz
Stolen Thunder (1993)
Dragon Jet (1994)

Written as Deanna Dwyer

The Demon Child (1971)
Legacy of Terror (1971)
Children of the Storm (1972)
The Dark of Summer (1972)
Dance with the Devil (1973)

Written as John Hill

The Long Sleep (1975)

Written as K. R. Dwyer

Chase (1972)
Shattered (1973), rewritten as *Winter Moon*
Dragonfly (1975)
Face of Fear (1978)

Written as Leigh Nichols

The Key to Midnight (1979)
The Servants of Twilight (1984)
The Door to December (1987)
The Eyes of Darkness (1981)

The House of Thunder (1982)
Twilight (1984), also published as *The Servants of Twilight* (1990)
Shadow Fires (1987)

Written as Owen West

The Funhouse (1980)
The Mask (1981)

Written as Richard Paige

New American (1985)

Nonfiction

The Pig Society, with Gerda Koontz (1970)
The Underground Lifestyles Handbook, with G. Koontz (1970)
Writing Popular Fiction (1972)
CIA Flaps and Seals Manual (1975)
How to Write Best Selling Fiction (1981)

Screenplays

CHiPs (1979), television episode "Counterfeit" as Brian Coffey
Cold Fire (1998), screenplay

Adaptations in Other Media

Demon Seed (1977), motion picture based on novel
Shattered (1977), motion picture based on novel; also titled *Les Passagers*
Watchers (1988), motion picture based on novel
Whispers (1989), motion picture based on novel
The Face of Fear (1990), teleplay based on novel
Watchers II (1990), motion picture based on novel
Servants of Twilight (1991), motion picture based on novel
Watchers III (1994), motion picture based on novel
Hideaway (1995), motion picture based on novel
Intensity (1997), television miniseries based on novel
Sole Survivor (1997), television miniseries
Phantoms (1997), motion picture from Koontz script based on his novel
Mr. Murder (1998), television miniseries
The Face of Fear (1998), television production from Koontz script based on his novel
Watchers Reborn (1998), motion picture based on *Watchers*
Black River (2001), television production based on novella
Frankenstein (2004), television production

For Further Information

Brown, Scott, "Oddest Proposal." *Entertainment Weekly,* May 30, 2003.

Chapman, Jeff, and Pamela S. Dean, eds., Dean R. Koontz entry, *Contemporary Authors New Revision Series*, volume 52. Detroit, MI: Gale Research, 1996.

Christopher Snow Web page. http://www.randomhouse.com/features/koontz/ christophersnow/world.html (viewed May 30, 2003).

Collings, Michael R., Dean R. Koontz entry, *St. James Guide to Mystery & Crime Writers*, 4th ed., Jay P. Pederson, ed. Detroit, MI: St. James Press, 1996.

Dean Koontz interview, Barnes & Noble. http://www.bookbrowse.com/index/ cfm?page=author&authorID=260&view=interview (viewed May 27, 2003).

Dean Koontz long fiction. http://web.tiscali.it/no-redirect-tiscali/luigiurato/ longfiction/.long.htm (viewed May 27, 2003).

Dean Koontz nonfiction. http://web.tiscali.it/no-redirect-tiscali/luigiurato/ nonfiction/nonfiction.htm (viewed May 27, 2003).

Dean Koontz pseudonyms. http://web.tiscali.iot/no-redirect-tiscali/luigiurato/ pseudo/pseudo1.htm (viewed May 27, 2003).

Dean Koontz Web site. http://www.deankoontz.com (viewed November 14, 2008).

Dean Koontz Web site. http://www.randomhouse.com/features/koontz/ index2.html (viewed May 27, 2003).

Gillespie, Nick, and Lisa Snell, "Contemplating Evil: Novelist Dean Koontz on Freud, Fraud and the Great Society, reasononline. http://web.tiscali.it/no- redirect-tiscali/luigiurato/interv/cont_evil.htm (viewed May 27, 2003).

Greenberg, Martin H., Ed Gorman, and Bill Munser, eds. *The Dean Koontz Companion.* New York: Berkley, 1994.

Halem, Dann, "Night Light: Dean Koontz Finds Brightness in Life's Dark Mysteries." *Pages,* January/February 2003.

Hartlaub, Joe, *Odd Thomas* review, Bookreporter. http://www.bookreporter. com/reviews/0553584499.asp (viewed January 7, 2008).

Hatchigan, Jessica, "Born to Write." *The Writer*, December 2003.

Koontz, Dean, "Koontz on Koontz." *Mystery Scene* No. 59, 1997.

Lybarger, Dan, "Unread Books and the Ancient Enemy: An Interview with Dean Koontz." *Pitch Weekly*, January 28–February 4, 1999.

Memmott, Carol, "Five Questions." *USA Today*, November 29, 2007.

Munster, Bill. *Sudden Fear: The Horror and Dark Suspense Fiction of Dean R. Koontz.* San Bernardino, CA: Borgo, 1990.

Olsen, Ray, *Brother Odd* review. *Booklist*, November 15, 2006.

Ramsland, Katherine Marie. *Dean Koontz: A Writer's Biography*. New York: Eos. (1998).

Springen, Karen, "The Cheery Titan of Terror." *Newsweek*, February 11, 1991.

Taylor, Marlene, and Sean Doorly, Dean Koontz interview, Doorly. http://www.doorly.com/writing/DeanKoontz/htm (viewed May 27, 2003).

Wiater, Stanley, "Dark Dreamer: Dean R. Koontz." http://web.tiscali/it/no-redirect-tiscali/luigiurato/interv/deramers.htm (viewed May 27, 2003).

Wiater, Stanley, "Dean R. Koontz in the Fictional Melting Pot." *Writer's Digest*, November 1989.

John le Carré (John Cornwell)

Adventure; Crime-Suspense; Espionage

Benchmark Title: *The Spy Who Came in from the Cold*

Poole, Dorsetshire, England

1931–

About the Author and the Author's Writing

John le Carré delves into the darkest of secret governmental worlds in his novels such as *The Constant Gardener*, in which the British high commissioner in Nairobi consorts with the international pharmaceuticals industry to test drugs on the unsuspecting poor. Le Carré's main character deeply loves his homeland, however, as does the author, who minces no words in criticizing England's participation in the Iraq War. "I believe the sin was greater than simply taking us to war," he told the *Guardian's* Stuart Jeffries. "It destroyed our relationship with the Middle East and with southeast Asia and took us on a flight of fantasy about our relationship with the U.S. These are terrible sins."

John le Carré nee David John Moore Cornwell has personally known the darker world of deceit and treachery, certainly better than he knows the open warfare he recently decried.

Born in Poole, Dorsetshire, England, in 1931, he attended Sherborne School. From 1948 to 1949, he studied French and German at the University of Berne, after which he joined the British Army Intelligence Corps. He later completed his studies at Lincoln College, Oxford, from which he received a first-class honors degree in modern languages in 1956. He has been twice married and has three children by his first wife, Alison Sharp, one by his second, Valerie Eustace.

The author taught junior school in England for two years, then from 1956 to 1958 was a tutor at Eton College, Buckinghamshire, England. Over the years, according to his publisher, he also sold bath towels, washed elephants, and accidently wiped out a flock of Welsh sheep when he failed to follow the instructions of his gunnery officer. Ultimately, he became second secretary in the British Foreign Office in Bonn, West Germany, and as political consul in Hamburg, from 1959 to 1964. It was in this period, he began to write. He adopted the pseudonym John le Carré, so as not to draw attention to his primary occupation.

Le Carré recruited Soviet agents from refugees living in Austria—not particularly James Bond stuff. "I am a writer who, when I was very young, spent a few ineffectual but extremely formative years in British Intelligence. The relationship between agent and agent-runner was sacrosanct," he told reporter Tim Sullivan. "You promised that you would never reveal what he did."

If his intelligence work came easy, it was because he knew firsthand of deceit from his childhood. His father was a confidence man and convicted felon. His mother fled the home by the time he was three. The author and his younger brother attended private British schools and pretended they were of the upper crust. In fact, he never knew when his father might next go to jail. He grew up much as an undercover agent. The entire world was the enemy, and he risked discovery at any turn.

The author's keen sense of the morally vague world of Cold War espionage emerges in his novel *The Spy Who Came in from the Cold* (1963). The character, Alec Leamas, is fifty, tired of the spy game, and anxious to lead a normal life. But he must complete one more assignment. Reviewer Anthony Boucher appreciated the intricacies of the agent's life of deception: "[Although he] earn[s] a fortune, his role may forbid him the purchase of a razor; though he may be erudite, it can befall him to mumble nothing but banalities; though he be an affectionate husband and father, he must under all circumstances withhold himself from those in whom he should naturally confide."

Le Carré identifies with another character, Oliver Single in *Single and Single* (1999), who eludes his corrupt father to become a magician. In le Carré's uncomfortable childhood, he was often the entertainer to the rest of the family. The cathartic, autobiographical *A Perfect Spy* (1986) is about a British spy about to turn traitor, a con man much like his father. The character of Rick Pym is something of an exception; the author told reporter Mary Ann Gwinn, "There is no such thing as a fictional character literally drawn from life—you can draw an inflection or a mannerism (from an actual person), but finally you have to fill that person with the possibility of your own character."

That book bears a lighter tone than most of le Carré's works, something he attributes to his maturity: given the world situation, at his age, one either laughs or commits suicide, he says.

Le Carré lives above a cliff on the Cornish coast. In conducting the considerable background research for his books, he often travels to actual locations and then fills his head with the main character's thoughts and motivations.

"I write in longhand," he told interviewer Chris Nashawaty in *Entertainment Weekly*. "And I always write first thing in the morning. If it's really going, I'll start at 4 or 5 o'clock and that will go through until lunchtime. And if it's gone well, I'll have a couple glasses of wine with lunch as a reward."

When the Cold War ended, le Carré simply shifted his focus to mobsters, gun runners, and deceiving Western governments for plot ideas. In *The Tailor of Panama* (1996), for example, ex-con Harry Pendel, blackmailed into becoming an informant, but lacking any crucial information to pass on, invents a plot about Asians who want to stir up a revolution and grab the Panama Canal. In *Absolute Friends*, the author circled around to espionage again and a very current topic: The war in Iraq.

George Smiley, the glum-but-solid British spy, has figured in many of le Carré's books, beginning with the first, *Call for the Dead*, and perhaps reaching his pinnacle in the trilogy in which he faces the Communist master spy Karla. That sequence took inspiration from the case of the treacherous British spy Kim Philby, the author has said.

He explained the genesis of *The Honourable Schoolboy* to Michael Barber for the *New York Times*: he had the characters, Jerry Westerby from an earlier book, *Tinker, Tailor*, along with the reliable George Smiley. He simply set them in the Far East and watched to see what happened. " I found myself referring to Jerry and George as 'my secret sharers.' So it was an act of complicity, I suppose, between myself and the characters, that we finally drew the story out of their motivations."

Le Carré makes a distinction that his books are credible, but not authentic. In the real world of spies, he points out, there is seldom resolution. Characters aren't always caught in the dilemma of wrong or right. And their motives may not always be dangerous.

Reviewer Bill Ott noted a change in the author's work with *The Constant Gardener*, a "profound cynicism" with a hero who feels betrayed by his own country. George Smiley, at least, always felt his government, whatever its shortcoming, was better than anyone else's.

The world of international politics and espionage is ever changing, and so is le Carré. His *A Most Wanted Man* takes place after the events of September 11 and involves new issues of global economics and religion. "We know so little, we understand so little, about Islam—the cultural differences that separate us, the thought processes that separate us," he told Jill Lawless for Associated Press.

Despite the enormity of the topic, the writer grasps for universal meaning. "I hope to provide a metaphor for the average reader's daily life," le Carré said to Andrew Ross for a Salon interview. "Most of us live in a slightly conspiratorial relationship with our employer and perhaps with our marriage. I think what gives my works whatever universality they have is that they use the metaphysical secret world to describe some realities of the overt world."

Works by the Author

A Small Town in Germany (1968)
The Naïve and Sentimental Lover (1971)
The Little Drummer Girl (1983)
A Perfect Spy (1986)
The Russia House (1989)
The Night Manager (1993)
Our Game (1995)
The Tailor of Panama (1996)
Single and Single (1999)
The Constant Gardener (2001)
Absolute Friends (2004)
The Mission Song (2006)
A Most Wanted Man (2008)

Smiley Series

Call for the Dead (1961), retitled *The Deadly Affair* (1966)
A Murder of Quality (1962)
The Spy Who Came in from the Cold (1963)
The Incongruous Spy (1964), includes first two books
The Looking Glass War (1965)
Tinker, Tailor, Soldier, Spy (1974)

The Honourable Schoolboy (1977)

Smiley's People (1980)

The Quest for Karla (1982), omnibus includes *Tinker, Tailor, Soldier, Spy; The Honorable Schoolboy*; and *Smiley's People*

The Secret Pilgrim (1990)

John le Carré: Three Complete Novels (1995), includes *Tinker, Tailor, Soldier, Spy; The Honourable Schoolboy*; and *Smiley's People*

Teleplays and Screenplays

Stage 66 (1966), television episode "Dare I Weep, Dare I Mourn"

Smiley's People, with John Hopkins, (1982)

The Clandestine Muse (1986)

Vanishing England, with Gareth H. Davies (1987)

The Tailor of Panama (2001)

Nonfiction

The Clandestine Muse (1986)

Vanishing England, with Gareth H. Davies, (1987)

Not One More Death, with Richard Dawkins, Brian Eno, Michael Faber, Harold Pinter, and Haifa Zangana (2006)

Adaptations in Other Media

The Spy Who Came in from the Cold (1965), motion picture

The Deadly Affair (1967), motion picture based on *Call for the Dead*

The Looking Glass War (1970), motion picture

Tinker, Tailor, Soldier, Spy (1980), motion picture

The Little Drummer Girl (1984), motion picture

A Perfect Spy (1997, BBC-TV and PBS), television production

The Russia House (1990), motion picture

A Murder of Quality (1991), television production (BBC)

The Constant Gardener (2005), motion picture

For Further Information

Barber, Michael, "John le Carré: An Interrogation." *New York Times*, September 25, 1977.

Boucher, Anthony, "Temptations of a Man Isolated in Deceit." *New York Times,* January 12, 1964.

Freeman, Alan, *Absolute Friends* review. Waterbury (CT) *Sunday Republican,* January 18, 2004.

Gwinn, Mary Ann, "Author John le Carré Digs Deep in His Own Past for the Themes of His Work." *Seattle Times*, March 25, 1999.

Harris, Mark, *Absolute Friends* review. *Entertainment Weekly*, January 16, 2004.

Homberger, Eric. *John le Carré*. New York: Ungar, 1985.

Jeffries, Stuart, "'I Do Give a Damn.'" *Guardian*, October 6, 2005.

John le Carré Web site. http://www.johnlecarre.com (viewed January 7, 2008).

Jones, Daniel, and John J. Jorgenson, eds., David Cornwell entry, *Contemporary Authors New Revision Series*, volume 59. Detroit, MI: Gale Research, 1998.

Lawless, Jill, "Le Carre Makes Angry Point." *Hartford* (CT) *Courant*, October 6, 2008.

le Carré Breaks His Silence, Random House. http://www.randomhouse.com/features/lecarre/author/html (viewed May 30, 2003).

le Carré, John, "The United States of America Has Gone Mad," Times/UK (January 15, 2003). http://www.commondreams.org/views03/0115-01.htm (viewed April 9, 2009).

Lelyveld, Joseph, "Le Carré's Toughest Case." *New York Times Magazine,* March 16, 1986.

Memmott, Carol, "Le Carré's 'Mission' Shows How the World Works." *USA Today*, September 18, 2006.

Monaghan, David. *The Novels of John le Carré*. Oxford: Blackwell, 1985.

Monaghan, David. *Smiley's Circus; A Guide to the Secret World of John le Carré*. London: Orbis, 1986.

Nashawaty, Chris, "The Spy Who Came in from the Cold War." *Entertainment Weekly*, January 16, 2004.

Ott, Bill, *Constant Gardener* review. *American Libraries,* February 2002.

Ross, Andrew, "John le Carré on Deception, Storytelling and American Hubris," Salon.com. http://www.salon.com/weekly/lecarre961021.html (viewed January 7, 2008).

Snyder, John, John le Carré entry. *St. James Guide to Crime & Mystery Writers,* 4th ed., Jay P. Pederson, ed. Detroit, MI: St. James Press, 1996.

Sullivan, Tim, "John le Carré Still Holding Back Some Secrets," Associated Press (November 22, 1996). http://cgi.canoe.ca/JamBooksFeatures/lecarre_john.html (viewed May 30, 2003).

Wolfe, Peter. *Corridors of Deceit: The World of John le Carré*. Bowling Green, OH: Bowling Green University Popular Press, 1987.

Dennis Lehane

Adventure; Espionage; Crime-Suspense; Thrillers: Terrorists

Benchmark Title: *Mystic River*

Dorchester, Massachusetts

1965–

Photo credit: Terri Ruth Unger

About the Author and the Author's Writing

Dennis Lehane counseled abused children and the mentally disabled by day, and he had the manuscript for a private detective novel in the drawer. He wanted to write professionally. But he wanted to establish himself for a long run. His agent passed along an offer for his first book from a paperback house. The author stood firm. He insisted on a hardcover contract, even if it ended up bringing only an $8,500 advance. After obtaining a hardcover contract, *A Drink before the War* won a Shamus Award for Best P.I. Novel in 1994. By the time he published his fifth book, he had better than a $100,000 advance. And his most recent contract called for a $3 million advance on three novels, two of which became best sellers, *Mystic River* and *Shutter Island*.

The author was born in Dorchester, Massachusetts, in 1965, the son of Irish American parents, a foreman and a school cafeteria worker. He received a bachelor of applied science degree from Eckerd College in 1988. From 1986 to 1991, he worked as a therapeutic counselor. He wrote his first novel, and an agent circulated it while he earned a master of fine arts degree in creative writing from Florida International University in 1993. He taught English at the university for two years. After graduation, he worked as a chauffeur at the Ritz-Carlton Hotel in Boston for two years. All this time, he continued to write in his spare time. By 1995, he became a full-time writer.

Lehane was a Bostonian through and through, and the city provided the backdrop for his first five books, a series featuring investigators Patrick Kenzie and Angela Gennaro. Their first case is to find a U.S. senator's missing cleaning woman. Their third case finds them becoming lovers, in the course of helping a ruthless but dying billionaire find his equally ruthless daughter.

The author mentions as influences authors ranging from William Kennedy and Pete Dexter to Elmore Leonard and Graham Greene,

Lehane lets his characters shape the plots, he said in a *Writer* interview in 2004. "I put a character on the page and I have him want something—it could be as simple as a cup of coffee—and he goes out to get that thing. And hopefully, he bumps into another character and then another and conflict will gradually develop." If he fumbles, in the early stages of a book, he revises and rewrites. He has said he dropped two hundred pages from an early draft of *Mystic River* before he got into the full swing of writing it. His wife, Sheila, and selected friends often read and commented on his manuscripts while in draft to help soften any missteps.

Only with *Shutter Island*, a tightly plotted, gothic novel set during a hurricane, did the author outline first. "I knew everything that was going to happen before I wrote it," he said in an interview with Edward Nawotka of *Publishers Weekly*. "A full third of the people who read it will figure it out before the end. The book is not *Mystic River*. It's something different, and it's always a danger to change when you have success."

Lehane had already made a change to write *Mystic River*. He'd decided it was time to give his glib crime solving characters a break. "I noticed one of my characters—probably the most popular character I've ever created, Bubba Rogowski—in the fifth book, he started getting cute. Just a little bit. And I felt myself doing it," he told interviewer Dave Weich.

It was time to put to paper a darker plot that had been formulating in his head for ten years. He had put some of the material, about a Boston neighborhood, into a novella that was part of his graduate thesis. *Mystic River,* brought to the big screen by director Clint Eastwood, is about three childhood friends who share a big secret—a secret that comes out when the daughter of one of the men is found murdered.

The dark *Mystic River* riveted readers. The author told *Mystery Scene* that it "grew out of a dawning realization that violence is never a solitary event. Even the smallest act of violence reverberates in ways the people involved in the original act can never foresee."

Lehane has seen Boston change—family-run pizza shops have become Starbucks—and he wanted to work out what that meant to the people living there. *Mystic River* was Lehane's opportunity to place minor-scale characters with modest lives on a large-scale stage.

"The job of the fiction writer is to create a believable cloth of lies and myth and could be—accent on the 'could'—a mirror of a life we all know," he said in a Bookreporter conversation.

Lehane has written and directed the screenplay for the as-yet-unreleased film *Neighborhoods*. His next novel, *The Given Day* (2008)—probably the start of a trilogy—is historical, set at the time of the Boston police strike in 1919. It was a time of rioting and union busting, influenza, and, in Boston, a great molasses flood in the warehouse district and the sale of Babe Ruth to the Yankees. "Back then, domestic terrorism was at an all-time high. We had just come through an unpopular war and no one could explain why we were there," the author told *The Boston Globe*'s Pagan Kennedy.

Lehane defied expectations with his historical novel *The Given Day* (2008), an epic novel set in Boston during the 1919 police strike. Five years in creation, the sprawling novel marks a new direction for the crime fiction master.

Pleased with his progress as a writer, and the special moments in the struggle to shape a manuscript, Lehane said on his Web site: "And then a moment occurs in which two or maybe three of these seemingly disparate things click. It's almost an audible click, a snapping sound in your head as these pieces slide into each other's slots and mesh. That moment is special."

Works by the Author

Mystic River (2001)
Shutter Island (2003)
Coronado: Stories (2006)
The Given Day (2008)

Patrick Kenzie and Angela Gennaro Series

A Drink before the War (1994)
Darkness, Take My Hand (1996)
Sacred (1997)
Gone, Baby, Gone (1998)
Prayers for Rain (1999)
Sacred; Gone, Baby, Gone; and Prayers for Rain (2002), omnibus
A Drink before the War and Darkness, Take My Hand (2007), omnibus

Screenplays

Neighborhoods (unreleased; also directed the film)
The Wire (2004), television episode "Dead Soldiers"
The Wire (2006), television episode "Refugees"

Adaptations in Other Media

Mystic River (2003), motion picture

For Further Information

Abbott, Jillian, "Three Writers on Plot: Dennis Lehane, Gayle Lynds and Stuart Woods Tell You How to Create a Great Plot." *The Writer*, May 2004.

Dennis Lehane interview, Bookreporter. http://www.bookreporter.com/authors/au-lehane-dennis.asp (viewed December 27, 2007).

Dennis Lehane Web site. http://dennislehanebooks.com/ (viewed November 14, 2008).

Kennedy, Pagan, "Q&A with Dennis Lehane." *Boston Globe*, December 16, 2007.

Nawotka, Edward, "Boston's Uncommon Bestseller: Dennis Lehane Takes Life, Success and the Mystery Genre in Hand." *Publishers Weekly*, April 14, 2003.

Richards, Linda, Dennis Lehane interview, January magazine, March 2001. http://januarymagazine.com/profiles/lehane.html (viewed January 27, 2007).

Taylor, Art, "Uncharted Waters: Dennis Lehane Sets a Course for Literary Adventure," *Mystery Scene*, Holiday 2003.

Weich, Dave, "Dennis Lehane Meets the Bronte Sisters," Powells. http://www.powells.com/authors/lehane.html (viewed December 27, 2007).

John Lescroart

Crime; Thrillers: Legal

Benchmark Series: <u>Dismas Hardy</u>

Houston, Texas

1948–

Photo credit: Courtesy of the author

About the Author and the Author's Writing

John Lescroart flailed a couple of times in his career until he found success writing legal and crime thrillers. Twice, serious health afflictions redirected him.

Three-quarters Irish, one-quarter French (his last name is pronounced less-kwah), he was born in Houston in 1948. His family moved frequently. He graduated from high school in San Mateo, California, in 1966. Four years and four schools later, he earned a B.A. in English with honors at the University of California at Berkeley. While in college, he wrote a mystery featuring Auguste Lupa, the son of Sherlock Holmes and Irene Adler (and, it is strongly hinted, is really Nero Wolfe). He wrote a sequel after graduation but set both manuscripts aside as he went to work in computer services.

Dissatisfied with his work, he quit in 1972 and traveled to Africa seeking a new direction. "I had malaria, dysentery, pneumonia and E. coli, all at once," he told interviewer Cathy Cassinos-Carr. The serious illness gave clarity to what he wanted to do: play music. He wrote his own songs and performed in Europe and this country. He relocated to Los Angeles in 1975 with a portfolio of some four hundred tunes. In 1976, he married Leslee Ann Miller. Three years later they divorced. As Johnny Capo and His Real Good Band, he continued to play guitar and sing in clubs and bars in the San Francisco Bay area. By 1978, he admitted success was elusive, but he completed a new novel, *Sunburn*, about his time in Spain. It wouldn't be published until four years later, but when a friend submitted it to the San Francisco Foundation for Best Novel by a California author, it won the Joseph Henry Jackson Award in 1979. Maybe he would have a future in writing after all.

He lists as an influence particularly Lawrence Durrell's <u>Alexandria Quartet</u> books. "They are profoundly 'literary,' and yet there is plenty of intrigue and suspense," he said in a Meet the Writers interview. He also admits to having read Scott Turow's *Presumed Innocent* three times.

He decided to enter graduate school at the University of Massachusetts at Amherst. A lucrative job opportunity writing technical papers for a legal consulting firm ended that plan. Meanwhile, he had remarried, to Lisa M. Sawyer, in 1984; they live in El Macero, California, and have two children.

As Lescroart worked as a house painter, furniture mover, bartender, legal secretary, and professional fundraiser, he wrote three more novels. Pinnacle Books accepted his unagented *Sunburn* for paperback publication, but other sales were elusive. At his architect-wife's urging, he dug out the two Auguste Lupa books and sent them out; they found a hardcover publisher. He then wrote screenplays and published three more books.

Illness a second time brought clarity to what he wanted to do. He contracted spinal meningitis after body surfing in contaminated water. He was in a coma for a week and a half and doctors had little expectation he would survive.

When he returned home, he quit his day job. From now on, he would only write fiction (and take care of the house and children while his wife worked as an architect). He had begun a series of books featuring the lawyer Dismas, an erratic character who still grieves for a lost child and an ended marriage. The books rose steadily on the best-seller lists as the author honed his craft. Lescroart took a secondary character, Abe Glitsky, a San Francisco homicide detective, and spun him into his own series.

"I needed a new protagonist, maybe because I had changed," the author told Catherine Maclay of *Publishers Weekly*. "Hardy is an ambivalent thinker. Abe is not conflicted. He knows what he believes in, what he's after."

Although they are categorized as mysteries, Lescroart sees the <u>Hardy</u> and <u>Glitzky</u> novels as something more. "I write them in the same way Patrick O'Brien wrote his stories," Lescroart told interviewer Jackie K. Cooper. "If people read them as who done it's, I haven't done my job. These are books to be read for the richness of the people not just to solve a crime."

Writing is now his day job. But Lescroart has not given up his music; his latest CD, country-tinged *Whiskey and Roses*, came out in 2007.

Works by the Author

Sunburn (1981)

<u>Abe Glitsky Series</u>

Certain Justice (1995)

Guilt (1996)

Hearing (1999)

Oath (2002)

Auguste Lupa Series

Son of Holmes (1986)

Rasputin's Revenge (1987)

Dismas Hardy Series

Dead Irish (1989)

Vig (1990)

Hard Evidence (1993)

13th Juror (1994)

Mercy Rule (1998)

Nothing but the Truth (1999)

Hearing (2001)

Oath (2002)

First Law (2003)

Motive (2004)

Second Chair (2004)

Betrayal (2007)

A Plague of Secrets (2009)

Wyatt Hunt Series

Hunt Club (2005)

Suspect (2007)

Treasure Hunt (announced 2010)

For Further Information

Cassinos-Carr, Cathy, "John Lescroart." *Sacramento Magazine*, December 2005.

Cooper, Jackie K., "John Lescroart: The Music of His Writing," Jackie K. Cooper Hollywood.   http://www.jackiekcooper.com/BookReviews/InterviewJohnLescroart.htm (viewed October 26, 2007).

"John Lescroart: As in less-kwah!," Mystery News. http://www.blackravenpress.com/Author%20pages/lescroart.htm (viewed October 26, 2007).

John Lescroart profile, Bookreporter. http://www.bookreporter.com/authors/au-lescroart-john.asp (viewed October 26, 2007).

John Lescroart profile, Meet the Writers, Barnes & Noble. http://www.barnesandnoble.com/writers/writer.asp?cid=883454 (viewed October 26, 2007).

John Lescroart Web site, http://www.johnlescroart.com/ (viewed November 14, 2008).

Jordan, Diana, "On the Hunt: Lescroart Mingles Old, New in Thriller," *Costco Connection*, January 2006.

Maclay, Catherine, "John T. Lescroart: No Day Job, Just Time to Write." *Publishers Weekly*, August 14, 1995.

Laura Lippman

Crime-Suspense

Benchmark Series: Tess Monaghan

Atlanta, Georgia
1955–

Photo credit: Jan Cobb

About the Author and the Author's Writing

Writing is forever a learning experience for Laura Lippman. She teaches at workshops such as Writers in Paradise and at institutions such as Goucher College. "I like thinking about fiction—what works, what doesn't, how to articulate those points. The more I think about other people's work and how it might be improved, the more I apply those lessons to my work," she said in a Noir Writer interview.

The author was born in 1959 in Atlanta, Georgia, and grew up in Baltimore, Maryland, where she still lives. She was captain of the Wilde Lake High School "It's Academic" team. Her father was a journalist, her mother a librarian, so books and writing were part of her life from the start. After studying at Northwestern University's Medill School of Journalism, she became a reporter. She worked for the *Tribune-Herald* in Waco, Texas, from 1981 to 1983; the *San Antonio Light* in Texas from 1983 to 1989; and with the *Evening Sun* in Baltimore from 1989 until 2002. She is married to David Simon, executive producer of the television series *Homicide* and *The Wire*.

Enamored of Baltimore, it became practically a character in her Edgar-, Shamus-, and Gumshoe-award-winning private detective series. "I started writing the Tess Monaghan books in part because I'm fascinated by my hometown," she told Suzanne Fox of *Publishers Weekly*. "Because I live, work and volunteer here, I'm aware of the changes Baltimore is going through." Against this backdrop, she explores such themes as child molestation, divorce, provoked suicide, even Edgar Allan Poe. *Another Thing to Fall* has the investigator on the set of a TV series—wonder where that idea came from?

Lippman wrote her first seven books while she reported full time for the *Sun*. She was inspired to write the first one, *Baltimore Blues* (1997), by an incident that happened to a friend, involving a rude employer. She began to speculate how someone in that situation might kill that abusive boss. "I made Tess a former journalist because I could imagine how a journalist could become a private detective drawing on what she knew as a journalist and other skills she'd picked up along the way," Lippman told *Publishers Weekly*'s Tracy Cochran.

Monaghan, the author allows, shares her temperament and may have had some of the same experiences, but otherwise she is entirely a creation of her mind.

Lippman's background as a reporter gave the author inquisitiveness and comfort with words. She credits a former editor with helping shape a narrative approach. "In journalism, with the tradition of the inverted paragraph, there's a tendency to load the best information at the top of the story. But this editor taught me that there's a way to make an implicit covenant with the readers that you're building toward something, that these portends of doom will pay off," she told interviewer Jeff Abbott.

The professional jealousy of another editor put so much pressure on her, Lippman quit her job. Her next book, *Every Secret Thing* (2003), was her first stand-alone thriller. It is about the media sensationalizing a news story when a baby is stolen and then murdered. Since then, Lippman alternates thrillers with her mystery novels. She says she roughs out her story before she begins to write. "I try to think it through beforehand, but I also know some things will become clear only after I'm in the thick of it," she said in a Bookbytes interview.

She's adopted a ritual to her writing. "I spend most weekday mornings at a local coffeehouse," she says on her Web site, "intent on writing at least 1,000 words. At that pace, I can usually finish a first daft in four–five months, which leaves time for quite a bit of redrafting."

Another benefit of having been a reporter for many years—"I work well on deadline," Lippman told interviewer Sara Nelson.

 # Works by the Author

Every Secret Thing (2003)
To the Power of Three (2005)
What the Dead Know (2007)
Life Sentences (2009)

Tess Monaghan Series

Baltimore Blues (1997)
Charm City (1997)
Butcher's Hill (1998)
In Big Trouble (1999)
The Sugar House (2000)
In a Strange City (2001)
The Last Place (2002)
By a Spider's Thread (2004)
No Good Deeds (2006)
Another Thing to Fall (2008)
Hardly Knew Her (2008), short stories

Editor

Baltimore Noir (2006), includes "Easy as A-B-C"

Contributor

First Cases, edited by Robert J. Randisi (2002), includes "Orphans Court," a Tess Monaghan story

Murderers' Row, edited by Otto Penzler (2003), includes "Ropa Vieja," a Tess Monaghan story

Thrilling Detective (2003) includes "The Half Monty," a Tess Monaghan story

Like a Charm, edited by Karin Slaughter (2004), includes "Not Quite U"

Plots with Guns, edited by Anthony Neil Smith (2005), includes "The Babysitter's Code"

Murder ... and All That Jazz, edited by Robert J. Randisi (2005), includes "The Shoeshine Man's Regrets," a Tess Monaghan story

The Best American Mystery Stories, 2005, edited by Joyce Carol Oates and Otto Penzler (2005), includes "The Shoeshine Man's Regrets"

Tart Noir, edited by Stella Duffy and Lauren Henderson (2005), includes "What He Needed"

Dangerous Women, edited by Otto Penzler (2005), includes "Dear Penthouse Forum, A First Draft"

The Cocaine Chronicles, edited by Gary Phillips and Jervey Tervalon (2005), includes "The Crack-Cocaine Diet"

The Best American Mystery Stories, 2006, edited by Scott Turow and Otto Penzler (2006), includes "The Crack-Cocaine Diet"

Dublin Noir, edited by Ken Bruen (2006), includes "The Honor Bar"

D.C. Noir, edited by George P. Pelecanos (2006), includes "ARM and the Woman"

Murder in the Rough, edited by Otto Penzler (2006), includes "A Good F**k Spoiled"

Damn Near Dead, edited by Duane Swierczynski (2006), includes "Femme Fatale"

Relationships Can Be Murder, edited by Harlan Coben (2006), includes "One True Love"

Bloodlines, edited by Jason Starr and Maggie Estep (2006), includes "Black-Eyed Susans"

Pulp Fiction — The Dames, edited by Otto Penzler (2008), includes introduction

For Further Information

Abbott, Jeff, "A Conversation with Laura Lippman, Writer2Writer. http://www.jeffabbott.com/writer_lippman.html (viewed March 6, 2008).

Cochran, Tracy, "The Baltimore Beat: Charmed City Scribe Laura Lippman Covers Crime in Her Own Way." *Publishers Weekly*, July 5, 2004.

Fox, Suzanne, "Topical Crimes." *Publishers Weekly*, June 5, 2006.

Jordan, Jon, "Interview with Laura Lippman," BookByte. http://www.bookbyte.com/auth_interviews/laura_lippman.html (viewed March 6, 2008).

Laura Lippman interview, Noir Writer. http://noirwriter.blogspot.com/2007/04/sunday-interview-laura-lippman-html (viewed March 6, 2008).

Laura Lippman Web site. http://www.lauralippman.com (viewed November 15, 2008).

Nelson, Sara, "Lady Baltimore." *Publishers Weekly*, February 11, 2008.

Elizabeth Lowell
(Ann Elizabeth Maxwell)

Crime-Suspense; Historical Fiction; Romantic Suspense; Science Fiction

Benchmark Series: St. Kilda

About the Author and the Author's Writing

In a writing career of more than three decades, Elizabeth Lowell has used several pennames and worked in all genres but horror and western. Whatever the style, whether writing alone or in collaboration, her work is marked by carefully crafted characters—and romance.

"I will always include a constructive relationship between a man and a woman in a book," the author said in a 2001 interview with Isolde Weir, noting her own now four-decades-long happy marriage. "My heroines have always been independent, intelligent, and capable of love; my heroes have always been stubborn, intelligent, and capable of love."

The author was born Ann Elizabeth Charters in Milwaukee, Wisconsin, in 1944. Her father was a manufacturer, her mother a teacher. She attended the University of California at Davis in 1962 and 1963 and received a bachelor of arts degree from the University of California at Riverside in 1966. She married journalist Evan Lowell Maxwell in 1966. He spent fifteen years with the *Los Angeles Times* before the couple moved to Washington State. They have two children, who are now adults.

Ann Maxwell began her writing career with her 1975 science fiction novel, *Change*. With a toddler in the house, the author was bored by television and was without a car most days. Her husband worked the night shift as a reporter on the international crime beat.

"So I sat down at the old manual typewriter that had seen two generations through college and started to write the kind of science fiction book I would enjoy reading," she told interviewer Claire E. White. She completed a second manuscript, and bore a second child, before the book found a publisher. But the book was nearly a Nebula Award finalist, and her career took off. Her science fiction books appeared under the pen name Ann Maxwell. Later, that name became familiar with her romantic suspense books, some of which she wrote alone, some with her husband.

Eventually, her husband began to write with her, and the two, as A. E. Maxwell, produced Fiddler and Flora mysteries. When they wrote together, the author once explained, he often established the background and they jointly shaped characters and plot. Evan wrote a first draft, while Ann independently wrote an Elizabeth Lowell book. Then Ann revised her husband's draft, with an eye toward pacing, consistency, and characterization. Evan then read the manuscript one more time before sending it to the editor. The author has written historical as well as contemporary novels.

Two advents sent the author in a new direction. The speed with which she could use a word-processing computer quickly took her ahead of her book contracts. And the appearance of Silhouette Desire paperback romance titles, beginning with *Corporate Affair* by Stephanie James (Jayne Ann Krentz), gave the author ideas about changing genres. Silhouette accepted her outline, she wrote the book, and in 1982 the Elizabeth Lowell pseudonym (a combination of Ann and Evan's middle names) was born. These days, the Lowell books are thrillers of the romantic-suspense variety.

The author's writing schedule varies with each book. "I work as many hours a day, as many days a week, as it takes me to get a book done on time," she says on her Web site. "As writing is only part of the work of a novel—research, especially on the suspense books, takes several months per book—there are too many times when my work is illegal!" She tries to write seven pages a day. She writes a long synopsis for each book.

Although her books have lots of twists and turns, the author told Contemporary Authors she is more concerned with character. "I create a sketch for each character, to bring them up to the moment the book will begin. I do not try to recreate an historical 'slice of life'…, but I do try to create characters my readers will respond to."

The author also pays great attention to setting. "Ninety-nine percent of the time, I go there," she said in an interview on the RBL Presents Web site. "When that's not possible (or downright dangerous for a lone tourist, as in China's Silk Road), I get videos, books, photos from people who have been there."

Her fans often request new books in the <u>Donovan</u>, <u>Fire Dancer</u>, or other series; on occasion she will comply, although she prefers to concentrate on the direction her recent thrillers have taken. Her books in the <u>Rarities Unlimited</u> series, for example, involve history, art, and unusual artifacts to trigger the action.

Although Lowell's writing has brought the author several awards, including a Romance Writers of America Lifetime Achievement Award in 1994, her identification with particular genres, and the grumblings of mainstream reviewers, has at times annoyed the author. In the essay "Popular Fiction: Why We Read It, Why We Write It," she wrote: "Readers of popular fiction judge an author by his or her ability to make the common language uncommonly meaningful, and to make an often told tale freshly exciting. The amount of effort a reader puts into this fiction is minimal. That, after all, is the whole point: to entertain readers rather than to exercise them."

Works by the Author

Written as A. E. Maxwell, with Evan Maxwell

Golden Empire (1979)
Steal the Sun (1983)
The Redwood Empire (1987), Harlequin Historical 267

<u>Fiddler and Flora Mysteries</u>

Just Another Day in Paradise (1985)

The Frog and the Scorpion (1986)
Gatsby's Vineyard (1987)
Just Enough Light to Kill (1988)
The Art of Survival (1989)
Money Burns (1992)
The King of Nothing (1992)
Murder Hurts (1993)

Written as Annalise Sun

The Golden Mountain (1990)

Written as Ann Maxwell, some with Evan Maxwell

Change (1975)
The Singer Enigma (1976)
A Dead God Dancing (1979)
The Jaws of Menx (1981)
Name of a Shadow (1984)
Timeshadow Rider (1986)
The Diamond Tiger (1992)
The Secret Sisters (1993)
The Ruby (1995)
Shadow and Silk (1997), sequel to *The Ruby*

Dancer Series

Fire Dancer (1982)
Dancer's Luck (1983)
Dancer's Illusion (1983)

Written as Elizabeth Lowell

The Danvers Touch (1983), Silhouette Intimate Moments 18, expanded as *To the Ends of the Earth* (1998)
Lover in the Rough (1983/expanded 1994), Silhouette Intimate Moments 34
Summer Thunder (1984), Silhouette Desire 77, expanded as *Desert Rain* (1996)
Summer Games (1984), Silhouette Intimate Moments 57, expanded as *Remember Summer* (1999)
Forget Me Not (1984/expanded 1994), Silhouette Intimate Moments 72
A Woman without Lies (1985/expanded 1995), Silhouette Intimate Moments 81
Traveling Man (1985), Silhouette Intimate Moments 97, expanded as *Where the Heart Is* (1997)
Valley of the Sun (1985), Silhouette Intimate Moments 109, expanded as *Beautiful Dreamer* (2001)

Sequel (1986), Silhouette Intimate Moments 128, expanded as *This Time Love* (2003)

The Fire of Spring (1986), Silhouette Desire 265

Too Hot to Handle (1986), Silhouette Desire 319

Fires of Eden (1986), Silhouette Intimate Moments 141, expanded as *Eden Burning* (2002)

Sweet Wind, Wild Wind (1987), Silhouette Intimate Moments 178

Love Song for a Raven (1987), Silhouette Desire 355

Chain Lightning (1988), Silhouette Intimate Moments 256

Fever (1988), Silhouette Desire 415

Dark Fire (1988), Silhouette Desire 462, sequel to *Fever*

Reckless Beach (1990)

Autumn Lover (1996)

Winter Fire (1996), sequel to *Autumn Lover*

Winter Fire/To the Ends of the Earth/Remember Summer (2001), omnibus

Death Is Forever (2004), rewrite of *The Diamond Tiger*

The Secret Sister (2005)

Forget Me Not/Beautiful Dreamer (2005), omnibus

Whirlpool (2006), rewrite of *The Ruby*

Donovan Series

Amber Beach (1997)

Jade Island (1998)

Pearl Cove (1999)

Midnight in Ruby Bayou (2000)

Amber Beach/Jade Island/Pearl Cove (2002), omnibus

MacKenzie-Blackthorn Series

Reckless Love (1990), Harlequin Historical 38

Fire and Rain (1990), Silhouette Desire 546

Outlaw (1991), Silhouette Desire 624

Granite Man (1991), Silhouette Desire 625

Warrior (1991), Silhouette Desire 631

Granite Man/Warrior (2007), omnibus

Fire and Rain/Outlaw (2007), omnibus

Medieval Series

Untamed (1993)

Forbidden (1993)

Enchanted (1994)

Only Series

Only His (1991)
Only You (1992)
Only Love (1995)
Only Mine (2003)

Rarities Unlimited Series

Moving Target (2001)
Running Scared (2002)
Die in Plain Sight (2003)
Color of Death (2004)

St. Kilda Series

Always Time to Die (2005)
The Wrong Hostage (2006)
Innocent as Sin (2007)
Blue Smoke and Murder (2008)

Contributor

Dangerous Men and Adventurous Women (1992)
Forever Mine, with Heather Graham and Nora Roberts (1998)
Summer Lovers: First, Best and Only/ Granite Man/Chain of Love, with Barbara Delinsky and Anne Stuart (1998)
Finding Home: Duncan's Bride/Chain Lightning/Popcorn and Kisses, with Linda Howard and Kasey Michaels (2001)
Love Song for a Raven/The Five-Minute Bride, with Leanne Banks (2001)
Summer Gold, with Barbara McCauley (2003)
At the Edge; Dark Fire/Wildcat/Return to Sender, with Rebecca Brandewyne and Merline Lovelace (2003)

Written as Lowell Charters

Thunderheart (1992), novelization of screenplay

Nonfiction

The Year-Long Day, written with Evan Maxwell as A. E. Maxwell (1976)

For Further Information

Ann Elizabeth Maxwell entry, Contemporary Authors Online. Reproduced in Biography Resource Center. Farmington Hills, MI: Thomas Gale, 2007. http://galenet.galegroup.com/servlet/BioRC (viewed November 16, 2007).

Elizabeth Lowell interview, RBL Romantica. http://www.geocities.com/interviews/lowellinterview.html (viewed December 24, 2007).

Elizabeth Lowell Web site. http://www.elizabethlowell.com/ (viewed November 16, 2008).

Lowell, Elizabeth, "Popular Fiction: Why We Read It, Why We Write It," Elizabeth Lowell Web site. http://www.elizabethlowell.com/popularfiction.html (viewed December 24, 2007).

Wehr, Isolde, "Interview with Elizabeth Lowell," Die romantische Bücherecke, April 2001. http://www.die-buecherecke.de/lowell2.HTM (viewed December 24, 2007).

White, Claire E., "A Conversation with Elizabeth Lowell," Writers Write, September 2000. http://www.writerswrite.com/journal/sep00/lowell.htm (viewed November 16, 2007).

Robert Ludlum

Adventure; Assassins; Espionage; Thrillers: Political, Biography, Nazis

Benchmark Title: *The Bourne Identity*

New York, New York

1927–2001

About the Author and the Author's Writing

Robert Ludlum's name appears on posthumously published espionage thrillers. A trilogy of films starring Matt Damon has topped the box office lists. There are even *Bourne Ultimatum* mobile phones and *Bourne Conspiracy* video games.

Robert Ludlum has become a brand.

"People expect something from a Robert Ludlum book, and if we can publish Ludlum books for the next 50 years and satisfy readers, we will," Ludlum estate executor Jeffrey Weiner told *New York Times* writer Richard Sandomir in 2007.

Ludlum was popular with readers from the start.

"Robert Ludlum [became] an eagerly collected author because of sheer immense popularity," in the view of Otto Penzler in *The Armchair Detective*. "His type of action-espionage thriller has influenced so many subsequent writers that the term 'Ludlum-esque' has become an accepted shorthand definition of the sort of novel that he single-handedly made so incredibly popular." Ludlum's stories have the sharpness of a dramatic script, and his characters speak with the crispness of actors, thanks to the author's first career as a stage performer and television actor. Born in 1927 in New York City, Ludlum was the son of a businessman and his wife. He grew up in Short Hills, New Jersey, and went to school at Cheshire Academy in Connecticut. At age sixteen, he landed a part in the Broadway show, *Junior Miss*. While on the road with the show in Michigan, he crossed the border and tried to enlist in the Canadian Air Force. Rejected for his youth, he returned home and eventually joined the U.S. Marine Corps. He saw action in the South Pacific from 1945 to 1947. He graduated with a bachelor of arts degree from Wesleyan University in 1951. While there, he met Mary Ruducha, an actress who became his wife. They had three children. For eight years, from 1952 to 1959, the Ludlums acted in summer stock and on and off Broadway. Robert Ludlum appeared in some two hundred television drama episodes including *Studio One, Robert Montgomery Presents*, and *Kraft Television Theater*. He also established and produced plays at North Jersey Playhouse in Fort Lee, New Jersey, from 1957 to 1969; then, for the next decade produced shows in New York City and Paramus, New Jersey. His first novel, *The Scarlatti Inheritance*, about a group of European financiers who after World War I put up the cash for Adolf Hitler's charge into the Third Reich, climbed onto the best-seller list, as did each of the nearly dozen books that followed.

Ludlum theorized it was his storytelling that set him apart from his contemporaries. "Life is extremely complicated," Ludlum said in an interview for Bookreporter. "I try as best I can to enter the realm of nuances of human behavior and alternatives of that behavior."

Ludlum's hallmark is the arena of mega-power. His twisting, turning tales delve into governmental secrets, huge conspiracies, and vile corruption. From such a dark morass rises the Ludlum hero, an idealist, a democrat, an individualist, tolerant yet strong and loyal. "Ludlum chooses somewhat ordinary men as his heroes to fight against these evils [cabals and enemy governments]. They are often in their 40s, of upper-middle class backgrounds, and with strong ideas of what is morally right," explained Karen Hinckley in *St. James Guide to Crime & Mystery Writers*.

Never a typist, much less a computer user, Ludlum wrote his manuscripts by hand on a yellow pad. A book typically took three months to research and as long as fifteen months to write. Ludlum put together the concept for a series of books to feature an elite, top-secret team of troubleshooters headed by Colonel Jonathan Smith, whose mission was to fight crime and corruption at the highest levels. Other authors have continued that <u>Covert-One Series</u> following his death in 2001. One of those authors, Gayle Lynds, observed on Mystery Ink, "As a writer of fiction, Robert Ludlum opened many doors for all of us not only politically but literarily. He brought passion, an informed sense of history, and a deep concern for the future to all his works. He was also unafraid to create strong female characters."

 # Works by the Author

The Scarlatti Inheritance (1971)
The Osterman Weekend (1972)
The Matlock Paper (1973)
The Rhinemann Exchange (1974)
The Gemini Contenders (1976)
The Chancellor Manuscript (1977)
The Holcroft Covenant (1978)
The Parsifal Mosaic (1982)
The Aquitaine Progression (1984)
The Icarus Agenda (1988)
Four Complete Novels (1988), includes *The Scarlatti Inheritance* and *The Osterman Weekend*
The Osterman Weekend, The Matlock Paper, and *The Gemini Contenders*
The Road to Omaha (1992)
The Scorpio Illusion (1993)
The Apocalypse Watch (1995)
The Prometheus Deception (2001)
The Sigma Protocol (2001), completed by Keith Kahla
The Janson Directive (2002), completed by Keith Kahla
The Tristan Betrayal (2003), completed by Keith Kahla
The Ambler Warning (2005)
The Bancroft Strategy (2007)

Brandon Scofield Series

The Matarese Circle (1979)
The Matarese Countdown (1995)

Jason Bourne Series

The Bourne Identity (1980)
The Bourne Supremacy (1986)
The Bourne Ultimatum (1990)
Three Great Novels (2003), omnibus
Robert Ludlum's The Bourne Legacy, by Eric Van Lustbader (2004)
Robert Ludlum's The Bourne Betrayal, by Eric Van Lustbader (2007)
Robert Ludlum's The Bourne Sanction, by Eric Van Lustbader (2008)
Robert Ludlum's The Bourne Deception by Eric Van Lustbader (2009)

Covert-One Series Created by Robert Ludlum

The Hades Factor, with Gayle Lynds (2000)
The Cassandra Compact, with Jonathan Smith (2001)
The Paris Option, with Gayle Lynds (2002)
The Altman Code, by Gayle Lynds (2003)
The Lazarus Vendetta, by Patrick Larkin (2004)
The Moscow Vector, by Patrick Larkin (2005)
The Arctic Event, by James Cobb (2007)
The Infinity Affair, by James Cobb (2009)

Written as Michael Shephard

The Road to Gandolfo (1975), reissued as by Robert Ludlum (1992)

Sherlock Holmes Series

Sherlock Holmes and the Case of Dr. Freud (1985), chapbook

Written as Jonathan Ryder

Trevayne (1973), reissued as by Robert Ludlum (1989)
The Cry of the Halidon (1974), reissued as by Robert Ludlum (1996)

Adaptations in Other Media

The Rhinemann Exchange (1977), television miniseries
The Osterman Weekend (1983), motion picture
The Holcroft Covenant (1985), motion picture
The Bourne Identity (1988), television film
The Apocalypse Watch (1997), television film
The Bourne Identity (2002), motion picture

The Bourne Supremacy (2004), motion picture
Covert One: The Hades Factor (2006), television film
The Bourne Ultimatum (2007), motion picture

For Further Information

Greenberg, Martin H., ed. *The Robert Ludlum Companion*. New York: Bantam, 1993.

Hinckley, Karen, Robert Ludlum entry. *St. James Guide to Crime & Mystery Writers*, 4th ed., Jay P. Pederson, ed. Detroit, MI: St. James Press, 1996.

Lynds, Gayle, "How I Came to Collaborate with Bob Ludlum." *Mystery Scene* No. 68 (2000).

Lynds, Gayle, "Remembering Robert Ludlum (1927–2001)," Mystery Ink. http://www.mysteryinkonline.com/ludlumrip.htm (viewed June 10, 2003).

MacDonald, Gina. *Robert Ludlum: A Critical Companion*. Westport, CT: Greenwood Press.

Maryles, Daisy, "Ludlum's Legacy." *Publishers Weekly,* October 28, 2002.

Penzler, Otto, "Collecting Mystery Fiction: Robert Ludlum," *The Armchair Detective* (Fall 1989).

Robert Ludlum biography, Barnes & Noble. http://www.barnesandnoble.com/writers/writerdetails.asp?userid=2UHJZHFY29&cid=91353#bio (viewed October 23, 2007).

Robert Ludlum entry. *Newsmakers*, volume 1. Detroit, MI: Gale Group, 2002.

Robert Ludlum interview, Bookreporter. http://www.bookreporter.com/features/020614-ludlum.asp (viewed October 23, 2007).

Robert Ludlum obituary, ashgroveaudiobook.com. URL: http//www.ashgroveaudiobook.com/grove/info_authors_ludlum.html (viewed June 10, 2003).

Robert Ludlum profile, Books and Writers. http://www.kirjasto.sci.fi/ludlum.htm (viewed October 23, 2007).

Robert Ludlum Web page. http://www.ludlumbooks.com (viewed October 23, 2007).

Sandomir, Richard, "The Ludlum Conundrum: A Dead Novelist Provides New Thrills." *New York Times*, July 30, 2007.

Valby, Karen, "Tome Raiders: Reports of Their Demise Are Greatly Exaggerated: How Dead Authors Are 'Writing' New Books." *Entertainment Weekly,* May 4, 2001.

"Vivendi Games Mobile Brings Robert Ludlum's Best-Selling Novel and Upcoming Movie *The Bourne Ultimatum* to Mobile Phones Worldwide." PR Newswire, August 3, 2007.

Eric Lustbader

**Adventure; Crime;
Espionage; Fantasy;
Thrillers: Political, Global**

Benchmark Series: <u>Nicholas Linnear</u>

New York, New York

1946–

Photo credit: Victoria Lustbader

About the Author and the Author's Writing

Many thriller writers aspire to become Robert Ludlum, but Eric Lustbader actually *did* become Robert Ludlum, writing best-selling sequels in the <u>Bourne</u> espionage series.

Lustbader didn't come out of nowhere to contract with the Ludlum estate to write the books in the frantic-paced Ludlum vein; he had already carved out a name for himself with his <u>Nicholas Linnear/Ninja</u> series and his <u>Sunset Warrior</u> fantasy novels.

Eric Van Lustbader was born in New York City's Greenwich Village in 1946 and graduated from Stuyvesant High School. His father was director of the state Social Security bureau. Lustbader was a music producer from 1963 to 1967 then received a bachelor of arts degree in sociology from Columbia University in 1968 and, with certification in elementary education, taught for two years. A music lover ever since he saw the Beatles on the *Ed Sullivan Show* in 1964, he wrote reviews for and eventually joined *Cashbox* magazine as an associate editor in 1970 (he was one of the first to anticipate the success of Elton John, Santana, and The Who). In 1972, he left to become director of international artists and repertory with Elektra records. He worked for other music-related businesses and was a writer and field producer with NBC-TV in New York in 1976, leaving to work with CBS records as a publicist and album cover designer in 1976. In 1978, he became a full-time fiction writer, after the success of his first <u>Sunset Warrior</u> books.

He married freelance editor Victoria Schochet in 1982. Their Long Island home is planted with unusual Japanese maple and beech species. Lustbader is a second-level master in Reiki, an energy healing practice.

Lustbader has long been fascinated with Japanese culture and used his knowledge in his fantasy novels about the Bladesman Ronin.

"I started out reading fantasy and science fiction, spy novels, when I was a teenager," Lustbader told interviewer Claire E. White, "but I was very much affected by the poetry of Walt Whitman and John Donne. I was particularly taken with *Moby Dick,*

Dracula, and *Frankenstein.* I also learned a great deal from the ancient Greek playwrights."

Before he finished this series, the author wrote a contemporary novel with a similar background, *The Ninja* (1980), which, although rejected by several editors, proved a best seller for publisher M. Evans. The protagonist, Nicholas Linnear, of English-Asian extraction honed in the mystical ways of the ninja, investigates murders on Wall Street. The <u>Linnear</u> books became a series.

With these books, Lustbader began to ground his contemporary novels in Far Eastern tradition. "I've been fascinated by how history informs the thinking and actions, not only of individuals, but of groups and, even, countries," the author said in an interview on his Web site. "That's why, before I wrote a word of my first thriller, *The Ninja,* in 1980, I steeped myself in the history, legends and lore of Japan."

Lustbader wasn't finished with fantasy. *The Ring of Five Dragons* (2001) began a trilogy set against the opposition of the technologically advanced Vornn and the more spiritual Kundalan. Another of Lustbader's interests found in *Ring* is the ways the two sexes act differently in certain circumstances and how often men and women are unable to communicate at critical times.

Lustbader and Robert Ludlum had the same agent, and when the two writers met, they became friends. They had several conversations about the mechanics of writing thrillers. After Ludlum's death, his agent asked Lustbader to continue the <u>Bourne</u> books, which enjoyed enormous popularity thanks to a motion picture (the first of three) starring Matt Damon.

On his Web site, the author confesses that he never outlined his books before he took the <u>Bourne</u> assignment—he felt too strict a road map would inhibit a sense of spontaneity in his writing. But his <u>Bourne</u> contract called for an outline, and he found he could simply describe what the character would do in particular chapters while leaving himself considerable room for creativity. The outline, in fact, kept him on track and eliminated the frequent experience of having to shed digressive chapters.

With *The Bourne Legacy,* Lustbader immediately picked up with Ludlum's characters to establish continuity with the original books—then immediately killed most of them off. "I know Bourne inside and out," the author said in an interview with Aaron Hughes. "I know what makes him tick. So it was very easy for me to write about him, and tremendous fun. I've had the most fun writing this book since I wrote *The Ninja.* I think it's the best thriller I've ever written."

So did readers, who, naturally, demanded sequels.

 # Works by the Author

Sirens (1981)

Black Heart (1983)

Jian (1986)

Zero (1987)

Shan (1988), sequel to *Jian*

French Kiss (1989)

Angel Eyes (1991)

Batman: The Last Angel (1992), graphic novel

Black Blade (1993)
Dark Homecoming (1997)
Pale Saint (1999)
Art Kills (2002), chapbook
The Bravo Testament (2006), in United States as *The Testament*
First Daughter (2008)

Nicholas Linnear/Ninja Series

The Ninja (1980)
The Miko (1984)
White Ninja (1990)
The Kaisho (1993)
Floating City (1994)
Second Skin (1995)

Pearl Series

The Ring of Five Dragons (2001)
The Veil of a Thousand Tears (2002)
The Cage of Nine Banestones (2004), in United States as *Mistress of the Pearl*

Robert Ludlum's Bourne Series

The Bourne Legacy (2004)
The Bourne Betrayal (2007)
The Bourne Sanction (2008)
The Bourne Deception (2009)

Sunset Warrior Series

The Sunset Warrior (1977)
Shallows of Night (1978)
Dai-San (1978)
Beneath an Opal Moon (1980)
Dragons on the Sea of Night (1997)

Anthologies

David Copperfield's Beyond Imagination, edited by Janet Berliner, David Copperfield, and Martin H. Greenberg (1982)
Peter S. Beagle's Immortal Unicorn, edited by Peter S. Beagle, Janet Berliner, and Martin H. Greenberg (1984)
David Copperfield's Tales of the Impossible, edited by Janet Berliner, David Copperfield, and Martin H. Greenberg (1995)
Excalibur, edited by Richard Gilliam, Martin H. Greenberg, and Edward E. Kramer (1995)

Murder for Revenge, edited by Otto Penzler (1996)
Vampires: The Greatest Stories, edited by Martin H. Greenberg (1997)
Off the Beaten Path: Stories of Place, edited by Joseph Barbato (1998)
999, edited by Al Sarrantonio (1999)
Murder and Obsession, edited by Otto Penzler (2000)
Thriller: Stories to Keep You Up All Night, edited by James Patterson (2006)

For Further Information

Eric Lustbader entry, Contemporary Authors Online, reproduced in Biography Resource Center. Farmington Hills, MI: Thomson Gale, 2007. http://galenet.galegroupcolm/servlet.BioRC (viewed December 1, 2007).

Eric Van Lustbader Web site. http://www.ericvanlustbader.com (viewed November 15, 2008).

Hughes, Aaron, "Eric Van Lustbader Interview," Fantastic Reviews. http://www.geocities.com/fantasticreviews/lustbader_interview.htm (viewed December 1, 2007).

White, Claire E., "A Conversation with Eric Van Lustbader," Writers Write. http://www.writerswrite.com/journal/Jul01/lustbader.htm (viewed December 1, 2007).

John T. Lutz

Crime-Suspense; Horror; Thrillers: Serial Killers

Benchmark Title: *The Night Caller*

Dallas, Texas

1939–

Photo credit: Jennifer Lutz

About the Author and the Author's Writing

Injured in the line of duty as a police bomb squad officer, Will Harper takes an early retirement and begins to fix up the family home. He is lured back to unofficial duty when his ex-partner Jimmy Fahey is blown up along with his employer, a best-selling author of techno thrillers. The killer, in John Lutz's *Final Seconds* (1998), is a terrorist with his eye on celebrity targets. Harper tracks the killer, with the help of a mysterious FBI profiler and a female agent who is African American. They must capture the mad man before he kills a British princess.

Lutz was born in Dallas, Texas, in 1939. He attended Meramec Community College in 1965, then worked as a construction laborer, truck driver, and civilian employee to the St. Louis Police Department. In 1958, he married Barbara Jean Bradley, and they have three children. He lives in St. Louis.

Lutz began his professional writing career as a specialist in the short form. In 1966, he sold his first story to *Alfred Hitchcock's Mystery Magazine*; since 1971, he has produced more than two hundred more stories, as well as some forty novels in four series.

"Some of the best [of Lutz's early stories] took off from the wildest premises: a lunatic trying to solve a murder in the asylum, the last hours of a tycoon accidentally locked into his walk-in vault by a watchdog," observed Francis M. Nevins in *St. James Guide to Crime & Mystery Writers*.

Lutz had no difficulty transferring to the longer form; both required the same commitment, although "I think the novel is the more forgiving discipline," he said in a Bookreporter interview. "The short story only seems easier because it takes less time and doesn't nag like a novel. It's really a high-wire act; one misstep and it will fall flat."

Where does the author get his ideas? He smiled at the question, and suggested on his Web site the unlikelihood of researching his latest novel about a serial killer. "I've

265

often heard that oft-given advice on writing about what you know, while I was sitting on a panel with four or five other people who wrote about mayhem and murder and were mostly afraid to step on a spider. Keep in mind we get paid for lying convincingly."

In blog comments on Amazon.com Lutz explains that an idea for *Chill of Night* came to him while on jury duty: What if someone dissatisfied with an acquittal verdict thinks otherwise, and seeks revenge? *Fear the Night*, he said, grew in part from an experience one night walking in Midtown Manhattan when he heard the reverberating bang of what he later learned was a construction crane falling to the street. How might a serial killer use an unexpected, shocking wham to terrorize the city?

Two of Lutz's free-standing thrillers were made into films, *SWF Seeks Same* and *The Ex*. But the author has been comfortable with four continuing series, beginning with the <u>Alo Nudger</u> books in 1976. Nudger is a private detective in St. Louis. Something of an anti-Mike Hammer, he has an office above Danny's Donuts, thrives on baseball trivia, and has little physical courage, but he does what he has to for his clients, even if they are deadbeats. Lutz's second series features a more traditional P.I., Floridian Fred Carver, who had to leave the police force when incapacitated by a bullet in the knee.

In *Mystery Scene*, Lutz said his heroes have both similarities (as required by the genre) and differences. They inspire different plot directions. "A few degrees' difference on the compass at the beginning of the journey can result in a variance of miles as the traveler progresses," he explained. "Slight differences in the characters will increasingly make them two distinct individuals."

"Both Carver and Nudger have feelings of inadequacy and physical problems so they have steeper uphill climbs," he explained further in a Bleeker Books interview.

In the 1990s, Lutz was busy writing the <u>Be Puzzled</u> books and then began a loose series with an ensemble police cast, all (until recently) with "Night" in the title. *In for the Kill* (2007), puts homicide detective Frank Quinn on the trail of "The Butcher." Bookreporter reviewer Joe Hartlaub said the book "grabs you at the very beginning and does not let go until, utterly spent, you have reached the last page."

That, after all, is the thriller writer's task, ably accomplished.

Works by the Author

The Truth of the Matter (1971)
Bonegrinder (1976)
Lazarus Man (1979)
Jericho Man (1980)
The Shadow Man (1981)
The Eye, with Bill Pronzini (1984)
Dancer's Debt (1988)
Shadowtown (1988), sequel to *The Eye*
Time Exposure (1989)
SWF Seeks Same (1990)
Dancing with the Dead (1992)
The Ex (1996)

Final Seconds, with David August (David Lindze) (1998)
Night Kills (2008)

Alo Nudger Series

Buyer Beware (1976)
Night Lines (1984)
The Right to Sing the Blues (1986)
Ride the Lightning (1987)
Dancer's Debt (1988)
Time Exposure (1989)
Diamond Eyes (1990)
Thicker than Blood (1993)
Death by Jury (1995)
Oops! (1998)
The Nudger Dilemmas (2001), stories

Be Puzzled Series

Double Cross (1989)
Feline Frenzy (1991)
Burning Evidence (1993)
Flowers from a Stranger (1994)
Grounds for Murder (1995)
Taxed to Death (1996)
Undercover Cat (1996)
Murder on the Titanic (1997)

Fred Carver Series

Tropical Heat (1986)
Scorcher (1987)
Kiss (1988)
Flame (1990)
Bloodfire (1991)
Hot (1992)
Spark (1993)
Torch (1994)
Burn (1995)
Lightning (1996)

Night Series

The Night Caller (2001)
The Night Watcher (2002)

The Night Spider (2003)
Darker than Night (2004)
Fear the Night (2005)
Chill of Night (2006)
In for the Kill (2007)

Collections

Better Mousetraps, edited by Francis M. Nevins (1988)
Shadows Everywhere (1994)
Until You Are Dead (1998)
Endless Road (2005)

Anthologies

The Eyes Have It, edited by Robert J. Randisi (1984), includes "Typographical Error"
Mean Streets, edited by Robert J. Randisi (1986), includes "The Thunder of Guilt"
The New Adventures of Sherlock Holmes, edited by Martin H. Greenberg and Carol-Lynn Rossel Waugh (1987), includes "The Infernal Machine"
An Eye for Justice, edited by Robert J. Randisi (1988), includes "Libra," written with Josh Pachter
Raymond Chandler's Philip Marlowe, edited by Byron Preiss (1988), includes "Star Bright"
Mistletoe Mysteries, edited by Charlotte MacLeod (1989), includes "The Live Tree"
Justice for Hire, edited by Robert J. Randisi (1990), includes "Someone Else"
Dick Tracy—the Secret Files, edited by Max Allan Collins and Martin H. Greenberg (1990) includes "Old Saying"
Cat Crimes, edited by Martin H. Greenberg (1991), includes "Finicky"
The Ultimate Dracula, edited by Byron Preiss (1991), includes "Mr. Lucrada"
Invitation to Murder, edited by Bill Pronzini (1991), includes "Open and Shut"
Solved (1991), includes "White Mustangs"
Deadly Allies, edited by Robert J. Randisi (1992), includes "Before You Leap"
Cat Crimes III, edited by Martin H. Greenberg (1992), includes "Kitty"
Danger in D.C.: Cat Crimes in the Nation's Capital, edited by Ed Gorman (1993) includes "The President's Cat Is Missing"
Deals with the Devil, edited by Mike Resnick, Martin H. Greenberg, and Loren Estleman (1993), includes "Jelly Reds"
Santa Clues, edited by Martin H. Greenberg and Charles G. Waugh (1993), includes "Slay Belle"
The Mysterious West, edited by Tony Hillerman (1994), includes "Bingo"
Dracula: Prince of Darkness, edited by Martin H. Greenberg (1994), includes "After the Ball"

Feline and Famous, edited by Martin H. Greenberg (1994), includes "Crazy Business"

Deadly Allies II, edited by Robert J. Randisi (1994), includes "The Romantics"

Murder Is My Business, edited by Mickey Spillane and Max Allan Collins (1994), includes "With Anchovies"

Vampire Detectives, edited by Martin H. Greenberg (1995), includes "Shell Game"

Dark Love, edited by Nancy A. Collins, Edward E. Kramer, and Martin H. Greenberg (1995), includes "Hanson's Radio"

Celebrity Vampires, edited by Martin H. Greenberg (1995), includes "Plague"

Unusual Suspects, edited by James Grady (1996), includes "Shock"

Homicide Hosts Presents, edited by Robert J. Randisi (1996), includes "You Belong to Me"

Guilty as Charged, edited by Scott Turow (1996), includes "Dogs and Fleas"

Cat Crimes Goes on Holiday, edited by Martin H. Greenberg, Ed Gorman, and Larry Segriff (1997), includes "But Once a Year"

Murder on Route 66, edited by Carolyn Wheat (1998), includes "Endless Road"

Once upon a Crime, edited by Ed Gorman (1998), includes "Swan Song"

Diagnosis Dead, edited by Jonathan Kellerman (1999), includes "Image"

Mystery in the Sunshine State, edited by Stuart M. Kaminsky (1999), includes "Machete"

Death Cruise, edited by Lawrence Block (1999), includes "S.O.S."

First Lady Murders (1999), includes "Political Decision"

Irreconcilable Differences, edited by Lia Matera and Martin H. Greenberg (1999), includes "Stutter Step"

Till Death Do Us Part (1999), includes "Traveling Alone," with Barbara Lutz

The Shamus Game, edited by Robert J. Randisi (2000), includes "The Litigants"

Unholy Orders, edited by Serita Stevens (2000), includes "Dilemma"

The Blue and the Gray Undercover, edited by Ed Gorman (2002), includes "Hobson's Choice"

Flesh and Blood: Dark Desires, edited by Max Allan Collins and Jeff Gelb (2002), includes "Lily and Men"

Death Dance (2002), includes "Tango Was Her Life"

Murder Most Confederate, edited by Martin H. Greenberg (2003), includes "Veterans"

Guilty as Sin (2003), includes "Nighthawks"

A Hot and Sultry Night for Crime, edited by Jeffery Deaver (2003), includes "El Palacio"

Show Business Is Murder, edited by Stuart M. Kaminsky (2004), includes "Arful"

Murder ... and All That Jazz, edited by Robert J. Randisi (2004), includes "Chop Suey"

Manhattan Noir, edited by Lawrence Block (2006), includes "The Laundry Room"

Screenplays

The Ex, with Larry Cohen (1997), motion picture based on the novel

Adaptations in Other Media

Single White Female (1992), based on *SWF Seeks Same*

For Further Information

"Alo Nudger," Thrilling Detective. http://www.thrillingdetective.com/nudger_a.html (viewed February 4, 2008).

"Fred Carver," Thrilling Detective. http://www.thrillingdetective.com/carver_f.html (viewed February 4, 2008).

In for the Kill review, Barnes & Noble. http://search.barnesandnoble.com/booksearch/isbnInquiry.asp?z=y&EAN=9780786018437&itm=1 (viewed February 4, 2008).

In for the Kill review, Bookreporter. http://www.bookreporter.com/reviews2/9780786018437.asp (viewed February 4, 2008).

John Lutz entry, Bookreporter. http://www.bookreporter.com/suspense_thriller/0710lutz/facts.asp (viewed February 4, 2008).

John Lutz entry, Wikipedia. http://en.wikipedia.org/wiki/John_lutz (viewed February 4, 2008).

John Lutz interview, Bookreporter, 2007. http://www.bookreporter.com/authors/au-lutz-john.asp (viewed February 4, 2008).

John Lutz Online. http://www.johnlutzonline.com (viewed February 4, 2008).

John Thomas Lutz entry, Contemporary Authors Online. Reproduced in Biography Resource Center. Farmington Hills, MI: Thomson Gale, 2008. http//galenet.galegroup.com/servlet/BioRC (viewed February 4, 2008).

"Lutz for Life," Bleeker Books. http://www.bleekerbooks.com/features/Lutzinterview.asp (viewed February 4, 2008).

Lutz, John, "Two-Timers." *Mystery Scene*, No. 41, 1993.

Nevins, Francis M., John Lutz entry. *St. James Guide to Crime & Mystery Writers*, 4th ed., Jay P. Pederson, ed. Detroit, MI: St. James Press, 1996.

Gayle Lynds

Adventure; Espionage; Thrillers: Crime, Political

Benchmark Title: *The Last Spymaster*

Omaha, Nebraska

1945–

Photo credit: Jay Farbman

About the Author and the Author's Writing

It surprises many that the woman author who co-developed the <u>Covert-One</u> series with Robert Ludlum actually cut her thriller teeth on the dime-novel hero Nick Carter in his 1970s incarnation as an American counterpart to James Bond.

Gayle Lynds has carved out a solid reputation for her own espionage novels as well those in series developed by others. Her late husband, Dennis Lynds (1924–2005), was a prolific writer under his own name, as well as under the names Mark Sadler, Maxwell Grant, and—perhaps the best known—Michael Collins. He also wrote a few Nick Carter paperbacks, which is how Lynds became interested in the genre.

Born in Omaha, Nebraska, in 1945, Gayle Hallenbeck grew up in Council Bluffs, Iowa, in a family that loved to read. She earned a journalism degree (with a minor in social studies) from the University of Iowa; married; was managing editor of the *Daily Iowan*; worked as an investigative reporter for the *Arizona Republic;* raised two children, Julia and Paul Stone; worked for a private think tank in California; divorced; wrote literary short stories for several journals; and found herself needing a reliable income.

"That's when I went to work for a magazine and a friend asked whether I could write <u>Nick Carter</u> novels," she said in an interview with Cathy Sova of Mystery Reader. "By then I was desperate, and so I lied: 'Of course I can.'" She wrote not one, but five novels, two <u>Mack Bolan</u> action series entries, also three books in the <u>Alfred Hitchcock and the Three Investigators</u> young adult series before writing the first novel to appear under her own name, *Masquerade*. Despite her background, she ran into a gender block when an initially receptive New York publisher ultimately rejected the book and told Gayle Lynds no woman could have written it, the author told Tom Nolan of the *Wall Street Journal.*

It's the hard reality of breaking into a competitive field, Lynds said in a conversation with mystery author Sue Grafton in 2003. "That's part of the process. Even if you publish with a New York publisher as a beginning mystery writer, you're going to get a $5,000 advance and honey, you'd better keep your day job."

But Gayle Lynds had good training. Her second husband, Dennis Lynds, whom she married in 1986, nurtured her fiction writing. She credits his spare, lyrical prose as influencing her own style—a style that caught the attention of thrill-master Robert Ludlum. Ludlum invited her to work with him to develop the Covert-One series. She wrote *The Hades Factor* and two more books about Lieutenant Colonel Jonathan "Jon" Smith M.D. and a team of ultra-secret technicians and political specialists who face corruption, crime, and terrorism at the highest levels.

"I grew up on Bob Ludlum books," Lynds said on her Web site. "He opened the world to me in a way no other author of international affairs had, including John le Carré and Graham Greene. Bob was the first novelist to write about the CIA's operating illegally in the United States, and he popularized the unthinkable notion that American and Soviet spies could work together."

Lynds came to the Ludlum partnership with a particular strength; she had worked with top security clearance at a California think tank for the military. She'd gotten the idea of working for a think tank from author Kurt Vonnegut, with whom she once took a writing class. Her tenure there introduced her to the world of "spookspeak," with which she peppers her novels, and gave her an appreciation for the latest in technology (the illegal weapons trade figures in *The Last Spymaster*).

With *Masquerade* (placed with Doubleday) Lynds was able to leave her day job. She continued to write her own stand-alone espionage novels, including two, *Mesmerized* (2001) and *The Coil* (2004) that delved into the families and entangled private lives of undercover operatives. Lynds is also cofounder and copresident with David Morrell of International Thriller Writers Inc.

Lynds has become so attuned to the global political world that her books have anticipated world events. *Mesmerized*, for example, about a corrupt spy, came out just as Robert Hanssen was arrested as a mole and an American traitor. *The Paris Option* (2002), written before 9/11, has a subplot involving al-Qaeda.

"The malaise of the post–Cold War, pre-9/11 years is over. Americans hunger to understand this new, dangerous world in which we can no longer close our eyes. Certainly we can't escape it. Topics, ideas and characters permeate the dynamic.... A novelist's dream come true," Lynds said in a Bookreporter interview in 2006.

Works by the Author

Masquerade (1996)

Mosaic (1998)

Mesmerized (2001)

The Coil (2004), sequel to *Mesmerized*

The Last Spymaster (2005)

Covert-One Series with Robert Ludlum

The Hades Factor (2000)

The Paris Option (2003)
The Altman Code (2003)

Written with Mark Sadler (Dennis Lynds)

Common Enemy (1990), never distributed

Mack Bolan Series, with Mark Sadler (Dennis Lynds) as by Don Pendleton

Moving Target (1989)
Blood Fever (1989)

Nick Carter Series as by Nick Carter

Day of the Mahdi (1984)
Mayan Connection (1984)
Pursuit of the Eagle (1985)
White Death (1985)
Execution Exchange (1985)

Anthologies

Mayhem in the Midlands, edited by Robert J. Randisi and Christine Matthews (2002)

I'd Kill for That (2004), serial novel with Rita Mae Brown, Marcia Talley, Lisa Gardner, Linda Fairstein, Kay Hooper, Kathy Reichs, Julie Smith, Heather Graham, Jennifer Crusie, Tina Wainscott, Anne Perry, and Katherine Neville

Thriller: Stories to Keep You Up All Night, edited by James Patterson (2006)

Young Adult Fiction written as G. H. Stone

Alfred Hitchcock and the Three Investigators Crimebusters Series
Rough Stuff (1989)
Reel Trouble (1990)
Fatal Error (1990)

Nonfiction

Intimacy: Strategies for Successful Relationships, as by Gayle Stone, with C. Edward Crowther (1988)

Adaptations in Other Media

The Hades Factor (CBS miniseries, 2006)

For Further Information

"Down and Dirty Dialogue between Gayle Lynds and Sue Grafton." *The Independent*, September 18, 2003.

Gayle Lynds interview, Bookreporter. http://www.bookreporter/com/authors/au-lynds-gayle.asp (viewed October 8, 2007).

Gayle Lynds Web site. http://www.gaylelynds.com (viewed November 15, 2008).

"Interview with Gayle Lunds," Readers Read, July 2006. http://www.readersread.com/feature/gaylelynds.htm (viewed October 8, 2007).

Lynds, Gayle, "Working with Robert Ludlum," Gayle Lynds Web site. http://www.gaylelynds.com/ludlum.html (viewed October 8, 2007).

Nolan, Tom, "Women Writers Infiltrate the Realm of Spy Novels." *Wall Street Journal*, May 18, 2004.

Sova, Cathy, "Meet Gayle Lynds," The Mystery Reader. http://www.themysteryreader.com/lynds.html (viewed October 8, 2007)

Phillip Margolin

Crime-Suspense; Thrillers: Legal, Political

Benchmark Title: *Gone, but Not Forgotten*

New York, New York

1944–

About the Author and the Author's Writing

Phillip Margolin wasn't old enough to have appreciated firsthand America's first popular fictional lawyer—Arthur Train's Ephraim Tutt. But in the 1950s and 1960s, he became hooked during the era of the next popular fictional lawyer—Erle Stanley Gardner's Perry Mason. And by the time John Grisham and Scott Turow ushered in the latest docket of courtroom thrillers, he was ready to put his own spin on the popular literary subgenre.

"Perry Mason novels made me want to be a criminal defense attorney, and I was one for twenty-five years," the author said in a Meet the Writers interview. "All of my novels have been legal thrillers. If it weren't for Perry, I might not have been a criminal defense attorney and written about what I know."

Margolin was born in New York City in 1944. After earning a bachelor of arts degree in government from American University in 1965, he served in the Peace Corps in Liberia for two years. Back in New York, he taught in public schools for two years and studied at New York University School of Law, which granted him a juris doctorate in 1970. In 1971–1972, he clerked for the chief justice of the Oregon Court of Appeals in Salem, Oregon. He was a deputy district attorney and special agent for Multnomah County during that same period. He went into private practice in 1972 and was a partner with Nash & Margolin from 1974 to 1980 and Margolin & Margolin from 1986 to 1996. He married Doreen Stamm in 1968. She is also an attorney. They have two children.

Margolin wrote his first short story while establishing his law practice. "The Girl in the Yellow Bikini" appeared in *Mike Shayne's Mystery Magazine* and was later reprinted as a booklet in *Elle* magazine and as an Amazon Shorts digital story. The sale gave Margolin the confidence to work on a novel, which he passed on to a friend from law school, who gave it to a client who was a literary agent, who then sold it to Pocket Books. *Heartstone* (1978), about the murder of a couple at a lover's lane, was nominated for a Mystery Writers of America award for best original paperback. Inspiration came from a well-known Oregon crime, the murders of college students Larry Peyton and Beverly Allen. With the 800-page appeal brief (prepared by another counsel) as bedside reading, he had ample background material for the book.

Margolin wrote one more novel, *The Last Innocent Man* (1981), but felt over-whelmed at his budding second career. The book was made into an HBO movie. Margolin nevertheless concentrated on law and didn't write another book for more than a decade.

As a lawyer, Margolin handled thirty murder trials and filed eighty appeals. He appeared before the U.S. Supreme Court, as well as federal circuit and state courts. He worked with some thirty clients who were charged with murder. He was the first coun-sel in Oregon to present the battered woman's syndrome during one client's trial.

"If I were in New York, it probably would have been different; there would have been parties and stuff, but I just went about my business," the author said in an AbsoluteWrite.com interview.

In 1993, Margolin's third novel leapt onto the *New York Times* best-seller list. *Gone, but Not Forgotten* grew out of a dinner conversation about moral dilemmas. He crafted a heroine, Betsy Tannenbaum, who specialized in women clients but is hired by an alleged serial killer, Martin Darius, to represent him at a murder trial.

Comfortable with women characters, Margolin introduced Amanda Jaffe in *Wild Justice*, gave her a small role in *The Associate,* then featured her again in *Ties That Bind* and *Proof Positive*. In the last book mentioned, the author tips crime scene inves-tigation on its head.

Margolin became president and chairman of the board of Chess for Success, a Portland school program, in 1996. He has said that chess, an avocational passion, helped him anticipate his opponent's moves and devise intricate plots. He roughs out his books much as a screenwriter might block scenes, then shapes the scenes into chapters.

"To me, writing a novel is like solving a puzzle, and I love to do crossword puz-zles. I try to have as many surprises and twists as possible," he told *Portland Life*'s Paul Duchene. "If everything doesn't fit, people get mad at me."

 Works by the Author

Heartstone (1978)

The Last Innocent Man (1981)

Gone, but Not Forgotten (1993)

After Dark (1995)

The Burning Man (1996)

Rookgordijn (1997) (or *Smokescreen*), published only in Holland

The Undertaker's Widow (1998)

The Girl in the Yellow Bikini (2002), *Elle* magazine chapbook (2007), Amazon
    Shorts digital story

Sleeping Beauty (2004)

Lost Lake (2005)

Executive Privilege (2008)

Fugitive (2009)

Amanda Jaffe Series

Wild Justice (2000)

The Associate (2002)
Ties That Bind (2003)
Proof Positive (2006)

Anthologies

Murder for Revenge, edited by Otto Penzler (1998), includes "Angie's Delight"
Legal Briefs, edited by William Bernhardt (1998), includes "The Jailhouse Lawyer"
The Best American Mystery Stories 1999, edited by Ed McBain (1999), includes "The Jailhouse Lawyer"

Adaptations in Other Media

The Last Innocent Man (1987), HBO film
Gone, but Not Forgotten (2004), Hallmark television film
Angie's Delight (2006), short film based on the short story

For Further Information

Dirks, Jennifer, "The Mystery behind Phillip Margolin's Best-Sellers," Absolute Write. http://www.absolutewrite.com/novels/phillip_margolin.htm (viewed January 14, 2008).

Duchene, Paul, "The Best Defense Is a Really Good Story." *Portland Tribune*, March 11, 2003.

Phillip Margolin interview, Meet the Writers. http://www.barnesandnoble.com/writers/writerdetails.asp?z=y&cid=1066615 (viewed January 14, 2008).

Phillip Margolin profile, NYU Law. http://www.law.nyu.edu/alumni/almo/2004_2005/margolin.html (viewed February 1, 2008).

Phillip Margolin Web site. http://www.phillipmargolin.com/ (viewed November 14, 2008).

Brad Meltzer

Crime; Thrillers: Political, Legal

Benchmark Title: *The Book of Fate*

Brooklyn, New York

1970–

Photo credit: Jackie Merri Meyer

About the Author and the Author's Writing

He's not likely to give up writing best-selling political thrillers any day soon, but Brad Meltzer has used them as a springboard to an interesting sideline. He also scripts DC comic books.

Meltzer was born in Brooklyn, New York, in 1970. His family moved to Florida, where he attended high school. In 1989, he was a Capitol Hill intern. After graduating from the University of Michigan with a bachelor of arts degree in 1992, he worked in advertising sales for *Games Magazine* in Boston and began work on his first novel. Twenty-four editors refused it before he put it on a shelf. He received his law degree from Columbia University School of Law in 1996. While at law school, he completed a second manuscript, *The Tenth Justice*, which was accepted for publication under the new Rob Weisbach Books imprint. The book leaped onto the best-seller lists and brought instant fame to the author—to the extent that he played himself in the Woody Allen film *Celebrity* (1998).

Each of Meltzer's novels has a high-charged Washington, D.C., setting. *The Tenth Justice* is about Supreme Court clerk Ben Addison, who is arm-twisted into leaking information about key decisions. *Dead Even* is about a husband defense counsel and a wife district attorney who face each other in a case that is not all it seems. *The Zero Game* features Congressional staffers who gamble on Congressional actions. With this book, in the opinion of Bookreporter reviewer Joe Hartlaub, "Meltzer continues to demonstrate his ability to present a complex plot in an understandable manner while using it as a method to propel his characters, and the reader, through a reading experience that is unstoppable."

Meltzer works hard to make each book different. On his Web site, he explains that he starts each book with a small premise. In *The First Counsel*, for example, it's a

White House lawyer who is dating the president's daughter. "Then I take the characters and throw them into the plot. If I'm doing it right, I hit a point where I stop telling them what to do, and they start telling me what they want to do. If all else fails, it's back to Parcheesi."

The author works with a rough outline but spends more time on character profiles and in research. The colors, smells, and sounds give his prose a necessary vitality. "I love digging around for the details," he said in a BookPage interview. "They are the most fun. Hollywood lies so much to us that when you take the time to get it right, it becomes amazing."

Through his writing, he has descended into caverns and Disney World attics. Networking never hurts. "Former President George H. W. Bush sent me a letter complimenting me on one of my novels," he told *Library Journal*'s Jeff Ayers, "and then kindly put up with me after I asked to visit him at the White House to see what life there was like."   Former President Bill Clinton, whom Meltzer met when *The Tenth Justice* was published, gave the author access to his staff in Harlem.

In 2004, the Department of Homeland Security's Analytic Red Cell office invited Meltzer to take part in a brainstorming session: What devious ways might al-Qaeda find to again attack the United States? Meltzer found it a satisfying experience. "If I can help the government on terrorism, that's better than being on the best-seller list," he told *Washington Post* Staff Writer John Mintz.

There are less-than-serious elements to Meltzer's writing. In *The Tenth Justice*, he named all but one of the Supreme Court justices after characters in Alan Moore's graphic novel *The Watchmen*. The other one he named Cori Flam, after his wife since 1995, who is an attorney. They have two children and live in South Florida. A peripheral character in *The Tenth Justice*, law clerk Joel Westman, shows up in every book. He is an upstairs neighbor in *Dead Even*, for example. Why? Just to show how everyday lives weave in and around, he explains on his Web site.

Meltzer has a further tie to comic books. He's long loved the characters and jumped at the opportunity to script DC Comics' *Justice League of America* (featuring Superman and Batman), *Green Arrow*, and *Identity Crisis* (a 2004 miniseries).

Several of Meltzer's books have been optioned by Hollywood producers, although none has been filmed. With Steve Cohen, however, Meltzer co-created the WB television series *Jack & Bobby*, which ran for twenty-two episodes in 2006. The main characters are teenage brothers, one of whom, years in the future, will become president of the United States. "Making it anyone's game is what makes America great," Meltzer said in a *Washington Post* interview. "Everyone can relate to that."

 # Works by the Author

The Tenth Justice (1998)

Dead Even (1999)

The First Counsel (2001)

The Millionaires (2002)

The Zero Game (2005)

The Book of Fate (2006)

The Book of Lies (2008)

Comic Books and Graphic Novels

Green Arrow, No. 16 to 21 (DC, 2002-2003), collected in graphic novel format
Identity Crisis (DC, 2004), miniseries collected in graphic novel format
Justice League of America, No. 0 to 11 (DC, 2006)
Buffy the Vampire Slayer, Season Eight (Dark Horse)

Creator and Scriptwriter

Jack & Bobby (2006), television program

For Further Information

Ayers, Jeff. *The Book of Fate* review. *Library Journal*, August 1, 2006.

Ayers, Jeff, 'Q&A: Brad Meltzer." *Library Journal*, August 1, 2006.

Brad Meltzer Web site. http://www.bradmeltzer.com (viewed November 17, 2008).

Frutkin, A.J., "Presidential Seedlings." *Washington Post*, May 9, 2004.

Hartlaub, Joe, *The Zero Game* review, Bookreporter. http://www.bookreporter.com/reviews/0446530980.asp (viewed November 30, 2007).

Mintz, John, "Homeland Security Employs Imagination: Outsiders Help Devise Possible Terrorism Plots." *Washington Post*, June 18, 2004.

Russo, Tom, "Murder Ink." *Entertainment Weekly*, June 18, 2004.

Swilley, Stephanie, "Meltzer Magic," BookPage, January 2002. http://www.bookpage.com/0201bp/brad_meltzer.html (viewed November 30, 2007).

Stephenie Meyer

Fantasy; Romantic Suspense: Vampires

Benchmark Series: Twilight Quartet

Hartford, Connecticut

1973–

About the Author and the Author's Writing

One of the hottest fiction writers of the decade dusted off a century-old fantasy figure from the catacombs of a castle in Transylvania, the blood-lusting vampire, and remade him as a charming, handsome teenager in rural Washington State. Stephenie Meyer's quartet of novels starting with *Twilight* sold some 25 million copies by the time the motion picture *Twilight* came out in 2008.

Meyer scoffed at comparisons with mega-selling J. K. Rowling (some 110 million Harry Potter books are in print). Her primary mission was to tell her stories and entertain an audience, not outshine a publishing icon.

Born in Hartford, Connecticut, in 1973, Meyer was named for her father, Stephen, with an "ie" tacked on, and grew up in Phoenix, Arizona. She majored in English at Brigham Young University, which she attended as a National Merit Scholar. She and her husband, Christiaan "Pancho" Meyer, an accountant, have three sons. Meyer had no background in writing when she had a dream about a girl and a vampire falling in love. At the urging of her sister, she wrote a manuscript in a mad rush of creativity.

"It gushed," she told *School Library Journal*. "I would write 10 or 12 pages [a day], single-spaced. That's a good chapter and then some."

Meyer finished the manuscript in three months and, encouraged by her writers' group, sent it to an agent. Little, Brown bought the rights for $500,000.

Twilight (2005) is about teenage Bella Swan, who shuns her mother's invitation to move to Florida and instead joins her father in Forks, Washington, where he is police chief. Forks is the wettest town in the continental United States and a comfortable place to live, apparently, if you're a vampire. Bella, feeling isolated at her new school, meets another outcast, attractive Edward Cullen, who is obviously different, although how different Bella will only learn with time. Edward, of course, is a vampire and instinctively wants to bite Bella's neck. But he's in love. He can't hurt her. There ensues, over the 2,552 pages of the four books, the longest description of an unusual, unconsummated love in literature. Or, as the *Twilight* film director Catherine Hardwicke, put it, "the most extended foreplay ever."

Although the sex is missing from the Bella-Edward relationship, the sexual tension is not. As relationship expert Gilda Carle said in a *USA Today* story by Susan Wloszcyna, teenage girls experiencing their first love often face the dilemma: Is it

281

them, or sex, the boy is after? In the <u>Twilight</u> books, there's no doubt. It's Bella who Edward wants. It's love.

"They're 'chick books,' with rival vampire clans, butt-kicking werewolves and lots of blood, so they have appeal to some boys, too," Susan Dunne wrote in the *Hartford Courant*.

Meyer claimed she'd not read Bram Stoker's *Dracula* or Anne Rice's Lestat novels, nor had she seen *Buffy the Vampire Slayer* or *True Blood* on television when she created her own vampire mythos. Edward is more than a hundred years old, his age frozen from when he was first infected. He never sleeps. He plays basketball and drives a fast car. He absorbs people's thoughts. He glitters in sunlight. The only way to destroy him is to tear his body apart and burn it. There's enormous tension in the secrecy—will the community learn that Edward and his family are blood-suckers?—and the rivalry—will a handsome werewolf, Jacob Black, seduce Bella away from Edward?

Meyer told *Time* magazine that a major theme of the series is choice: "I really think that's the underlying metaphor of my vampires. It doesn't matter where you're stuck in life or what you think you have to do; you can always choose something else. There's always a different path." In the <u>Twilight</u> books, the Cullens, who traditionally would have been the villains, are instead the heroes.

Meyer's Mormon faith has a lot to do with the low tone of sexuality in her books. Her church affiliation "has a huge influence on who I am and my perspective on the world," she said on her Web site, "and therefore what I write (though I have been asked more than once, 'What's a nice Mormon girl like you doing writing about vampires?')."

But as Liesl Schillinger commented in the *New York Times Book Review*, "Luckily for her, while her religion's teachings may frown on caffeine and alcohol for humans, the Word of Wisdom has a flexible attitude toward human blood for monsters; and there's no ban on big love in the mythical world."

Meyer lists among literary favorites the classic works of Jane Austen and the Brontë sisters and Lucy Maud Montgomery's Anne of Green Gables books, and also the science fiction of writer Orson Scott Card.

She still writes her books in her kitchen, often listening to the music of Linkin Park, Coldplay, or Weezer. With five books in four years, her career had a whirlwind start. Shifting gears slightly, she brought out a science fiction thriller, *The Host*, in 2008, just months before concluding the <u>Twilight</u> quartet with *Breaking Dawn*. *The Host*, described by the publisher as "the only love triangle involving two bodies," relates the internal struggle of teen Melanie Stryder, who refuses to allow an alien soul called Wanderer to take over her mind and body.

Although the <u>Twilight</u> books are marketed to young adult readers, they have enjoyed a broad appeal. "I think some of it's because Bella is an everygirl," Meyer told EW.com's Gregory Kirschling. "She's not a hero, and she doesn't know the difference between Prada and whatever else is out there. She doesn't always have to be cool, or wear the coolest clothes ever. She's normal. And there aren't a lot of girls in literature that are normal."

Works by the Author

The Host (2007)

Twilight Quartet

Twilight (2005)
New Moon (2006)
Eclipse (2007)
Breaking Dawn (2008)

Contributor

Prom Nights from Hell, with Meg Cabot, Kim Harrison, Lauren Myracle, and Michele Jaffe (2007)

Adaptations in Other Media

Twilight (2008), motion picture

For Further Information

Dunne, Susan, "Young Blood." *Hartford Courant*, November 16, 2008.

Elgin, Susan, "The Secret Life of Vampires." *Newsweek*, July 26, 2008

Grossman, Lev, "Stephenie Meyer: A New J. K. Rowling?" *Time*, April 24, 2008.

Kirschling, Gregory, "Stephenie Meyer's 'Twilight' Zone." EW.com. http://www.ew.com/ew/article/0,,20049578,00.html (viewed November 12, 2008).

Margolis, Rick, "Love at First Bite." *School Library Journal*, October 2005.

Meadows, Bob, and Kari Lydersen, "Stephenie Meyer Written in Blood." *People Weekly*, September 8, 2008.

Memmott, Carol, "'Twilight' author Stephenie Meyer unfazed as fame dawns." *USA Today*, August 1, 2008.

Moyer, Jessica., *The Host* review. *Booklist*, September 15, 2008.

Schillinger, Liesl, *Eclipse* review. *New York Times Book Review*, August 12, 2007.

Stephenie Meyer Web site. http://www.stepheniemeyer.com/bio.html (viewed September 13, 2008).

Truitt, Brian. "The Twilight Zone." *USA Weekend*, November 14, 2008.

Turakhia, Vikas, "The Twilight Saga." *St. Petersburg Times*, August 1, 2008.

"Twilight: To Die For." *Entertainment Weekly*, November 14, 2008.

Valby, Karen, "Stephenie Meyer: Inside the 'Twilight' Saga, EW.com. http://www.ew.com/ew/article/0,,20213067_20213068_20211938,00.html (viewed November 13, 2008).

Valby, Karen, and Kate Ward, "The Vampire Empire." *Entertainment Weekly*, July 18, 2008.

Wloszczyna, Susan, "Vampires Seduce a New Generation." *USA Today*, November 20, 2008.

David Morrell

Adventure; Assassins; Espionage; Horror; Thrillers: Political

Benchmark Title: *First Blood*

Kitchener, Ontario

1943–

Photo credit: Jennifer Eperanza

About the Author and the Author's Writing

He accepts the designation as the "father" of modern action novels on his Web site. But David Morrell, who indeed pioneered the thriller beyond the boundaries of horror, war, or mystery fiction with his 1972 novel *First Blood*, is also quick to acknowledge a host of forebears, beginning with Edgar Allan Poe and including Robert Louis Stevenson, Bram Stoker, Edgar Rice Burroughs, and John Buchan.

First Blood appeared after the Cold War–era heyday of James Bond–inspired spy novels. It had a psychological, as well as political, social, and historical edge that none of the secret agent books had. Its hero, Rambo (he acquired his first name John in the movies starring Sylvester Stallone), was a returned Green Beret veteran of the Vietnam War. He suffered posttraumatic stress syndrome. He just wanted to be left alone, as he hitchhiked through Kentucky. But small-town sheriff Wilfred Teasle thought he was a no-good. Despite being a Korean War veteran himself, Teasle didn't recognize the shell-shocked ex-soldier's pain. Rambo snapped, killed one of Teasle's deputies, and fled to the woods, where he waged his own small guerilla war. In the book, the ending was not a happy one. In the movie, perhaps with sequels in mind, he survived to rescue POWs in Vietnam and to save his former commanding officer from the Afghanis.

"Rambo may be the boldest embodiment of a system that trains men to kill," reviewer Joseph Catinella said in *Saturday Review*.

Morrell was a teacher at Pennsylvania State University in the late 1960s when he wrote the book. He explained on his Web site, "I encountered young men recently returned from the war who had a lot of trouble accepting me as an authority figure. We got to talking. I learned about their difficulties in adjusting to civilian life: nightmares, lack of sleep, depression, defensive reactions to loud noises." He recognized the veterans were greatly overlooked, and decided to bring the war home—in an action thriller.

The author was not a Vietnam vet, but he had plenty of experience with stress and anxiety. Born in Kitchener, Ontario, in 1943, he grew up living for several years in an orphanage and boarding house while his mother struggled to find work and sort out her life. His father died in World War II. His new stepfather had no use for children. "There were never-ending family fights. I slept under the bed, fearing for my safety. These events left me anxious about the stability of everyday life," the author said in a Writers Write interview.

Morrell received a bachelor of arts degree from the University of Waterloo in 1966 and a master's from Pennsylvania State University the next year. An influential instructor at that school was Philip Klass, better known as a fiction writer under the name William Tenn. In 1970, Morrell earned his Ph.D. from Penn State. He and his wife, Donna Maziarz, whom he married in 1965, have two children.

From 1969 to 1970, Morrell taught rhetoric at Penn State, then became an assistant professor at the University of Iowa, working his way up to professor of American literature before he retired in 1986 to write full time.

As his action novels found a wide audience, Morrell continued his education in directions that may seem atypical—unless you write thrillers. He graduated from the National Outdoor Leadership School in Wyoming and the G. Gordon Liddy Academy of Corporate Security in California in 1986.

His popular novel *The Brotherhood of the Rose* (1984)—the first of a loose, like-themed series of novels with different characters—was made into a television miniseries featuring Robert Mitchum. It is about two orphans raised as brothers and trained as assassins. "Though he is occasionally chided for constructing flat characters or over-complicated plots in these novels, he inevitably wins recognition as a born story-teller," said *Contemporary Authors*.

Morrell lost his son, Matthew, age fifteen, to a rare bone cancer. The loss informed a memoir, *Fireflies*, and created the background for a novel, *Desperate Measures* (1994), in which the suicidal hero, reporter Matthew Pittman, has just lost his own son.

An avid researcher, the author learned about photography for *Double Image* and artists' painting for *Burnt Sienna*. He's taken instruction in firearms, electronic eavesdropping, hostage negotiation, and antiterrorism driving. Over the years, Morrell has also written short fiction, much of it in the horror genre.

Dark elements infect much of Morrell's prose, and come center stage in books such as *Testament* and *The Totem*. "There's even horror embedded in my espionage novels," the author admitted in a *Mystery Scene* interview. "For the most part, my horror stories are studies of psychological breakdowns, more than anything else."

Morrell's designation as "father" of the modern thriller is apt for a second reason. As co-president (with Gayle Lynds) of the International Thriller Writers Association, he works diligently to publicize and legitimize the thriller genre and nurture new and upcoming writers. He has no qualms about the genre's value. Noting the thriller varieties that range from medical to legal to espionage, he wrote in a Thriller Writers Web page, "One of their common denominators is that they quicken the reader's heartbeat."

Besides his frequent contributions to the Web site, Morrell has written a book about his career, *Lessons from a Lifetime*, which *Booklist* reviewer David Pitt commended: "There is never the sense that Morrell is telling us what to do; rather, he describes what has worked for him (and other writers), noting mistakes that many have made and how we might avoid them."

One of the author's recent books, *Creepers* (2005), is an urban fantasy about a group of city dwellers who explore a boarded-up, condemned monstrosity of an old hotel, on the eve of its demolition, never expecting to encounter the accelerating menaces of vagrants, a kidnapper, and a venal building.

"I dramatize every instant of every breath of the harrowing eight hours that the 'creepers' endure within the walls of that crumbling edifice," Morrell wrote for Backspace. In other words, it's the essence of a thriller by a master.

Works by the Author

Testament (1975)

Last Reveille (1977)

The Totem (1979), unaltered edition (1994)

Blood Oath (1982)

The Hundred-Year Christmas (1983)

The Brotherhood of the Rose (1984)

The Fraternity of the Stone (1985)

The League of Night and Fog (1987)

The Fifth Profession (1990)

The Covenant of the Flame (1991)

Assumed Identity (1993)

Desperate Measures (1994)

Extreme Denial (1996)

Double Image (1998)

The Unpublished Testament *Prologues* (1998), chapbook

Black Evening (1999), collection

Burnt Sienna (2000)

Long Lost (2002)

The Protector (2003)

Nightscape (2004)

Creepers (2005)

Scavenger (2007)

The Spy Who Came for Christmas (2008)

Rambo Series

First Blood (1972)

Rambo: First Blood Part II (1985), adaptation of screenplay

Rambo III (1988), adaptation of screenplay

Anthologies

Ellery Queen's Crookbook (1974), includes "The Dripping"

Horrors, edited by Charles L. Grant (1981), includes "Black Evening"

Ellery Queen's Book of First Appearances (1982), includes "The Dripping"

Fears, edited by Charles L. Grant (1983), includes "The Dripping"

Dodd, Mead Gallery of Horror, edited by Charles L. Grant (1983), includes "The Typewriter"

Shadows 6, edited by Charles L. Grant (1983), includes "But at My Back I Always Hear"

Shadows 7, edited by Charles L. Grant (1984), includes "The Storm"

The Year's Best Fantasy Stories (1985), includes "The Storm"

Whispers 5, edited by Stuart L. Schiff (1985), includes "For These and All My Sins"

Night Visions: Dead Image, edited by Charles L. Grant (1985), includes "Black and White and Red All Over," "Mumbo Jumbo," and "Dead Image"

The Best of Shadows (1988), includes "The Storm"

Prime Evil, edited by Douglas E. Winter (1988), includes "Orange Is for Anguish, Blue for Insanity"

Masters of Darkness III, edited by Dennis Etchison (1990), includes "But at My Back I Always Hear"

Ghosts of the Heartland, edited by Frank McSherry, Charles G. Waugh, and Martin Greenberg (1990), includes "But at My Back I Always Hear"

Short, Sharp Shocks, edited by Julian Lloyd Webber (1990), includes "But at My Back I Always Hear"

Psycho Paths, edited by Robert Bloch (1990), includes "Remains to be Seen"

Hollywood Ghosts, edited by Frank McSherry, Charles G. Waugh, and Martin Greenberg (1991), includes "Dead Image"

Final Shadows, edited by Charles L. Grant (1991), includes "The Beautiful Uncut Hair of Graves"

Year's Best Fantasy and Horror 5 (1992), includes "The Beautiful Uncut Hair of Graves"

Dark at Heart, edited by Joe and Karen Lansdale (1992), includes "The Shring"

Metahorror, edited by Dennis Etchison (1992), includes "Nothing Will Hurt You"

Nursery Crimes, edited by Martin H. Greenberg (1993), includes "Black and White and Red All Over"

Dark Crimes 2, edited by Ed Gorman (1993), includes "The Dripping"

Grifters and Swindlers (1993), includes "The Partnership"

Mists from Beyond (1994), includes "But at My Back I Always Hear"

The King Is Dead: Tales of Elvis Postmortem, edited by Paul M. Sammon (1994) includes "Elvis .45"

Stalkers III, edited by Martin Greenberg (1995), includes "The Dripping"

A Century of Horror: 1970–1979, edited by David Drake (1996), includes "The Dripping"

Night Screams, edited by Ed Gorman and Martin H. Greenberg (1997), includes "The Dripping"

Revelations, edited by Douglas E. Winter (1997), in Great Britain as *Millennium* (1997), includes "If I Should Die before I Wake"

Murder for Revenge, edited by Otto Penzler (1997), includes "Front Man"

999, edited by Al Sarrantonio (1999), includes "Rio Grande Gothic"

World's Best Crime and Mystery Stories, edited by Ed Gorman (2000), includes "Rio Grande Gothic"

Opening Shots, edited by Lawrence Block (2000), includes "The Dripping"

Speaking of Greed, edited by Lawrence Block (2001), includes "Front Man"

Redshift, edited by Al Sarrantonio (2001), includes "Resurrection"

Year's Best SF 7, edited by David Hartwell (2002), includes "Resurrection"

Murder Is My Racquet, edited by Otto Penzler (2002), includes "Continental Grip"

The Mammoth Book of Best New Horror, edited by Stephen Jones (2007), includes "They"

Comic Books

The Bank Street Book of Mystery (1989), adapts "The Good Times Always End"

Captain America: The Chosen (Marvel, 2007–2008)

Nonfiction

John Barth: An Introduction (1976)

Fireflies: A Father's Tale of Love and Loss (1988)

Lessons from a Lifetime of Writing: A Novelist Looks at His Craft (2002)

The Successful Novelist (2008)

Adaptations in Other Media

First Blood (1982)

Rambo: First Blood, Part II (1985)

Rambo: The Force of Freedom (1986), syndicated animated television series

Rambo III (1988)

Monster (syndicated television series, 1989), episode based on "Habitat"

Brotherhood of the Rose (1989), NBC miniseries

The Hunger (Showtime series 1997), episode based on "But at My Back I Always Hear"

Rambo (2008)

For Further Information

David Morrell Web site. http://www.davidmorrell.net/ (viewed November 17, 2008).

Catinella, Joseph, *First Blood* review. *Saturday Review*, December 2, 1972.

Morrell, David, "Must-Read Thrillers," International Thriller Writers. http://www.thrillerwriters.org/index.php?option=com_content&task=view&id=12&Itemid=29 (viewed November 16, 2007).

Morrell, David, "What Is a Thriller?," Backspace: The Writer's Place. http://bksp.org/secondarypages/articles/authors/DMorrell2.htm (viewed September 13, 2007).

Rosen, Judith, "Morrell Tries 20% Solution." *Publishers Weekly*, September 5, 2005.

Wiater, Stanley, David Morrell profile, *Mystery Scene*, June 1990.

White, Claire E., "A Conversation with David Morrell," Writers Write, October 2002. http://www.writerswrite.com/journal/oct02/morrell.htm (viewed October 8, 2007).

John J. Nance

Photo credit: Patricia Davenport

Adventure: Military; Crime; Thrillers: Political, Bio

Benchmark Title: *Blackout*

Dallas, Texas

1946–

About the Author and the Author's Writing

John J. Nance's aviation thrillers have such a ring of authenticity, they could have been written aboard an airplane. In fact, he did write most of *Blackout* (2000) inside the cabin of his company aircraft, while his home office was being remodeled. The plane was in the hangar. He installed a coffeepot to get through the late fall months.

Nance in a Bookreporter interview said he generally sets a ten-page goal each day. Some days he fails. "Some days the story flies (no pun intended), and I rack up twenty to twenty-five pages. So the average is ten. Interestingly enough, those multipage days need the least editing, because they represent the parts of a story where my engagement is so total, you couldn't interrupt me if you tried."

The Lone Star State native was born in Dallas in 1946. His father was an attorney, his mother an English professor and poet. Nance went to the University of Hawaii for a year. In 1968, he received a bachelor of arts degree from Southern Methodist University; the next year he earned a juris doctorate from SMU School of Law. He graduated with distinction from U.S. Air Force Undergraduate Pilot Training in 1971. From 1971 to 1975, Nance was an Air Force pilot and aircraft commander. He served in Vietnam and later, as a reservist with the rank of lieutenant colonel, served in Operation Desert Storm, 1990–1991. Decorated for his military service, he became project officer for the Cockpit Resource Management and Aircrew Flight Safety Program for the 97th Military Aircraft Squadron from 1988 to 1993.

Nance has been a journalist, columnist, professional airline pilot of 727s, 737s, 747s, and Air Force C-141s (for Braniff International 1975 to 1982, and Alaska Airlines since 1985), as well as a television consultant and commentator and as a lawyer. He has been ABC News' aviation analyst since 1995 and aviation editor for *Good*

Morning America since 1996. Two of his books, *Pandora's Clock* and *Medusa's Child*, were made into television movies.

Nance's first books were nonfiction. *Splash of Colors* (1984) told the story of the rise and demise of Braniff Airlines. *Blind Trust* (1986) decried deregulation in the airline industry. "*Blind Trust* put me into the crucible of being about the only one with any credibility in the country to be standing up and pointing at the Reagan administration and saying, 'Now, wait a minute, deregulation is having an effect on safety,'" Nance told *Pages* magazine.

Nance eventually turned to novels but continued the flying theme. His books are technically accurate, Nance stresses, but they are not futuristic in the vein of some techno writers. In 2003, *Publishers Weekly* described one of his novels as the latest "in a subgenre he has established almost single-handedly, the aviation thriller."

Nance's novels put the scare into airline travel, but the author vouches flights are safer today than ever, largely through airline dedication to safety improvements. Most accidents were proved to be the result of human mistakes, and technology today anticipates most, if not all, those mistakes. Still, the surge in scheduled flights has put enormous pressure on air traffic controllers. An advocate for a modern approach to airplane management, Nance also took his campaign to the military, where he and others were able to persuade officials of the need to adopt a command setup in which the highest-ranking officer will listen to and act with his crew at critical moments.

The author appreciates his readers' interest in all aspects of aviation but pushes himself as a novelist to provide more. "I wanted to continue to prove something to my audience and to the critics: that just because a thriller is paced at high-speed (one critic called *Blackout* an exercise in aerobic page-turning, which I like), that does not mean the author must, or should, fail to fully develop the characters," he told interviewer Richard Rennicks.

In a typical Nance book, *Blackout* (2000), some of the hairiest action takes place aboard a 747 in which the crew has become incapacitated. An announcement is made to passengers, asking if there is anyone aboard who is a licensed pilot willing to help. "John Nance keeps you on the edge of your seat," said a FlightSim.com reviewer, whose only complaint was that some of the action took place on the ground.

Blackout was Nance's second book to feature FBI Special Agent Kat Bronsky, brought back from *The Last Hostage*. "She embodies what I value and admire in so many women today: a capable, self-confident woman, smart, innovative, and thoroughly professional, who more than holds her own in a male-dominated world, but without surrendering her femininity," he told Bookreporter's Joe Hartlaub.

That, in sum, is the key to Nance's success: rock-solid detail, breath-taking suspense, and a commitment to strong characters.

Works by the Author

Final Approach (1990)
Scorpion Strike (1992)
Phoenix Rising (1994)
Pandora's Clock (1995)
Medusa's Child (1997)
The Last Hostage (1998)

Blackout (2000), sequel to *The Last Hostage*
Headwind (2001)
Turbulence (2002)
Skyhook (2003)
Fire Flight (2003)
Saving Cascadia (2005)
Orbit (2006)

Nonfiction

Splash of Colors (1984)
Blind Trust (1986)
On Shaky Ground (1988)
What Goes Up: The Global Assault on Our Atmosphere (1991)
Golden Boy: The Harold Simmons Story (2003)
Why Hospitals Should Fly (2008)

Contributor

Transportation Safety in an Age of Deregulation, edited by Leon N. Moses and Ian Savage (1989)

Adaptations in Other Media

Pandora's Clock (1996), NBC television film
Medusa's Child (1997), ABC television film

For Further Information

Blackout review, Flightsim.com. http://www.flightsim.com/cgi/kds?$=main/review/blackout.htm (viewed February 18, 2008).

Cohen, George, *Orbit* review. *Booklist*, February 15, 2006.

Hartlaub, Joe, John J. Nance interview, Bookreporter. http://www.bookreporter.com/authors/au-nance-john.asp (viewed January 14, 2008).

Hogan, John, "Taking Off." *Pages*, January/February 2000.

John J. Nance Web site. http://johnjnance.adhostclient.com (viewed November 19, 2008).

Rennicks, Richard, "A Conversation with John J. Nance," Borders. http://johnjnance.adhostclient.com/tvradio/intrvw_borders.htm (viewed February 14, 2008).

Skyhook review. *Publishers Weekly*, March 24, 2003.

Peter O'Donnell

Adventure, Espionage; Romance

Benchmark Series: <u>Modesty Blaise</u>

London, England
1920–

Photo credit: Bernard A. Drew

About the Author and the Author's Writing

When Peter O'Donnell's thriller novels are likened to a comic strip, it is no insult; his tales of Modesty Blaise and Willie Garvin began in a daily three-panel in the London *Evening Standard,* after all. And they are among the most roundly characterized, skillfully plotted, daringly adventurous series to emerge at the height of the James Bond era. On top of the novels and short stories, O'Donnell's characters have found a robust continuing audience worldwide with a motion picture, a uniform series of graphic-novel-format reprints and new American editions of his prose.

O'Donnell was born in 1920 in London, England, the son of a crime reporter. He studied at Catford Central School in London. He wrote his first story when he was sixteen, and sold it to *Scout* magazine. "My father and elder brother were journalists on national newspapers," he said in *Million* magazine. "It didn't occur to me to do anything else."

After working for Amalgamated Press, publisher of juvenile periodicals and comic books, from 1937 to 1939; he joined the British Army's Royal Signal Corps, where he served in the Near East and Mediterranean, 1939 to 1946. After World War II, he was an editor with the book publisher Clerke & Cochran until 1951, when he became a freelance writer. He scripted newspaper comic strips including "Garth" in the *Daily Mirror* (1953–1966), "Tug Transom" (1954–1966), and "Romeo Brown" (1956–1962). He wrote a half-dozen (text only) Western and mystery stories and romantic serials a week in the 1950s, in addition to the comics. It proved good training for his succinct writing style. Then, in 1963, he created "Modesty Blaise" for the *Evening Standard;* it was syndicated worldwide for thirty-three years. Modesty Blaise and her companion Garvin appeared in 98 strip adventures, 11 novels, and 11 short stories —120 adventures in all.

293

O'Donnell spent a year developing "Modesty Blaise." Because he intended to feature a woman character, he had to create a believable background, he said in an interview with Contemporary Authors in 1986. He recalled someone he had seen during the war, when he was posted in northern Iran. "Moving through those mountains ahead of the advancing German armies was a steady stream of refugees, among them small children. One of them, a girl surely no more than seven, came back to mind all these years later and became the inspiration for my character."

The girl, in O'Donnell's mind, was a survivor. He imagined Modesty Blaise was a displaced person fleeing from Greece, tutored by an old Jewish professor; she joined a gang when she was sixteen, learned self-defense and the skills of a criminal sufficient that she eventually developed her own organization in Tangier, The Network. It was an organization that never dealt in narcotics or prostitution. When the comic strip began, she had retired, as had her right hand, Garvin, a man she had rescued from prison. Modesty and Willie shared the closest of bonds, platonically. They think alike in desperate situations; they complement each other in combat (she is skilled with firearms and a kongo, he with knives). Although Blaise was sometimes likened to James Bond, and she undertook several assignments for Sir Gerald Tarrant, head of a British security agency, O'Donnell never intended her to be a Bond imitation.

Modesty Blaise turned out to be an immediate hit. "I was taken to lunch by the editor of the *Evening Standard* a few weeks after the launch, and he was in great glee because of reader response," O'Donnell said in a conversation with Kent Hedlundh in 2002.

O'Donnell worked for many years from a fourth-floor office on Fleet Street, reached by an alley entry next to the El Vino wine shop. His spacious room was decorated with art by Jim Holdaway, the first Modesty Blaise artist. He wrote with a typewriter, standing at a tall, Dickensian desk. Shelves brimmed with foreign-language editions of his books. "I obviously could do my writing at home," he told interviewer Bernard A. Drew in 1983, "but I've always tried to keep the work side of life separate from the family side. It can cut into your family life, if you do it at home." O'Donnell and Constance Doris Green married in 1940 and have two daughters.

Once he had a villain in mind, O'Donnell said, he would start writing and see where things went. For his comics, he had to shape action to fit daily and weekly sequences; he often drew stick figures to pass along to his artists. O'Donnell developed several regular continuing characters in the strips and books—Blaise's houseman Weng, Tarrant's agents Frasier and Maude Tiller, Willie's friend Lady Janet among them.

"She [Blaise] does other things besides kick people in the head," O'Donnell jokingly told a *Guardian* interviewer in 2000. "She's very compassionate and vulnerable."

O'Donnell wrote his first novel for Souvenir Press in 1965, based on a failed screenplay. He continued to write a book every few years, his readers not knowing that he alternated with his alter ego, Madeleine Brent. Brent made her reputation as a solid author of rapid-paced gothic romances—nine in all, from 1971 through 1987. O'Donnell only revealed his second career to a fan publication in 1991.

The author kept tight control of his character, allowing her to appear in one radio series, two motion pictures, and one telefilm. He was never completely satisfied that the producers achieved the right portrayal of Modesty Blaise. In his last book, a 2001 collection of stories, he wrote one in which his heroes, by then in their fifties, died. Knowing what it is about, many fans refuse to read that story. O'Donnell retired the comic strip April 11, 2001, his eighty-first birthday. Since then, he has revisited each strip and written new introductions as Titan Books has packaged the adventures in uniform format for international sale. For the most intense fans, publisher Lawrence Blackmore in 2005 issued an oversized, 418-page hardcover concordance, *The Modesty Blaise Companion*, with accompanying CD to document every story, every character O'Donnell ever put to paper. It's the sort of tribute reserved for only the most admired of fictional characters.

"It's difficult to find the right word for my reaction when I saw it," O'Donnell wrote in a foreword. "'Gobsmacked' would be the most accurate, but as I pretend to be a literary sort of cove I'd better settle for 'astounded.'"

 Works by the Author

Modesty Blaise and Willie Garvin Series

Modesty Blaise (1965)

Sabre-Tooth (1966)

I, Lucifer (1967)

A Taste for Death (1969)

Impossible Virgin (1971)

Pieces of Modesty (1972), short stories

Silver Mistress (1973)

Last Day in Limbo (1976)

Dragon's Claw (1978)

Xanadu Talisman (1981)

Night of Morningstar (1982)

Dead Man's Handle (1985)

Cobra Trap (1996), short stories

Comic Strip and Graphic Novels

Modesty Blaise (*Evening Standard* comic strip, 1963–2001)

Modesty Blaise: In the Beginning (1978)

Modesty Blaise: The Black Pearl and The Vikings (1978)

Modesty Blaise: First American Edition Series 1, introduction by Cat Yronwode (1981)

Modesty Blaise: First American Edition Series 2, introduction by Chris Claremont (1981)

Modesty Blaise: First American Edition Series 3, introduction by Don McGregor (1982)

Modesty Blaise: First American Edition Series 4, introduction by Cat Yronwode (1983)

Modesty Blaise: First American Edition Series 5, introduction by Cat Yronwode (1984)

Modesty Blaise: First American Edition Series 6, introduction by Bernard A. Drew (1985)

Modesty Blaise Book One: The Gabriel Setup, introduction by Peter O'Donnell (1985)

Modesty Blaise: First American Edition Series 7 (1986)

Modesty Blaise: First American Edition Series 8 (1986)

Modesty Blaise Book Two: Mr. Sun, introduction by Peter O'Donnell (1985)

Modesty Blaise Book Three: The Hell-Makers, introduction by Peter O'Donnell (1986)

Modesty Blaise Book Four: The War-Lords of Phoenix, introduction by Peter O'Donnell (1987)

Modesty Blaise Book Five: Death of a Jester, introduction by Peter O'Donnell (1987)

Modesty Blaise Book Six: The Puppet Master, introduction by Peter O'Donnell (1987)

Modesty Blaise Book Seven: The Iron God, introduction by Peter O'Donnell (1989)

Modesty Blaise Book Eight: Uncle Happy, introduction by Peter O'Donnell (1990)

Dark Angels (2002)

Modesty Blaise: The Gabriel Set-Up, introduction by Peter O'Donnell, revised edition (2004)

Modesty Blaise: Mister Sun, introduction by Peter O'Donnell, revised edition (2004)

Modesty Blaise: Top Traitor, introduction by Peter O'Donnell (2004)

Modesty Blaise: The Black Pearl, introduction by Peter O'Donnell (2005)

Modesty Blaise: Bad Suki, introduction by Peter O'Donnell (2005)

Modesty Blaise: The Hell Makers, introduction by Peter O'Donnell, revised edition (2005)

Modesty Blaise: The Green-Eyed Monster, introduction by Peter O'Donnell (2005)

Modesty Blaise: The Puppet Master, introduction by Peter O'Donnell, revised edition (2006)

Modesty Blaise: The Gallows Bird, introduction by Peter O'Donnell (2006)

Modesty Blaise: Cry Wolf, introduction by Peter O'Donnell (2006)

Modesty Blaise: The Inca Trail, introduction by Peter O'Donnell (2007)

Modesty Blaise: Death Trap, introduction by Peter O'Donnell (2007)

Modesty Blaise: Yellowstone Booty, introduction by Peter O'Donnell (2008)

Modesty Blaise: Green Cobra, introduction by Peter O'Donnell (2008)

Modesty Blaise: The Lady Killers, introduction by Peter O'Donnell (2009)

Plays and Screenplays

Take a Pair of Private Eyes (1966), teleplay

The Vengeance of She (1968), screenplay

Murder Most Logical (1974), two-act play, published as *Mr. Fothergill's Murder: A Play in Two Acts* (1983)

Written as Madeleine Brent

Tregaron's Daughter (1971)

Moonraker's Bride (1975)

Stranger at Wildings (1975), in United Kingdom as *Kirby's Changeling*

Merlin's Keep (1977)

Capricorn Stone (1979)

Long Masquerade (1981)

Heritage of Shadows (1983)

Stormswift (1984)

Golden Urchin (1987)

Adaptations in Other Media

Modesty Blaise (1966), motion picture

Modesty Blaise (1977), British radio series

Modesty Blaise (1982), television production

My Name Is Modesty: A Modesty Blaise Adventure (2003), motion picture

For Further Information

Beckett, Simon, "Blazing a Trail." *Guardian*, September 15, 2002.

Blackmore, Lawrence. *The Modesty Blaise Companion*. London: Book Palace Books, 2005.

Cobra Trap review. *Publishers Weekly*, April 9, 2001.

Cunningham, John, "Adventures in Old Fleet Street," *Guardian*, September 16, 2000.

Drew, Bernard A., "He Nails 'Em with Modesty." *Armchair Detective*, volume 20 no. 1, 1985.

Drew, Bernard A., "Modesty Blaise—Two Decades of Adventure." *Comics Collector*, Fall 1984.

Drew, Bernard A., "PO and MB." In *Modesty Blaise: First American Edition Series 6*. Park Forest, IL: Ken Pierce Inc., 1985.

Glass, Kristy Lyn, "Peter O'Donnell aka Madeleine Brent." *Gothic Journal*, November–December 1991.

Hendlundh, Kent, "Exclusive Interview with Peter O'Donnell," Modesty Blaise homepage, August 2002. http://www.cs.umu.se/~kenth/Modesty/podint2.html (viewed November 6, 2008).

O'Donnell, Peter, "Girl Walking: The Real Modesty Blaise." *Crime Time*, July 29, 2005. http://www.crimetime.co.uk/features/modestyblaise.php (viewed July 29, 2005).

O'Donnell, Peter, Introduction. *Modesty Blaise: Death Trap*. London: Titan Books, 2007.

Ross, Jean W., "Peter O'Donnell Interview." *Contemporary Authors*, volume 117. Detroit, MI: Gale Research, 1986.

Wells, Gordon, "Peter O'Donnell Interview. "*Million*, January–February 1993.

Perri O'Shaughnessy
(Pseudonym for Mary and
Pamela O'Shaughnessy)

Crime; Thrillers: Legal

Benchmark Series: <u>Nina Reilly</u>

Mary O'Shaughnessy

California

Birth date not disclosed

Photo credit: Ardyth Brock

Pamela O'Shaughnessy

Missouri

Birth date not disclosed

Photo credit: Courtesy of the author

About the Authors and the Authors' Writing

The sisters O'Shaughnessy, one with three young children, the other with a toddler, say they began to write fiction together as a creative, fulfilling outlet. Both voracious readers, they felt blessed with their family's gift for blarney. And they thought they could write together. Their heroine, they decided, would be Nina Reilly, a woman in a one-person law practice. Pamela O'Shaughnessy knew her way around the law books. She was a lawyer in South Lake Tahoe in California. Mary O'Shaughnessy had an idea for a surefire plot.

Their first courtroom drama, *Motion to Suppress*, came out in 1995. They published it under the joint pseudonym Perri O'Shaughnessy—the family name with a merging of their own first names. (The byline was also a subtle nod to Erle Stanley Gardner's popular crime solver, Perry Mason.) With their sixth book, *Move to Strike* in 2000, the authors leapt onto the *Publishers Weekly* and *New York Times* best-seller lists.

Mary O'Shaughnessy was born in Northern California. She graduated from the University of California in Santa Barbara with a bachelor of arts degree in English literature, magna cum laude. She has worked as a production designer and documentary editor in Washington, D.C., New York, and the Virgin Islands. She married an engineer and has three children; they live in California.

Pamela O'Shaughnessy was born in Missouri. She earned her bachelor of science degree in political science from Long Beach State University and her juris doctorate from Harvard University. She has practiced law with her late mother and on her own. She married a surveyor and has a son; they live in Hawaii.

The sisters led nomadic childhoods. Their parents moved at least once a year. Why they moved long puzzled the daughters, and they never pressed their now-deceased folks for a reason. Their father once said he was a spy. More likely, they think, the family long experienced financial instability.

The women bring different personalities to their writing. Mary O'Shaughnessy considers herself an optimist, whereas Pamela O'Shaughnessy considers herself a realist. They don't always agree, but they know what works on the written page. If nothing else, they learned from their father that an air of certainty can overcome facts in most arguments. "Always attack, never defend," he told them.

Thus Nina Reilly, who is shorter, of darker hair, and different in personality from either one of the sisters: "She's a very impetuous person and an impulsive person," Pamela O'Shaughnessy told Bridget Kinsella of *Publishers Weekly*. "She's blunt," her sister said in the same interview.

Their first manuscript made the circuit of publishers for a year. They wrote another story, and, with an agent's help, sold it through auction to Delacorte. In it, Nina Reilly, recovering from a bad marriage, opens a business on her own in South Lake Tahoe. From the start, the authors planned to have their heroine gain legal experience and grow in personality.

Their female protagonist affords a different perspective on the courtroom. *Motion to Suppress*, for example, wasn't shy about discussing the old-boy network. "The 'ah-ha' moments come every week," Pamela O'Shaughnessy said in a Random House Web site for *Presumption of Death*, "realizing the (male) judge just doesn't feel comfortable chatting with you, that you have to have meetings rather than informal get-togethers at lunch or dinner because you or the (male) lawyer are married."

The authors nevertheless are strong supporters of the law and lawyers. "It's easier to take cheap shots at lawyers, and sometimes we indulge," one of the sisters (they aren't always identified in joint interviews) told Bookreporter. "In fact, we have great respect for the profession as a whole. It's stressful, unforgiving, challenging, and attracts the brightest minds."

The writers acknowledge a debt to family. "We'd like to think we are [as] charming and inventive as Dad, as ambitious and optimistic as Mom. They both loved the law and writing and singing, and we do too. We honor those hardworking, lovable, creative, frustrated people, and so many others like them, raising families, reaching high, trying," the O'Shaughnessys said on their Web site.

The authors work in different ways with different books, or different parts of books. Mary O'Shaughnessy did the initial draft of their first book. Pamela O'Shaughnessy corrected the legal malapropisms and honed the prose. Since then, they have edited each other's chapters, written alternating chapters, even written alternating scenes.

"Before any fingertips begin skittering over keyboards, we create a detailed proposal and outline together," the authors said in a Readers Read interview. "In practice, one person almost never completes a first draft. A stopping point arrives, and the other sister takes over for a while."

The sisters find comfort in writing together, and neither feels she has the time to devote to a book on her own. They have written short stories individually. Their first collection appeared in 2006. They also have written one non-series crime novel, based in part on the enigma of why their family moved so often.

Pamela O'Shaughnessy once mentioned the French term *folie à deux*, or craziness of two. "That's what Mary and I have," she said in *Publishers Weekly*, "but it results in something constructive—imaginary murders."

Works by the Authors as Perri O'Shaughnessy

Sinister Acts (2006), short stories
Keeper of the Keys (2006)

Nina Reilly Series

Motion to Suppress (1995)
Invasion of Privacy (1997)
Obstruction of Justice (1997)
Breach of Promise (1998)
Acts of Malice (1999)
Move to Strike (2000)
Writ of Execution (2001)
Unfit to Practice (2002)
Presumption of Death (2003)
Unlucky in Law (2004)
Case of Lies (2005)
Show No Fear (2008)

For Further Information

"Interview with Perri O'Shaughnessy," Readers Read. http://www.readersread.com/features/perrioshaughnessy.htm (viewed November 30, 2007).

Kinsella, Bridget, "Sisters in Crime: Perri O'Shaughnessy." *Publishers Weekly*, August 19, 2002.

Maryles, Daisy, "Sisters in Crime." *Publishers Weekly*, August 28, 2000.

Melvin, Beth, Perri O'Shaughnessy interview about *Presumption of Death*, Random House. http://www.randomhouse.com/catalog/display.pperl?isbn=9780440240877&view=auqa (viewed November 30, 2007).

Perri O'Shaughnessy interview, Bookreporter, July 8, 2005. http://www.bookreporter.com/authors/au-oshaughnessy-perri.asp (viewed December 2, 2007).

Perri O'Shaughnessy Web site. http://www.perrio.com (viewed November 19, 2008).

Pitt, David, *Keeper of the Keys* review. *Booklist*, October 1, 2006.

T. Jefferson Parker

Crime-Suspense

Benchmark Series: <u>Merci Rayborn Series</u>

Los Angeles, California

1954–

About the Author and the Author's Writing

With the story of a disgraced Los Angeles cop's pursuit of a psychopath who sets his victims on fire (*Laguna Heat*, 1985), author T. Jefferson Parker leapt into the thriller genre. HBO snapped up the book rights and made it a television movie that aired in 1987 with Harry Hamlin and Jason Robards.

It was a great payoff for a manuscript put together by a newspaper reporter in spare hours and weekends, edited and edited again, over five years. The process would only get easier.

In the two decades since, Parker has gained valuable experience. "I think I'm more economical, more imaginative, less prone to easy situations and emotions, better at creating suspense," he said in a Fiction Addiction interview.

The author was born in Los Angeles, California, in 1954, and grew up in Orange County. As a boy, he read Jack London and the Hardy Boys. In 1976, he received a bachelor of arts degree from the University of California at Irvine. He began his writing career as a reporter for *The Newport Ensign*, a California weekly where he was responsible for crime, political, and cultural stories. He has been twice married (his first wife died) and has two children. While he worked for the *Daily Pilot*, also in California, he began to write fiction. Eventually he quit a job as a technical writer to compose fiction full time. In addition to his passion for writing, he is an avid hiker, hunter, diver, and fisherman and plays tennis. Favorite contemporary authors include Elmore Leonard, Norman Mailer, Thomas Harris, John Gregory Dunn, and Thomas McGuane.

Parker has said his interest in writing was triggered by a "Mythology and Folklore" class in high school and a teacher's assignment to read a book selected from a dozen in a box. He picked Joseph Heller's *Catch-22*. "I couldn't believe how funny it was, how hip and right-on. I told myself that if I could ever write something that would give someone 1/1000th the pleasure that Heller gave me, I'd be proud," he told BookBrowse.

Parker found journalism a direct route to a career in fiction because "it teaches a young person how the world works. It's not the writing itself, because that is fairly straightforward and desirably formulaic. It's the exposure that's valuable," he said in a Writers Write interview.

Parker won Mystery Writers of America's Edgar Allan Poe Award and the Los Angeles Times Book Prize for Best Mystery Thriller for his novel *Silent Joe*. The 2001 novel follows prison guard Joe Trona, who doggedly pursues the murder of his adoptive father, Will Trona, the powerful (and deal-making) Orange County supervisor. According to *Booklist* reviewer Wes Lukowsky, the book "offers another compelling take on one of [Parker's] favorite themes: damaged souls forced to confront their own inner demons while battling others made of flesh and blood."

Most of Parker's books stand alone, but he has written three books about crime solver Merci Rayborn, who exposed department corruption and brought down the former sheriff. If that wasn't enough to turn some officers against her, in pursuit of that sheriff, she nearly implicated her father and her lover. The author does well with female leads; *L.A. Outlaws* (2007) is about a history teacher, Allison Murrieta, who by night holds up diners and steals cars—and one day chances on a robbery scene and makes off with a bag of diamonds.

Parker has no shortage of ideas. He says they come from current news, from bits of overheard conversation, from brief experiences. By the time they are shaped into a plot, they have that already mentioned thread of loss and striving for understanding.

"Loss just seems to me such a common, universal thing," he said on his Web site. "I mean in the end you're stripped of everything, even your heartbeat. And along the way you will lose many, many things. No one is immune. Everyone can understand it."

Southern California, he has found, is a rich setting, as it is home to both the ultra-wealthy and the desperately poor. Parker works with a diverse cast of characters. He has depicted everything from child molesters and right-wing extremists to rapists to Vietnam War veterans in his stories.

The author aims to write five pages a day. He roughly outlines, although he says the multigenerational plot of *California Girl* made it difficult. "So I quickly gave up any idea of outlining. I just winged it, changing characters and years and decades when it felt right. *Silent Joe*, on the other hand, I outlined in 85 single-spaced pages, then found out 200 pages into the manuscript that the outline was worthless," he said in an interview with Kevin Tipple.

However a story comes together, Parker aims to make a connection with the reader. "I defy you to read one of my books and not have some kind of emotional reaction to it," he told Timothy Peters of *Publishers Weekly*, "It may not matter a lot, it's not going to change the course of the world, but it's going to mean something during the time you're reading if it's done right."

Works by the Author

Laguna Heat (1985)

Little Saigon (1987)

Pacific Beat (1991)

Summer of Fear (1993)

The Triggerman's Dance (1996)

Where Serpents Lie (1998)

Silent Joe (2001)

Cold Pursuit (2003)

California Girl (2004)
The Fallen (2006)
Storm Runners (2007)
L.A. Outlaws (2008)

Merci Rayborn Series

The Blue Hour (1999)
Red Light (2000)
Black Water (2002)
The Renegades (2009)

Nonfiction

My California: Journeys by Great Writers, with Mark Arax, Michael Chabon, Firoozeh Dumas, Edward Humes, Aimee Liu, Mary Mackey, Devorah Major, Thomas Steinbeck, Hector Tobar, Donna Wares, and Matt Warshaw (2004)

Adaptations in Other Media

Laguna Heat (1987), HBO television movie based on novel

For Further Information

Cold Pursuit review. *Publishers Weekly*, February 10, 2003.

Jacobsen, Teresa L., *L.A. Outlaws* review. *Library Journal*, October 15, 2007.

Lukowsky, Wes, *Silent Joe* review. *Booklist*, February 15, 2001.

Peters, Timothy, "T. Jefferson Parker: The Dark Side of the California Dream." *Publishers Weekly*, February 6, 2006.

T. Jefferson Parker interview, BookBrowse. http://www.bookbrowse.com/author_interviews/full/index.cfm?author_number=890 (viewed March 14, 2008).

T. Jefferson Parker interview, Fiction Addiction. http://interviews.fictionaddiction.net/tjeffersonparker.html (viewed March 14, 2008).

T. Jefferson Parker Web site. http://www.tjeffersonparker.com/ (viewed November 19, 2008).

Tipple, Kevin, "T. Jefferson Parker Interview." Hardluck Stories. http://www.hardluckstories.com/fall2004/Hardluck%20Stories/Parker1.htm (viewed March 14, 2008).

White, Claire E., "A Conversation with T. Jefferson Parker," Writers Write. http://www.writerswrite.com/journal/apr03/parker.htm (viewed March 14, 2008).

James Patterson

Crime-Suspense: Legal, Historical; Science Fiction

Benchmark Title: *Four Blind Mice*

Newburgh, New York

1947–

Photo credit: Rankin

About the Author and the Author's Writing

James Patterson is a writing dervish. He typically is writing one book; outlining another, perhaps from the <u>Alex Cross</u> series; revising another outline for the <u>Maximum Ride</u> books; and tweaking yet another manuscript from a cowriter. He loves every minute of it.

"Since I work on a lot of projects at the same time, I can flit around," he said in an interview on the International Thriller Writers Web site. "I tend to do a draft in a month/month-and-a-half. And I do seven or eight drafts. Because I'm working on a number of projects, I never got blocked."

Patterson was born in Newburgh, New York, in 1947. His family moved to Massachusetts after his senior year of high school. He took a job at a mental hospital to pay his way through college. Then something clicked. He discovered how much he enjoyed books. "I'd hang out in the library," he said in *TV Guide*. "I became a serious reader. And I was scribbling on the side."

An English major, the author graduated summa cum laude from Manhattan College in 1969 and earned a master's degree summa cum laude at Vanderbilt University the next year. He became a copywriter for J. Walter Thompson advertising agency, working on Toys 'R' Us, Ford Motor Company, and other campaigns. He rose to chief executive officer in 1988 and chairman in 1990.

All the while, he wrote on the side. Thirty-one publishers refused his first manuscript. Finally in print, *The Thomas Berryman Number* (1976) won the Mystery Writers of America Edgar Award for best first novel. It wasn't until his *Along Came a Spider* (1993), about a deranged math teacher who has kidnapped two students, that he leapt into the upper bracket of popular writers. In 1996, he retired from advertising.

Spider was the first of Patterson's <u>Alex Cross</u> series, about a detective psychologist in Washington, D.C. Those kidnapped children weren't just any high school students; they were the daughter of a Hollywood actress and the son of the secretary of the U.S. Treasury. Cross, tall and athletic (Morgan Freeman played him on screen), lost his wife to a drive-by killer. The murder was never solved. Now a widower with three children, Cross, who calls himself Dragonslayer, relentlessly pursues psychopaths and high-profile killers.

Patterson said he made Cross an African American because of a family he had known and respected when growing up in Newburgh in the 1950s.

The author switched the gender of his main characters for a second series, the <u>Women's Murder Club</u>. The main characters are homicide detective Lindsay Boxer, reporter Cindy Thomas, medical examiner Claire Washburn, and lawyer Jill Bernhardt. They work together to show up men.

Patterson has found a different voice for these books. "I think frequently women solve problems differently than men do," he said in a CanMag conversation. "Women when they come in and there's a problem, they'll go, 'What do you think? What do you think? What do you think?' Men kind of come in and just blurt out, 'Well, here's the answer.'"

Patterson, who lives with his wife, Susan Solie, and son in Florida, has accelerated his book production in recent years, working on some manuscripts with co-authors.

Besides thrillers and crime-mystery novels, Patterson has written a romance, *Suzanne's Diary for Nicholas*; a novel with spiritual overtones, *Cradle and All*; a medieval romantic adventure, *The Jester*; and a legal thriller, *The Beach House*. The last, he said in a BookBrowse interview, "seemed like a fun idea to take on John Grisham at his own game. I generally like his stuff and the legal world is incredibly dramatic."

In discussing his writing, Patterson says he never bases his characters on real people. But his personal experience may figure in a story; when he was in his early thirties, he lost a close woman friend to cancer. It was several years before he loosened up enough to establish a new, close relationship with someone. *Thus Suzanne's Diary for Nicholas* is about love lost, love regained. It was his best-selling book up to that time.

To save time, he outlines his books but omits specifics that will emerge in the course of writing; he is never quite sure how things will turn out until he gets there. He employs professional researchers to dig up some information for his books but pursues those topics that intrigue him the most. He writes seven days a week.

Patterson trademarks are his short, rapid-paced chapters and his character-driven plots. "I think it's an easier way of reading," he said in a Lycos conversation. Each chapter is built around a dramatic moment that propels the story. "And turns on the movie projector in our heads. That's what I'm trying to do with the short chapters."

Patterson has bridged younger and older reading niches with the <u>Maximum Ride</u> books, which in 2008 his publisher Little, Brown promoted heavily in front-of-the-store promotions, usually reserved for adult fare, to maximize crossover.

Each book, Patterson said in an iVillage interview, is an attempt "to create the perfect amusement park ride: lots of twists and turns, swoops and heights on the ride."

Works by the Author

The Thomas Berryman Number (1976)

The Season of the Machete (1977)

The Jericho Commandment (1979), retitled *See How They Run* (1997)

Virgin (1980), rewritten as *Cradle and All* (2000)

Black Market (1986), retitled *Black Friday* (1989)

The Midnight Club (1989)

The Thirteen (1995)

Hide and Seek (1996)

Miracle on the 17th Green (1996), with Peter de Jonge

Suzanne's Diary for Nicholas (2001)

The Beach House (2002), with Peter de Jonge

The Jester (2003), with Andrew Gross

Sam's Letters to Jennifer (2004)

Honeymoon, with Howard Roughan (2005)

Beach Road, with Peter de Jonge (2006)

Judge & Jury, with Andrew Gross (2006)

The Quickie, with Michael Ledwidge (2007)

Step on a Crack, with Michael Ledwidge (2007

You've Been Warned, with Howard Roughan (2007)

Sundays at Tiffany's (2008)

Sail, with Howard Roughan (2008)

Dangerous Days of Daniel X, with Michael Ledwidge (2008)

Run for Your Life, with Michael Ledwidge (2009)

Alex Cross Series

Along Came a Spider (1993)

Kiss the Girls (1995)

Jack and Jill (1996)

Cat and Mouse (1997)

Pop! Goes the Weasel (1999)

Roses Are Red (2000)

Violets Are Blue (2001)

Four Blind Mice (2002)

The Big Bad Wolf (2003)

London Bridges (2004)

Mary, Mary (2005)

Cross (2006)

Double Cross (2007)

Cross Country (2008)

Winged Children Series

When the Wind Blows (1998)
The Lake House (2003)

Women's Murder Club Series

1st to Die (2001)
2nd Chance (2002) with Andrew Gross
3rd Degree, with Andrew Gross (2004)
4th of July, with Maxine Paetro (2005)
The 5th Horseman, with Maxine Paetro (2006)
The 6th Target, with Maxine Paetro (2007)
7th Heaven, with Maxine Paetro (2008)
The 8th Confession, with Maxine Paetro (2009)

Editor

Thriller: Stories to Keep You Up All Night (2006)

Juvenile Fiction

Santakid (2004)

Young Adult Fiction

Maximum Ride Series, written with Gabrielle Charbonnet
The Angel Experiment (2005)
School's Out—Forever (2006)
Saving the World and Other Extreme Sports (2007)
The Final Warning (2008)
Max (2009)

Nonfiction

The Day America Told the Truth: What People Really Believe about Everything That Matters, with Peter Kim (1991)
The Second American Revolution, with Peter Kim (1994)
Against Medical Advice, with Hal Friedman (2008)

Adaptations in Other Media

Child of Darkness, Child of Light (1991), television film based on *Virgin*
Kiss the Girls (1997), motion picture
Miracle on the 17th Green (1999), television film
Along Came a Spider (2001), motion picture
1st to Die (2003), television film
Suzanne's Diary for Nicholas (2005), television film
Women's Murder Club (ABC, 2007), television series
When the Wind Blows (announced)
Maximum Ride (announced)

For Further Information

Brookman, Rob, "Have You Read a Patterson Lately?" *Book,* March-April 2003.

"James Patterson: A Cross between Black and White," International Thriller Writers. http://www.thrillerwriters.org/index.php?option=com_content&task=view&id=406&Itemid=29 (viewed September 21, 2007).

James Patterson biography, Bookbrowse. http://www.bookbrowse.com/index/cfm?page=author&authorID-289 (viewed April 11, 2003).

James Patterson entry. *The Mammoth Encyclopedia of Modern Crime Fiction,* Mike Ashley, ed. New York: Carroll & Graf, 2002.

James Patterson interview, Bookbrowse. http://www.bookbrowse.com/author_interviews/full/index.cfm?author_number=289 (viewed October 25, 2007).

James Patterson interview, Bookreporter. http://www.bookreporter.com/reviews/0316969680.asp (viewed April 11, 2003).

James Patterson interview, Lycos (March 20, 2003). http://clubs.lycos.com/live/Events/Transcripts/james_patterson.asp (viewed May 17, 2003).

James Patterson interview, Written Voices. http://www.writtenvoices.com/authorfeature.asp?namelast-patterson (viewed April 11, 2003).

James Patterson on Women's Murder Club," CanMag. http://www.canmag.com/nw/9271-james-patterson-womens-murder-club (viewed October 25, 2007).

James Patterson Web page. http://www.twbookmark.com/features/jamespatterson/press.html (viewed May 17, 2003).

James Patterson Web site. http://www.jamespatterson.com (viewed November 19, 2008).

"James Patterson: I Never Stop Writing," iVillage. http://www.ivillage.com/books/intervu/myst/articles/0,11872,240795_219210,00.html (viewed April 11, 2003).

Jones, Daniel, and John D. Jorgenson, eds., James Patterson entry, *Contemporary Authors New Revision Series*, volume 72. Detroit, MI: Gale Research, 1999.

Kotler, Joan G. *James Patterson: A Critical Reader.* Westport, CT: Greenwood, 2004.

Lake House review. *Publishers Weekly,* May 19, 2003.

Morris, Edward, "A Jester on Crusade: James Patterson Plumbs Medieval History for His Newest Hero." *BookPage,* March 2003.

Murphy, Mary, "Along Came a Writer." *TV Guide,* February 22, 2003.

Rich, Motoko, "An Author Looks beyond Age Limits," *New York Times*, February 20, 2008.

"2007 Thriller Master James Patterson," International Thriller Writers. http://www.thrillerwriters.org/index.php?option=com_content&task=view&id=479&Itemid=83 (viewed October 25, 2007).

Womack, Steve, "Stretching the Boundaries of the Thriller, BookPage. http://www.bookpage.com/0006bp/james_patterson.html (viewed April 11, 2003).

Richard North Patterson

Thrillers: Legal, Political

Benchmark Title: *Degree of Guilt*

Berkeley, California

1947–

About the Author and the Author's Writing

Richard North Patterson, a lawyer, has written several courtroom novels. But he doesn't want to be categorized as simply a writer of legal thrillers. His topics often have national and international implications. He's written about gun control in *Balance of Power*, about abortion in *Protect and Defend*, and about Israel and the Palestinians in *Exile*.

In each case, although his stance is obvious, he presents a multifaceted story. Of *Conviction*, for example, which is about the death penalty, reviewer Stacy Alesi noted in *Library Journal*, "Patterson provides compelling evidence for both sides of the argument. In his sure hands, this fascinating and often agonizing in-depth look at the death-penalty process becomes a personal journey for the lawyers, the convicted, and the reader."

Perhaps his most ambitious book is *Exile*, in which he uses the courtroom drama to explore geo-politics. "*Exile* represents what, to me, is an exciting fusion of my established territory," Patterson told Bookreporter in 2007, "with a new focus: the conflict between Israelis and Palestinians, and the lethal politic of the Middle East, shadowed by the threat of a nuclear Iran. The result, I hope, is the most compelling fiction of my career."

Born in Berkeley, California, the author grew up in Bay Village in suburban Cleveland. In 1968, he graduated from Ohio Wesleyan University with a bachelor of arts degree, and he earned his juris doctorate from Case Western Reserve Law School in 1971. After a stint as assistant attorney general in Ohio, he served on the special prosecutor's staff during the Watergate hearings as a liaison from the Securities and Exchange Commission. He has practiced law in Washington, D.C., Alabama, and California, and has been active with several advocacy groups and has chaired the National Governing Board of Common Cause. He had two children from his first marriage, to Anne Riggs, and four with his second, to Laurie Anderson. He has homes in San Francisco and Martha's Vineyard.

Patterson was well established in his law career when he took a creative writing course at the University of Alabama at Birmingham. After thirteen rejections and three rewrites, a manuscript from that class found a publisher. *The Lasko Tangent* (1979)

310

won an Edgar Award as Best First Mystery Novel. The author subsequently won the Grand Prix de Littérature Policière.

Books that have influenced him include Dashiell Hammett and Ross Macdonald crime novels, James Gould Cozzens's social dramas, and Alan Drury's political sagas. Patterson explained his general philosophy of writing to Absolute Write's RoseEtta Stone: "I try to write novels in which interest is not only in the story, but in exploration and development of the characters. The danger is less physical. It's psychological or moral."

Patterson took an eight-year break from writing in the 1980s, returned with *Degree of Guilt*, and since 1993 has been a full-time writer. His 1998 book *No Safe Place* drove deep into the national political arena in the story of liberal New Jersey Senator Kerry Kilcannon's tense campaign for the presidential nomination. The late Bobby Kennedy inspired Patterson's hero, and while researching for the book, he got to know several other Washington politicos, including Senator John McCain.

"I came away with a sense that the good politicians are better than we know and better than we have a right to expect," he told BookPage interviewer Alden Mudge, "given the corrosive nature of the fundraising system that exists, the demands of the office, the absolute loss of privacy, dignity, and even respect."

The Columbine school killings begged for Patterson treatment, and his *Balance of Power* (2003) makes a clear case for sound regulation of weapons. "I wanted to imagine a situation that not only moved the reader but also galvanized the country to focus on the insanity of gun death," he said in an interview with Linda Kutman of *U.S. News & World Report*. He upbraids the National Rifle Association for distorting the aim of proponents of gun regulation

His solid writing and consistent growth has brought Patterson to a strong position of being pretty much able to write what he wants. "And this has caused me to reflect on how to use that gift, and to pursue what, to me, is one of the most important functions of a writer:" to address some of the central political and social issues of our time," he said in an interview on Macmillan's Web site.

Works by the Author

The Outside Man (1981)
Escape the Night (1983)
Private Screening (1985)
The Final Judgment (1995), also issued as *Caroline Masters* (2000)
Silent Witness (1996)
No Safe Place (1998)
Dark Lady (1999)
Protect and Defend (2000)
Balance of Power (2003)
Degree of Guilt/The Final Judgment (2003), omnibus
Conviction (2005)
Exile (2007)
The Race (2007)
Eclipse (2009)

Christopher Paget Series

The Lasko Tangent (1979)
Degree of Guilt (1992)
Eyes of a Child (1994)
The Lasko Tangent/Degree of Guilt (2005), omnibus

For Further Information

Alesi, Stacy, *Conviction* review. *Library Journal*, December 1, 2004.

Huntley, Kristine, *The Race* review. *Booklist*, September 1, 2007.

"An Interview with Richard North Patterson," Pan Macmillan Web site. http://www.panmacmillan.com/interviews/displayPage.asp?PageID=5461 (viewed January 3, 2008).

Kulman, Linda, "He's Not Gun-Shy.*U.S. News & World Report*, October 6, 2003.

Mudge, Alden, "Patterson Tackles National Politics, and Timely Issues in *No Safe Place*," BookPage. www.bookpage.com/9809bp/richard_north_patterson.htm (viewed January 3, 2008).

Richard North Patterson interview, Bookreporter, January 12, 2007. http://www.bookreporter.com/authors/au-patterson-richard.asp (viewed January 3, 2008).

Stone, RoseEtta, "A Discussion with Richard North Patterson," Absolute Write. http://www.absolutewrite.com/ novels/richard_north_patterson.htm (viewed January 3, 2007).

Ridley Pearson

Adventure; Crime; Fantasy; Thrillers: Medical, Global

Benchmark Series: <u>Lou Boldt/Daphne Matthews Mysteries</u>

Glencove, New York

1953–

Photo credit: Timathea Shays

About the Author and the Author's Writing

The hero swings on a rope across a ship's deck, knife in his teeth, sabre in his hand, to fend off the pirates in one of Ridley Pearson's recent novels. That this swashbucker is Peter Pan shouldn't detract from our appreciation of Pearson's prose abilities; he and his cowriter, Dave Barry, are simply taking a break from their routines (in Pearson's case, thrillers; in Barry's, humor) to satisfy their inner children.

"We both have kids under seven, and they can't read much of what we normally write," Pearson explained in a BookPage interview, "so it was nice to create something they could finally read of ours."

Pearson's recent *Killer Weekend* (2007), the first in a new series featuring Idaho Sheriff Walt Fleming, has plenty of action and suspense for adults. In addition to his regular duties, Fleming has to protect a New York state attorney general, Elizabeth Shaier, who intends to announce her candidacy for the U.S. presidency at a weekend conference at a major resort. That's when she receives a death threat. Fleming has little time to find the assassin among the prominent business people at the gathering.

Pearson was born in Glencove, New York, in 1953. His father was a writer, his mother an artist. He grew up in suburban Connecticut. In 1972, he graduated from the University of Kansas and Brown University in 1974. He and his second wife, Marcelle Marsh, have two children and live in Missouri. He has been everything from a dishwasher to a songwriter (he composed the orchestral score for the documentary *Cattle Drive*).

After finishing college, Pearson moved to Sun Valley, Idaho, and played in a rock band. He began to write fiction, selling his first novel, *Never Look Back*, to St. Martin's in 1985. He continued to write freestanding crime and suspense novels and books in a series featuring Lou Boldt, a police detective based in Seattle. Pearson says that he never anticipated the first <u>Boldt</u> book, *Undercurrents* (1988) becoming a series. Had he known, he said in a Bookreporter interview in 2004, he might have slipped in more backstory. "It's the relationships between these characters that has surprised me—and in this way, these characters really have written the book on their own in many places, and I've felt much like a spectator," he said.

Sensitive to emotional themes, the author has said he graphs his characters so he can track their progress in the course of the books. He outlines his books closely but often ends up changing the endings.

Sometimes the author uses familiar settings—such as Sun Valley for the Sheriff Fleming novel—but he researches others. "I put a significant emphasis on research because I think one way to suspend the reader's disbelief is to base the novel in as much truth as possible," he told Katie Struckel for *Writers Digest*. Interestingly, Pearson's novel *Undercurrents*, describes certain research methods regarding tide flow employed by the hero that a real-life prosecuting attorney in Washington State used to dig up information for his own use in a trial.

In 1991, Pearson became the first American to attend Oxford University under the Raymond Chandler Fulbright Fellowship. During the program, which was created for established writers, he researched and developed outlines for the novels *The Angel Maker* (1993) and *No Witnesses* (1994).

Pearson occasionally plays bass guitar at book conferences with the Rock Bottom Remainders, a literary garage band made up of fellow writers including Stephen King, Amy Tan, and Dave Barry, among others. The musical connection has produced literary benefits. He crafted the fictional diary of Ellen Rimbauer, as she relates her sexually charged early 1900s experiences at haunted Rose Red manor in Seattle, based on the King novel *Red Rose*. Only several months after publication did King let on that Pearson had written the book, under the pseudonym Steven Rimbauer. The revelation came on the eve of publication of Pearson's own ironically titled *The Art of Deception*. (Both King's novel and Pearson's pastiche were made into television films.)

"The game here was to take the existing script and write a prequel to it that would explain much of what we would later see [in the television movie]," Pearson told *Publishers Weekly*. "I had to come up with lives of these people and what they had been through in order to justify what Stephen was going to put their ghosts through. What a fun game that was."

Pearson worked with another band-mate, Dave Barry, to devise more prequels when they took on the Peter Pan tales, based on the stories of J. M. Barrie. These and series featuring the Kingdom Keepers and Steel Trapp are not Pearson's first venture into stories for younger readers. Using the penname Wendell McCall, he wrote three books about Chris Klick, a lumbering former songwriter who traces missing musicians. Does the character sound reminiscent of the author?

"Being a fiction writer is really like being an actor, because if you're going to write convincingly it has to sound right and play right," Pearson said on his Web site. "The only way that works is to emotionally and technically act out and see the scene you're in."

Works by the Author

Never Look Back (1985)
Blood of the Albatross (1986)
The Seizing of the Yankee Green Mall (1987), retitled *Hidden Charges*
Probable Cause (1990)
Hard Fall (1992)
Chain of Evidence (1995)
Parallel Lies (2001)
Cut and Run (2005)

Lou Boldt/Daphne Matthews Mysteries

Undercurrents (1988)
The Angel Maker (1993)
No Witnesses (1994)
Beyond Recognition (1997)
The Pied Piper (1998)
The First Victim (1999)
Middle of Nowhere (2000)
The Art of Deception (2002)
The Body of Peter Hayes (2004)

Sheriff Walt Fleming Series

Killer Weekend (2007)
Killer View (2008)
Killer Summer (2009)

Contributor

Diagnosis: Terminal, edited by F. Paul Wilson (1996), includes "All Over but the Dying"
The Putt at the End of the World, edited by Les Standiford (2000)
Murder Is My Racquet, edited by Otto Penzler (2005), includes "Close Shave"

Screenplay

The Diary of Ellen Rimbauer (ABC, 2003), television film

Written as Steven Rimbauer

The Diary of Ellen Rimbauer: My Life at Rose Red (2001)

For Young Adults and Juveniles

Science Fair with Dave Barry (2008)

Kingdom Keepers Series

The Kingdom Keepers: Disney After Dark (2005)
Kingdom Keepers II: Disney at Dawn (2008)

Neverland Books

Escape from the Carnivale, with Dave Barry (2006)
Cave of the Dark Wind, with Dave Barry (2007)
Blood Tide, with Dave Barry (2008)

Starcatchers Series

Peter and the Starcatchers, with Dave Barry (2004)
Peter and the Shadow Thieves, with Dave Barry (2006)
Peter and the Secret of Rundoon, with Dave Barry (2007)

Steel Trapp Series

The Challenge (2008)

Chris Klick Mystery Series, as by Wendell McCall

Dead Aim (1988)
Aim for the Heart (1990)
Concerto in Dead Flat (1999)

For Further Information

Croog, Dena, "'Rimbauer' Author Unmasked." *Publishers Weekly*, July 8, 2002.

Kinsella, Bridget, "Ridley Pearson Gets Real in Sun Valley." *Publishers Weekly*, May 7, 2007.

Ridley Pearson profile and interview, Bookreporter, 2004. http://www.bookreporter.com/authors/au-pearson-ridley.asp (viewed February 15, 2008).

Ridley Pearson Web site. http://www.ridleypearson.com/about.html (viewed November 19, 2008).

"Shiver Me Timbers! It's a Peter Pan Prequel," BookPage. http://www.bookpage.com/0409bp/dave_barry_ridley_pearson.html (viewed February 15, 2008).

Struckel, Katie, "Conducting Research with Ridley Pearson," WritersDigest. http://www.writersdigest.com/articles/interview/pearson_conducting_research.asp (viewed February 15, 2008).

Weich, Dave, "Dave Barry and Ridley Pearson Will Never Grow Up," Powells. http://www.powells.com/authors/pearson.html (viewed February 15, 2008).

Thomas Perry

Adventure; Espionage; Thrillers

Benchmark Series: <u>Jane Whitefield Series</u>

Tonawanda, New York

1947–

Photo credit: Jo Perry

About the Author and the Author's Writing

In trouble with the mob? Need to get out of the reaches of a North Korean spy cell? You could do worse than hire Jane Whitefield of Thomas Perry's rapid-paced series. Usually found leading a quiet life with her husband in upstate Amherst, New York, she has Native American skills and instincts that would make a Navy SEAL take notice. She has the resources to manufacture birth certificates, driver's licenses, and passports at a moment's notice and whisk you to Remote Place, Kansas, or Neverfindem, Arkansas, without leaving a trace.

Perry was born in 1947 in Tonawanda, New York. In 1969, he received a bachelor of arts degree from Cornell University; and five years later he earned a Ph.D. in English literature from the University of Rochester. His career covers the gamut: park maintenance worker, commercial fisherman, factory laborer, teacher, university administrator, weapons mechanic, television writer, and program producer. Not the least, he is author of five books in the best-selling <u>Whitefield</u> series, along with ten-and-counting freestanding novels.

Perry and his wife, Jo, wrote television scripts together as staff writers for such programs as Universal Television's *Simon & Simon*, Disney's *Sidekicks* and *The Oldest Rookie*, and Viacom's *Snoops*. They also freelanced for Steven J. Cannell's *21 Jump Street* and Paramount's *Star Trek: The Next Generation*. They stopped television work to raise their two daughters. Thomas Perry now concentrates on writing thrillers.

Perry's first novel, *The Butcher's Boy* (1982), won an Edgar Award from the Mystery Writers of America. He wrote a half-dozen more novels before the first <u>Jane Whitefield</u> book, *Vanishing Act*, was published in 1994. His editor almost immediately wanted it to become a series. Perry has temporarily abandoned her exploits, explaining he

317

has built up a pile of other ideas, and he'd like the character to grow a little older, so he has other themes to explore.

Series are good for a writer, he said in an Identity Theory interview. "You know when you are finished with this book—then you have a million wonderful things that you are thinking that you know that you can't possibly fit into this plot, you're going to have another chance at it." Stand-alone books, on the other hand, potentially waste character traits and plot deviations that could clutter the action.

Perry likes to explore facets of evil. "I've never written about the really mentally ill killers, the barking mad Jeffrey Dahmers and Joyn Wayne Gacys of the world. What I usually write about is mild sociopaths, people who do evil things because they don't see any reason not to," he said in a Crime and Suspense interview.

Perry's books contain violence and death, subjects he does not deal with lightly, he has said in interviews. He strives for as much realism as he can achieve, given the popular entertainment medium in which he is working. On his Web site, Perry says he strives to become a better writer with each novel. "The best way for me to improve was to strain a bit and work on new stories with new characters I knew little about and needed to study…. I continue to experiment and explore, and to try to make each day's work a little better than the last."

Although he admires the writing of Lawrence Block, Donald Westlake, and Joe Gores, among others, he generally does not read a lot in the genre, so he won't inadvertently borrow. He strives for an unobtrusive writing style. Ultimately he wants to entertain himself, and that means keeping things tight. "I do edit myself to keep from becoming the Village Explainer," he told Bookreporter's Ann Bruns. "It's important, I think, for a writer of fiction to maintain an awareness of the pace and shape of the book as he's writing it. That is, he should be making an object, not chattering."

Jane Whitefield hoped to retire and lead a quiet life as a surgeon's wife, Mrs. Jane McKinnon. But there's always one more person to hide. In the character's return, in the 2009 novel *Runner*, a bomb explodes during a hospital fundraiser. Whitefield has had to assimilate a whole new repertoire of tricks as she takes a young pregnant woman on the run from hired killers. The world's technology has caught up with and soared beyond her old skills. Perry said on his Web site that he waited to bring his heroine back until he had a good new story to tell.

Perry, as we've come to appreciate, is seldom without a good new story.

Works by the Author

The Butcher's Boy (1982)
Metzger's Dog (1983)
Big Fish (1985)
Island (1987)
Sleeping Dogs (1992)
Pursuit (2001)
Death Benefits (2001)
Dead Aim (2002)
Nightlife (2006)

Silence (2007)
Fidelity (2008)

Jane Whitefield Series

Vanishing Act (1994)
Dance for the Dead (1996)
Shadow Woman (1997)
The Face-Changers (1998)
Blood Money (2000)
Runner (2009)

For Further Information

Birnbaum, Robert, Thomas Perry interview, Identitytheory, 2003. http://www.identitytheory.com/people/birnbaum85.html (viewed February 15, 2008).

Bruns, Anne, Thomas Perry interview, Bookreporter, 2003. http://www.bookreporter.com/authors/au-perry-thomas.asp (viewed February 15, 2008).

"Interview with Thomas Perry," Crimeandsuspense.com, 2005. http://www.crimeandsuspense.com/archives/perry_intv.htm (viewed February 15, 2008).

Thomas Perry Web page, Random House. http://www.randomhouse.com/features/thomasperry.bio.html (viewed February 21, 2008).

Thomas Perry Web site. http://www.thomasperryauthor.com (viewed November 19, 2008).

Jodi Picoult

Crime; Mainstream; Romance; Thriller: Legal

Benchmark Title: *Nineteen Minutes*

New York

1966–

Photo credit: Simon & Schuster

About the Author and the Author's Writing

Jodi Picoult's script for the iconic female comic book character Wonder Woman in 2007 brought her a new audience—not that she lacked for readers. Her novels, produced at an accelerating rate since 1992, and variously categorized as legal thrillers, mysteries, family dramas, women's fiction, and romances, have brought her an enormous following worldwide.

Writing about the author for the *New York Times*, Janet Maslin summarized her appeal: "She writes articulately and clearly.... Her stories are more reassuring than disturbing, and their surprise twists pose no threats. These novels have soap-opera momentum, and they guarantee comforting closure."

Born in New York in 1966, the daughter of a securities analyst and a nursery school director, the author received a bachelor of arts degree in English from Princeton University in 1987. While there, she studied creative writing with Mary Morris and sold two short stories to *Seventeen* magazine. In 1990, she earned a master's degree in education from Harvard University. She worked in several jobs including as a developmental editor for Allyn & Bacon in Newton, Massachusetts, in 1987 and 1988; she then taught English and creative writing in Concord and Natick, Massachusetts, from 1989 to 1991. After that, she became a writer while raising three children with her husband, Timothy Warren van Leer. The family lives near Hanover, New Hampshire.

Picoult began her first novel while pregnant with her first child. Among authors who inspired her, she says, is Margaret Mitchell and her *Gone with the Wind*. Other favorites include Ernest Hemingway, Alice Hoffman, and William Shakespeare. That first novel, *Songs of the Humpback Whale*, came out right after her son was born. Her second book was about juggling parental responsibilities and work. Being a mother-writer had its advantages, however. "I learned how to write quickly and efficiently, and never had writers block," she said in a Writers Write interview. "Some days, I write pure dreck, but I can always edit that the next day. I just plow through and then go back and edit."

Picoult is drawn to timely subjects. "I do like to deal with hard topics like child abuse," she told *Publishers Weekly* in 2005. "When you throw it into fiction, you almost hook the reader by accident because you get people involved with the story of a family, the story of a person. You sort of go in the back door and crack open their thinking." The author has written a story about a couple conceiving a second child purposely so it can donate organs to an ailing sibling (*My Sister's Keeper*, her breakthrough novel), and she has written about a father tracking his daughter's kidnapper (*The Tenth Circle*).

"Picoult has become a master—almost a clairvoyant—at targeting hot issues and writing highly readable page-turners about them," said *Washington Post* reviewer Anne Hood of *Perfect Match,* a novel about an abusive priest.

The Columbine school shootings in 1999 in Colorado sparked the plot for the novel *Nineteen Minutes*, which presciently came into print within a week of the Virginia Tech shootings in 2007. The author tells the story from the perspective of seventeen-year-old Peter Houghton, who shoots up his New Hampshire high school after suffering years of abuse and bullying from fellow students. She says her intention was not to forgive the spree, but spur people to try to understand it.

"As a mom of three, I've seen my own children struggle with fitting in and being bullied," Picoult told Bookreporter. It was listening to their experiences, and my own frustrations, that led me to consider the topic."

The book was difficult to research, she said. But through a colleague, she obtained material from the Jefferson County Sheriff's Office relating to Columbine, and she spoke with survivors. For *Plain Truth*, set among the Amish, she spent a week on a Pennsylvania farm, rising at 4:30 to help milk cows.

Picoult's books often include trial scenes. "I always work with an attorney to make sure I get it right, since I'm not a lawyer myself. When we work on the courtroom scenes, we role play," she told interviewer RoseEtta Stone.

Known for twist endings, Picoult said on her Web site she has the conclusion worked out before she begins writing. "When I start a book, I juggle a what-if question in my head, and push it and push it until I feel like I have a good story."

Because of their topicality, the author's work has found a wide audience with book clubs, whose members discuss issues in the context of the novels. "My job is not to answer the questions but to get you talking," Picoult said in a *USA Today* interview. "If I can get you hooked on a plot, you go along for the ride and start thinking about an important issue… If I can lift the curtain on certain topics, I don't think that's a bad thing."

Works by the Author

Songs of the Humpback Whale: A Novel in Five Voices (1992)

Harvesting the Heart (1993)

Picture Perfect (1995)

Mercy (1996)

The Pact (1998)

Keeping Faith (1999)

Plain Truth (2000)

Salem Falls (2001)
Perfect Match (2002)
My Sister's Keeper (2004)
Vanishing Acts (2005)
The Tenth Circle (2006)
Nineteen Minutes (2007)
Change of Heart (2008)
Handle with Care (2009)

Graphic Novels

The Tenth Circle: Wildclaw (2006)
Wonder Woman: Love & Murder (2007)

Adaptations in Other Media

The Pact (2002), television film
Plain Truth (2004), television film
The Tenth Circle (2008), television film

For Further Information

Connolly, Paul, "Chilling Timing for This Tale of a Killer in Class." *Evening Standard*, April 24, 2007.

Dellasega, Cheryl, "Mothers Who Write: Jodi Picoult," Writers Write, September 2001. http://www.writerswrite.com/journal/sep01/picoult.htm (viewed January 4, 2008).

Donahue, Deirdre, "Curiosity Produces a Novel Every 9 Months," *USA Today*, April 11, 2006.

Donahue, Deirdre, "Picoult Draws Readers in to Her 'Circle' of Ideas." *USA Today*, April 11, 2006.

France, Louise, "The Great Unknown." *Guardian*, April 25, 2007.

"From Quiche to Corvette Steve: From a Safe Haven, Jodi Picoult Explores the Dark Side." *Publishers Weekly*, February 14, 2005.

Hood, Anne, *Perfect Match* review. *Washington Post*, May 5, 2002.

Jodi Picoult interview, BookBrowse. http://www.bookbrowse.com/author_interviews/full/index.cfm?author_number=601 (viewed January 4, 2008).

Jodi Picoult interview, Bookreporter. http://www.bookreporter.com/authors/au-picoult-jodi.asp (viewed January 4, 2008).

Jodi Picoult Web site. http://www.jodipicoult.com/ (viewed November 19, 2008).

Maslin, Janet, "From This Moment On: After the Shooting Is Over," *New York Times*, March 16, 2007.

Stone, RoseEtta, "Interview with Jodi Picoult," Absolute Write. http://www.absolutewrite.com/novels/jodi_picoult.htm (viewed January 4, 2008).

Wyatt, Neal, "Beyond the Funny Pages: Comics in Fiction." *Library Journal*, July 1, 2007.

Kathy Reichs

Crime

Benchmark Series: <u>Dr. Temperance Brennan</u>

Chicago, Illinois

1948–

Photo credit: Marie-Reine Matera

About the Author and the Author's Writing

The body of a Canadian missionary, killed in a skirmish in Guatemala, buried in a small town in New Brunswick, is exhumed and examined by a forensic anthropologist to determine whether the man had been tortured before he died and whether it was a government explosive that blew his body to bits.

Bones are unearthed in a pizza parlor basement. Police think they are as old as the buttons found nearby, but a forensic anthropologist uses Carbon 14 dating of their tooth enamel to determine when the victims—three women—were born.

Which one is the real case, which one is made up? The first one is real. The body was that of Raoul Léger. Forensic specialist Kathy Reichs was on the 1981 team that probed for clues to help his family learn the truth in his violent death.

And forensics specialist Kathy Reichs was involved in the second case as well. It was a puzzle she crafted for her mystery series heroine, Temperance "Tempe" Brennan, *Monday Mourning* (2004).

Reichs leads a double—or is it quadruple?—life. She's a forensic anthropologist for the Office of the Chief Medical Examiner for the state of North Carolina. She's a forensic anthropologist for the Laboratoire des Sciences Judiciaries et de Médecine Légale for the province of Québec. She writes mystery novels. And she serves as a producer for the popular Fox Network drama series *Bones*, which debuted in 2005.

Born in Chicago in 1948, Kathleen Joan Toelle earned her undergraduate degree from American University and her Ph.D. from Northwestern University. In 1968, she married attorney Paul Reichs; they have three children. She has been a professor of anthropology at the University of North Carolina at Charlotte and has taught at the FBI's academy at Quantico and at the Canadian Police College.

Reich's original career path was as an archaeologist. "I was studying doing bio-archeology, which is the study of ancient skeletons. Police started bringing me cases about skeletons they'd found, so it was a natural progression," she said in an interview on the Bibliofemme Web site. Now one of only fifty forensic anthropologists certified by the American Board of Forensic Anthropology, hers is a specialized craft.

Her expertise initially took her to Canada as part of the National Faculty Exchange program. At the end of a year, in 1990, she signed on to commute once a month to Québec to work on its cases. At the same time, she performed the same role in North Carolina. Experiences from both countries serve her fiction writing.

"A serial killer case gave rise to *Deja Dead*," she said in a Bookreporter interview in 2002. "Two investigations triggered *Death du Jour*: seeing the victims of a murder-suicide cult, and working on the bones of a woman, dead in 1714, who had been proposed for sainthood. *Deadly Decisions* grew out of a number of cases I have done involving people killed by outlaw motorcycle gangs."

Most writers enjoy a distance from their subjects. Reichs is up to her elbows in bodies. She handles as many as eighty cases a year. Coroners or police often bring her in when "the body is compromised. It's mummified. It's burned, decomposed. It's dismembered. It's putrified. It's just a torso out of the river. It's just a skeleton," she said in a question-and-answer with HBO.com. First she must figure out who it is, then what killed the person.

Bones, she has said, are the common denominator in her cases. And *Bones* is the name, conveniently, of the Fox Network television show based on Reichs and her character. She serves as executive producer. "I'm a producer and I work on every script," she said in a Strand Magazine interview. "I help them [staff writers] mainly with getting the science right."

Those familiar with her books notice the characters and characterizations are different from the television portrayals. Reichs considers the TV program as presenting Tempe Brennan when she's in her thirties. "She's less sophisticated, her people skills clearly need some work.... And she's in Washington, which I find particularly appropriate because I started my career at the Smithsonian," she said in a *TV Guide* interview with Angel Cohn.

Although Reichs monitors scripts, she agreed that another writer should write a separate series of novels based on the TV show. While she appreciates the need for dramatic impact, she's keen on keeping the scripts, and the novels that come from them, faithful to science.

The writing and the television show are short-term relief from her work, which can at times be wrenching. "You have to remain objective," she said in an interview for *Smithsonian Magazine*. "My colleague Clyde Snow has said, 'If you have to cry, you cry at night at home. While you're doing your job, you do your job.' The cases that stay in your mind are the ones that haven't been resolved."

Works by the Author

Dr. Temperance Brennan Mystery Series

Deja Dead (1997)
Death du Jour (1998)
Deadly Decisions (2000)

Fatal Voyage (2001)
Grave Secrets (2002)
Bare Bones (2003)
Monday Mourning (2004)
Cross Bones (2005)
Break No Bones (2006)
Bones to Ashes (2007)
Devil Bones (2008)

Bones Series

Buried Deep by Max Allan Collins (2006), based on the television series

Nonfiction, Editor

Hominid Origins: Inquiries Past and Present (1983)
Forensic Osteology: Advances in the Identification of Human Remains (1986)

Television Series Based on the Author's Work

Bones (Fox, 2005–)

For Further Information

Cohn, Angel, "Kathy Reichs Talks about Bones' Brennan Meeting Her Maker." *TV Guide*, November 8, 2006.

Demont, John, "An Agonizing Wait." *MacLean's*, March 18, 2002.

Gulli, Andrew F., "Interview: Kathy Reichs." *Strand Magazine*, October 2008.

"Interview with Kathy Reichs," Bibliofemme. http::/www.bibliofemme.com/interviews/reichs.shtml (viewed October 12, 2007).

Kathy Reichs interview, Bookreporter. http://www.bookreporter.com/authors/au-reichs-kathy.asp (viewed October 12, 2007).

Kathy Reichs Web site. http://www.kathyreichs.com/ (viewed November 19, 2008).

Lineberry, Cate, "On the Case." *Smithsonian Magazine*, August 2007.

MacDonald, Don, "Famed Author Helps Tackle Real Mystery: Kathy Reichs to Autopsy Slain N.B. Missionary." *Montreal Gazette*, November 24, 2001.

MacDonald, Don, "Novelist Aims to Get Facts." *Montreal Gazette*, December 16, 2001.

Mudge, Alden, "Meet This Season's Best Discovery: Kathy Reichs," BookPage, September 1997. http://www.bookpage.com/9709bp/firstperson1.html (viewed October 12, 2007).

"Q&A with Forensic Anthropologist, Kathy Reichs," HBO.com. http://www.hbo.com/autopsy/forensics/qa_with_kathy_reichs_html (viewed October 12, 2007).

Ruditis, Paul, with foreword by Kathy Reichs. *Bones: The Official Companion*. London: Titan Books, 2007.

Matthew Reilly

Adventure: Military; Science Fiction; Thrillers: Techno

Benchmark Title: *Ice Station*

Photo credit: Natalie Reilly

About the Author and the Author's Writing

Matthew Reilly not only set his first thriller in a library, he self-published it. *Contest* (1996) kicked off a successful writing career. After five best sellers, the ever-innovative Reilly launched his futuristic *Hover Car Racer* novel by giving it away free on the Internet.

Born in 1974 in Sydney, Australia, Reilly was a popular entertainment junkie as a youth. He went to movies and watched television, and he went to see his actor-parents perform at the theater. It wasn't until late in his high school years that he discovered the pleasures of reading—thanks to Harper Lee's *Kill a Mockingbird* and William Golding's *Lord of the Flies*. His all-time favorite author, and an inspiration for his work, he has said, is Michael Crichton.

Reilly attended the University of New South Wales and earned a bachelor of arts degree in 1994. In his spare time, he wrote an adventure book, *Contest*; when it failed to find a publisher, he printed copies and distributed them to bookstores around Sydney. An editor with Pan Macmillian read the book, liked it, and gave Reilly a two-book contract. The young author continued his studies and earned a bachelor of law degree in 1997, all the while completing his next novel, *Ice Station*. The 540-page book sold a remarkable 140,000 copies in Australia, and went on to find publishers in more than a dozen countries.

Ice Station introduces Marine Lieutenant Shane "Scarecrow" Schofield, who with his highly trained team investigates an apparent spaceship discovered in a cavern below the Antarctic ice. The discovery touches off a wave of murders, plottings, and cross-plottings as different governments seek to get their hands on the chilly UFO.

Ice Station grew from Reilly's fascination with Hollywood action films, the author said on his Web site. "I figured that when you make a movie, you are limited by

326

your budget, it costs you a lot of money to do action scenes. But when you write a book, you can create the wildest and biggest action scenes and it doesn't cost you a cent. The only limit is the limit of your imagination."

A *Publishers Weekly* reviewer found the book both derivative and breathtakingly innovative. "The outrageously heroic Schofield comes off as less a real Marine than a fantasy action figure on a par with [James] Bond ... but Reilly doesn't really need to be original, not at the pace at which he whips his story line past readers."

Rivaling *Ice Station* in popularity, Reilly's next adventure, *Temple*, is set in both present and past, as the hero searches for clues in an old Incan manuscript. Strong sales prompted the publisher to ask for revisions to *Contest,* so it could be issued traditionally, reviewed, and so on. Meanwhile, the author continued the Schofield series with *Area 7*, in which the hero and his team are assigned to protect the president of the United States during a visit to a top-secret below-level air base in the Nevada desert. "The action is nonstop and includes shootouts, crazed convicts, wild animals, and, in an eerily timely subplot, a new strain of racially selective biological warfare that has been developed at Area 7," said *Library Journal*'s reviewer, Robert Conroy.

Reilly tunes in to favorite songs by performers such as Green Day, Pink, or Christine Aguilera for inspiration. But he doesn't lack ideas and ambition. "I have an inbuilt determination that just keeps on driving forward," he said in a Reach Out! interview. "I think you must draw on something inside yourself to get strength or inspiration."

The author says he has a good grip on his plot's destination before he begins writing. "I don't even begin writing a novel until I have the last scene of the book firmly pictured in my mind," he said in a Panorama Magazine interview. "My books have a lot of twists and narrow escapes in them and to effect these things, you have to know what you're going to do well in advance." Recent works have taken the author into both the past and the future. *7 Deadly Wonders* hinges on Schofield finding the Golden Capstone that was once on the Great Pyramid of Giza as a preventive to a dreaded solar blast that would trigger a flood every 4,500 years.

Bookreporter reviewer Joe Hartlaub noticed that Reilly's writing in the next Schofield adventure, *Scarecrow*, includes the "ticking clock" plot device: "The writer has to set up a scenario whereby resolution of a problem has to be obtained within a certain amount of time, or adverse consequences will occur. Reilly scatters a couple of hundred clocks through *Scarecrow* and sets them to go off within a few seconds of each other."

Hover Car Racer, set a few years in the future, is about a fourteen-year-old ace at the wheel who competes in competitions against the best of professionals, the meanest of villains, and the least-expected of twists and turns. Long a fan of car racing, and one of the few motorists in Australia who owns a classic gull-wing DeLorean sports car from the early 1980s, Reilly knew he wanted a younger audience for this story. And he wanted to reach new readers. "I'm taking a big risk here," he said in a Teenreads.com interview. "I spent eight months writing *Hover Car Racer*, and yes, I could have sold it to a publisher for lots of money and royalties, but honestly, there's more to life than money. I think *Hover Car Racer* can be a phenomenon." The book came out on the Internet in installments in 2004 and was broken into thirds for print publication.

Reilly has also tried his hand at screenplays. "Literary Superstars," a pilot for a television series, looked promising in 2007, according to Angela Cuming's story in the *Sydney Morning Herald*. If it doesn't make it, the author will surely find an innovative way to take it to his loyal and growing audience.

Works by the Author

Contest (1996; revised, 2000)
Temple (1999)

Jack West Jr. Series

Seven Ancient Wonders (2005)
The Six Sacred Stones (2007)
The Five Greatest Warriors (2009)

Shane Schofield Series

Ice Station (1998)
Area 7 (2002)
Scarecrow (2003)
Hell Island (2006)

Juvenile Fiction

Hover Car Racer Series
Hover Car Racer (2004)
Crash Course (2005), United States publication of first third of *Hover Car Racer*
Full Throttle (2006), United States publication of second third of *Hover Car Racer*
Photo Finish (2007), United States publication of last third of *Hover Car Racer*

For Further Information

Ayers, Jeff, "Q&A: Mathew Reilly." *Library Journal*, January 1, 2006.

Carlson, Joseph L., *Hover Car Racer* review. *Library Journal*, September 1, 2005.

Conroy, Robert, *Area 7* review. *Library Journal*, December 2001.

Cuming, Angela, "Author Goes to the Sauce of Publishing." *Sydney Morning Herald*, October 21, 2007.

Hartlaub, Joe, *Scarecrow* review, Bookreporter. www.bookreporter.com/reviews/0312937660.asp - 22k (viewed October 26, 2007).

Ice Station review. *Publishers Weekly*, July 26, 1999.

Matthew Reilly interview. *Panorama Magazine*, November/December 1998. http://www.matthewreilly.com/media_ansett.htm (viewed October 26, 2007).

Matthew Reilly interview, Reach Out. http://www.reachout.com.au/default.asp?ti=1492 (viewed October 26, 2007).

Matthew Reilly interview, Teenreads.com. http://www.teenreads.com/authors/ au-reilly-matthew.asp (viewed October 1, 2007).

Matthew Reilly Web site. http://www.matthewreilly.com (viewed November 19, 2008).

Pearl, Nancy, "Macho Heroes! Evil Villains! Adventure!!" *Library Journal*, February 15, 2004.

John Ringo

Science Fiction; Thrillers: Techno, Military, Mercenary

Benchmark Series: <u>Posleen War</u>

Miami-Dade, Florida

1963–

Photo credit: Courtesy of the author

About the Author and the Author's Writing

Author John Ringo—along with fellow writers David Weber, Eric Flint, and David Drake and savvy publisher Jim Baen of Baen Books—skirts convention with hard-edged military science fiction. His first novel, *A Hymn before Battle* (2000), finds Earth inhabitants fighting for survival against the Posleen. Only an ex-Special Ops soldier named Michael O'Shea can save the world.

Ringo was born in Miami-Dade, Florida, in 1963, the son of an ex-Navy civil engineer who worked with an international company. According to his Web site, Ringo had attended fourteen schools and had been to twenty-three countries (including Iran, Egypt, Switzerland, and Greece) by the time he completed his high school education. After attending the University of Georgia and the University of South Florida in pursuit of a degree in marine biology, he served with a parachute infantry regiment with the Army's 82nd Airborne Division and earned a Combat Infantry Badge and a Parachutists Badge through Grenada and Desert Storm tours. He spent four years with the Florida Air National Guard. He sold cameras, managed a catfish pond, and administered a quality control database before he began writing science fiction. His hobbies have included scuba diving, hunting, spearfishing, sailing, and climbing and repelling. He and his wife, Karin, have two children and raise Arabian horses in Georgia.

Ringo's writing career began in an unusual way. He submitted a manuscript to publisher Baen. Ringo had used strong language in an Internet chat room exchange with Baen and figured the chances of his novel finding a home with him were next to none. Baen read the manuscript, suggested changes, and published *A Hymn before Battle* (2000). "Foul-mouthed, tough and quirky, Ringo's good guys are forced to deal with alien technologies they've never dreamed of, face foes that make previous human adversaries look like prom dates, and work around short-sighted bureaucrats pursuing personal agendas," said reviewer John C. Snider.

Critics said that the sequel, *Gust Front*, published the next year, demonstrated a deepening grasp of prose technique. The book was a page-turner.

In 2001, Ringo collaborated with Honor Harrington Series writer David Weber on *March Upcountry*, kicking off that series. Ringo also wrote series books with Tom Kratman, Travis S. Taylor, and Michael Z. Williamson over the next several years.

His heroes are invariably military trained in combat (armed and unarmed), muscular, sharp, and quiet. And this is in either gender. The author's novel *Road to Damascus*, written with Linda Evans, is about ex-Deng infantrywoman Kafari Khrustinova's struggle to defeat a political alliance that has decimated her country. *Cally's War*, which springs from Ringo's Posleen epic and was written with Julie Cochrane, features an ace assassin for the sisterhood of Bane Sidhe, who fights battles not overtly on the streets but darkly in the alleys. This is how Ringo describes one of O'Neal's conquests: "She walked over to the body and tilted her head appraisingly a moment before carefully and deliberately spitting on it. 'The name's Cally O'Neal, and that's for trying to kill me when I was eight.'"

Following a creative burst in early 2004, Ringo says on his Web site, he abandoned the future to write of the present. *Ghost* is the tale of discharged Navy SEAL Mike Harmon, who witnesses a kidnapping and follows the perps to Syria, where he witnesses a remarkable international conspiracy—and brings back to the American president a most unusual and welcome terrorist trophy. Ringo was unsure the book would fit with his usual SF fare, but Baen liked it and, although the publisher attempted to market it as a techno thriller, its telltale Baen cover art and Ringo's backlist finds it generally shelved with science fiction in bookstores.

Protagonist Harmon is a tough cookie. Bleeding from his wounds, two hastily trained young women at his side, he won't give up. "Mike could barely see the landing anymore," we read in *Ghost*, "his vision was tunneling out. But he shot at the figures, like ghosts, that moved in the red light, as the pain from each recoil racked his broken body, kept firing and firing until he couldn't see anymore."

The author is very serious about his craft and, at the same time, allows that a greater force may be at work.

"There are times, and *Ghost* was one of them, when they [stories] seem to be an external force, like a giant wall of water pressing against the dam of my psyche and saying 'Write me or else,'" Ringo said on his Web site.

Works by the Author

The Road to Damascus, with Linda Evans (2004)
Von Eeumann's War, with Travis S. Taylor (2006)
Princess of Wands (2006)
The Last Centurion (2008)

Council Wars Series

There Will Be Dragons (2003)
Emerald Sea (2004)

Against the Tide (2005)
East of the Sun, West of the Moon (2006)

Empire of Man Series with David Weber

March Upcountry (2001)
March to the Sea (2001)
March to the Stars (2003)
We Few (2005)

Looking Glass Series

Into the Looking Glass (2005)
Vorpal Blade, with Travis S. Taylor (2007)
Manxome Foe, with Travis S. Taylor (2008)
The Claws That Catch, with Travis S. Taylor (2008)

Paladin of Shadows Series

Ghost (2005)
Kildar (2006)
Choosers of the Slain (2006)
Unto the Breach (2006)
A Deeper Blue (2007)

Posleen War Series

A Hymn before Battle (2000)
Gust Front (2001)
When the Devil Dances (2002)
Hell's Faire (2003)
The Hero, with Michael Z. Williamson (2004)
Cally's War, with Julie Cochrane (2004), spinoff from series
Watch on the Rhine, with Tom Kratman (2005)
Yellow Eyes, with Tom Kratman (2007)
Sister Time, with Julie Cochrane (2007), sequel to *Cally's War*
Eye of the Storm (2009)
Honor of the Clan, with Julie Cochrane (2009), sequel to *Sister Time*

Anthologies

The Service of the Sword, edited by David Weber (2003), "Let's Go to Prague" and "A Ship Named Francis"

For Further Information

Cassada, Jackie, *Vorpal Blade* review. *Library Journal*, September 15, 2007.

Danielson, Scott D., *Cally's War* review, SFFaudio. http://www.sffaudio.com/?p=671 (viewed December 1, 2007).

John Ringo Web site. http://www.johnringo.com (viewed November 19, 2008).

Snider, John C. *A Hymn before battle* review, SciFiDimensions. http://www.scifidimensions.com/jan01/hymnbeforebattle.htm (viewed December 8, 2007).

J. D. Robb (Nora Roberts)

Crime; Romance: Paranormal, Historical; Science Fiction

Benchmark Series: <u>Eve Dallas and Roarke Mysteries</u>

Washington, D.C.

1950–

About the Author and the Author's Writing

J. D. Robb's futuristic series of police procedural novels, with a romantic twist, had already climbed onto the best-seller lists well before the publisher, Putnam/Berkley, revealed in 2001 the author's real identity to be popular romance author Nora Roberts. A prolific writer with more than 175 titles—selling some 50 million copies a year, *Forbes* reported in 2004—Roberts simply turned out so many books, her editors couldn't keep up. The solution was to create a new name. And the science fiction element of the <u>Eve Dallas and Roarke</u> series gave the books a distinction in the market.

The penname incorporates the initials of her sons' first names, Jason and Dan, and Robb is a variation on Roberts, which is itself a variation on the writer's birth name. Eleanor Marie Robertson was born in Washington, D.C., in 1950. She married high school sweetheart Ronald Aufdem-Brinke in 1968 and had two children before they divorced in 1983. She worked as a legal secretary. She did not attend college. She married her second husband, Bruce Wilder, in 1985.

For the author, the new pseudonym was an opportunity to stretch. "I wanted to explore these people and peel the layers off book by book," Roberts said on the J. D. Robb Web site. "Each book resolved the particular crime or mystery that drives it, but the character development, the growth and the changes, the tone of the relationships go more slowly. I'm enjoying that tremendously."

In the first book, in 1996, Eve Dallas investigates the murder of a high-priced call girl and finds herself romantically drawn to one of the suspects, an Irish billionaire named Roarke. By the fourth book, they've married.

Roberts has been a full-time writer since being confined to the house during a blizzard in 1979, which allowed her the time to write a manuscript. She sold her first, *Irish Thoroughbred*, in 1981, and found a steady market writing romance books for paperback publishers. *Honest Illusions* (1992) was her first hardcover, although she continued to write paperback originals.

Roberts writes at a frantic pace. While she does some research for settings, usually on the Internet (she intensely dislikes flying), her novels tend to be character-, rather than story-, driven. Her stories are filled with emotions, successes, and losses. Several of her series revolve around families, albeit sometimes unusual families, such as the Donovan Legacy Trilogy about three cousins who have strange powers, or the Royal Family of Cordina Series, which is set in an imaginary Mediterranean country.

Roberts seldom writes issue-oriented books. "I write strictly for entertainment, romances with a lot of suspense. If issues are a part of the story, that's a plus. But I don't seek to raise issues or write about them," she said in an interview with Susan Farrington.

The author has been innovative, introducing multiple viewpoints—including male narrators. She has introduced premarital sex and humor, as well as suspense.

Roberts and Robb jointly "wrote" *Remember When* (2003). While the character Laine Tavish in the present grapples with the sudden reappearance and death of her fugitive father, Detective Dallas in the future sorts out issues surrounding Laine's secret fortune.

"I just have a steady pace," Roberts told *Publishers Weekly* in 1988, "it's like having green eyes." She writes six to eight hours a day. She generally writes a fast and slim first draft to be sure of the story. She then goes back over the manuscript, fleshing out the story and characters. A final pass is to buff the language.

"I really love the entire process of writing," she said on Subversion Parlor. "The crafting of the story, the building of characters, the surprises when I'm doing both and each goes its own way. I love the fiddling and polishing to make it the best story I can at that time. And I'm madly in love with the basic writer perks. No makeup, no pantyhose, no commuting in traffic."

What's the secret of her success? Her answer: "My people win. That's what people buy me for. They're not buying me to write King Lear," according to *The Writer* in 2003.

 # Works by J. D. Robb

For a list of works by Nora Roberts, visit her Web site http://www.noraroberts.com.

Eve Dallas and Roarke Mysteries

Naked in Death (1995)

Glory in Death (1995)

Immortal in Death (1996)

Rapture in Death (1996)

Ceremony in Death (1997)

Vengeance in Death (1997)

Holiday in Death (1998)

Conspiracy in Death (1999)

Loyalty in Death (1999)

Witness in Death (2000)

Judgment in Death (2000)

Betrayal in Death (2001)

Seduction in Death (2001)

Reunion in Death (2002)
Purity in Death (2002)
Portrait in Death (2003)
Imitation in Death (2003)
J. D. Robb Collection 1: Naked in Death, Glory in Death, Immortal in Death (2003), omnibus
Remember When (2003), written with Nora Roberts
Dividend in Death (2004)
Visions of Death (2004)
J. D. Robb Collection 2: Rapture in Death, Ceremony in Death, Immortal in Death (2004), omnibus
J. D. Robb Collection 3: Holiday in Death, Conspiracy in Death, Loyalty in Death (2004), omnibus
J. D. Robb Collection 4: Witness in Death, Judgment in Death, Betrayal in Death (2004), omnibus
Survivor in Death (2005)
Midnight in Death (2005), novella
Origin in Death (2005)
Memory in Death (2006)
Born in Death (2006)
Innocent in Death (2007)
Creation in Death (2007)
Strangers in Death (2008)
Salvation in Death (2008)
Promises in Death (2009)
Kindred in Death (2009)

Anthologies

Silent Night, with Dee Holmes, Susan Plunkett, and Claire Cross (1998), includes "Midnight in Death"
Out of This World, with Laurell K. Hamilton, Susan Krinard, and Maggie Shayne (2001), includes "Interlude in Death"
Bump in the Night, with Mary Blayney, Ruth Ryan Langan, and Mary Kay Comas (2006), includes "Haunted in Detroit"
Dead of Night, with Mary Blayney, Ruth Ryan Langan, and Mary Kay McComas (2007), includes "Eternity in Death"
Suite 606, with Mary Blayney, Ruth Ryan Langan and Mary Kay McComas (2008), includes "Ritual in Death"

<u>Concannon Sisters Series</u>, written as Sarah Hardesty

Born in Fire (1994)
Born in Ice (1995)
Born in Shame (1996)
Irish Born (1996), omnibus
Born in Fire/Born in Ice/Born in Shame (1998), omnibus

For Further Information

Burke, Jan, "Success in Death: An Interview with Nora Roberts aka J. D. Robb." *Mystery Scene*, Winter 2004.

Donahue, Dick. "Roberts Rules Redux." *Publishers Weekly,* September 8, 2003.

Farrington, Susan, "An Interview with Nora Roberts." *Sanford Herald,* April 24, 2003.

Foege, Alec, "Close to Home: Romance Writer Nora Roberts Found Her Own True Love with the Man Who Came to Build Her a Bookcase." *People Weekly,* April 12, 1999.

Imitation in Death review. *Publishers Weekly,* August 25, 2003.

J. D. Robb interview, Paranormal Romance Reviews. http://pnr.thebestreviews.com/author2 (viewed June 17, 2003).

J. D. Robb Web site. http://www.noraroberts.com/jdrobb.htm (viewed November 19, 2008).

Kellner, Thomas, "Who Needs a Muse?" *Forbes*, November 15, 2004.

Kloberdanz, Kristin, "Thought You Could Dismiss It? Think Again: Meet Nora Roberts, the Queen of the Genre, Who Reigns over a Changed Landscape." *Book,* March/April 2002.

Little, Denise, and Lara Hayden. *The Official Nora Roberts Companion.* New York: Berkley, 2003.

Maryles, Daisy, "Breaking Her Record." *Publishers Weekly,* July 16, 2001.

Maryles, Daisy, "Roberts Rules." *Publishers Weekly,* November 1, 1999.

McMurran, Kristin, "Page Churner." *People Weekly,* July 1, 1996.

Nora Roberts bibliography, Fantastic Fiction. http://www.fantasticfiction.co.uk/r/nora-roberts/ (viewed October 26, 2007).

"Nora Roberts: I'm Not Planning to Retire," iVillage. http://www.ivillage.com/books/intervu/romance/articles/0,11872,192493_82603,00.html (viewed June 17, 2003).

Nora Roberts interview, BookBrowse. http://www.bookbrowse.com/author_interviews/full/index.cfm?author_number=296 (viewed October 25, 2007).

Quinn, Judy, "Nora Roberts: A Celebration of Emotion." *Publishers Weekly,* February 23, 1998.

Remember When review. *Library Journal,* September 1, 2003.

"Resolved." *People Weekly,* May 4, 1998.

Rist, Curtis, "Bodice Rip-Off." *People Weekly,* August 18, 1997.

Tichemer, Louise, "Drive, Discipline, and Desire." *Writer's Digest,* February 1997.

Wachsmith, Maudeen, "No Makeup, No Commuting: Nora Roberts on Reading, Writing, and Relaxing," Subversion Parlor. http://www.booksquare.com/subversion/parlor/int002.cfm (viewed June 17, 2003).

"What Makes Readers Love Nora Roberts' Romances?" *The Writer,* September 2003.

James Rollins
(James Czajkowski)

Adventure: Military, Historical; Fantasy; Science Fiction; Thrillers: Bio, Cipher

Benchmark Title: *Subterranean*

Chicago, Illinois

1961–

Photo credit: David Sylvian

About the Author and the Author's Writing

"My goal when I set out to write is not to examine the human condition or explore the trials and tribulations of modern society," author James Rollins said in a Bookbrowse interview, "When I set out to write, I aim for pure balls-to-the-wall adventure, pure escape and entertainment. I follow the three M's of storytelling: murder, magic, and mayhem."

James Rollins isn't his only name. It's the one he uses for adventure fiction. And it's not his real name. Born James Czajkowski in Chicago in 1961, to a family of seven children, the author in his first writings used the penname James Clemens. And he still uses that name for his fantasy books.

Czajkowski grew up fascinated with adventure—true and made-up. He delighted in learning of the exploits of archaeologist Howard Carter, who discovered King Tut's tomb. He read Edgar Rice Burroughs's Tarzan novels and L. Frank Baum's Oz books. He turned page after page of Jules Verne, H. G. Wells, and H. Rider Haggard. (Today he enjoys contemporary equivalents Michael Crichton, Stephen King, and Clive Cussler.) But mostly as a teen, he collected and devoured Lester Dent's Doc Savage magazine stories (issued under the house name Kenneth Robeson), also tales of The Shadow, The Spider, and other pulp magazine heroes.

Rollins came to the writing profession in a circuitous manner. In 1985, he graduated from the University of Missouri with a doctorate in veterinary medicine and established a practice in Sacramento, California. He treated animals by day and dreamed of being a writer by night. He was a veterinarian until his fifth book gave him sufficient income to switch careers.

Rollins felt well equipped to write. His fiction reading gave him a keen sense of suspense, of how to craft a cliffhanger, and perhaps most of all, of how to accelerate cliffhangers to the brim of peril.

However, even this isn't enough for a great book, he said on his Web site: "I think for a book to resonate with a reader at a deeper level it should offer more. A book should challenge the reader, involve them and immerse them in histories and speculations that will still echo after the last page is turned."

In the summer of 1996, Czajkowski decided to act on his dream. He enrolled in the Maui Writers Conference. He wrote the first two hundred pages of a fantasy novel and submitted it to the conference's writing contest. While in Hawaii, the author immediately met one of his favorite authors, Terry Brooks, master of the Shannara fantasy books. Brooks, it turned out, not only was one of the judges for that year's fiction-writing contest, he showed the sample pages to his publisher. The publisher liked what he read, and Czajkowski soon had a three-book contract.

The first book was *Wit'ch Fire* (1998). In a Writers Write interview, the author says it is a traditional fantasy quest, with a key difference: "I never saw this 'quest' story taken from a woman's perspective. The more I thought about this, a world of different possibilities opened.... From this kernel of an idea, the character of Elena, the young wit'ch, was born."

Because of the complexities of his fantasies, the author says, he outlines his books from beginning to end. Within that frame, he leaves sufficient flexibility to make changes, to allow characters to assert themselves, to take on their own voice. Characters don't emerge overnight; Elena, he has said, took shape over five years, and even as the books were written, changed in response to suggestions from women readers.

Creating a fantasy universe also brings its structures; a magical world can't exist on its own, the author asserts; it needs boundaries, a certain order, and a past. As he worked out what became the five-book Banned and Banished Series, the author crafted freestanding books such as *Subterranean* (1999), which is about an archaeological expedition in search of a lost underground world. Here was opportunity to free-associate on all he knew about the Egyptologist Howard. Despite already having a series in progress, Czajkowski sent this manuscript to forty-nine publishers before he signed on with an agent, who put the book to bid to two top publishers and sold the film rights to NBC. That book and others came out under the James Rollins name.

Rollins developed a new series featuring the Sigma Force, with *Sandstorm* in 2004. In a recent entry, *The Judas Strain*, the high-tech team of heroes vies with the terrorist Guild to isolate a strain of lethal virus that threatens world calamity.

"One of the joys of writing," Rollins said in a Slushpile interview, "is to create your own character: piecemeal their bones, flesh out their musculature, get their heart beating and loins stirring. Each book is an adventure of discovery."

In the same conversation, the author commented that he didn't want to write books based on characters created by others. An exception, he allowed, might be Doc Savage. Or, as it turns out, Indiana Jones. Rollins wrote the book version of *Indiana Jones and the Kingdom of the Crystal Skull* in 2008. How could he resist?

Works by the Author

Written as James Clemens

Banned and Banished Series
Wit'ch Fire (1998)
Wit'ch Storm (1999)
Wit'ch War (2000)
Wit'ch Gate (2001)
Wit'ch Star (2002)
Godslayer Series
Shadowfall (2005)
Hinterland (2006)

Written as James Rollins

Subterranean (1999)
Excavation (2000)
Amazonia (2002)
Ice Hunt (2003)
The Last Oracle (2008)
Indiana Jones Series
Indiana Jones and the Kingdom of the Crystal Skull (2008)
Sigma Force Series
Sandstorm (2004)
Map of Bones (2005)
Black Order (2006)
The Judas Strain (2007)
The Last Oracle (2009)

For Juvenile Readers

Lost Tribes Series
The Stone Dragon (2008)

Anthology

Thriller, edited by James Patterson (2006), includes "Kowalski's in Love"

For Further Information

James Rollins interview, BookBrowse. www.bookbrowse.com/author_interviews/full/index.cfm?author_number=1155 (viewed November 16, 2007).

James Rollins interview, HarperCollins. http://www.harpercollins.com/author/authorExtra.aspx?authorID=19188&displayType=interview (viewed November 16, 2007).

James Rollins interview, Slushpile. http://www.slushpile.net/index.php/2005/07/01/interview-james-rollins-autho/ (viewed November 16, 2007).

James Rollins Web site. http://www.jamesrollins.com/ (viewed November 19, 2008)

White, Claire E., "A Conversation with James Clemens," Writers Write. http://www.writerswrite.com/journal/oct00/clemens.htm (viewed November 4, 2007).

M. J. Rose (Melissa Shapiro)

Adventure; Crime-Mystery:
Paranormal; Horror:
Psychological; Thriller:
Legal

Benchmark Title: *The Halo Effect*

New York, New York

Photo credit: Kelly Campbell

Birth date not disclosed

About the Author and the Author's Writing

Despite her agent's confidence in the story, she couldn't place Melisse Shapiro's first manuscript. "I write books that don't fit a category. A little too erotic, a little too commercial to be literary, a little too literary to be commercial…. I started to think about those authors I'd read about—Virginia Woolf and Mark Twain included and more—who'd also struggled to get published and struck out on their own," the author commented in a Go Publisher Yourself Web site interview.

A seasoned marketer, the author hired an editor and book designer and created an e-book as well as printed copies of *Lip Service*, a steamy tale of a woman who resists her overbearing husband and is at the same time caught up in a telephone sex scam. She issued it under the name M. J. Rose, a blend of her own and her mother's first initials. She spent hours persuading appropriate webmasters to look at the book and promote it to their women audiences. After six months, the books sold 2,500 print and electronic copies. An editor picked it up for Doubleday Book Club and Literary Guild; Doubleday Direct sold 18,000 e-book copies within a year. Rose's agent placed the book with Pocket Books for mainstream publication.

And a career was launched.

Rose does not recommend self-publishing to everyone. It has worked for her, and for other talented authors such as Zane, but the author says her main intent was to prove to publishers the viability of cross-genre fiction. Although she was a pioneer in self-marketing and Internet publication, she prefers traditional print. "E-publishing is still talking to itself," she told *Publishers Weekly*.

One of the founding members of International Thriller Writers, the author was born in New York City and earned a BFA degree from Syracuse University. She worked in the advertising field in the 1980s and became creative director of Rosenfield Sirowitz and Lawson. A commercial she produced for the New York Police Department is in the collection of the Museum of Modern Art. She has been a journalist for wired.com and maintains three blogs. She lives in Connecticut with her partner, Doug Scofield, a composer and musician, and their dog Winka.

Rose knew from childhood she wanted to be a writer. "I was eight years old, sitting at my grandfather's typewriter pecking out a short story about a man who wore five hats and very large green shoes," she said on the M. J. Rose Web site. "My mother asked me what I was doing and I told her I was practicing writing for when I grew up."

Two writers particularly influenced the author. Frances Hodgson Burnett's *Secret Garden* made her realize the value of imagination. She also cites Ayn Rand as an influence, a writer whom "I devoured [as a teenager] because her iconoclastic view of the world and the loneliness of her heroes appealed to me," she said in a BookBrowse interview.

Rose's <u>Butterfield Institute</u> series, featuring sex therapist Dr. Morgan Snow, began with *The Halo Effect* in 2004. Snow learns deep secrets from her patients—and struggles to maintain confidentiality while at the same time dealing with horrific illegalities. In *The Delilah Complex* (2006), Snow is drawn into the world of sex clubs and men who want to be dominated by women.

The author's recent *The Reincarnationist* bends genres. The main character, a photojournalist, survived a bombing while in Italy. But he is haunted by memories that are not his own. They are from another place and time and involve a vestal virgin, Sabina. Through a foundation in New York that documents past life experiences, "he finds himself trying to unravel the mystery of his own past lives as well as several present-day murders with a connection to his past and a handful of ancient stones with powers that are practically magical," the author told January magazine interviewer Linda L. Richards.

The author notes that she likes to map her books out in advance. It took her two years to write *The Reincarnationist*, both because of the research involved and her caution in not wanting to come off as bizarre. Josh Ryder, the hero, proved stubborn. "When I first thought about writing this book the main character was an entirely different person," she said in a Murderati interview. "As I started doing the research and thinking about the book the original character started to morph. I don't remember when exactly he stopped being the other person and became Josh."

Rose followed with *The Memorist* (2008), in which the heroine, Meer Logan, is haunted by locked away memories of the past. She confronts unexpected old secrets with the help of a journalist, David Yalom, who is trying to recover from his own family losses at the hands of terrorists.

Rose hopes to find new audiences with these books, as well as to give her readers something tangible even after reading her work. As she told *Publishers Weekly* in 2007, "I hope that after a reader turns the last page, he or she is left with something to think about, to wonder about, something that I would love to think might even offer some solace, the way reincarnation has offered me solace and hope."

Works by the Author

Lip Service (1998)
In Fidelity (2001)
Flesh Tones (2002)
Sheet Music (2003)

Lying in Bed (2006)
The Reincarnationist (2007)
The Memorist (2008)

Dr. Morgan Snow Series

The Halo Effect (2004)
The Delilah Complex (2006)
Venus Fix (2006)

Contributor

Thriller, edited by Richard Patterson (2006), includes "The Portal," a Dr. Morgan Snow story written with John Lescroart

Nonfiction

How to Publish and Promote Online, with Angela Adair-Hoy (2001)
Buzz Your Book, with Doug Clegg (digital, 2001)

For Further Information

Abbott, Charlotte, "M. J. Rose: E-book Queen Inks Print, Digital Deals." *Publishers Weekly*, April 3, 2000.

Ellison, J. T., "A Glimpse into the Life (Lives?) of M.J. Rose," Murderati. http://murderati.typepad.com/murderati/2007/09/a-glimpse-into-.html (viewed November 4, 2007).

Kleckner, Karen, "The Erogenous Book Zone." *Library Journal*, June 15, 2006.

M. J. Rose biography, BookBrowse. http://www.bookbrowse.com/biographies/index.cfm?author_number=301 (viewed November 4, 2007).

M. J. Rose interview, Go Publish Yourself. http://www.go-publish-yourself.com/community/interview-rosem.php (viewed November 4, 2007).

M. J. Rose Web site. http://www.mjrose.com/ (viewed November 19, 2008).

M. J. Rose Web site. http://www.readlipservice.com/ (viewed November 4, 2007).

Richards, Linda L., M. J. Rose interview, January magazine. http://januarymagazine.com/profiles/rose.html (viewed November 4, 2007).

Sia, Nicole K., "PW Talks with M. J. Rose; Accessing Past Lives." *Publishers Weekly*, July 23, 2007.

S. J. Rozan

Crime

Benchmark Series: <u>Lydia Chin and Bill Smith</u>

Bronx, New York

Birth date not disclosed

Photo credit: Marion Ettlinger

About the Author and the Author's Writing

Lydia Chin, a bright, savvy young private investigator, remains respectful of—if not always in agreement with—the traditions of New York City's Chinatown, where she grew up. But when the Chinese Restaurant Workers' Union tries to organize waitresses, busboys, and other restaurant workers, against the wishes of powerful owners, she finds herself caught in the vice grip of cultural change. After four workers, including one organizer, disappear, Chin and her frequent partner Bill Smith are hired to find out what happened. In S. J. Rozen's novel *A Bitter Feast*, the duo have to navigate a power maze of city and federal investigators before they solve the puzzle. And then there's Chin's mother.

"My mother shook her head. 'This union,' she said. 'I knew this union was a bad idea. Now you can see I was right.'"

Rozen's main course of eight Chin-Smith novels, plus a generous side offering of short stories, serve generous helpings of humanity and cultural exploration along with the requisite searches, chases, crisp conversations, and gunplay.

"Rozan delivers strong characters, deft plotting, and a hard-driving narrative," said *Booklist* reviewer Stuart Miller of a later entry, *Winter and Night*.

Characters Chin and Smith work well together. They take turns narrating the events in their novels. In interesting counter to Chin's Chinese-American background, Smith is an older, rumpled, cynic who lives over a bar. The two love each other but have never been lovers, not that they haven't considered it.

Shira J. Rozan was born in the Bronx, New York. She received a bachelor of arts degree from Oberlin College and a master's degree in architecture from State University of New York at Buffalo. Before completing her studies, she worked as a custodian, self-defense instructor, jewelry clerk, and photographer. After graduation, she joined

345

the architect firm Stein, White, Nelligan Architects in New York City. In 2004 she left to write full time. She is a devoted New York Knicks fan.

As an architect, Rozan specialized in police stations, fire stations, hospital facilities, and zoo buildings—and thus knows inside-out the city that her characters inhabit. Her first fiction works were short stories for *P.I. Magazine, Alfred Hitchcock's Mystery Magazine,* and *Ellery Queen's Mystery Magazine.* The author says short stories are harder to write than novels. "They still demand attention to setting, character development, and the sound of the language; but the storyline itself has to be simple. That makes it harder than a novel to hide what you're really getting at from the reader, and therefore they're a great exercise for the novelist," she said in a conversation with Steven Torres.

Over her decade-plus writing career, the author has garnered Anthony, Edgar, Macavity, Nero, and Shamus awards. She explained to John McAuley, interviewer for Casa Mysterioso, that Bill Smith is the traditional rumpled, morally ambiguous private dick. "Lydia [Chin] was created at first as a sidekick for Bill, and to be as different from him as possible, so there would be a voice able to counter each of his assumptions about how the world works. But she wouldn't sit still for that sidekick business."

In 2001, the terrorist attack on the World Trade Center shocked Rozan's writing sensibility. "Moving right into the next Lydia Chin book, set in downtown New York, was impossible for me," she said on her Web site. "I needed Smith and Chin to get some time and distance from 9/11; I needed to see what New York could become before I wrote about their New York again."

So she wrote for the *New York Times* a nonfiction account of vicious crimes that caught the public's attention. She also wrote a stand-alone novel, *Absent Friends,* in 2004, about a heroic firefighter who was killed in the collapse of the Twin Towers— only to have revelations about his real life emerge. "It's clear that her desire to write about social issues is one of Rozan's driving motivations," said Sybil Steinberg in *Publishers Weekly.* "The central theme of *Absent Friends* is whether getting at the truth is always a good thing, and whether one person's conceptions of morality and justice may carry their own unusual validity."

The book was not an easy one to write, she said in a Mystery News interview. "You have to pin your emotions on a story framework and the problem was to find a story that could deal with this unprecedented enormously emotional situation without being overwhelmed by it or making it trivial."

In This Rain (2007) tells the story of Joe Cole, a former city building inspector who was sent to prison for crimes he didn't commit. Now on parole, he can't help jumping in when he recognizes there's a pattern to a series of accidents at construction sites.

In this novel particularly Rozan draws on her background as an architect. As she said in an essay for MysteryNet.com. "I pull out the pieces of experience that have meaning for me, organize them in a way that says something I think is worth saying, and hand them back to the reader for attention…. Life is what it is; fiction tries to tell you what it's about."

Works by the Author

Absent Friends (2004)
In This Rain (2007)

Lydia Chin and Bill Smith Series

China Trade (1994)
Concourse (1995)
Mandarin Plaid (1996)
No Colder Place (1997)
A Bitter Feast (1998)
A Tale about a Tiger (1998), audiobook
Stone Quarry (1999)
Reflecting the Sky (2001)
Winter and Night (2002)
The Shanghai Moon (2009)

Contributor

The Chopin Manuscript, with Lee Child, David Corbett, Jeffery Deaver, Joseph Finder, Jim Fusillli, John Gilstrap, James Grady, David Hewson, John Ramsey Miller, P. J. Parrish, Ralph Pezullo, Lisa Scottoline, Peter Spiegelman, and Erica Spindler (2007)

Anthologies

The Fourth Womensleuth Anthology, edited by Irene Zahava (1991), includes "Prosperity Restaurant"
Women of Mystery II, edited by Cynthia Manson (1994), includes "Body English"
Deadly Allies II, edited by Robert J. Randisi and Susan Dunlap (1994), includes "Film at Eleven"
Lethal Ladies, edited by Barbara Collins and Robert J. Randisi (1996), includes "Once Burned"
The Best American Mystery Stories 1997, includes "Hoops"
Year's 25 Finest Crime and Mystery Stories: Sixth Annual Edition, edited by Joan Hess, Ed Gorman, and Martin H. Greenberg (1997), includes "Hoops"
Vengeance Is Hers, edited by Mickey Spillane and Max Allan Collins (1997), includes "Subway"
Lethal Ladies II, edited by Christine Matthews and Robert J. Randisi (1998), includes "Prosperity Restaurant"
Canine Crimes, edited by Jeffrey Marks (1998), includes "Cooking the Hounds"
Crime after Crime, edited by Joan Hess, Ed Gorman, and Martin H. Greenberg (1999), includes "Hoops"

The Shamus Game, edited by Robert J. Randisi (2000), includes "Marking the Boat"

Gift of the Magi (2000), *Mysterious Bookshop* chapbook

Créme de la Crime, edited by Janet Hutchings (2000), includes "Hoops"

Mystery Street, edited by Robert J. Randisi (2001) includes "Crossing Delancey Street"

World's Finest Crime and Mystery Stories II (2001), includes "Childhood"

Wild Crimes, edited by Dana Stabenow (2004), includes "Birds of Paradise"

Dangerous Women, edited by Otto Penzler (2005), includes "The Last Kiss"

Manhattan Noir (2006), includes "Building"

The Blue Religion: New Stories about Cops, Criminals, and the Chase (2008), includes "Passline"

Editor

Bronx Noir (2007)

For Further Information

Aldrich, Chris, "S. J. Rozan: Telling Everyone's Story," Mystery News. http://www.blackravenpress.com/Author%20pages/rozan.htm (viewed October 8, 2007).

Fitzgerald, Marianne, *In This Rain* review. *Library Journal*, November 15, 2006.

McCauley, John, "Interview with S. J. Rozan," Casa Mysterioso. http://www.casamysterioso.com/interviews.htm (viewed October 8, 2007).

Miller, Stuart, *Winter and Night* review. *Booklist*, January 1, 2002.

Rozan, S. J., "Mystery Writer Job Requirements," MysteryNet. http://www.mysterynet.com/books/testimony.mystery-writer-job.shtml (viewed January 24, 2008).

Rozan, S. J., "New York Numb." *New York Times*, March 12, 2006.

S. J. Rozan interview, Bookreporter. http://www.bookreporter.com/authors/au-rozan-sj.asp (viewed October 8, 2007).

S. J. Rozan Web site. http://www.sjrozan.com/ (viewed November 19, 2008).

Steinberg, Sybil, "Scoping 9/11 Morality: S. J. Rozan." *Publishers Weekly*, November 1, 2004.

John Sandford (John Camp)

Crime-Suspense: Serial Killers; Thrillers: Political

Benchmark Series: <u>Prey</u>

Cedar Rapids, Iowa

1944–

About the Author and the Author's Writing

John Camp is on his second successful career. Having garnered a Pulitzer Prize for a series of newspaper articles about the farming crisis in the Midwest, he now writes best-selling fiction. As John Sandford, his <u>Prey</u> police procedurals are wildly popular.

Born in Cedar Rapids, Iowa, in 1944, John Roswell Camp showed a knack for writing while still in grade school. A high school English teacher commended him for his essays. In 1965, he married Susan Lee Jones; they have two children. He wrote a few pieces for the newspaper at the University of Iowa, where he earned a degree in American Studies in 1966. But it wasn't until he was in the Army in 1966, at a base newspaper in Korea during the Vietnam War, that he considered writing as a career.

Stateside in 1968, Camp was a reporter for the *Cape Girardeau S.E. Missourian* for two years. In 1971, he obtained a master's degree in journalism from the University of Iowa, and he worked for the *Miami Herald* from 1971 to 1978, when he became a feature reporter for the *St. Paul Pioneer Press*. His articles on Native Americans in Minnesota and North Dakota in 1980 earned a nomination for a Pulitzer, but it wasn't until 1986 that he won the prize. He left the *Pioneer Press* in 1989. In 1996, he wrote a follow-up to the farm story, "Life on the Land." And he has written occasional book reviews for other newspapers. Otherwise, journalism is in his past.

The author wrote two novels that found no market before he wrote two that did. In fact, the books were scheduled by publishers Henry Holt (*The Fool's Run*, the first of the <u>Kidd</u> series) and Putnam (*Rules of Prey* to start the <u>Prey</u> series) three months apart. Putnam asked Camp to come up with a penname. He chose his paternal grandmother's maiden name, Sandford. When Sandford outsold Camp, the Kidd and later books were reissued under the Sandford name.

Lucas Davenport is a Minneapolis police detective who, in the first book, confronts the vicious murders of several women. The serial killer leaves behind notes, and soon cop and criminal are caught in a tense game of cat-and-mouse.

As first conceived, Davenport was something of a womanizer. "Even when he was in a relationship, he'd [have an affair with other] women," the author states on the John Sandford Web site. "But then he changed, mellowed out. He began to seem like

349

he was searching for something. I want him to have a happy ending. I don't want him to wind up a bitter, lonely guy."

Sandford's reportorial work sometimes includes stories about serial killers, and thus they frequently appear in the books. His articles about Native Americans provided grounding for *Shadow Prey,* in which Davenport as investigator for the Minneapolis PD's Office of Special Intelligence sets out to solve a series of Indian-hater killings. These days Sandford is keenly interested in archaeology, and particularly a dig in Israel near the Sea of Galilee, although it has yet to work into the background of one of the novels.

Kidd, a corporate con artist, has been around for four books, most recently *The Hanged Man's Song* (2003) in which the professional thief tracks down a missing cyber hacker named Bobby. Protagonist Anna Batroy and the freelance videographers of *Night Crew* (1997) drew many requests from readers—which Sandford so far has resisted—for a sequel.

The author found it different to write a novel from a woman's perspective. "This is a violent book. And Anna has a hand in the violence in *Night Crew*. So there's a psychology that I had to work out of how a woman would relate to taking part in these very violent acts," he told Bookreporter interviewer Sean Doorly.

Another character, Investigator Virgil Flowers, who was introduced in *Invisible Prey*, has his own book in *Dark of the Moon* (2007), in which he helps solve the murder of an elderly couple. This is an instance, among several, in which secondary characters in the Davenport books fleshed out enormously in the writing. Another character whom Sandford hasn't been able to shake at first seemed so inconsequential, the author has said, he was given a name right off the computer keyboard: Del Capslock. Capslock returned several times as Davenport's partner in the books.

An arduous researcher, Sandford is proud of his accomplishments and the authentic details in his work. With good humor, he told interviewer David Finkle for *Publishers Weekly,* "You could go to the bathroom … in the Pillsbury Building by following the instructions in my book."

 # Works by the Author

Night Crew (1997)
Dead Watch (2006)
Murder in the Rough (2006), short stories

Kidd Series

The Fool's Run (1989 as by John Camp, reissued 1996 as by John Sanford)
The Empress File (1991 as by John Camp, reissued 1995 as by John Sanford)
The Devil's Code (2000)
The Hanged Man's Song (2003)

Prey Series

Rules of Prey (1989)
Shadow Prey (1990)
Eyes of Prey (1991)

Silent Prey (1992)
Winter Prey (1993)
Night Prey (1994)
Mind Prey (1995)
Sudden Prey (1996)
Secret Prey (1998)
Certain Prey (1999)
Easy Prey (2000)
Chosen Prey (2001)
Mortal Prey (2002)
Naked Prey (2003)
Hidden Prey (2004)
Broken Prey (2005)
Invisible Prey (2007)
Phantom Prey (2008)
Wicked Prey (2009)

Virgil Flowers Series

Dark of the Moon (2007)
Heat Lightning (2008)

Nonfiction

The Eye of the Heart (1988)
Plastic Surgery (1989)

Adaptations in Other Media

Mind Prey (1998), television film

For Further Information

Doorly, Sean, John Sandford profile and interview, April 1997, Bookreporter. http://www.bookreporter.com/authors/au-sandford-john.asp (viewed October 25, 2007).

Finkle, David, "John Camp/John Sandford: The Award-Winning Journalist Mines his Experiences for Background to His Pseudonymous Novels." *Publishers Weekly*, June 29, 1990.

John Sandford interview, Tangled Web. http://www.twbooks.co.uk/authors/jsanfordinterview.html (viewed October 25, 2007).

John Sandford Web site. http://www.johnsandford.org/faq.html (viewed November 19, 2008).

Maryles, Daisy, "Let Us Prey." *Publishers Weekly*, May 24, 2004.

Schleier, Curt, "Double Identity: 'Prey' Author on Why He Had to Reinvent Himself." *New York Post*, June 2, 2002.

Lisa Scottoline

Crime; Thrillers: Legal

Benchmark Title: *Everywhere That Mary Went*

Philadelphia, Pennsylvania

1956–

About the Author and the Author's Writing

Lisa Scottoline's first published writing was a little on the dry side. She was an associate editor of the *University of Pennsylvania Law Review*. Her next attempt at writing, while she was newly separated from her husband and raising a daughter, was a women's novel. Although it generated some interest among agents, she withdrew it when she realized she'd far rather write a crime story set in the world of a Philadelphia law firm. John Grisham and Scott Turow had just made it big with their legal thrillers. So she wrote *Everywhere That Mary Went*, which HarperCollins snapped up and published in 1993.

Scottoline got in on the ground floor when the subgenre of legal thrillers mushroomed. With her crisp style, female protagonists (several with an Italian-American bent), and Philadelphia setting, she was guaranteed high visibility. In 1994, she garnered a Mystery Writers of America Edgar Award with her second novel, *Final Appeal*.

Although often categorized as a writer of legal thrillers, Scottoline doesn't confine her characters to the courtroom. "Of course, I'm writing about a law firm, so there are legal issues at the heart of every book," she told interviewer Jon L. Breen, "but I don't force a courtroom scene just for the sake of having it. It needs to be appropriate to the book, and needs to maintain the pace of the book."

Born in South Philadelphia in 1956, the author graduated with honors from the University of Pennsylvania in 1976, having earned a bachelor of arts degree in English with a concentration in the contemporary American novel. One of her professors was Philip Roth. In 1981, she graduated from the University of Pennsylvania Law School cum laude.

After graduation, Scottoline clerked for Judge Edmund B. Spaeth Jr. of the Pennsylvania Superior Court. She then joined the Philadelphia firm Dechert, Price, and Rhoads as an associate with a specialty in litigation. When her daughter was born in 1986, she left that position. Her marriage broke up, and she soon began to write part time.

Once her writing career was underway, she became an administrative law clerk for Chief Judge Dolores K. Sloviter of the U.S. Court of Appeals, Third Circuit. She writes at home at a horse farm she shares with her several dogs. She has taught creative writing, including a course, "Justice and Fiction," at the University of Pennsylvania Law School. Since 2007, she has also written a column for the *Philadelphia Inquirer*.

The author, who actively promotes her books through gift bookbags and unabridged audio versions of her stories, received an unusual boost when Diet Coke included excerpts from her book *Mistaken Identity* in a promotion in 1999. That book became her first on the *New York Times* best-seller list.

Acknowledging she has been a fan of Erle Stanley Gardner and other writers of courtroom crime, the author says she found Grisham particularly influential. "Grisham opened my eyes to the possibility that lawyers could have rich interior lives…, and from him I learned that these lives could make for first-rate suspense fiction," she said in a Meet the Writers Web page conversation.

Scottoline has found rich material for her books in her own background. She grew up with a brother but didn't know, until years later, that she also had a half-sister. From the experience, she wrote *Mistaken Identity*, in which her law firm heroine, Bennedetta Rosato, is revealed to have a twin sister. The sister, an evil twin, as it turns out, returned in *Dead Ringer*.

"Bennie" Rosato, the good twin, has figured in several Scottoline books beginning with *Legal Tender* in 1996. (That book also marked the author's transition from paperback originals to hardcover.) The tall blond and keen rower Rosato initially belonged to a small Philly firm. By *Rough Justice*, Rosato brought together Mary DiNunzio, Judy Carrier, and other characters from previous books to form their own law office, Rosato and Associates. All women lawyers. All rich characters from Scottoline's word processor.

The author explains her inspiration to run with women lead characters in a conversation with *Time* magazine's Andrea Sachs: "I don't think women characters were well realized. They were the subordinate characters. They were the wife, the spouse, the girlfriend. I thought, I'm a woman trial lawyer. I'm not that rare a bird."

To make things even more interesting, Scottoline brings in elements of the predominantly Italian and Jewish neighborhood in which she grew up. "I remember thinking, 'Why are there no Italians in these books?' There are Italian lawyers. And there are also Italian criminals! But I think what was lacking in a lot of legal thrillers was characterization. Really fully fleshed out, specific characters," she told *Publishers Weekly*.

In another instance of real life instigating a plot thread, a house painter at her home gave her the idea to incorporate the world of pigeon racing in her novel *The Vendetta Defense* (2001). She had to do a good deal of research for that book, as well as for others.

"I'm an admitted bookworm, but I'm also addicted to Web surfing, so books and the Internet provide me with lots of terrific research," she said in a Crime & Suspense interview. There's no substitute, though, for the real thing. She's taken boxing lessons, visited a Montana internment camp, and driven up the steps of the Philadelphia Museum. Scottoline explains, "I do it because I think the details matter and I want to get them right for my readers."

Of course, it's handy she lives in the same city she writes about so lovingly.

Works by the Author

Final Appeal (1994)
Running from the Law (1996)
Devil's Corner (2005)
Dirty Blonde (2006)
Daddy's Girl (2007)
Look Again (2009)

Rosato & Associates Series

Everywhere That Mary Went (1993)
Legal Tender (1996)
Rough Justice (1997)
Mistaken Identity (1999)
Moment of Truth (2000)
The Vendetta Defense (2001)
Courting Trouble (2003)
Dead Ringer (2003)
Killer Smile (2004)
Lady Killer (2008)

Anthologies

Legal Briefs, edited by William Bernhardt (1998), includes "Carrying Concealed"

Naked Came the Phoenix, edited by Marcia Talley (2001)

A Century of Great Suspense Stories, edited by Jeffery Deaver (2001), includes "Carrying Concealed"

Murder Is My Racquet: Fourteen Original Tales of Love, Death, and Tennis by Today's Great Writers, edited by Otto Penzler (2005), includes "Love Match"

For Further Information

Adriani, Lynn, "Writing Novels and Having Fun, That's Amore: With Funny, Italian-American Lawyers and Fascinating Story Lines, Lisa Scottoline Turns the Legal Thriller on Its Head." *Publishers Weekly*, April 26, 2004.

Block, Allison, *Dirty Blonde* review, *Booklist*, January 1, 2006.

Bren, Jon L. "A Talk with Lisa Scottoline." *Mystery Scene*, Summer 2003.

Lady Killer review. *Publishers Weekly*, December 3, 2007.

Lisa Scottoline Web site. http://scottoline.com/ (viewed November 19, 2008).

Ohnstad, Dorinda, Lisa Scottoline interview, CrimeandSuspense. http://www.crimeandsuspense.com/archives/07-04/lisa_scottoline_interview.pdf. (viewed January 28, 2008).

Sachs, Andrea, "Pinstripes and Pearls." *Time*, May 29, 2005.

Segretto, Mike, Lisa Scottoline interview, Meet the Writers. http://www. barnesandnoible.com/writers/writerdetails.asp?z=y&cid=968085#interview (viewed January 21, 2008).

"Suspense Novelist Lisa Scottoline to Write Philadelphia Inquirer Column." *Editor & Publisher*, March 1, 2007.

M. R. Sellars

Crime: Paranormal, Serial Killers; Fantasy

Benchmark Series: <u>Rowan Gant Investigations</u>

St. Louis, Missouri

1962–

Photo credit: K. J. Epps

About the Author and the Author's Writing

When his first paranormal fantasy crime novel *Harm None* came out in 2000, M. R. "Murv" Sellars was not popular in the Wiccan community. They expected the worst—assuming he would mock witches. He circulated a lot of free copies, so people would actually read the book. By the eighth in the thriller series, he's gained a strong following not only in that community but also among mainstream readers of crime fiction and urban fantasy.

Born in 1962, Sellars learned to read by the time he was four. He studied journalism and literature in college but pursued a career as a senior-level computer technician and Internet systems administrator. A self-described hippie and tree hugger, he is an active member of The Nature Conservancy and the World Wildlife Fund. His St. Louis home, which he shares with his wife and daughter, is a haven for abandoned pets. In his spare time, he hikes, camps, cooks, and takes nature photos. And writes. By 2004, he quit most of his computer work and just wrote.

Sellars grew up in a liberal home. His mother was Wiccan, his father a secular humanist. He was exposed to many of the world's religions, from the familiar to the obscure. Wicca, a nature-based pagan religion, had the greatest appeal. He is an elder of The Grove of the Old Ways and an honorary elder of Mystic Moon, both covens. He frequently gives pagan lectures.

That grounding provided the background for *Harm None* (2000), his first novel. Homicide Detective Ben Storm of the Major Case Squad asks his friend Rowan Gant, a practicing witch, for help when a woman is brutally and ritualistically murdered in her St. Louis apartment. Other officers think it's a cult killing. Storm thinks a serial killer is at work. Gant, who can see things through the eyes of others, knows so.

Gant and Storm are bantering, on-again–off-again partners throughout the series, and Gant's wife, Felicity O'Brien, also makes regular appearances. In fact, in a recent trilogy, she becomes a suspect in a series of brutal murders (her imprisonment spurred fans to wear "Free Felicity" buttons), and Gant's powers are put to the test in tracking the real perpetrator. Readers instantly admired the author's authenticity, his clever plotting, and his ability to portray Wicca without relying on clichés. His characterizations are honest and unusual (Storm is a Native American). Sellars said there's a little of himself in each of his main characters. And Gant's cat, Emily, was based on his own cat named Data.

It's not easy to write about witches without resorting to cliché. In an interview with Michael Samhain of *New Witch*, Sellars said an editor once urged him to have his characters cast spells and ride brooms. "I was told that I hadn't researched my witchcraft enough. I almost dropped the phone. Then I said, 'What do you mean, researched my witchcraft? Have you read my bio?' The editor said, 'Yeah, but you practice the wrong kind of witchcraft.' Not enough Sabrina the Teenage Witch or Harry Potter to suit the editor, apparently."

While his own practice of Wicca is eclectic, Sellars strives for authenticity. He incorporates realistic rituals, as well as proper police procedures. "I wanted [the books] to be entertaining and educational to the non-pagan populace…. While [Gant] has no problem with magic and he does practice magic, he is more of a psychic practitioner. And certainly in the books I go over the top. I have to, it's there for entertainment," he said in an interview for *Minnesota Pagan Press*.

"The hero's powers are increasing with each crime he becomes involved in and it's fascinating to watch him learn to cope with them in his everyday life," said reviewer Harriet Klausner on AllReaders.com.

Sellars is accustomed to people's reactions to his paganism; and he responds with good humor. About witches and brooms, the author said on his Web page, "The Industrial Revolution changed all that many years ago. We now ride on vacuum cleaners, preferably cordless with extended life batteries."

 # Works by the Author

Rowan Gant Investigations Series

Harm None (2000)
Never Burn a Witch (2001)
Perfect Trust (2002)
The Law of Three (2003)
Crone's Moon (2004)
Blood Moon (2008)

Rowan Gant Investigations Series Miranda Trilogy

Love Is the Bond (2005)
All Acts of Pleasure (2006)
The End of Desire (2007)

For Further Information

Buedel, Matt, "Author Works Off Misperception," (Peoria, IL) *Sunday Journal Star*, September 9, 2001.

Klausner, Harriet, *Perfect Trust* review, AllReaders. http://www.allreaders. com/Topics/info_12879.asp?BSID=85369441 (viewed October 11, 2007).

M. R. Sellars Web page. http://www.mrsellars.com/biography.html (viewed November 19, 2008).

Rakasha, "Pagan Fiction: An Interview with M. R. Sellars, Author of The Rowan Gant Investigations." *Minnesota Pagan Press*, Lammas Issue, Volume 5, 2002.

Samhain, Michael, "Candles, Corpses & Cauldrons: The Magical Mysteries of M. R. Sellars," *New Witch*, December 2004.

Daniel Silva

Adventure: Assassins; Espionage; Thrillers: Historical, Nazis

Benchmark Series: Gabriel Allon

Michigan

1960–

About the Author and the Author's Writing

Interests in art, World War II, and Switzerland's secret past coalesced for author Daniel Silva as he wrote *The English Assassin*, featuring his morose, on-again–off-again Israeli Massad agent Gabriel Allon, this time in Zurich with the body of a Swiss banker named Rolfe on his hands. Allon must examine the past to solve the crime of the present. Rolfe collected art—art, it turns out, the Nazis had appropriated in their assault on European museums.

"The history of Nazi art looting, and of how all these paintings and other works of art made their way into Switzerland, was a natural," the author said in a BookBrowse interview. He said he was shocked, during his research, to find evidence that Swiss art dealers, and regular citizens, "capitalized on the extermination of a people in a way that is somehow unfathomable."

Born in Michigan in 1960, Silva grew up in California. He abandoned studies toward a master's degree in international relations at San Francisco State University to take what he expected would be a temporary job with United Press International, covering the 1984 Democratic National Convention. By year's end, he had joined UPI full time. He left San Francisco for the foreign desk in Washington and later became Middle East correspondent in Cairo and the Persian Gulf. In 1987, he met NBC correspondent Jamie Gangel, when both covered the Gulf War. They married that year. The Silvas live in Georgetown, Virginia, with their twin children.

Silva went to work as a producer and journalist with CNN in Washington. He produced programs such as "Inside Politics," "The World Today," and "Prime News."

Gangel was a supportive wife; when Silva told her in 1995 that he really wanted to be a novelist, she encouraged him. Over the next year, he wrote *The Unlikely Spy*. In 1997, when the book found a large audience, he left the world of reality writing for a full-time career in the world of fiction.

His first Gabriel Allon novel grew out of a dinner conversation with an art restorer friend. The idea was to mix a secret agent with an art technician—thus, Gabriel Allon. He liked the destroyer/healer dichotomy. As it turned out, one book wasn't enough.

Allon has emerged as a complex character. Recruited when he was an art student in Jerusalem, he hunted the Black September terrorists who were responsible for killing Israeli athletes at the 1972 Munich Olympics. Allon's Mossad spymaster linked the young man with a master art restorer in Venice, establishing a permanent cover with which he could circulate anywhere in Europe. But Allon's life went awry when a car bomb killed his son and left his wife mentally scarred and in an institution. He quit the Office, only to be repeatedly lured back for special assignments.

In *The Kill Artist* (2000), Allon is assigned to protect Yasir Arafat at the Oslo peace meetings. The next three books became an unofficial trilogy as Silva delved into the history of Swiss banks, enemy collaboration, and Nazi art thefts. In *The Messenger* (2006), Allon is assigned to find a Saudi intelligence agent before he can assassinate Pope Paul VII.

While he has resisted writing a book directly about September 11, the author has danced close. "*The Messenger* dealt with Saudi Arabia and its financial links to the global jihadist movement," he told *Publishers Weekly*'s Allen Appel in 2007. "*The Secret Servant* has two general themes: the threat from the radicalized young Muslims in Europe and those in Egypt."

All the while, Silva delves deep into his characters, to show the toll the fight against terrorism takes on people. "It's awful work, and it leaves scars.... I wanted to show what this kind of work does to people," he told interviewer Adam Dunn in 2002. "As a technique for developing a major character, I often prefer to work from the outside in. I like to watch them from a distance, through the eyes of a perfect stranger, before I go inside their head."

Silva does most of his research before he begins writing. He has appropriated the basement of the Georgetown home he shares with his wife and children for his writing. He told Michele Norton of National Public Radio that it's the only place he can concentrate. It is decorated in colors that make him think of the Mediterranean, where most of his thrillers are set. "I'm a prisoner of my space," he told NPR. "It's comfortable down here, it's where I spend all my days."

Ah, but Silva now has the luxury of visiting some of the locales in his books, for veracity. "I usually do much of my travel near the end of the [writing] process," he said on his Web site, "when I need a specific touch of atmosphere or factual research. I finished a rough first draft of *A Death in Vienna* over the summer.... In October I hit the road to complete the book in Europe and Israel."

With a growing international audience, Silva's novels of intrigue have brought him firmly into the heady world of John le Carré and Graham Greene.

◆ Works by the Author

The Unlikely Spy (1997)
The Mark of the Assassin (1998)
The Marching Season (1999)
Moscow Rules (2008)
The Defector (2009)

Gabriel Allon Series

The Kill Artist (2000)
The English Assassin (2002)
The Confessor (2003)
A Death in Vienna (2004)
Prince of Fire (2005)
The Messenger (2006)
The Secret Servant (2007)

For Further Information

Appel, Allen, "PW Talks with Daniel Silva." *Publishers Weekly*, June 4, 2007.

Daniel Silva interview, BookBrowse. http://www.bookbrowse.com/author_interviews/full/index.cfm?author_number=730 (viewed November 2, 2007).

Daniel Silva interview, Bookreporter. http://www.bookreporter.com/authors/au-silva-daniel.asp (viewed November 2, 2007).

Daniel Silva Web site. http://www.danielsilvabooks.com/ (viewed November 19, 2008).

Dunn, Adam, "The Allure of Intelligence." *Publishers Weekly*, April 1, 2002.

Norris, Michele, "Creative Spaces: Daniel Silva's Spy Den," National Public Radio. http://www.npr.org/templates/story/story.php?storyId=3844570 (viewed November 5, 2007).

Michael Slade

Crime; Horror: Serial Killers

Benchmark Series: <u>Special X</u>

Lethbridge, Alberta
1947–

Photo credit: Oraf

About the Author and the Author's Writing

Michael Slade is really one pseudonymous horror and crime fiction writer who has had several partners. Jay Clarke, a Vancouver attorney, first worked with John Banks and Richard Covell, then with his wife, Lee Clarke. Since 2000, Clarke's daughter, Rebecca, has shared the byline. Clarke's hand has provided the consistency; the collaborators have brought their individual ranges and thrust.

The first Michael Slade book, *Headhunter*, Jay Clarke claims, came about because of a governmental reduction in the budget for public defenders. Why not write a novel in the extra time? he thought. The publisher Penguin quickly agreed to bring out the first and all the subsequent books. A collective penname was chosen—Michael (a name from the Bible) Slade (sounded solid). Although the partnerships have varied, Clarke has final say on the manuscripts.

His first real-life murder case as a lawyer "involved a man who was found standing on his head in a urinal in the men's room of an upcountry bus station, screaming he was Jesus Christ," the author said in a ChiZine interview. The man was sent to prison for three months on a stolen-car charge. Guards ignored his bizarre behavior and threatening notes. The day he was released, he beat his wife to death with a baseball bat. Clarke and Banks defended the man, who was found insane. In another case, they represented a Vietnam War machine gunner who frequently tripped on acid. Discharged, he killed a hiker in the woods, splaying the body over a boulder. Again, a killer who was found to be insane. "That's why Slade writes what he writes," Clarke said.

In *Headhunter* (1984), a serial murderer decapitates his victims and taunts members of the Royal Canadian Mounted Police, including Robert DeClerq (Clarke wouldn't let a good name go to waste). By the time of *Cutthroat*, in which a series of murders in San Francisco and Vancouver are linked, the Special X squad has materialized, including DeClerq, Zinc Chandler, and Nick Craven. It's a squad, the author said in a conversation on the CultureDose Web site, "Canada's law enforcement unit for dealing with serial killers and other assorted psychos."

Each of Clarke's books stands alone. But together, they are carefully contrived in a bigger picture. "If you know it, the series is more enjoyable because all the smaller plots lock like a jigsaw puzzle into a larger whole," Clarke said in a conversation with Gord Rollo. "The good part about coming into any series later is then you have lots more books to read instantly if you like the stuff."

Jay Clarke has cited several authors as inspiring his writing, from Robert Louis Stevenson and Robert Bloch (human monsters); to John Dickson Carr, Agatha Christie, and Ellery Queen (whodunits); to Ed McBain (police procedurals).

In one book, a killer thinks he's Jack the Ripper. In another, the repeat murderer is fixated on the occult writer H. P. Lovecraft. Often shocking in their gruesome villains, much of Slade's work can be considered horror. In fact, *Ghoul* (1987) was named one of the top forty horror novels of all time by the Horror Writers Association.

Jay Clarke was drawn to horror at a young age, when he discovered the notorious EC Comics in the 1950s. "From then on, I was fascinated by the criminal mind," he told *BC Bookworld*. Couple that with a major shock Clarke experienced as a boy—his father, Jack Clarke, a former RAF bomber who went on to fly for Air Canada—went missing in 1956, when his DC-4 crashed in the Cascade Mountains. The wreckage wasn't found for months. That was an experience of real psychological horror for a nine year old.

Family experiences spurred several plot threads in Clarke's books. His great-grandfather was George Murdoch, the Leather Man, one of the forces behind early Calgary, Alberta. Clarke made good use of the setting in *Headhunter* when he introduced a puzzle involving the long-frozen body of a headless man, dressed in the scarlet tunic of the North-West Mounted Police. The experiences of Jay Clarke's mother, Vivian Murdoch, as a wartime nurse inspired the story of atrocities at a hospital in Hong Kong in the 1940s in another novel, *Kamikaze* (2006).

Clarke's daughter, Rebecca Clarke, majored in literature and history at the University of British Columbia. Her participation, and Jay Clarke's keen interest in research, have given recent books in the series strong World War II overtones. A cache of his father's World War II souvenirs, found after his mother's death in 2003, spurred the father and daughter Clarke to research what they suggest was a major cover-up of Werner von Braun's German war record so that he could develop a missile program for the United States. The plot figures in *Swastika* (2005).

"I truly believe that Slade's books are more than just grisly stories of 'cops chasing killers,'" Jay Clarke said on the Specialx.net Web site.

"They offer complex plots for complex characters. They offer an homage to one of the most popular police forces in the world, the R.C.M.P. through which we make the acquaintance of amazing courage and determination."

Works by the Author

Special X Series

Headhunter (1984), by Jay Clarke, John Banks, and Richard Covell
Ghoul (1987), by Jay Clarke, John Banks, and Lee Clarke
Cutthroat (1992), by Jay Clarke and John Banks
Ripper (1994), by Jay Clarke
Zombie (1996), in United States called *Evil Eye* (1996) by Jay Clarke
Shrink (1998), in United States called *Primal Scream* (1998) by Jay Clarke
Burnt Bones (1999), by Jay Clarke
Hangman (2000), by Jay Clarke and Rebecca Clarke
Death's Door (2001), by Jay Clarke and Rebecca Clarke
Bed of Nails (2003), by Jay Clarke and Rebecca Clarke
Swastika (2005), by Jay Clarke and Rebecca Clarke
Kamikaze (2006), by Jay Clarke and Rebecca Clarke
Crucified (2008), by Jay Clarke and Rebecca Clarke

Young Adult Books

The Horses of Central Park (1992)

Adaptations in Other Media

The Headhunter (in production), motion picture

For Further Information

Hangman review, CultureDose. http://culturedose.150m.com/review_10002214. html (viewed October 8, 2007).

"Interview with Michael Slade about Swastika," SpecialX. http://specialx. net/swastika_interview.html (viewed October 8, 2007).

Jay Clarke profile, BC Book World. http://www.abcbookworld.com/?state= view_author&author_id=588 (viewed October 25, 2007).

Michael Slade interview, Chizine. http://www.chizine.com/michael_slade_ interview.htm (viewed October 8, 2007).

Michael Slade Web site. http://specialx.net/ (viewed November 19, 2008).

Rollo, Gord, "Exclusive Interview with Canadian Horror Author Michael Slade," Official Website of Gord Rollo. http://home.mountaincable.net/~grollo/ new.htm (viewed October 8, 2007).

Karin Slaughter

Crime: Medical, Serial Killers

Benchmark Series: <u>Grant County</u>

Georgia

1971–

About the Author and the Author's Writing

First things first. If Karin Slaughter has a title, she as good as has a book. "The title does define the story for me and I feel very close to it from a creativity standpoint," she said in a Bookreporter interview. "I consider the title that helps pry the story from my brain."

The author was born in Georgia in 1971 and still lives there. An avid rock climber, fencer, and runner, she owned a sign shop before she became a full-time writer.

Most of her books have been in the <u>Grant County</u> crime series. A depiction of the underbelly of small-town Southern life, the books feature a trio of characters: pediatrician/coroner Sara Linton; her ex-husband, the police chief, Jeffrey Tolliver; and the only woman on the police force, Lena Adams. Why a pediatrician? "I like that medicine can offer clues to violence and what's happened to someone," she told CNN interviewer Adam Dunn, "that murder … doesn't stand alone, that there are clues that lead you toward how something was done."

In the first book in the series, *Blindsighted* (2001), Adams's twin sister is raped and murdered, and the serial killer haunts the community. The author said in a Mystery One interview that she purposely wrote counter to the expectations of veteran thriller readers. "What I wanted to do was turn those [roller-coaster plot] situations around so that the reader says, 'Oh, I know what comes next,' then is shocked when it doesn't."

Grant County is fictional, but there's enough truth in characters and situations to represent the present-day South. The violence, of course, is an expectation of the genre, and the author embraces it. "I want to show violence for what it is. For so long, women weren't expected to talk about these crimes, even though we were more likely to be the victims. I think it's time we started talking about rape and violence against women," she said on her Web page.

Although she had to apologize for muffing some details about guns, when savvy readers complained, Slaughter extensively researches her work—in legal and medical books as well as firsthand.

Characters are uppermost to Slaughter. She generally maps out relationships several books ahead. "When I first started thinking about Jeffrey and Sara and Lena, I had specific plans about where they would be at the end of the third book," she said in an interview with Laura Lippman. Lena, however, was something of a problem child. "Lena is the most difficult to write because she's always changing the story," the author admitted in a New Mystery Reader conversation. "I never want Lena to appear to be a victim or a bad person, but there are things she does that are unlikable." When Lena makes a bad choice, Slaughter has to "show that she made these choices because she is, at heart, a person with flaws."

The characters' passions always ring true. Reviewer Joanne Wilkinson in *Booklist* said of *Beyond Reach* (2007) that it "offers both wrenching emotional highs and lows and a gripping plot, but what gives it emotional heft is its unwavering focus on the grim social ills of the rural South."

The author does not sleight secondary characters either. "I have a soft spot for Bill Brock, who runs the funeral home," she told Bookreporter. "He's very goofy and he lives with his mama and has a crush on Sara, yet he seems to still have a very happy outlook on life."

Slaughter leans toward unusually dark plot angles—pornography, pedophilia, rape, and crucifixion. "Fortunately, it's not illegal yet to think of dastardly things, as long as you don't do them," she told *Time* interviewer Andrea Sachs. "But a friend of mine who's a crime writer said that we share the same interests as serial killers."

So what new evil is she plotting?

 Works by the Author

Triptych (2006)

Grant County Mystery Series

Blindsighted (2001)

Kisscut (2002)

A Faint Cold Fear (2003)

Indelible (2004)

Faithless (2005)

Beyond Reach (2007), issued in United Kingdom as *Skin Privilege*

Fractured (2008)

Genesis (2009)

Editor

Like a Charm: A Novel in Voices (2004)

For Further Information

Dunn, Adam, "A Sweet Woman Writing about Ugly Things: Karin Slaughter's Latest Is 'A Faint Cold Fear,'" CNN.com, October 30, 2003. http://www.cnn.com/2003/SHOWBIX/books/10/30/karin.slaughter/index.html (viewed March 2, 2008).

Karin Slaughter interview, Bookreporter, 2005. http://www.bookreporter.com/authors/au-slaughter-karin.asp (viewed March 2, 2008).

Karin Slaughter interview, Mystery One. http://www.mysteryone.com/KarinSlaughterInterview.htm (viewed March 17, 2008).

Karin Slaughter interview, New Mystery Reader. http://www.newmysteryreader.com/karin_slaughter.htm (viewed March 2, 2008).

Karin Slaughter Web site. http://www.karinslaughter.com (viewed November 19, 2008).

Lippman, Laura, Karin Slaughter interview. http://www.karinslaughter.com/interviewLL.html (viewed March 2, 2008).

Sachs, Andrea, "Between the Lines with Karin Slaughter." *Time*, October 4, 2005.

"Slaughter Slays with New Series." *Book*, September-October 2003.

Wilkinson, Joanne, *Beyond Reach* review. *Booklist*, June 1, 2007.

Wilbur Smith

Adventure: Historical

Benchmark Series: <u>Egyptian</u>

Broken Hill, Northern Rhodesia

1933–

About the Author and the Author's Writing

When Wilbur Smith was thirteen, growing up on his father's 25,000-acre African plantation, he was presented with his first rifle, a well-used .22 Remington. Wilbur was left in nominal charge while his parents went away for vacation. When lions got inside the fences and killed some cattle, he recounted in *The Observer* in 2003, "I took my father's rifle, got on my pony and found the cattle dead in a field. I heard a growl and suddenly, looking over the top of a dead ox, were these big golden eyes. The lioness charged straight at me and I shot her. She fell at my feet."

His agent once advised Smith to write what he knew. With Smith's experiences in Africa, he knew enough for dozens of novels—as he proceeded to produce them over the next several decades.

Wilbur Addison Smith was born in Northern Rhodesia (now Zambia) in 1933, to English parents. At the time, his father worked for a copper company, but eventually he acquired a ranch. Barely eighteen months old, Smith suffered cerebral malaria. He survived to grow up with the sons of black ranch workers as his playmates. He attended boarding school, Cordwalles, in Natal, South Africa, where one of his instructors presented him with a copy of W. Somerset Maugham's *Introduction to Modern English Literature* as reward for writing an English essay. It opened his eyes to the possibilities of writing.

In 1954, he received a bachelor of commerce degree from Rhodes University in Grahamstown, South Africa. His mother was an avid reader, but his father was not and discouraged his son's interest in writing as a profession. As a result, Smith went to work for Goodyear Tire & Rubber, 1954 to 1958; then for H.J. Smith & Son, 1958 to 1963. During that time, he sold a story to *Argosy* magazine for 70 pounds, to test the waters.

Depressed in the aftermath of a divorce from his second wife, he completed a manuscript that never sold, then finished *When the Lion Feeds*, which was picked up by an enthusiastic editor at Heinemann, Charles Pick. Pick later became Smith's literary representative following the death of his original agent, Ursula Winant. The 1964 novel was the first to feature the cattle ranching Courtney family and described in robust language the colonial era, European pioneers, native Zulus, gold, and violence. Smith continued to write about Africa, and although some suggest his writing is not critical enough of colonialism, his market broadened considerably in the United States following the end of apartheid.

Smith left his position as a tax accountant with the Deceased Estates Department of Salisbury Inland Revenue to write full time. Success meant the author would eventually own his own 60,000-acre preserve in Zambia, as well as an island in the Seychelles. His third marriage, to Danielle Thomas in 1971, was a happy one. After her death to a brain tumor in 1999, he met and married Mikhiniso Rakhimova.

Smith has written blockbuster books in several series. Besides the dozen Courtney family novels, there are books featuring the Ballantynes, set in the days of fierce colonialism, and the Egyptian novels, which take place in the time of the pharaohs. In addition, from time to time Smith writes novels that stand alone. His novels are at times violent. This, he has said, reflects reality, and he only has to mention the recovery of bodies from latrines, while he was in National Service in Rhodesia, to drive the point home.

A second piece of advice his agent, Pick, gave Smith also struck home. "'Do not write for your publishers or for your imagined readers. Write only for yourself,'" Smith says on his Web site. "This was something that I had learned for myself, Charles merely confirmed it for me."

Smith's readers are drawn in by his well-delineated, exotic settings; his robust characters; his complex and luring plots; and his relentless pace. Echoing his childhood ailment, Smith often introduces characters who have physical disabilities. "It is because I had polio when I was a child and have a withered right leg, though now it only shows up when I am tired," he said in a *Publishers Weekly* interview.

Now on a schedule of a book every two years, Smith generally writes from February to October, then travels the rest of the year to fish or ski. Past are the days when hunting brought pleasure, when he sampled lion, leopard, crocodile, or python meat. Although he has shot two elephants, he never wants to again, both out of concern for the species and from a recollection of stalking the huge animals, day after day, and coming upon a waterhole only to take a drink and realize the elephant had been there before him and peed in the pool.

The author relishes his African estate, "where there are many reintroduced animal species that had become extinct in the region," he said in *Geographical*. "When I am there I have the place to myself so I can live with the illusion that I am one of the forefathers to the territory."

Smith is admittedly old-fashioned about his writing. Until *River God* (1994), he created each first draft by pen. "I believe in the triumph of good over evil and that love conquers all," he told a BookBrowse interviewer. "I haven't gotten really cynical."

Works by the Author

The Train from Katanga (1965), issued in United Kingdom as *The Dark of the Sun*

Shout at the Devil (1968)

Gold Mine (1970)

The Diamond Hunters (1971)

The Sunbird (1972)

Eagle in the Sky (1974)

Cry Wolf (1975)
Hungry as the Sea (1977)
Wild Justice (1978)
The Delta Decision (1981)
Elephant Song (1991)

Ballantyne Series

A Falcon Flies (1979), retitled *Flight of the Falcon* (1982)
Men of Men (1980)
The Angels Weep (1983)
The Leopard Hunts in Darkness (1984)

Courtney Series

When the Lion Feeds (1964)
The Sound of Thunder (1971)
A Sparrow Falls (1976)
The Burning Shore (1985)
Power of the Sword (1986)
Rage (1987)
The Courtneys (1988)
A Time to Die (1989)
Golden Fox (1990)
Birds of Prey (1997)
Monsoon (1999)
The Blue Horizon (2003)
The Triumph of the Sun (2005)
Assegai (2009)

Egyptian Series

River God (1994)
The Seventh Scroll (1995)
Warlock (2001)
The Quest (2007)

Adaptations in Other Media

The Mercenaries (1968), motion picture, titled *Dark of the Sun* in the United States, based on *The Dark of the Sun*
The Last Lion (1972), motion picture
Gold (1974), motion picture, retitled *The Great Gold Conspiracy* in the United States, based on *Gold Mine*
The Kingfisher Caper (1975), motion picture, retitled *Diamond Lust* (Canada) and *The Diamond Hunters* (South Africa), based on *The Diamond Hunters*

Shout at the Devil (1976), motion picture based on the novel

Mountain of Diamonds (1991), television production, based on the novel, also titled *The Burning Shore* in United Kingdom

Wild Justice (1994), motion picture, also titled *Covert Assassin* and *Dial*

The Seventh Scroll (1999), television miniseries based on the novel

The Diamond Hunters (2001), television miniseries based on the novel

For Further Information

Field, Michele, "Wilbur Smith: His 25th Book Is a Winner Here." *Publishers Weekly*, May 1, 1995.

Hooper, Brad, *The Quest* review. *Booklist*, April 15, 2007.

Janes, Hilly, "This Much I Know." *Observer Magazine*, March 9, 2003.

Wilbur Smith interview, BookBrowse. http://www.bookbrowse.com/biographies/index.cfm?author_number=381 (viewed March 2, 2008).

Wilbur Smith interview. *Geographical,* April 2001.

Wilbur Smith Web site. http://www.wilbursmithbooks.com (viewed November 19, 2008).

Erica Spindler

Crime-Suspense: Serial Killers; Espionage; Romance

Benchmark Title: *Copycat*

Rockford, Illinois
1957–

Photo credit: David Anthony

About the Author and the Author's Writing

There's an old adage often passed on to new writers: Write what you know. A corollary might be: Write what you read. It worked for Erica Spindler. Suffering the sniffles, she picked up some tissues and cold medication at a pharmacy. The clerk added a Silhouette Romance novel to the bag. When she got home, she snuggled in a chair with the book, was hooked, and not long after, began to write her own. Two years later, she sold her first novel.

The author was born in Rockford, Illinois, in 1957. She received a bachelor of fine arts degree from Delta State University master's in fine arts degree from the University of New Orleans. She has taught in Southeastern Louisiana University's fine arts program. She and her husband, advertising executive Nathan Spindler, have two children.

Several of Spindler's books have been nominated for Romance Writers of America Rita awards. However, the author gradually began to introduce serial killers and assassins to her romances, and eventually changed genres. Her novel *Bone Cold* (2002) won the Daphne du Maurier Award for excellence.

"The writing transition was organic," she explained in a Bookreporter interview. "In 1996 I came up with a story in which the hero was an NOPD [New Orleans Police Department] homicide detective and there was a serial killer subplot." She found she enjoyed writing the suspense, and increased that aspect of the story with each new book.

Spindler grew up reading the Trixie Belden teen novels and the stories of Phyllis Whitney and Mary Stewart. Today she enjoys reading other writers in the suspense and thriller genre, from David Baldacci and Iris Johansen to Michael Connelly and Janet Evanovich.

Her 2006 novel *Copycat* has the intriguing concept of a serial killer, apparently long retired, who is known for suffocating his young victims, offering to help the Violent Crimes Bureau when a copycat stalks a new set of girls. Veteran detective Kitt Lundgren, who was going through marital troubles when she investigated the first killing binge, and M. C. Riggio, her young protégé, can't refuse the offer. "The detectives must overcome their personal problems in order to catch the monsters, a tack culminating in a breathless finale," explains a reviewer in *Publishers Weekly*. In the author's *Last Known Victim* from 2007, a serial killer takes advantage of Hurricane Katrina–distracted New Orleans to kill police Captain Patti O'Shay's husband.

The writer generally keeps regular business hours, working overtime, if necessary, when a deadline approaches. She writes out concepts on a legal pad, shapes and fits elements until she is ready to outline—often fifty pages worth. She begins with a plot concept. Characters have traits that Spindler draws from those of people she knows, but they are not directly based on real people.

Ideas come from anywhere. *Bone Cold*, she said in an Escape to Romance interview, "was sparked by a fan letter from a child; *Fortune,* the message in a fortune cookie. The spark for *Dead Run* occurred one Sunday during my pastor's sermon on how the notion of universal evil or the forces of darkness had become politically incorrect."

The author creatively adapts things she hears. "No matter how innocent the story being relayed to me is, I can twist it into something pretty damn frightening," she said on her Web site. "I've learned the real trick is not sharing these versions with those relaying the story. It tends to make people avoid me."

Readers, meanwhile, have had no reluctance seeking out Spindler's books.

Works by the Author

Heaven Sent (1987)
Read between the Lines (1989)
Rhyme or Reason (1990)
Wishing Moon (1991)
Longer Than … (1991)
Baby Mine (1992)
Tempting Chance (1993)
Baby, Come Back (1994)
Slow Heat (1995)
Red (1995)
Forbidden Fruit (1996)
Fortune (1997)
Chances Are (1998)
Shocking Pink (1998)
Cause for Alarm (1999)
All Fall Down (2000)
Bone Cold (2001)
Dead Run (2002)

In Silence (2003)
See Jane Die (2004)
Killer Takes All (2005), sequel to *See Jane Die*
Baby Mine/Longer Than ... (2005), omnibus
Copycat (2006)
Last Known Victim (2007)
Breakneck (2009)

Blossoms of the South Series

A Winter's Rose (1992)
Magnolia Dawn (1993)
Night Jasmine (1993)
Night Jasmine/Magnolia Dawn (2005), omnibus

Contributor

The Chopin Manuscript, with Lee Child, David Corbett, Jeffery Deaver, Jim Fusilli, John Gilstrap, James Grady, David Hewson, John Ramsey Miller, P. J. Parrish, Ralph Pezullo, S. J. Rozan, Lisa Scottoline, Peter Spiegelman, and Joseph Finder (2007)

Adaptations in Other Media

Red (Japanese daytime TV drama)

For Further Information

Copycat review. *Publishers Review*, April 24, 2006.

Erica Spindler entry, Contemporary Authors Online. Reproduced in Biography Resource Center. Farmington Hills, MI: Gale, 2008. http://galenet.galegroup.com/servlet/BioRC (viewed February 15, 2008).

Erica Spindler interview, Escape to Romance. http://www.escapetoromance.com/interviews/spotlight-spindler.html (viewed February 15, 2008).

Erica Spindler Web site. http://www.ericaspindler.com (viewed November 20, 2008).

Fitzgerald, Carol, and Wiley Salchek, Erica Spindler interview, Bookreporter. http://www.bookreporter.com/authors/au-spindler-erica.asp (viewed February 15, 2008).

Last Known Victim review. *Publishers Weekly*, August 6, 2007.

Richard Stark
(Donald E. Westlake)

Crime: Capers

Benchmark Series: <u>Parker</u>

Brooklyn, New York
1933–2008

Photo credit: Abby Adams

About the Author and the Author's Writing

Richard Stark wrote with the kind of economy and muscle that makes Ernest Hemingway's prose look almost bloated. This is how Stark's 2001 crime novel *Firebreak* opens: "When the phone rang, Parker was in the garage, killing a man." As David Wright asked in an essay in *Booklist*, "How are you going to put down a book that begins like that?"

"Richard Stark" is one of a dozen pennames of prolific and multitalented author Donald E. Westlake. Westlake didn't expect Parker would be around long; he invented the name for a one-off novel about a professional criminal, *The Hunter*, in 1962. "If I'd known he'd be back in more than 20 books, I'd have given him a first name," Westlake said in a Bookreporter interview in 2001. "Anyway, in that first book I gave him none of the softnesses you're supposed to give a series character and no band of sidekicks to chat with, because he was going to pound through one book and goodbye." Parker was newly out of prison at the book's beginning and was back in again at its end. But Westlake's editor wanted a series. And Westlake, tired of writing low-paying erotic novels for a marginal publisher, obliged.

Donald Edwin Westlake was born in 1933 in Brooklyn, New York. He attended three colleges in New York State, including Champlain and Harpur. He did not graduate, but in 1996 State University of New York at Binghamton awarded him a doctorate in letters. From 1954 to 1956, he served in the U.S. Air Force. He was twice wed and twice divorced before he married Abigail Adams in 1979. Between them, they had seven children. He lived in Yonkers, Albany, Plattsburgh, Troy, Binghamton, and

Manhattan in New York. Toward the end of his life, he spent a good deal of time on a former farm in upstate Dutchess County.

Out of school, out of the military, Westlake strode through several jobs before he joined the Scott Meredith Literary Agency, reading cold-submission manuscripts and taking a few writing assignments that came in the door. He sold his first story, "Or Give Me Death," to *Universe Science Fiction*—which promptly went out of business. His first novel and career-starter was *The Mercenaries,* published in 1960 by Random House. The publisher contracted four more novels. After a dozen or so books, Westlake got the sillies. He couldn't write *The Fugitive Pigeon* (1965) with a straight face. Although it took some persuading from the publisher, the book created a second direction for the idea-filled author. "Before *The Fugitive Pigeon*, there was no such thing as a comic mystery novel; within a few years such a category did in fact exist, and Westlake essentially owned it," wrote fellow mystery writer Lawrence Block in The Scribner Writers Series.

Under the name Tucker Coe, Westlake wrote five books about a guilt-ridden former policeman, Mitch Tobin, who preferred to be in his backyard constructing a stone wall to solving crime. As Samuel Holt, Westlake wrote four tales about an actor-detective. And as Stark, he wrote a dozen and a half taut crime thrillers. There's nothing funny about Parker.

"The greatest insights come from so-called comedy, I believe," Westlake asserted in a 2002 interview with his alter-ego Stark, published on the Hatchett Book Group Web site. "But how do you manage to maintain absolutely no sense of humor year after year?" "No sense of humor?" Stark responded. "Don't make me laugh."

Westlake told *Newsweek*'s Malcolm Jones that he adopted something of a different persona, an altered language, when writing the Parker novels. "The separation's in the language. I don't want to overstate it, but I bring out a different vocabulary. I'll be going along, and I'll think, wait a minute. Stark wouldn't say that. That's a little flowery. Because the Stark books are a little more of a construct."

Just because they're dead serious doesn't mean Westlake didn't let a little whimsy into the Stark novels. Chapters from an ersatz Parker escapade figure in one of the humorous crime caper novels about John Dortmunder, *Jimmy the Kid*, for example. The Dortmunder story, in fact, might have been a Parker novel. Westlake was writing a story in which Parker had to repeat the same crime, over and over. It wasn't serious enough. So he created Dortmunder, Murch, Kelp, and the rest of the inept gang for *The Hot Rock* in 1970. Westlake/Stark also wrote four books featuring Alan Grofield, a character from the Parker series.

"By the late 60's, Stark was better known and better paid than Westlake," Westlake wrote in the *New York Times*, "which felt a little odd. But after all, we were both me, so there was no reason for jealousy."

"I usually start with no more than a character or two and a setting and an opening scene," Westlake said in describing his routine to interviewer Paul Kane. "I make it up as I go along, so that makes me my first reader. This keeps up both the enthusiasm and the aggravation."

Ultimately, after the mega-heist novel *Butcher's Moon* in 1974, the candle burned out on Parker. Twenty-three years later, his senses again hardened with the award-winning script for *The Grifters*, Westlake/Stark revived Parker. It was as if he'd never been away.

"The tension builds with the thieves' reactions as the story winds tightly toward the ending," said reviewer Pam Johnson of *Nobody Runs Forever* (2005). "Stark's careful control over every element results in a fascinating novel, a look at the true price of crime, and an opportunity to enjoy another book by this master writer."

A master writer indeed, Westlake (or was it Stark? Or Coe?) deservedly received the Mystery Writers of America Grand Master Award in 1992.

The author died on the last day of 2008 of a heart attack while on vacation in Mexico.

Works by Richard Stark

For other works by Donald E. Westlake, see his Web site http://www.donaldwestlake.com.

Parker Series

The Hunter (1962), retitled *Point Blank* (1967), retitled *Payback*

The Man with the Getaway Face (1963), retitled *Steel Hit* (Great Britain)

The Outfit (1963)

The Mourner (1963)

The Score (1963), retitled *Killtown* (Great Britain, 1973)

The Jugger (1965)

The Seventh (1966), retitled *The Split* (1968)

The Handle (1966), retitled *Run Lethal* (Great Britain, 1973)

The Rare Coin Score (1967)

The Green Eagle Score (1967)

The Black Ice Score (1968)

The Sour Lemon Score (1969)

Slayground (1971)

Deadly Edge (1971)

Plunder Squad (1972)

Butcher's Moon (1974)

Child Heist (1974), a fake Parker novel included in the Dortmunder novel *Jimmy the Kid*

Comeback (1997)

Backflash (1998)

Flashfire (2000)

Firebreak (2001)

Breakout (2002)

Nobody Runs Forever (2004)

Ask the Parrot (2006)

Dirty Money (2008)

Grofield Series

The Damsel (1967)
The Dame (1969)
The Blackbird (1969)
Lemons Never Lie (1971)

Screenplays by Donald E. Westlake

Hot Stuff, with Michael Kane (1979)
The Stepfather (1986)
Father Dowlling Mysteries (TV series, 1987), episode "Fatal Confession"
The Grifters (1990)
Why Me? (1990)
Fallen Angels (television series, 1995), episode "Fly Paper"
Ripley Underground (2005)

Adaptations in Other Media

87th Precinct (1962), episode based on story "Feel of the Trigger"
Made in the USA (1966), based on *The Jugger*
Point Blank (1967), based on *The Hunter*
The Busy Body (1967), based on the novel
Mise en Sac (1967), based on *The Score*
The Split (1967), based on *The Seventh*
Journey to the Unknown (1969), episode based on story "One on a Desert Island"
The Hot Rock (1972), based on the novel
Cops and Robbers (1973)
Bank Shot (1974), based on the novel
The Outfit (1974), based on the novel
Jimmy the Kid (1982), based on the novel
Slayground (1984), based on the novel
Stepfather 2: Make Room for Daddy (television movie 1989), based on characters in *The Stepfather*
Stepfather 3: Father's Day (television movie, 1992), based on characters in *The Stepfather*
Payback (1999), based on *The Hunter*, reissued as *Payback: Straight Up—The Director's Cut* (2006)
Jimmy the Kid (1999), based on the novel
A Slight Case of Murder (1999), based on the novel
Le Jumeau (2001), based on *Two Much*
What's the Worst That Could Happen? (2001), based on the novel
Le Couperet (2005), based on *The Ax*

For Further Information

Donald E. Westlake checklist. http://www.imc.pi.cnr.it/~resta/westlake.html (viewed January 25, 2008).

Donald E. Westlake entry by Lawrence Block, in *The Scribner Writers Series Mystery & Suspense Writers: The Literature of Crime, Detection and Espionage*, 2 volumes, Robin W. Winks, ed. New York: Scribner's, 1998.

Donald E. Westlake Web site. http://www.donaldwestlake.com/ (viewed November 20, 2008).

Grondahl, Paul, "For Mystery Writer, It's One Story after Another," Albany (N.Y.) *Times-Union*, July 20, 1997.

Hahn, D. Kingsley, ed., *The ParkerPhile* newsletters, five issues, 1982–1983.

Hartlaub, Joe, Donald E. Westlake interview, Bookreporter. http://www.bookreporter.com/authors/au-westlake-donald.asp (viewed January 20, 2008).

Jones, Malcolm, "Lives of Crime," *Newsweek*, April 23, 2007.

Kane, Paul, "An Interview with Donald Westlake (aka Richard Stark)," The Compulsive Reader. http://www.compulsivereader.com/html/index.php?name=News&file=article&sid=1481 (viewed January 19, 2008).

"Mystery Author Donald E. Westlake Dies at 75." *Los Angeles Times*, January 2, 2009.

Poggiali, Chris, "Stark Views: The Violent World of Donald Westlake." http://www.violentworldofparker.com/articles/badazz.htm (viewed October 10, 2007).

Violent World of Parker Web site. http://www.geocities.com/SoHo/Nook/5171/ (viewed January 20, 2008).

Westlake, Donald E., "A Pseudonym Returns from an Alter-Ego Trip, with New Tales to Tell." *New York Times*, January 29, 2001.

Westlake, Donald E., "Interview Richard Stark," Hatchett Book Group. http://hachettebookgroupusa.com/authors/42/339/interview24295.html (viewed January 20, 2008).

Wright, David, "Cut to the Chase." *Booklist*, May 1, 2007.

S. M. Stirling

Fantasy; Science Fiction: Military, Techno, Action-Adventure

Benchmark Series: <u>Draka</u>

Metz, France

1953–

About the Author and the Author's Writing

In a post-apocalyptic world, in western Oregon, most of the technology we've come to enjoy in the last two centuries no longer functions. Rudi Mackenzie, the son of a high priestess, follows a mysterious traveler who has come from Nantucket Island—fabled land of Change—in quest of the Sword of the Lady. As it turns out, Mackenzie *is* the Sword of the Lady, and he accepts the challenge to cross the Valley of Paradise to fulfill his destiny, despite threats many and dire. That's the premise of *The Sunrise Lands*, the first one of S. M. Stirling's recent science fiction series. Although he uses it to explore political themes, he doesn't leave out the action. "Readers who have survived Stirling's usual high body count will recognize brilliant action fiction and alternate history when they see it and happily hang fire for more," observed reviewer Roland Green in *Booklist*.

Stephen Michael Stirling was born in 1953 in Metz, France, the son of a Royal Canadian Air Force wing commander. He later lived in Kenya before coming to Canada as a teenager. In 1976, he earned a bachelor of arts degree with honors in history and English from Carleton University in Ottawa, and in 1979 a law degree from Osgoode Hall Law School of York University in Toronto. For eight years, he worked at part-time jobs—variously as a farmhand, secretary, and bouncer—before becoming a full-time writer in 1988. That same year, he married Janet Cathryn Moore. They live in Santa Fe, New Mexico, where Stirling pursues his side interests in history, anthropology, archaeology, and karate.

Stirling considers himself politically conservative, with a strong feminist sympathy, and, although raised Anglican, religiously agnostic. Being Canadian gave him both a shot at a broader reading audience—Great Britain as well as the United States—and a different attitude. "Canada's history starts with an enormous disaster (the American Revolution, from our point of view) and then goes through a century or so of being a loyal Dominion of the Empire," he said in a *Locus* interview in 2006. "It tends to give you a somewhat different perspective; more pessimistic, and perhaps more modest. Nobody's ever talked about the 'Canadian Century'!"

Stirling sold his first story to editor Jim Baen for an anthology in the mid-1980s and since has produced books in his own series and those started by others. He has collaborated with other writers including Holly Lisle, Jerry Pournelle, and David Drake. He has also written entries for series based on popular films. He best likes stories set in alternate worlds (*Ice, Iron and Gold*, for example) and military science fiction (Man-Kzin series) but also writes fantasy (Fifth Millennium series), and urban fantasy (*Drakon*). In the last, a genetically improved warrior, Gwendolyn Ingolfsson, is flung through the universe to present-day New York City, where she inveigles to open an intradimensional gate so the Draka army can invade Earth. Only the agent Kenneth Lafarge stands between her and disaster. "Defeating this cheerfully bloodthirsty scheme involves nonstop action and Stirling's usual wealth of technical detail, wry wit, and superlatively drawn female characters, not the least of them the appalling Ms. Ingolfsson," said Roland Green in *Booklist*.

Stirling plies various genres and subgenres such as techno and post-apocalyptic science fiction with great ease, although some critics have cringed at the violence and at his occasional use of the villain's point of view. This, Stirling insists, should not be mistaken for his endorsement.

The author reads a great deal of history, which gives him lots of ideas. The books in the Raj Whitehall, or General, series, for instance, derive from the life of the Byzantine warrior Belisarius, restaged on a distant planet with only late-nineteenth-century technology. Stirling has said he finds science fiction writers are no more prescient than anyone else in anticipating future technologies. Thus he is comfortable with alternate worlds with lesser technologies, although no less conflict.

One of Stirling's collaborations was not with a writer but with actor James Doohan, who played the Enterprise's engineer Scottie on the original *Star Trek* television series. Together they crafted four books featuring starfighter pilot Peter Reeder. "The two have compatible senses of humor and the ability to exploit to the full the absurdities of the military and war," said reviewers Roland Green and Gilbert Taylor in *Booklist*. "At the same time, they don't let the tone turn silly. Solid astronautical fare."

For *The Sky People*, Stirling tipped his hat to pulp science fiction icons Edgar Rice Burroughs and Leigh Brackett. "They got a much more interesting solar system than we did: lost civilizations on a dying Mars, steamy jungles on Venus, … [which is] much less boring than the baking, sulfuric-acid hell and barren ice ball that reality handed us," he said in an interview on SciFi.com "So it occurred to me that it would be a lot of fun to do a living Mars and Venus and then hold everything else constant."

In a Chronicle interview, the author asserted that he likes science fiction, fantasy, and horror "because of the sense of limitless possibility, together with the acceptance of variety. Conventional 'literary' fiction has become entirely too tight-arsed for my taste. Which is not to say that I don't read some, of course."

 # Works by the Author

The Rose Sea, with Holly Lisle (1994)
Conquistador (2003)
The Sky People (2006)
Ice, Iron and Gold (2007), stories
In the Courts of the Crimson Kings (2008)

Babylon 5 Series

6. *Betrayals* (1996)

Change Series

The Sunrise Lands: A Novel of the Change (2007)
The Scourge of God (2008)
The Sword of the Lady (2009)
The High King (announced)

Dies the Fire Series

Dies the Fire (2004)
The Protector's War (2005)
A Meeting at Corvallis (2006)

Draka Series

Marching Through Georgia (1988)
Under the Yoke (1989)
The Stone Dogs (1990)
Drakon (1996)
The Domination (1999), omnibus of first three novels
Drakas!, edited by S. M. Stirling (2000), short stories by other authors

Fifth Millennium Series

Snowbrother (1985), expanded edition (1989)
The Sharpest Edge, with Shirley Meier (1986), expanded edition, retitled *Saber and Shadow* (1992)
The Cage, with Shirley Meier (1989)
Shadow's Son, with Shirley Meier and Karen Wehrstein (1991)
The Anthology of Fantasy and the Supernatural, edited by Stephen Jones and David Sutton (1994), includes "The Waters of Knowing"

Flight Engineer Series, with James Doohan

The Rising (1996)
The Privateer (1999)
The Independent Command (2000)

General Series, with David A. Drake

The Forge (1991)
The Hammer (1992)
The Anvil (1993)
The Steel (1993)

The Sword (1995)
The Chosen (1996)
The Reformer (1999)
The Warlord (2003), omnibus of first two novels
The Conquerer (2003), includes the next three novels

Island in the Sea of Time Series

Island in the Sea of Time (1998)
Against the Tide of Years (1999)
On the Oceans of Eternity (2000)
The First Heroes: New Tales of the Bronze Age, edited by Harry Turtledove and Noreen Doyle (2004), includes "Blood Wolf"

Legends of the Riftwar Series

Jimmy the Hand, with Raymond Feist (2003)

Magic: The Gathering Series

Tapestries, edited by Kathy Ice (1995), includes "The Lament"

Man-Kzin War Series

Man-Kzin Wars 2, edited by Larry Niven (1989), includes "The Children's Hour," with Jerry Pournelle
Man-Kzin Wars 3, edited by Larry Niven (1990), includes "The Asteroid Queen," with Jerry Pournelle
Man-Kzin Wars 4, edited by Larry Niven (1991), includes "The Man Who Would Be Kzin," with Greg Bear
Cats in Space, edited by Bill Fawcett (1992), includes "The Man Who Would Be Kzin," with Greg Bear
Man-Kzin Wars: The Best of All Possible Wars, edited by Larry Niven (1998), includes "The Man Who Would Be Kzin," with Greg Bear, and "In the Hall of the Mountain King," with Jerry Pournelle
Man-Kzin Wars 5, edited by Larry Niven (1992), includes "In the Hall of the Mountain King" with Jerry Pournelle
The Houses of the Kzinti (2004), reprints "The Children's Hour," with Jerry Pournelle

Peshawar Lancers Series

The Peshawar Lancers (2002)
Worlds That Weren't (2002), includes "Shikari in Galveston"

Ship Who Sang Series

The City Who Fought, with Anne McCaffrey (1993)

The Ship Avenged (1997)

The City and the Ship (2004), omnibus of the two novels

Terminator 2 Series

Infiltrator (2001)

Rising Storm (2002)

The Future War (2003)

War World Series

War World Vol. 1, edited by Jerry Pournelle (1988), includes "Necessity"

Go Tell the Spartans, with Jerry Pournelle (1991)

War World Vol. 3, edited by Jerry Pournelle (1991), includes "Shame and Honor"

Prince of Sparta, with Jerry Pournelle (1993)

War World: Blood Feuds, with Jerry Pournelle, Judith Tarr, Harry Turtledove, and Susan Schwartz (1993)

War World: Blood Vengeance, with Jerry Pournelle, Judith Tarr, Harry Turtledove, and Susan Schwartz (1994)

War World Vol. 4, edited by Jerry Pournelle (1994), includes "Kings Who Die"

The Prince, with Jerry Pournelle (2002), includes *Go Tell the Spartans* and *Prince of Sparta* and other Pournelle stories

Editor

The Fantastic World War II, with Frank D. McSherry Jr.

The Fantastic Civil War, with Frank D. McSherry Jr. (1990)

Power (1991) includes "Roachstompers"

Anthologies

Far Frontiers Vol. 4, edited by Jim Baen and Jerry Pournelle (1986), includes "Cops and Robbers"

New Destinies Vol. 8, edited by Jim Baen (1989), includes "Roachstompers"

Battlestation Book 1, edited by David Drake and Bill Fawcett (1992), includes "Comrades"

Bolos: Honor of the Regiment, edited by Bill Fawcett (1993), includes "Lost Legion"

Dragon's Eye, edited by Christopher Stasheff (1994), includes "Constant Never"

Bolos 2: The Unconquerable, edited by Bill Fawcett (1994), includes "Ancestral Voices"

The Day the Magic Stopped, edited by Christopher Stasheff and Bill Fawcett (1995), includes "The Thief of Eyes"

Lammas Night, edited by Josepha Sherman (1996), includes "The Mage, the Maiden, and the Hag" with Janet Stirling

Bolos 4: Last Stand, edited by Bill Fawcett (1997), includes "The Sixth Sun"

Urban Nightmares, edited by Josepha Sherman and Keith R. A. DeCandido (1997), includes "The Release"

More Than Honor, edited by David Drake and David Weber (1998), includes "A Whiff of Grapeshot"

Did You Say Chicks?! edited by Esther Friesner (1998), includes "Armor Propre" with Janet Stirling

Armageddon, edited by David Drake and Billie Sue Mosiman (1998), includes "Riding Shotgun to Armageddon"

Alternate Generals, edited by Harry Turtledove, Roland Green, and Martin H. Greenberg (1998), includes "The Charge of Lee's Brigade"

First to Flight, edited by Martin H. Greenberg (1999), includes "Flyboy"

Adventures of Swords and Sorcery No. 6 (1999), includes "The Thief of Eyes"

Foreign Legions, edited by David Drake (2001), includes "Three Walls-32nd Campaign"

Alternate Generals 2, edited by Harry Turtledove and Martin H. Greenberg (2002), includes "Compadres" with Richard Foss

Space, Inc., edited by Julie E. Czerneda and Martin H. Greenberg (2003), includes "Field Trip" with Janet Stirling

Live Without a Net, edited by Lou Anders (2003), includes "The Crystal Method"

The Enchanter Completed, edited by Harry Turtledove (2005), includes "The Apotheosis of Martin Padway"

For Further Information

Cassada, Jackie, *The Sky People* review. *Library Journal*, November 15, 2006.

Green, Roland, *Drakon* review. *Booklist*, February 1, 1996.

Green, Roland, *The Sunrise Lands* review. *Booklist*, September 1, 2007.

Green, Roland, and Gilbert Taylor, *The Privateer* review. *Booklist*, October 1, 1999.

Ice, Iron and Gold review. *Publishers Weekly*, October 1, 2007.

"In *Sky*, Mars and Venus Live," SciFiWire. http://www.scifi.com/scifiwire/index.php?category=0&id=38720 (viewed January 31, 2008).

S(tephen) M(ichael) Stirling entry. *St. James Guide to Science Fiction Writers*, 4th ed., Jay P. Pederson, ed. Detroit, MI: St. James Press, 1996.

S. M. Stirling interview, Chronicle No. 30. http://www.eternalnight.co.uk/chronicle/30/stirling.html (viewed January 21, 2008).

"S. M. Stirling: Turning Points." *Locus*, January 2006.

S. M. Stirling Web site. http://www.smstirling.com (viewed January 21, 2008).

The Privateer review. *Booklist*, October 1, 1999.

Scott Turow

Crime-Suspense; Thrillers: Legal, Business/Finance

Benchmark Title: *Presumed Innocent*

Chicago, Illinois

1949–

Photo credit: Courtesy of the author

About the Author and the Author's Writing

Author Scott Turow's ability to create complex characters and intricate plots grows from his eight years as a prosecutor and his subsequent career as a defense lawyer, dealing with witnesses and defendants on a daily basis.

In fact, he considered a literary career before he took up the legal profession. "I was headed for life as a university professor, and it didn't suit me," he told *Mason Gazette*'s Colleen Kearney Rich. "I needed another day job, and I chose law school rather than going to Hollywood and getting a studio job or going into advertising. I just didn't think I was going to be much of an English professor."

Turow was born in Chicago in 1949, the son of a physician and a writer. In suburban Winnetka, he edited the New Trier High School newspaper. He received a bachelor of arts degree in 1960 from Amherst College, and accepted a Mirrielees Fellowship to the Stanford University Creative Writing Center, 1970–1972. He married Annette Weisberg, an artist, in 1971, and they have three children. For three years he taught creative writing at Stanford as E. J. Jones Lecturer. In 1974, he completed requirements for a master's degree from Stanford. He received his law degree from Harvard University in 1978.

After graduating from law school, he clerked in the Suffolk County District Attorney's Office in Boston, then became assistant United States attorney in the United States Court of Appeals, Seventh District, in Chicago, from 1978 to 1986. Since 1986, he has been with the law firm Sonnenschein, Carlin, Nath & Rosenthal. He was president of the Authors Guild 1997–1998.

Turow's first published book was a work of nonfiction, *One L*, describing his first year as a law student at Harvard. A decade later, he published a novel, *Presumed Innocent*.

In the book, Rusty Sabich, chief deputy prosecuting attorney, is implicated in the murder of an attractive, sharp, corruptible coworker. As the novel progresses, "perceptions shift rapidly with each new piece of information," according to *St. James Guide to Crime & Mystery Writers*. "The result is not only a first-rate study of a metropolitan criminal-justice system from the inside, but a psychological study of a morose man seeking an ephemeral, beguiling illusion in a world of corruption, betrayal, and inescapable pain."

On his Web page, the author says the writers who have most influenced him are Saul Bellow and Charles Dickens; in an interview with *Book* magazine, he singled out Leo Tolstoy and James Joyce. In an *Observer* interview, he mentioned Ian Fleming and Alexandre Dumas.

His law experience was critical to his finding a voice for his fiction, he said in *The Writer* in 2005. "It made me comfortable with the kind of moral debate that is at the center of all the fiction that I write. I identify it as a central passion for me."

In another interview, with David Zivan, Turow spoke again about the world of the courtroom: "I am defined by the legal universe. I refuse to change its rules, so I have got to try to make people understand the way lawyers think about certain things."

The author sets his stories in a fictional Kindle County, modeled on Cook County in Illinois, with a hint of Boston thrown in.

He writes today while continuing his law practice. He works in the area of white-collar criminal litigation and does a lot of pro bono work. In 2000, he was appointed to an Illinois board to review the state's capital punishment laws and came away opposed to the death penalty. The experience became the grist for a nonfiction book, *Ultimate Punishment: A Lawyer's Reflections on Dealing with the Death Penalty*, in 2003. "This measured weighing of the facts will be most valuable to those who, like Turow, are on the fence—they will find an invaluable, objective look at both sides of this critical but highly charged debate," suggested *Publishers Weekly*.

Turow says he does not write a novel from beginning to end. Rather, he writes in blocks of text, scenes that, thanks to the flexibility of the word processor, he can rearrange as needed. "I used to read about [Vladimir] Nabokov who would write paragraphs out on index cards all over his books, and I thought, 'How can the guy do that? You've got to have it all in order in your head.' But I'll be damned. That's now the way I write," he said on his Web page. He doesn't put together an outline until he's in his second or third draft. This fractured writing method served him well on his daily commutes to and from work in the Windy City.

Turow often finds himself deeply entwined with his characters, such as black defense lawyer Hobie Tuttle in *The Laws of Our Fathers*. "Hobie's character is one of my favorites," he said to interviewer Alden Mudge for BookPage. "In each of my books a character begins to take over. In *The Burden of Proof* it was Sonny Klonsky. I wrote almost a third of the book in her voice until my editor reined me in. In this book it was Hobie Tuttle. He was originally just part of the mechanics of the novel, but he took over. I love his character. Hobie Tuttle is one clever dude."

Turow's books share a theme. "All my novels are about the ambiguities that lie beneath the sharp edges of the law," he told Robert McCrum of *The Observer*. "Criminal law in particular does indeed present human beings in extreme. You're always dealing with definitions of evil."

Works by the Author

Presumed Innocent (1987)
The Burden of Proof (1990)
Pleading Guilty (1993)
Scott Turow Omnibus (1993), includes first two novels
The Laws of Our Fathers (1996), sequel to *The Burden of Proof*
Personal Injuries (1999)
Reversible Errors (2002)
Ordinary Heroes (2005)
Limitations (2006)

Editor

Guilty as Charged (1996)
Best American Mystery Stories (2006)

Anthologies

The Best American Short Stories (1971)
The Best American Short Stories (1972)
The Writing Life: Writers on How They Think and Work, edited by Marie Arana (2003)

Nonfiction

One L: An Inside Account of Life in the First Year at Harvard Law School (1977)
Ultimate Punishment: A Lawyer's Reflections on Dealing with the Death Penalty (2003)

Adaptations in Other Media

Presumed Innocent (1990), motion picture
Scott Turow's Reversible Errors (CBS, 2004), television movie

For Further Information

Abbe, Elfrieda, "Building a Legal Thriller." *The Writer*, May 2005.

"Author of the Month: Scott Turow," Authors on the Web. http://www. authorsontheweb.com/features/authormonth/0211turow/turow-scott.asp#facts (viewed May 26, 2003).

Buckley, James Jr., "Going Undercover in Life and Law: A Talk with Scott Turow," BookPage. http://www.bookpage.com/9910bp/scott_turow.html (viewed April 5, 2003).

Flynn, Gillian, *Ultimate Punishment* review. *Entertainment Weekly,* September 26, 2003.

Jones, Daniel, and John D. Jorgenson, eds., Scott Turow entry. *Contemporary Authors New Revision Series*, volume 65. Detroit, MI: Gale Research, 1998.

MacDonald, Andrew F., and Gina MacDonald. *Scott Turow: A Critical Companion*. Westport, CT: Greenwood Press, 2005.

McCrum, Robert, "To Hell with Perry Mason." *The Observer*, November 24, 2002.

Mudge, Alden, "When Characters Slip from the Confines of Plot: A Talk with Scott Turow," BookPage. http://www.bookpage.com/9610bp0.mystery/thelawsofourfathers.html (viewed April 5, 2003).

Rich, Colleen Kearney, "The Five-Minute Interview: Author Scott Turow." *The Mason Gazette*, February 21, 2007.

Scott Turow entry, *St. James Guide to Crime & Mystery Writers*, 4th ed., Jay P. Pederson, ed. Chicago: St. James Press, 1996.

Scott Turow Web site. http://www.scottturow.com (viewed November 20, 2008).

Turow Scott, "Odyssey That Started with 'Ulysses.'" *New York Times*, November 22, 1999.

Ultimate Punishment review. *Publishers Weekly,* August 25, 2003.

Zivan, David, "The Double Life of Scott Turow." *Book*, September/October 1999.

Andrew Vachss

Crime

Benchmark Series: Burke

New York, New York
1942–

Photo credit: Courtesy of the author

About the Author and the Author's Writing

Andrew Vachss has fought to protect children from abuse his entire professional life. When he became a lawyer in New York City, he chose to represent only children and youth. Outside his law practice, he was a founding member of the National Association to Protect Children; he also writes influential nonfiction for periodicals, journals, and Web sites. And as a fiction writer, his long-running series character Burke pursues predators of children and other innocent victims.

The author and his violent protagonist overlap in their intensity and dedication. Vachss told interviewer Peter Pavia for the *New York Post*, "We share the same taste in music and women. Our politics are the same. We're both gamblers. I'm trying to show him as an abused child, hypervigilant, distrustful, and absolutely bonded to the family of his choice."

To keep the sordid, ultra-noir world of Burke interesting for readers, Vachss varies locale on occasion. But the plots never stray from their focus on empowering the underpowered. In *Safe House*, he helps a woman at a Manhattan refuge whose neo-Nazi husband is stalking her. In *Dead and Gone*, professionals kill his dog and send him to the hospital—and ultimately, to take refuge on the West Coast. In *Terminal*, Burke hires on to a dying career criminal who wants to blackmail three millionaires; three decades ago, they raped and murdered a girl. Burke just wants justice. "Vachss' prose is as taut and streetwise as ever," said reviewer Bruce DeSilva in the *Albany Times Union*, in discussing *Terminal*, "drawing his readers again into an evil underworld that is at once impossible to look away from and horrible to behold.

Vachss was born in New York City in 1942. In 1965, he received a bachelor of arts degree from Case Western Reserve University in Cleveland, Ohio. He worked as a field investigator for the U.S. Public Health Service in Ohio; a representative for the

Community Development Foundation working on behalf of Biafra; a casework supervisor for the Department of Social Services in New York; and a director of the intensive treatment unit, ANDROS II, a maximum security prison for "aggressive-violent" youth in Roslindale, Massachusetts, among other endeavors, before he returned to school and received his juris doctorate, magna cum laude, in 1975 from the New England School of Law in Boston. While there, he became editor in chief of the *New England Law Review* for a year. He also holds an honorary doctorate of law from Case Western Reserve University.

From 1975 to 1985, Vachss was director of the Juvenile Justice Planning Project in New York City. He has been an attorney and consultant since 1976. His wife, Alice, is former chief of the Special Victims Bureau of the Queens District Attorney's Office. The recurring character of Wolfe in the Burke series is based on Alice Vachss.

Vachss has said he doesn't have to research his plots; they happen around him. In the book *Down Here*, for example, Vachss works in a serious suggestion for a survey that law enforcement officials might employ to gain information to detect pattern rapists. He did this in a sincere desire to see it put to use, he told Dan Pearson of *Daily Southtown*. "Certain triggers set them off. The only way to find that out is to collect the data and make it available to every jurisdiction." He included the information at the risk of confusing or distracting readers, but conceded. "If you can't read the book to the end, then any information, any point of view I have, is wasted."

And Vachss cares about his readers. He has created a small stable of secondary characters—his "Family of Choice"—who populate the Burke novels and provide support as needed. They include Max the Silent, a mute martial artist with too many talents to list; the Mole, a techno-genius who lives in an underground bunker hidden in a junkyard; Michelle, a longtime friend and a pre-op transsexual (who later has gender-reassignment surgery), "married" to the Mole; Mama, who presides over the restaurant that serves as the command center of the family's operations; the Prof, a master burglar who speaks in rhyme, the only "father" Burke has known; and Terry, a computer-savvy victim of child abuse whom Burke rescued from a pimp and Michelle has adopted. Rest assured, the characters are far more complex than this description suggests.

However, Vachss isn't afraid to lose characters, or sharply change direction, as in *Dead and Gone*, when Burke has to alter his appearance, and in *Another Life* (2008), in which Vachss draws the series to a close.

The author has also written stand-alone novels. *The Getaway Man* (2003) is something of an Appalachian tale of a young career criminal. *Two Trains Running* (2005), set in the Midwest, takes place on the eve of the 1960 election, which had the highest voter turnout of any United States election ever. "It's much harder to keep a population count in a border town, which means you can deliver more votes than there are voters," Vachss said in a conversation with Adam Dunn for Cobrapost in 2006. Two factions, Irish and Italian, look to upset the power wielded by a political boss named Beaumont. Even if it means murder.

These occasional stand-alone novels demonstrate Vachss's versatility. His graphic novels, adapted from short stories, show his commitment to reaching everyone—including younger readers. "I have a message. Comics give me a chance to reach a group of people I couldn't otherwise," he told Calvin Reid of *Publishers Weekly*. "I want to make people angry. Early interdiction in the lives of victims is an alternative to the vigilantism in my books."

Andrew Vachss is one of a kind in his use of prose as a tool in his very large tool chest of seeking relief for a part of our society that has little voice, little strength—our children.

Works by the Author

Bomb Built in Hell (1973)
Shella (1993)
Born Bad: Stories (1994)
Everybody Pays: Stories (1999)
The Getaway Man (2003)
Two Trains Running (2005)

Burke Series

Flood (1985)
Strega (1987)
Blue Belle (1988)
Hard Candy (1989)
Blossom (1990)
Sacrifice (1991)
A Flash of White (1993), chapbook
Down in the Zero (1994)
Footsteps of the Hawk (1995)
False Allegations (1996)
Safe House (1998)
Choice of Evil (1999)
Dead and Gone (2000)
Pain Management (2001)
Only Child (2002)
Down Here (2004)
Mask Market (2006)
Terminal (2007)
Another Life (2008)

Graphic Novels

Predator: Race War (1995)
Batman: The Ultimate Evil (1995)
Cross, with James Colbert (1995)
Hard Looks (1996), includes "Drive By," originally published as a ten-issue an-
    thology series in 1992–1993
Underground (Alamaailma) (1997), published in Finland

Anthologies

A Matter of Crime, edited by Matthew Joseph Bruccoli and Richard Layman (1987), includes "It's a Hard World"

New Crimes (1989), includes "Exit"

Great Tales of Madness and the Macabre, edited by Charles Adai (1990), includes "Placebo"

Dark Crimes, edited by Ed Gorman (1991), includes "Exit"

Cold Blood (1991), includes "Lynch Law"

Invitation to Murder (1991), includes "Anytime I Want"

New Crimes 2, edited by Maxim Jakubowski (1990), includes "Hostage"

Kingpins (1992), includes "Cough"

Hard-Boiled (1992), includes "Treatment"

Year's Finest Crime & Mystery Stories (1992), includes "White Alligator"

The Deadliest Games, edited by Janet Hutchings (1993), includes "Born Bad"

Blood, Threat and Fears, edited by Cynthia Manson (1993), includes "Placebo"

Hard-Boiled (1995), includes "It's a Hard World"

The Killing Spirit (1996), includes "Cain"

Orion Book of Murder, edited by Peter Haining (1996), includes "A Flash of White"

Unusual Suspects, edited by James Grady (1996), includes "Homeless"

The Crow: Shattered Lives & Broken Dreams, edited by J. O. Barr and Edward E. Kramer (1998), includes "The Real Thing"

The Cutting Edge (1998), includes "Perp Walk"

Créme de la Crime, edited by Janet Hutchings (2000), includes "Big Sister"

Children's Book for Adults

Another Chance to Get It Right (1993, revised 2003)

Nonfiction

The Life-Style Violent Juvenile: The Secure Treatment Approach (1979)

The Child Abuse-Delinquency Connection—A Lawyer's View (1989)

For Further Information

Andrew Vachss Web site. http://vachss.com (viewed November 20, 2008).

Dunn, Adam, "PW Talks with Andrew Vachss." *Publishers Weekly*, August 27, 2001.

Dunn, Adam, "Trying to Get Away." *Publishers Weekly*, March 17, 2003.

Pavia, Peter, "Just Kidding: Andrew Vachss Writes Crime Novels—for the Children." *New York Post*, August 13, 2006.

Pearson, Dan, "Serious Issues Permeate Crime Thriller." *Daily Southtown*, May 23, 2004.

Reid, Calvin, "Why Andrew Vachss Gets Graphic." *Publishers Weekly*, November 18, 1996.

"Reinventing Vachss," Cobrapost. http://www.cobrapost.com/documents/ReinventingVachss.htm (viewed October 18, 2007).

Safe House review. *Publishers Weekly*, March 16, 1998.

Terminal review. *Albany Times Union*, October 7, 2007.

Minette Walters

Crime-Suspense

Benchmark Title: *The Ice House*

Bishop's Stortford, Hertfordshire, England
1949–

Photo credit: Kate Eshelby

About the Author and the Author's Writing

Minette Walters has spent a lot of time in prison. As a staunch supporter of programs to improve inmate literacy, she was a prison visitor in Winchester for two decades. "I have been banging a drum for so long that there's a correlation between illiteracy and going to prison," the author said in an interview with Peter Kingston of the *Guardian*. "Between 50 percent and 75 percent of all prisoners can't read."

Minette Jebb was born in 1949 in Bishop's Stortford, Hertfordshire, England, the daughter of an army captain and an artist. She attended Godolphin, a boarding school, and Durham University, where she studied French. A volunteer educator, she lived on a kibbutz in Israel. She married Durham classmate and businessman Alexander Walters in 1978. They have two adult sons.

Walters worked briefly as a secretary and as a barmaid before securing a sub-editorship (and later editor's position) with *Woman's Weekly Library*. She wrote some thirty romance novelettes under several pseudonyms. When her sons were in their teens, she attempted a full-length novel. *The Ice House* was published in 1992 and brought the author a John Creasey Award for best first mystery. She has written a novel a year since.

Psychological suspense was a departure from the author's earlier cozy romances. "I felt it was quite important to alert people fairly early on to the fact this wasn't going to be an Agatha Christie-style book, which was probably why I put 'fart' in the first sentence," she said in a *Who Weekly* interview.

From the time she was a youngster and devoured Grimm's fairy tales and surreptitiously read newspaper stories about the James Hanratty murder case in the 1950s, she was hooked on gritty stories. "I have always been fascinated by the challenge that crime fiction represents to an author," she said on her Web site. "I wanted to know if I

395

could carry an intricate plot for 100,000 words, and keep readers guessing while I was portraying characters under considerable tension."

Walters doesn't dance around. She starts the story right off with a murder. "I am not keen on reading 150 pages before I discover who is going to be murdered, and want no one to be in any doubt that this is a horrific act," she told interviewer Judith Spelman for *Writers News*. "I am interested in why somebody might have done it and what might have driven them to do it."

The author incorporates real settings in her work. She and her husband, a British Telecom executive, lived in Romsey, England, for a dozen years before moving to Dorset. She went to school in Salisbury. All show up in her books.

The author also uses her writing to explore important social themes. *The Chameleon's Shadow,* for instance, is about the effects of posttraumatic stress syndrome on Iraq War soldiers. *The Shape of Snakes* tells the story of a teacher who is not convinced her black neighbor, who suffered from Tourette's syndrome, died at the hands of a racist killer.

"I'm not trying to recreate real crimes, but I get ideas from them," Walters told interviewer Emma Baird. "*The Shape of Snakes,* for instance, was written round about the time of the Stephen Lawrence Inquiry."

Walters adds strength to her stories with her fictional personalities. *Library Journal* reviewer Michele Leber said Walters's novel "presents wonderfully complex, three-dimensional characters … and unravels their stories masterfully."

The author writes from a home office, usually early in the morning and early evening.

Walters was featured in a BBC-TV program in which, as an art detective, she attempted to solve a mystery involving a Van Eyck painting. The BBC also filmed her first five novels as crime dramas.

The author returned to the novella format for *Chickenfeed*, a contribution to the 2006 World Book Day Quick Reads program. It was voted the first Quick Reads Learners' Favorite.

Although she appreciates the popularity of mystery series, she says she prefers the freshness of independent stories. She also says she is sensitive to a common criticism "that it is formulaic writing: you use the same place, the same characters, but with a different death each time. In other words, you don't have to think too hard about the next book…. I really wanted to change direction with each book," she said in a Crime Time interview.

Certainly the human mind suffers from enough psychological deviations to keep the author busy for many more books.

Works by the Author

The Ice House (1992)

The Sculptress (1993)

The Scold's Bridle (1994)

The Dark Room (1995)

The Echo (1997)

The Breaker (1998)

The Shape of Snakes (2000)

Acid Row (2001)
Fox Evil (2002)
Disordered Minds (2003)
The Devil's Feather (2005)
Chickenfeed (2006), novella
The Chameleon's Shadow (2007)

Adaptations in Other Media

The Works (BBC-TV, 1996), episode "Minette Walters and the Missing Master-piece"
The Sculptress (BBC-TV and PBS, 1996), television film based on the novel
The Ice House (BBC TV, 1997), television film based on the novel
The Echo (BBC-TV, 1997), television film based on the novel
The Scold's Bridle (BBC-TV, 1998), television film based on the novel
The Dark Room (BBC, 1999), television film based on the novel

For Further Information

Bailey, Moira, "Murder She Writes." *Who Weekly*, April 14, 1997.

Baird, Emma, "Minette Walters—In It Together," *Upbeat, Magazine of the Strathclyde Police Department*, October 2004.

The Devil's Feather review. *Publishers Weekly*, June 12, 2006.

Gee, Eve Tan, "Minette Walters: My Glittering Career." *Crime Time*, January 20, 2008.

Kingston, Peter, "Minette Walters: New Readers Start Here." *The Guardian*, March 13, 2007.

Krangle, Karenn, "Bringing War Home." *Vancouver Sun*, January 12, 2008.

Leber, Michele, *The Shape of Snakes* review. *Library Journal*, June 1, 2001.

Minette Walters Web site. http://www.minettewalters.co.uk (viewed November 20, 2008).

Spelman, Judith, "Minette Walters: An Intelligent Approach to Crime." *Writers News*, June 1994.

David Weber

Photo credit: Portrait Innovations

Fantasy; Science Fiction: Action-Adventure, Techno, Military

Benchmark Series: Honor Harrington

Cleveland, Ohio

1952–

About the Author and the Author's Writing

David Weber's science fiction heroine Honor Harrington is such a dynamic creation that he's had to call in help in relating the stories of her universe. The Changer of Worlds anthologies, which feature his own short stories as well as those by other writers, satisfy fans between regular novels in the regular science fiction Honor Harrington series.

Weber's character shares initials—and not a little background—with C. S. Forester's earlier literary creation, Horatio Hornblower. Books in the respective series followed each character through training, assignments, commands, and wars. The Hornblower books are set in the time of Napoleon Bonaparte, the Harrington books in a parallel world that has facets of nineteenth-century Britain. Both are strong on detail. "Weber gives a real feel for the military chain of command—both the good and bad parts," said *Publishers Weekly* of the novelette "Ms. Midshipwoman Harrington."

Harrington, a graduate of the Saganami Naval Academy and an officer in the Royal Navy in the Star Kingdom of Manticore, is a sharp tactician and powerful leader. She rises rapidly through the ranks in Weber's universe, in which racial, gender, and faith distinctions are meaningless. There is turmoil, however. "Honor Harrington has to cope with the Havenites, the Masadans, the political opponents of the ruler of Grayson … and best of all, Reginald Houseman. Houseman is a Manticoran socialist," explains reviewer Elisabeth Carey on a New England Science Fiction Association Web page. Yes, Weber brings a political agenda to his books.

Weber had Harrington's entire background in mind—the "Honorverse"—before he wrote the first book. He knew from the start that it should be a series and planted hints in early books that he more fully developed in later ones. Weber has said it was simply ordained that his popular character be female. She's not meant to be a feminist, however. "I'm writing about a human being who happens to be female," he said in a Wild Violet interview. "And human beings are human beings."

Born in Cleveland in 1952, he began to write poetry and short stories as a twelve-year-old. None was very good, he has said on publisher Baen's Web site. The first science fiction he remembers reading is Jack Williamson's *Legion of Space*. He kept at his writing, won a few contests, found he had a knack for advertising copy for his parents' public relations business, did radio and television writing, wrote newspaper and magazine articles, and shaped video games. Meanwhile, he was discouraged in his hope to teach history at the college level. Writing full time was his next choice. He drew on his broad reading interests to shape his own writing: he enjoys reading authors ranging from Tom Clancy, Alastair McLean, and Louis L'Amour to Georgette Heyer, Ed McBain, Jack Higgins, and David and Leigh Eddings.

"It's pretty evident that my historian's background plays a major role in most of the stories I tell," he said on the Baen Web site. "In a way, I've managed to combine historical novels with science-fiction—I just create my own history for them."

Weber frequently collaborates with other writers, including John Ringo, Eric Flint, and Keith Laumer, and finds it a positive experience, as the end result is always different from what the individual authors would have crafted on their own.

Weber has developed several series. *Off Armageddon Reef*, for example, is the star of an epic space saga in which there has been a major galactic war with the alien race called Gbaba. Human survivors give up their basic rights as they regroup on the planet Safehold. "Shifting effortlessly between battles among warp-speed starships and among oar-powered galleys, Weber brings the political maneuvering, past and future technologies, and vigorous protagonists together for a cohesive, engrossing whole," said a *Publishers Weekly* reviewer.

Weber is more than happy he ended up outside the classroom. In a SciFi Weekly interview, he said, "The really neat thing for me is that despite the occasional bouts of fatigue (my wife prefers the word 'exhaustion') and deadline panic, I really, really enjoy what I do for a living. The fact that total strangers are actually willing to pay perfectly good money to read my stories only makes it even better."

Works by the Author

Path of the Fury (1992)
The Apocalypse Troll (1998)
The Excalibur Alternative (2001)
In Fury Born (2006)

Assiti Shards Series, created by Eric Flint

1633 (2002)
1634: The Baltic War (2007)

Bolos Series, created by Keith Laumer

Bolos! (2005)

Dahak Series

Mutineer's Moon (1991)
The Armageddon Inheritance (1993)
Heirs of Empire (1996)
Empire from the Ashes (2003), omnibus includes all three books

Empire of Man Series, with John Ringo

March Upcountry (2001)
March to the Sea (2001)
March to the Stars (2003)
We Few (2005)

Honor Harrington Series

On Basilisk Station (1993)
The Honor of the Queen (1993)
The Short Victorious War (1994)
Field of Dishonor (1994)
Flag in Exile (1995)
Honor among Enemies (1996)
In Enemy Hands (1997)
More Than Honor, with S. M. Stribling and David Drake (1997)
Echoes of Honor (1998)
Ashes of Victory (2000)
Worlds of Honor (1998), anthology includes "What Price Dreams?" and "The Hard Way Home"
Changer of Worlds (2001), includes "Ms. Midshipwoman Harrington"
War of Honor (2002)
The Service of the Sword (2003)
At All Costs (2005)

Honor Harrington Universe Series

Crown of Slaves, with Eric Flint (2003)
The Shadow of Saganami (2004)
Storm from the Shadows (2009)
The Torch of Freedom, with Eric Flint (2009)

New Multiverse Series, with Linda Evans

Hell's Gate (2006)
Hell Hath No Fury (2007)

Old Soldiers Series, created by Keith Laumer

Old Soldiers (2005)

Safehold Series

Off Armageddon Reef (2007)
By Schism Rent Asunder (2008)
By Heresies Distressed (2009)

Starfire Series, with Stephen White

Insurrection (1990)
Crusade (1992)
In Death Ground (1997)
The Shiva Option (2002)
The Stars at War (2004), omnibus includes *Crusade* and *In Death Ground*
The Stars at War II (2005), omnibus includes *Insurrection* and *The Shiva Option*

War God Series

Oath of Swords (1994)
The War God's Own (1998)
Wind Rider's Oath (2004)

Anthologies

The Williamson Effect (1996)
The Warmasters, with David Drake and Eric Flint (2002), includes "Ms. Midshipwoman Harrington"

Editor

Foreign Legions, with David Drake and Eric Flint (2001)
In Fire Forged (2003)

Adaptations in Other Media

Saganami Island Tactical Simulator (2005), based on Honor Harrington series

For Further Information

Adams, John Joseph, "David Weber Takes Readers on a Tour Off Armageddon Reef and Discusses Writing, Religion and Responsibility." *Sci Fi Weekly*, February 4, 2008.

Carey, Elisabeth, "The Honor Harrington Series," New England Science Fiction Association. http://www.nesfa.org/reviews/Carey/honorharrington/.htm (viewed February 8, 2008).

Changer of Worlds review. *Publishers Weekly*, February 19, 2001.

Crown of Slaves review. *Publishers Weekly*, September 1, 2003.

David Weber bibliography, Fantastic Fiction. http://www.fantasticfiction.co.uk/w/david-weber/ (viewed February 8, 2008).

David Weber entry, Contemporary Authors Online. Reproduced in Biography Resource Center. Farmington Hills, MI: Gale, 2008. http://galenet.galegroup.com/servlet/BioRC (viewed February 15, 2008).

Green, Roland, *March to the Stars* review. *Booklist*, January 1, 2003.

http://www.scifi.com/sfw/interviews.sfw15625.html (viewed February 8, 2008).

Off Armageddon Reef review. *Publishers Weekly*, November 27, 2006.

Weisskopf, Toni, "David Weber Internet Interview," Baen Books, 2003. http://www.baen.com./interviews/intdweber.htm (viewed February 8, 2008).

Wilson, Alyce, David Weber interview, Wild Violet, 2005. http://www.wildviolet.net/live_steel/david_weber/html (viewed February 8, 2008).

Stephen White

Crime: Medical

Benchmark Series: <u>Alan Gregory Books</u>

Long Island, New York

1951–

Photo credit: Reid Wilkening

About the Author and the Author's Writing

Moral medical issues, from doctor–client relationships to managed health care, doubly intrigue Stephen White—as a professional psychologist and a thriller writer. All of his books have featured Dr. Alan Gregory, a psychologist who has a practice in Boulder, Colorado, and his (eventual) wife, Lauren Cowder. When he completed his first novel, White didn't expect it would spark a series. However, today he has developed an ensemble cast of characters to people his popular series. Some come to the fore in various books (Lauren is featured in *Higher Authority* and *Remote Control*), some recede to the background (Gregory barely appears in *Kill Me*). He writes some books in the first person, some in the third. The books offer interesting plot twists, but are character-driven.

"I've written about hot-button contemporary issues and about small things that fascinate me," he told interviewer Patti Thorn for *Rocky Mountain News*. "I try to make the series work to my advantage."

"From a craft point of view," he went on, "the familiarity of the characters and the opportunity to allow them to grow over great swaths of time is certainly appealing."

"Psychology fascinates me," White confessed in a Bookreporter interview in 2007. "It's why I started in the field and it's why I continue to write about it." In a review for *Library Journal*, Craig Shufelt said *Kill Me* "is an outstanding page-turner that examines quality of life, what it means to be living or dying, and who should make that determination."

White's heroes and heroines evolve as the series progresses. Gregory, for example, grapples with over-drinking. White even brought back the killer Michael McClelland from the first book, *Privileged Information* (1991) for *Dry Ice* (2007), to look at how both Alan Gregory and McClelland had changed. "Reintroducing him provided an excellent vehicle for reexamining Alan," White told Bookreporter.

White was born on Long Island, New York, in 1951. He grew up in New York, New Jersey, and Southern California. He briefly attended the University of California campuses at Irvine and Los Angeles before he graduated from UCLA at Berkeley in 1972. For a time after graduating, he was a Universal Studios tour guide and a waiter at Chez Panisse in Berkeley. In 1979, he completed his Ph.D. requirements in clinical psychology at the University of Colorado. He worked with pediatric cancer patients at Children's Hospital in Denver. He was on the University of Colorado Health Services Center staff and had a private practice. His specialty is the psychological effects of marital disruption, according to his Web site. He is a registered pilot. His older brother, Richard White, is also an author. The author and his family live in Denver.

White began his first book in 1989 in spare moments from his practice. Two years later *Privileged Information,* centered on Gregory's concern that a patient might be a killer, found a publisher.

His medical background is a strong plus to his writing, White believes. "My work gave me a chance to observe and study the infinite varieties of motivation that human beings have for their behavior," he said on his Web site. As a psychotherapist, he has years of experience simply listening to people, lots of people. "I can't imagine a better training ground for writing dialogue."

He does not make a detailed outline before beginning a manuscript. "When I start a book I usually have no more than the kernel of an idea, often just a dilemma or a point of conflict in my mind," he said in a conversation with Paul Comstock of *California Literary Review.* "I've often envied writers who are capable of doing all the creative work before they begin writing, but for me it seems impossible."

Writing nevertheless is a major task, the author comments on his Web site, as he strives to improve himself with each book. To keep a strong focus, he finds topics that interest him—and that he in turn can make interesting to his readers.

"But if there are any lessons in the books, they have to be almost invisible," he said in *USA Today.* "People don't read crime fiction to learn. They read for entertainment."

Works by the Author

Alan Gregory Series

Privileged Information (1991)

Private Practices (1993)

Higher Authority (1994)

Harm's Way (1996)

Remote Control (1997)

Critical Conditions (1998)

Manner of Death (1999)

Cold Case (1999)

The Program (2001)

Warning Signs (2002)

The Best Revenge (2003)

Blinded (2004)

Missing Persons (2005)

Kill Me (2005)
Best Revenge/Warning Signs (2006), omnibus
Blinded/Missing Persons (2007), omnibus
Dry Ice (2007)
Dead Time (2008)
The Siege (2009)

For Further Information

Comstock, Paul, "An Interview with Thriller Writer Stephen White." *California Literary Review*, April 3, 2007.

Elias, Marilyn, "Psychology Group Feels Good about White's Mystery Tales." *USA Today*, August 25, 2002.

Shufelt, Craig, *Kill Me* review. *Library Journal*, December 1, 2005.

Stephen White interview, Bookreporter. http://www.bookreporter.com/authors/au-white-stephen.asp#view030131 (viewed January 20, 2008).

Stephen White Web site. http://www.authorstephenwhite.com (viewed January 20, 2008).

Thorn, Patti, "Author's Stretch Spawns a 'New Breed Of Thriller.'" *Rocky Mountain News*, March 3, 2006.

F. Paul Wilson

Horror: Vampires; Science Fiction: Paranormal; Thrillers: Global, Mercenary

Benchmark Series: <u>Repairman Jack</u>

Jersey City, New Jersey

1946–

Photo credit: Ellen Datlow

About the Author and the Author's Writing

Repairman Jack will take on unusual missions. Your sister is missing? Your boyfriend was caught with his hands in the till? A shadowy, amorphous creature lurks outside your window? Jack's your man.

In *Conspiracies* (1999), F. Paul Wilson's enterprising character attends a conference of UFO enthusiasts and is soon on the trail of a missing woman, Melanie Ehler. A story that begins as whodunit soon turns into a whatdunit. Clues increasingly suggest a demonic force is at work. On the Web site Fantasticfiction.com, reviewer Tom Piccirilli suggests the hero "is one part Travis McGee and one part the Saint, an enigmatic antihero without identity, working outside the system. Jack's moral imperative is sometimes questionable but always leads him into the heart of darkness and beyond."

Repairman Jack, interestingly, is in his second life. Between 1981 and 1992, Wilson wrote six books with the character, went on to other things, and after six years revived him for a new, extended run.

Repairman Jack is not easily pigeonholed among fictional heroes, nor does his creator fit neatly among fiction genres. Wilson writes primarily science fiction and horror, with side excursions into paranormal fiction, medical novels and mercenary series.

Born in 1946 in Jersey City, New Jersey, Wilson was the son of a business executive and his wife. He grew up reading Bill Gaines's horror EC comics and Uncle Scrooge comic book adventures by Carl Barks. He devoured the fiction of H. P. Lovecraft (the otherworldliness of the Repairman Jack books derives from Lovecraft's paranormal universe), Richard Matheson, Ray Bradbury, and Robert E. Heinlein. In 1968, he earned a bachelor of science degree from Georgetown University. He received his doctorate from Kirksville College of Osteopathic Medicine in 1973. He married teacher Mary Murphy the next year, and they have two daughters.

While still a medical student, Wilson wrote short stories, and he sold his first novel, *Healer*, in 1976. It was the opening book for his LaNague Federation series. He wrote a half dozen science fiction books, nine horror tales beginning with *The Keep*, and several medical thrillers. His 1999 novella, *Aftershock*, won a 1999 Stoker Award for short fiction. He earned Prometheus Awards for *Wheels within Wheels* (1979) and *Sims* (2004). With Matthew J. Costello, he created and wrote the 30-second "news" segments (purportedly from the year 2142) for the Sci-Fi Channel's first series, *FTL Newsfeeds*, which aired from 1992 to 1996.

With his growing success as a part-time writer, Wilson gradually diminished his medical practice to two days a week. He's not likely to quit his work as a physician, he said in an interview on Wotmania. "If you spend every day before the computer screen and much of your free time hanging out with other writers, you develop a sort of tunnel vision. You narrow the range of your human experience."

Regardless of his wide writing interests, Wilson is particularly fond of Repairman Jack and has indicated that he has several more novels in mind. He labels Jack a "gut libertarian," without a studied idea of life, but rather an organic moral code. He's a shadow mercenary, working mostly for himself for what he believes is right, against an overpowering evil. While the books may be read on their own, they fit into the author's broader universe as defined in the novel *Nightworld* (1992). Wilson's science fiction universe, similarly, began without structure. As he's written more books, he's begun to connect them, rewriting earlier books as they are reissued to maintain consistency and temporal logic.

Wilson has admitted having difficulty at times in finishing a manuscript. "I'd get a great idea, and I'd get a great start to the story, and then I'd lose interest in actually finishing it. I'd finished it in my head. You come to learn that finishing is the work of writing," he said in an interview with Russell Madden.

In an interview with Chris Kemp for fwomp, he said his plots emerge in different ways: "Sometimes a novel arises out of a character (Dr. Lathram in *Implant*); sometimes out of a theme (the vagaries of faith and belief in *The Haunted Air*); sometimes out of a single scene (the rooftop battle in *The Tomb* arose from a dream; I built the novel backward and forward from there)."

Whatever the origin of the story, Wilson always outlines. But he doesn't feel compelled to stick to it. As long as he knows how a book will end, he lets the writing take him there.

His mix between science fiction, horror, and thriller may make it difficult for booksellers to place him in stores, but it's satisfying to his creative instincts, Wilson asserts. On the Web site Sunni's Salon, he wryly states, "My rule has always been: Write the next book—that is, the story that's most ready to be told. Which has made me a genre hopper…. Slate magazine recently termed me a cult writer. Maybe they're right. Maybe they heard about my stock of Kool-Aid."

Works by the Author

Soft and Others: *16 Stories of Wonder and Dread* (1984)

Black Wind (1988)

Buckets (1989), chapbook

Midnight Mass (1990)

Ad Statum Perspicuum (1990), short stories
Pelts (1990)
Sibs (1991), also titled *Sister Night*
Barrens and Others (1992), short stories
Mirage, with Matthew J. Costello (1996)
Nightkill, with Steven Spruill (1997)
Masque, with Matthew J. Costello (1998)
The Beast and Me (2001), chapbook
Artifact: A Daredevils Club Adventure, with Kevin J. Anderson, Janet Berliner, and Matthew J. Costello (2003)
The Fifth Harmonic (2003)
Aftershock and Others: 19 Oddities (2009)

LaNague Federation Series

Healer (1976)
Wheels within Wheels (1978)
Enemy of the State (1980)
Dydeetown World (1989)
Tery (1989), revised as *The Tery: The Definitive Edition* (2006)
LaNague Chronicles (1992), omnibus

Repairman Jack: Adversary Cycle

The Keep (1981)
The Tomb (1984), reissued as *Rakoshi* (2004)
Touch (1986)
Reborn (1990)
Reprisal (1991), in United Kingdom as *Reprisals* (1991)
Nightworld (1992)

Repairman Jack Series

Legacies (1998), first issued as by Colin Andrews
Conspiracies (1999)
All the Rage (2000)
Hosts (2001)
The Haunted Air (2002)
Gateways (2003)
Crisscross (2004)
Infernal (2005)
Last Rakosh (2005)
Harbingers (2006)
Bloodline (2007)

The Long Way Home (2007), Amazon Shorts electronic story
Secret Histories (2008), for young adult readers
By the Sword (2008)

Sims Series

La Causa (2000)
The Portero Method (2001)
Meerm (2002)
Sims (2004), omnibus

Editor

Freak Show (1992)
Diagnosis: Terminal: An Anthology of Medical Terror (1996)

Contributor

Binary Star 2 (1979), includes *The Tery*
Masques: All New Works of Horror and the Supernatural, edited by J. N. Williamson (1984)
Whispers 6, edited by Stuart David Schiff (1987)
Night Visions 6: The Bone Yard (1988)
Silver Scream (1988)
Hot Blood: Tales of Erotic Horror, edited by Lonn Friend and Jeff Gelb (1989)
New Destinies 7, edited by Jim Baen (1989)
Year's Best Fantasy Second Annual Collection, edited by Ellen Datlow and Terri Windling (1989), issued in United States as *Demons and Dreams: The Best Fantasy and Horror 1* (1989)
Between Time and Terror, edited by Stefan R. Dziemianowicz, Martin H. Greenberg, and Robert E. Weinberg (1990)
Lovecraft's Legacy, edited by Martin H. Greenberg and Robert E. Weinberg (1990)
Mammoth Book of Terror, edited by Stephen Jones (1990)
Best New Horror 2, edited by Ramsey Campbell and Stephen Jones (1991)
The Mammoth Book of Vampires, edited by Stephen Jones (1992)
Dark at Heart, edited by Joe and Karen Lansdale (1992)
Predators, edited by Ed Gorman and Martin H. Greenberg (1993)
Weird Tales 305/306 Winter 1992/Spring 1993, edited by Nina Kiriki Hoffman, F. Paul Wilson, and Darrell Schweitzer (1993)
The Best of Weird Tales, edited by Marvin Kaye and John Gregory Betancourt (1995)
Cthulhu 2000: A Lovecraftian Anthology, edited by Jim Turner (1995)
David Copperfield's Tales of the Impossible, edited by David Copperfield and Janet Berliner (1995)
Great Writers and Kids Write Spooky Stories, edited by Martin H. Greenberg, Jill M. Morgan, and Robert E. Weinberg (1995)

Night Screams, edited by Ed Gorman and Martin H. Greenberg (1995)

100 Tiny Tales of Terror, edited by Stefan R. Dziemianowicz, Martin H. Greenberg, and Robert E. Weinberg (1996)

Rivals of Dracula, edited by Stefan R. Dziemianowicz, Martin H. Greenberg, and Robert E. Weinberg (1996)

Dancing with the Dark, edited by Stephen Jones (1997)

Magic-Lover's Treasury of the Fantastic, edited by Martin H. Greenberg and Margaret Weis (1997)

Mammoth Book of Dracula: Vampire Tales for the New Millennium, edited by Stephen Jones (1997)

Millennium, edited by Douglas E. Winter (1997)

999, edited by Al Sarrantonio (1999)

Vampire Slayers: Stories of Those Who Dare to Take Back the Night, edited by Martin H. Greenberg and Elizabeth Ann Scarborough (1999)

The Mammoth Book of Best New Horror 11, edited by Stephen Jones (2000)

Written as Colin Andrew

Foundation (1993), issued as by F. Paul Wilson as *The Select* (1994)

Implant (1995), issued as by F. Paul Wilson (1995)

Deep as the Marrow (1996), issued as by F. Paul Wilson (1997)

Written with Mary Murphy as Mary Elizabeth Murphy

Virgin (1995), reissued as by F. Paul Wilson (2007)

Juvenile Books as F. Paul Wilson

The Christmas Thingy (2000)

Graphic Novels as F. Paul Wilson

Completely Doomed, with Robert Bloch, Richard Matheson, and David J. Schow (2007)

Dark Voices 6: Sex Slaves of the Dragon Tong (2007)

Nonfiction Contributor, as F. Paul Wilson

Horror: The 100 Best Books, edited by Stephen Jones and Kim Newman (1988)

Adaptations in Other Media

The Keep (1983), motion picture

FTL Newsfeed (with Matthew J. Costello, Sci-Fi Channel, 1992–1996), television short-segment series

Midnight Mass (2003), motion picture

Others (2006), motion picture

For Further Information

F. Paul Wilson interview, Sunni's Salon. http://www.endervidualism.com/salon/ intvw/wilson.htm (viewed October 12, 2007).

F. Paul Wilson interview, Wotmania. http://www.wotmania.com/ fantasymessageboardshowmessage.asp?MessageID=45889 (viewed October 12, 2007).

F. Paul Wilson profile, Amazon. http://www.amazon.com/gp/pdp/profile/ AYR10UHMTDNZA (viewed October 12, 2007).

F. Paul Wilson profile, Scifipedia. http://scifipedia.scifi.com/index.php/F._ Paul_Wilson (viewed October 15, 2007).

Kemp, Chris, "Interview with F. Paul Wilson, fwomp. http://www.fwomp. com/int-fpaul.htm (viewed October 12, 2007).

Madden, Russell, F. Paul Wilson interview, 2000. http://www.home.earthlink. net/~rdmadden/webdocs/Wilson_Interview.html (viewed October 12, 2007).

Piccirilli, Tom, *Conspiracies* review, fantasticfiction. http://www. fantasticfiction.co.uk/w/f-paul-wilson/conspiracies.htm (viewed October 12, 2007).

Repairman Jack Web site. http://www.repairmanjack.com/ (viewed November 20, 2008).

Author/Title Index

Genre Index

About the Author

   BERNARD A. DREW is a freelance writer/editor and author of numerous articles and books, including *100 Most Popular African American Authors* (Libraries Unlimited, 2006) and *100 Most Popular Nonfiction Authors* (Libraries Unlimited, 2008). He lives in Great Barrington, Massachusetts. He has also written books about Hopalong Cassidy creator Clarence E. Malford and civil rights activist W. E. B. DuBois.

Recent Titles in the Popular Authors Series

The 100 Most Popular Young Adult Authors: Biographical Sketches and Bibliographies, Revised First Edition
Bernard A. Drew

Popular Nonfiction Authors for Children: A Biographical and Thematic Guide
Flora R. Wyatt, Margaret Coggins, and Jane Hunter Imber

100 Most Popular Children's Authors: Biographical Sketches and Bibliographies
Sharron McElmeel

100 Most Popular Picture Book Authors and Illustrators: Biographical Sketches and Bibliographies
Sharron McElmeel

100 More Popular Young Adult Authors: Biographical Sketches and Bibliographies
Bernard A. Drew

Winning Authors: Profiles of the Newbery Medalists
Kathleen L. Bostrom

Children's Authors and Illustrators Too Good to Miss: Biographical Sketches and Bibliographies
Sharron McElmeel

100 Most Popular Genre Fiction Authors: Biographical Sketches and Bibliographies
Bernard A. Drew

100 Most Popular African American Authors: Biographical Sketches and Bibliographies
Bernard A. Drew

100 Most Popular Nonfiction Authors: Biographical Sketches and Bibliographies
Bernard A. Drew